FOLKLIFE
and
SUPERSTITION

SANDRA ROLLINGS-MAGNUSSON

FOLKLIFE *and* SUPERSTITION

THE LUCK, LORE AND WORLDVIEWS OF PRAIRIE HOMESTEADERS

Heritage House Publishing Company Ltd.
heritagehouse.ca

Cataloguing information available from Library and Archives Canada
978-1-77203-506-3 (paperback)
978-1-77203-507-0 (e-book)

Edited by Audrey McClellan
Proofread by Anna Phelan
Cover and interior design by Jacqui Thomas
Cover image: McKinnon homestead, Foremost, Alberta (1910). NA-2604-32. Courtesy of Glenbow Library and Archives Collection, Libraries and Cultural Resources Digital Collections, University of Calgary.
Frontispiece: A group of men, women and children pose outside a stopping place on Alberta's Grande

Prairie–Edson Trail in 1912. NA-1328-2810 by Byron-May company limited. Courtesy of Libraries and Cultural Resources Digital Collections, University of Calgary.

The interior of this book was produced on 100% post-consumer recycled paper, processed chlorine free, and printed with vegetable-based inks.

Heritage House gratefully acknowledges that the land on which we live and work is within the traditional territories of the Lkwungen (Esquimalt and Songhees), Malahat, Pacheedaht, Scia'new, T'Sou-ke, and W̱SÁNEĆ (Pauquachin, Tsartlip, Tsawout, Tseycum) Peoples.

We acknowledge the financial support of the Government of Canada through the Canada Book Fund (CBF) and the Canada Council for the Arts, and the Province of British Columbia through the British Columbia Arts Council and the Book Publishing Tax Credit.

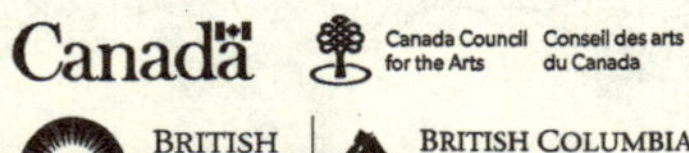

28 27 26 25 24 1 2 3 4 5

Printed in Canada

Early environment and experiences influence throughout our lives our feelings, behaviour, and personality. The child of the mountains loves the grandeur of the lofty peaks; the coast dweller is drawn to the sea; the desert person is at home on the sandy waste. Many of us who grew up on the Canadian prairie see beauty in a landscape which others may find monotonous and boring—the wide open spaces, the distant view, the big sky.

DORA MITCHELL, homesteader[1]

Contents

Publisher's Note

The era of homesteading was one of high emotion for many those moving to the west, from the excitement and optimism of a new start to the trepidation and anxiety of surviving in an unfamiliar place. The other side of these stories of pioneers and settlers is that of the original people who have inhabited this land for millennia, who were and continue to be deeply affected by the waves of newcomers who arrived on the Prairies with encouragement from the colonial enterprise to "settle the West."

What is today known as the province of Manitoba is located on the Treaty Territories and ancestral lands of the Anishinaabeg, Anishininewuk, Dakota Oyate, Denesuline, and Nehethowuk Nations, as well as the Homeland of the Red River Métis and lands in the north that were and are the ancestral lands of the Inuit.

Saskatchewan is located on lands covered by Treaties 2, 4, 5, 6, 8, and 10, the traditional lands of the Cree, Dakota, Dene, Lakota, Nakota, and Salteaux peoples, and the homeland of the Métis.

Alberta is located on lands covered by Treaties 6, 7, and 8, and is the traditional and ancestral territory of many peoples, namely: the Blackfoot Confederacy (Kainai, Piikani, and Siksika), the Cree, Dene, Saulteaux, Nakota Sioux, Stoney Nakoda, and the Tsuut'ina Nation, as well as the Métis People of Alberta. This includes the Métis Settlements and the Six Regions of the Métis Nation of Alberta within the historical Northwest Metis Homeland.

Preface

Ever since I was a graduate student at the University of Regina and discovered the vast amount of material that was available in the provincial archives, I have been fascinated with the homesteading era. Over the past thirty-plus years, I have researched many aspects relating to this time period, including the political and economic situation surrounding the National Policy and the implementation and effect of the *Dominion Lands Act.* I have written about the importance of child labour on prairie homesteads, the inequities of the homestead program for women, women's work on homesteads in the fields and in the family home, and the availability of homestead land through South African scrip. I also wrote an historical book as a tribute to Saskatchewan people, which detailed the lives of the men, women and children who homesteaded in the province. Most recently, I published a book of short stories that highlighted the homesteaders who settled in Alberta, Saskatchewan and Manitoba. Their immigration experiences were discussed, as were their experiences travelling on the ships and the trains. Stories of how they built their homes, cropped their fields and worked with farm animals were also included, as were the hardships of daily living.

While my research has been extensive, there was one aspect of homesteading life that always seemed elusive. I wanted to know how the homesteaders felt about the homesteading way of life. What were their personal thoughts? What aspects of life did they enjoy? What did they dislike? When they were visiting each other, what did they talk about? What made them laugh? Given that hundreds of thousands of people converged on the western prairies within a few decades, all with their own languages and customs, how did they form friendship ties with others in the community? Were there aspects of homesteading life that bonded these groups of people? If so, what were they? Could a researcher go so far as to argue that all of these people shared a unique folklife given their common circumstances?

These initial ideas guided my research. As I reviewed thousands of pages of archival materials, I was able to glean bits of information from here and there relating to the personal lives of the homesteaders. The pioneer questionnaires relating to folklore and farming experiences that are held by the Provincial Archives of Saskatchewan were invaluable to this research and gave me a strong starting point. From there, I followed up with searches in other archives, where I reviewed more historical material, including reports, letters, memoirs, interviews, homestead files, books and photographs. This book is the culmination of all those efforts.

There are a number of people I wish to thank. Without their help, this book would never have been written. First of all, I have greatly appreciated the assistance of Nadine Charabin, the director of Archival Services at the Provincial Archives of Saskatchewan. She and her staff have always generously offered their expertise as I reviewed the many archival materials that were made available to me over the years. I would also like to thank the staff of the Provincial Archives of Alberta and Manitoba. Closer to home, I extend my appreciation to all of my colleagues at MacEwan University. They are a great group of people who have always encouraged me with their kind words of support, their humour and their interest in my work. Appreciation is also extended to the librarians at MacEwan University, who unceasingly carried out my requests for inter-library loans over the past two years.

Thanks are also given to Heritage House Publishing, especially Lara Kordic, Nandini Thaker, Monica Miller, Kimiko Fraser, Jacqui Thomas, and to Audrey McClellan for all of her excellent editing suggestions.

Finally, I would like to thank Brad Johnson for his family photographs and homesteading stories; Jacqueline (Deighton) Pearson for her comments on Romanian superstitions; and Lydia (Kroening) Lanterman, my aunt, for her unwavering praise for my research. David Shiers was helpful with his suggestions, as was my mother, MaryEtta Rollings (a homesteader's grand-daughter), whose knowledge of farm life was invaluable. Thanks also to my daughter, Christina Magnusson, for her ongoing encouragement.

Introduction

Many words could be used to describe the homesteading era on the Canadian prairies. It was an exhilarating time, as hundreds of thousands of men, women and children decided to leave their mother countries and move half-way across the world to live in a foreign land. They travelled from such countries as England, Scotland, Germany, Switzerland, Poland, Belgium and Ukraine to immigrate to the provinces of Alberta, Saskatchewan and Manitoba.[1] Others migrated east from the Maritime provinces, Newfoundland, and the central provinces of Ontario and Quebec to begin their lives in a new undeveloped region, while still others travelled north from the United States to become Canadian homesteaders.[2] The vibrant excitement of the homesteading era was contagious. Just the utterance of one word—homesteading—invoked visions of hardy men, women and children working the hard prairie soil, day after day, month after month, and year after year, in order to make their mark on their own piece of land. Many of these people were poor, they were isolated, and they faced many dire and dangerous situations. However, they had patience, courage, fortitude and the drive and willingness to eke out a living on the prairie land. For many, even though homesteading was a challenging endeavour, they believed that they were working toward a better future in a land that promised democracy, financial opportunity, productivity, and freedom.

The Canadian homesteading era began under the direction of Sir John A. Macdonald, the first prime minister of Canada, through the implementation of the *Dominion Lands Act* in 1872. Under this act, western prairie land was partitioned into quarter-sections (i.e., 160 acres) and was offered to those who wished to farm for the price of a ten-dollar registration fee. Those who acquired land had to meet a number of stipulations in order to "prove" their homestead and gain title to the land: build a habitable home, reside on the property for six months every year for three years, and break and crop thirty acres within three years.[3] Initially, only men eighteen years of age and older could apply, regardless of their marital status. Women were finally allowed to apply in 1876, but only if they could confirm that they were heads of their own households.[4]

Given that all of these people were converging on one area of the country, the western Canadian prairies, it is not surprising to find that many of the homesteaders shared similar experiences. Whether they were travelling alone by Red River cart with their oxen or horses over well-worn North-West Mounted Police (NWMP) dirt roads, venturing off on buffalo trails or creating their own path through the wilderness, they made their way into the unknown. Unsure of what the future held for them and not knowing if they would ever return to their homeland, they made sure to bring all their worldly possessions with them. To ensure a successful start to their homesteading efforts, they purchased horses, cows, roosters, chickens and sometimes even a cat or dog. Agricultural implements like walking plows, harrows and disc harrows, as well as household furnishings such as camp stoves, tables, chairs, bed springs and straw ticks (mattresses), were hauled across the prairie. Families didn't leave anything to chance, so they also purchased a generous quantity of food staples—flour, oats, coffee, tea, sugar, salt and pepper—from Winnipeg, Manitoba, the last populated hub for supplies before they started on their way west.

Living in an undeveloped region meant that homesteaders were reliant on each other for survival. Helping each other out was part of the community spirit that developed over time, with many people providing assistance. Whether homesteaders were trying to help "greenhorns" (people unfamiliar with a farming lifestyle) with fieldwork or animal husbandry, or offering advice on how to ford local streams and rivers or cross gumbo-filled stretches of land, their guidance was invaluable to all newcomers. People also gathered together to build barns, sheds or granaries for each other, and they assisted their neighbours if they were ill and unable to work their fields or take care of their families. Such "working bees" were beneficial. Not only did they allow people to meet their neighbours, but those experiencing challenging times were always assured that there would be help available if needed.

Homesteaders were also reliant on each other for camaraderie. Given the distressing isolation that many homesteaders experienced, particularly during the relentlessly cold months of the year, every homesteader looked forward to those times when neighbours stopped by. Typically, visitors would come in for a meal or for a cup of coffee or tea, or they would come by in the evening. Discussing the current news or upcoming events, like pie or box socials, picnics, dances and other community events, would have been a highlight, as would trading novels or singing the newest tune with a harmonica or guitar accompaniment. If one neighbour was going to town (a rare event for all homesteaders given the distance that many of them had to travel), he or she would pick up outgoing mail from each neighbour along the way, and then, on the return trip, would distribute incoming mail.

Children were thrilled when other children came to visit. Being able to play games with others their own age, either indoors or out in the yard, was a joyful event, with much laughter and fun-filled rambunctiousness. Going to school was another highlight for many children, as they could socialize with their peers during recess, play baseball or Ante Over Pigtail, skip rope, race, swing on the swings, chase each other or climb through the trees. They also looked forward to the annual Christmas concert, a highlight of the school year, which was organized by their teacher and included singing Christmas carols, taking part in nativity plays and dressing up in costumes for their audience—an audience that consisted of proud parents and others from the community.

Many homesteaders and their families developed similar interests while living on the prairies. They took part in community associations, with some men being involved in gun clubs and literary and debate clubs, while others were drawn to Masonic and Orangemen organizations. Women tended to be involved with Women's Aid associations, where their efforts were focused on helping the poor. Sporting events such as boxing, baseball and football were appreciated by everyone, whether they were members of a team or the cheering onlookers. Similarly, country fairs, with their various competitions and races, were highly anticipated events that few could ignore. Knowing the location of the best hunting places and the best fishing holes also brought communities together. Identifying local landmarks helped to guide people from one place to another. Naming these places and landmarks, along with nearby rivers and streams, was a common pastime for many homesteaders, as was getting together to officially establish and name their villages, towns and school districts.

Another feature that many homesteading communities had in common was their ability to identify some of the remarkable people who lived in their midst. These people were well respected and well liked in the community, either for their skills or for their generosity. Some took the law into their own hands, using brass knuckles and guns to keep the peace when the NWMP was not available, while others were local shopkeepers who dealt fairly with their customers. Then there were teachers in the one-room schoolhouses, preachers who delivered sermons every Sunday, and owners of stopping places, who cooked up hearty meals and served their patrons with a smile. Of course, there were also people who were held in contempt and loathed by those who encountered them. From horse thieves and bank robbers to general miscreants who made life miserable, homesteaders knew how to deal with them when they caught them.

Climatic extremes could also make those who lived on the western prairies miserable. Whether homesteaders were being pelted by rain and hail, hunkering down during windstorms or diving for cover when they were caught in a blizzard, the hazards associated with the prairie climate could be inconvenient at best or life-threatening at worst. Many homesteaders tried to develop ways to predict what kinds of weather were on the horizon. They would commonly watch for unusual behaviour in their pets, or in the cattle, horses, pigs or chickens around the farmyard. Even birds flying overhead or frogs in the creek seemed to sense an impending storm or change in the weather. Some homesteaders studied the shape of the moon to determine the amount of rain that would fall, while others deliberated over the direction of the wind. Still others tried to determine the meaning behind northern lights and mirages, rainbows and cumulus clouds.

Some homesteaders were superstitious. They would take extra care to avoid evil spirits in the local graveyard. Or maybe they paid serious attention to the predictions of the cards, the Ouija board, the tea leaves in their cup or the lines in the palms of their hands. Whatever the source, they were wary of what the future held for them, especially if the results were less than desirable. Homesteaders were also familiar with signs of good and bad luck, and would try to remedy their situation if they happened across a sign of misfortune, hardship or tragedy. One homesteader long rued the day when he had a number of black cats cross his path one afternoon while he was on his way to town.

Given the similar conditions that homesteaders faced, it is not surprising that they acquired similar belief systems associated with the prairies that brought them together as a community. Even though they had come to western Canada with their own cultures, customs and religions that made each of them unique, they also became part of a new dynamic—a new social environment. Their prairie poetry, songs, tall tales, jokes, legends, traditions, beliefs, superstitions and proverbial sayings, as well as traditional aspects of family lore, all helped to create a new homesteading lifestyle. Homesteaders learned from each other as they interacted with each other, and each had an influence on the other.

Whether they were experiencing good times and revelling in each other's company, or facing difficulties on their farms, homesteaders were, in essence, part of a new microcosm of Canadian society. They might have worked on their own as they tried to develop their own homesteads, but they were also a part of the new social communities and towns that were being built across the prairies. These individuals and their stories created the prairie folklife of the region, and their motivations, struggle for survival, labour and tenacity made them a distinctive part of western Canadian social history.

Using information from the Provincial Archives of Alberta, Saskatchewan and Manitoba, and from the University of Alberta, this book is a compilation of tales and anecdotes relating to prairie folklife, as told by the homesteaders themselves. In particular, it gives readers insight into the mindset of the people who decided to settle on the prairies. Till now, little has been known about how homesteaders felt about their lives, their concerns, their interests, their friendships, their ability to work together and their shared social norms and values. The stories in this book help to reveal not only their thoughts and feelings about being homesteaders, but also how they survived, thrived and helped each other during a unique time in Canadian history.

Hunters, Cowboys, Trappers, Egg Collectors and Banjo Players

The skill sets of those who settled on the prairies varied depending on the types of jobs, hobbies and interests they had in the past. Whether they emigrated from European countries, migrated from central or eastern Canada or moved north from the United States, all of them were determined to be homesteaders. The following stories highlight the vast array of skills, life experiences and ethnic backgrounds held by those who eventually decided to make western Canada their home.

James Tulloch was a young man who hailed from the Shetland Islands (a group of islands in the north of Scotland).[1] He had faced a number of challenges in his young life; however, he valued the schooling that he had received, and he remembered the immigration agent who had influenced him to move from his homeland to the western prairie region of Canada when he was a young adult. As he stated:

> My parents never lived in Canada. My mother died when I was born in 1872 and my mother requested my grandmother to nurse and care for me. My father was a sailor and the boats he was employed on traded between London and the Far East, that is, the East Indies. I did not see my father very often as I lived in the Shetland Islands and steamboats were not in general use as they are now, therefore I only saw him once every three years. When I was really young, I was learned the alphabet and spelling two letters put together such as "in" and "to" (to make the word "into") by my grandmother. I was eventually sent to school. There were no Government Schools

The Federal Immigration Branch of Canada's Department of the Interior sent out immigration agents across Europe and the United States to convince people to become homesteaders on the Canadian prairies. In combination with these efforts, promotional materials like *Canada West: The Last Best West* magazine, with its exhilarating covers (as shown here), portrayed "an idyllic prairie life of blue skies, golden crops, happy families, friendly neighbours, sunshine, and independence."[2] It also included helpful hints for successful farming practices, such as the types of crops that should be planted and when they should be harvested. Building materials were discussed, as well as the progress of the rail line across the west. The amenities that were available in the small towns (i.e., mercantile stores, livery stables, dentists, doctors, blacksmithing shops and churches), notes on the variable climatic conditions, copies of township maps with fold-outs, and favourable testimonials from those who had previously homesteaded were all included in the various issues. COVER OF *CANADA WEST*, 1922, CU11054187. COURTESY OF LIBRARIES AND CULTURAL RESOURCES DIGITAL COLLECTIONS, UNIVERSITY OF CALGARY

[offering public education] then, that was in the spring of 1878. I was not six years of age 'til October. It was a Free Church School that I went to that was built from Church grants and contributions.[3] My grandfather gave them free land to build a school and house for the teacher. Fees were paid the teacher every three months; ten shillings per year to start. The student's fees increased as you passed your examinations. The Government schools started in 1880 for Scotland in the district I lived in. I left the Shetland Islands in 1890 when I was eighteen and worked in the south of Scotland on the border (with England) in Dumfriesshire. That was when I came in contact with a Mr. Waugh May of Winnipeg (a Canadian immigration agent). He was interested in securing immigrants for Manitoba. He advised me to come out to Winnipeg. This was in the fall of 1893. I came out to Winnipeg to homestead in June of 1894 when I was twenty-two years old.

Like James Tulloch, Sidney May had little to no knowledge of rural living, but this fact did not deter him.[4] Sidney left his hometown of London, England, in 1906 with the intention of becoming a homesteader in the province of Saskatchewan. He was an industrious and skilled young man, traits learned from his parents. His father had been a hard-working fisherman who manned his own fishing vessel in the cold waters of the North Sea of England in the early mornings, while his mother remained at home and "braided all of his father's trawl and shrimp fishing nets by hand." She also repaired and made the sails. Sidney worked alongside his father in his younger years, learning his father's craft. As time went by, both father and son supplemented the family income by hand-carving model fishing boats. In fact, Sidney became so proficient at wood-working that he received a certificate from the Home Arts and Industries Association of Great Britain during the Royal Albert Hall Exhibition in 1888.

Another Englishman, Fred Baines, was born in Manchester in 1875 but was raised in Lincolnshire and Norfolk County.[5] His father had made a decent living for the family as a boot and shoe dealer. In 1883, his father learned of the opportunities available in Canada and decided that the family should emigrate to Saskatchewan to homestead. Fred said that his father did not have any experience with farming. However, he was a determined man and quickly became a jack-of-all-trades as he not only worked to meet all of the homestead requirements by building a home and breaking and cropping his fields, but he also learned how to raise cattle, horses and poultry and how to be a hunter, cowboy, trapper, egg collector and banjo player. Due to his father's earnestness and positive attitude in learning all of these new skills, Fred was also influenced to become a homesteader when he turned eighteen years old. As for his mother, he said that she was "a hard-working woman who saved many lives by midwifery and nursing the sick and unfortunate."

Like Fred Baines and his father, Charles Davis also knew little about agricultural work.[6] However, he was well experienced in many other occupations before he made his way to Canada. As he stated:

> I was born in the parish of Ombersley in the county of Worcestershire, England, in 1882. There in the village of

> Stourport, I lived for the first twelve years of my life. After finishing in the Seventh Standard at the National School, I tried many, many vocations—designing, general mercantile, chenille works, and the co-op (grocery store) business. These kept me employed until February 1900. Then I joined the Royal Marine Artillery. Became a first-class gunner. Served in the old ironclad battleship, "Dreadnaught," in the Channel Fleet. Commissioned in his Majesty's Bullwark Flagship in the Mediterranean for eight years. In 1905, I came to Canada to take up homesteading in Glaslyn, Saskatchewan. Ten years later, in January of 1915, I married a widow who also held homestead land as she had filed on her husband's land after his death.

Compared to those immigrants who did not have any farming experience, Tobias Lanegraff found himself in an advantageous position.[7] He was well versed in agricultural pursuits as his parents had both been farmers. They came from Norway in 1867 and first took up residence in Houston County, Minnesota. Once settled, they purchased a team of oxen and with the help of fellow farmers cleared the land of brush that was more than six

Scottish parents pose with their three children in Glasgow in 1902 before embarking on their journey to western Canada to homestead. AUTHOR'S COLLECTION

feet tall. Unfortunately, even though a lot of physical labour had been expended to clear land and then seed and grow a successful crop, a grasshopper infestation wiped them out. His parents decided to move to Swift County, Minnesota. Shortly afterward, they relocated to the Hoople area in the state of North Dakota, where Tobias was born in 1880. In 1887, when he was seven years old, he started school. As he said,

> I soon learnt to speak and read and write. I also went to Concordia College in Moorhead, Minnesota. After that, I sold implements and worked in a mercantile store with my dad 'til 1905. In September of that year [when I was twenty-five years old], I made a trip to Canada. I bought a quarter-section of land near Wetaskiwin, Alberta, but sold it later on. In March 1906, I filed for a homestead on April 10, 1906, in Battleford, Saskatchewan. While working to meet the homestead requirements, I sold implements to make a living and I cooked in a railroad camp. In 1906, my dad joined me. We went back to Minnesota during the hard, cold winter of 1906 and 1907. We made a little cash buying furs and supplying the workers in the bush with beef (which I had bought and slaughtered). I made enough money to come back to Battleford in the spring of 1907. Even though we had arranged for a man to look after our cattle and oxen before we left for Minnesota, we found out that he had run short of hay and most of the cattle starved. We lost about 75% of our stock.

Tobias and his father continued to work on the homestead and broke thirty acres of land, which they seeded in 1907. Once again, luck was not on their side as the spring was late, with freezing temperatures that hampered germination. As well, the gophers ate all of the crops that did manage to break through the soil. As Tobias exclaimed,

> There were thousands of gophers! So, in 1907, there was no crop. We then moved into the bush eighteen miles east during the winter of 1908–09. We had put up hay there in August and September of 1908. So, we wintered there very

> good. Lots of wood close by. We earned some money wintering cattle and oxen for others. We took out wood to the railroad camp which we sold for $3 per load. In the spring, when all of the cattle were fat, we moved back to the homestead where we broke more land and we rented more land from others. We had rain and got a good crop. That saved the situation. I also made money by threshing for others in the fall with a big steam outfit. I threshed every year from 1912 'til 1926. My name became well established as a thresherman.

Marie Jordens also recounted her family's story of how they eventually became homesteaders in Saskatchewan.[8] They lived in the province of Quebec, but moved in 1880 to take up homesteading in the United States, where they could obtain 160 acres of free land. After they met all of the homesteading requirements there and received the title to their land, they sold it, and in 1885 the family moved to the Qu'Appelle Valley in Saskatchewan to take up homesteading in Canada.[9] Once they were settled, the rest of the family followed them. Marie mentioned that they all spoke French, and she sang all sorts of songs in French that she had learned from her parents. She was also impressed with her father's carpentry, farming and cobbler skills, stating that "he built his own log home, plowed the sod with oxen to cover the rails on the roof, made the sleighs, hayracks, tables, benches, even the willow chairs with split back seats, as well as all of our cow hide shoes." Her mother was a "housewife who spun yarn from sun up to sun down, knitted all of our stockings and mittens, plaited straw and made all our summer hats." As for Marie, soon after she was married in 1914, she began working as a midwife for neighbouring farm women.

Another young woman, Lena May Purdy, described her early life with her parents.[10] She said that she was born near Napanee, Ontario, where her parents, who were both born in Canada, farmed from 1873 to 1883. In 1896, they decided to move west and relocate near Condie, Saskatchewan. Her father supported the family by being a farmer, but he also worked as a bookkeeper for a variety of businesses. She said that he was a very imaginative and resourceful fellow and tried to create inventions such as sailing sleighs. Unfortunately, he had little success with them. A skilled carpenter, he also made furniture.

A common task for many farm women was to spin wool to make it into yarn. Once it was in yarn form, they could then knit or crochet clothes for their families. Here, Mrs. Floden from the Calmar district of Alberta is spinning wool on a spinning wheel in the early 1900s. NA-4174-10. COURTESY OF LIBRARIES AND CULTURAL RESOURCES DIGITAL COLLECTIONS, UNIVERSITY OF CALGARY

He was very fond of hunting, was a pretty good bass singer, and was a clever gymnast. As for games, he was a skilled pool player and he enjoyed playing checkers and chess. Her mother did needlework and sewed, batted, crocheted, knitted and spun wool. She made quilts and rugs, wrote articles for newspapers, homeschooled Lena and her siblings, and was very fond of botany. She also played the organ and sang. Lena read books, gardened, made quilts and rugs, and used to play the piano for her own amusement. When she was a girl, she skinned a good many animals and tanned the skins. She also hunted and fished to help supply the family table.

John Thiessen was born in Russia in 1891, and his family lived there until 1903, when he was twelve years old.[11] They immigrated to Manitoba, and in 1905 moved to Saskatchewan. His family knew how to speak both Russian and German. His father was a farmer but he also did a lot of carpentry work, such as making furniture out of wood, and making baskets out of willows. His mother enjoyed sewing, knitting and crocheting. John reported that he did some trapping and worked in a blacksmith

Blacksmithing skills were a benefit to those who homesteaded. Knowing how to create metal tools or fix farm implements not only made working life more bearable on the farm, but was also a vocation through which men in the family could earn extra money. In this photograph, August and Norman Kremer are working with hammers, a tong and an anvil in a blacksmith shop in Innisfail, Alberta, in 1910. The forge to heat the metal is located behind them. NA-1709-52. COURTESY OF LIBRARIES AND CULTURAL RESOURCES DIGITAL COLLECTIONS, UNIVERSITY OF CALGARY

shop, and that he liked making things from iron, like hammers, knives, shovels, picks, axes, door hinges, nails, plow blades, bolts, pots, pans and kitchen utensils.

Marion Anderson's parents were both from Ontario, with her mother hailing from Woodstock while her father was from Tiverton.[12] Even though her parents had lived their entire lives in Ontario, because of their Scottish backgrounds they both spoke Gaelic. Marion said that "when they wanted to have some fun with us [that is, with Marion and her siblings], they would talk to themselves in Gaelic and laugh because we were curious but would hold back what they were keeping secret and tell us later." In 1901 the family moved from Ontario to Sintaluta, Saskatchewan (eighty-five miles from Moosomin), where this knowledge of the "two talks" was useful to her father in business. He worked as the Massey Harris Implement Agent in Moosomin and could make sales easily to the Scottish Highlanders who lived in the area. Marion stated that her father, besides being an implement dealer, was a farmer, a homestead inspector and a land agent on the prairies. He also liked to tell stories. As for

Marion's mother, she enjoyed writing in her diary and kept daily accounts describing the trip the family made when they headed west from Ontario. Night after night, Marion said, her mother sat on the floor of the tent with the lantern beside her to write her diary entries. Marion's mother wrote that the family had a feather tick (a feather-filled mattress) and lots of clothes, and that they were quite comfortable on the week-long trip they were taking by horse and wagon. She also noted that she was getting used to cooking outside "but felt stupid at first about it. There were two men, one woman, and three children to cook for. Chief articles of food were bread and tea, fried pork, butter and eggs, and mush for breakfast."[13] Once they were settled on their homestead, Marion mentioned that her mother always offered assistance to other homesteaders in need. "Many a time in the early days, mother would be come for by husbands whose wives had gone into labour." Marion said that her mother would go with them, day or night, and be gone for several days. She also stated that "her mother had no special training as a nurse, but she did well." She also remembered that her mother made dresses for her and her four sisters when they were little, and she would bake bread for bachelors living alone on their homesteads.

Another homesteader, Eric Neal, was the son of immigrants who had travelled from England in 1880 to Manitoba.[14] The family homesteaded, with his father building up a large number of stock. His mother contributed her efforts to farm life and also enjoyed musical pursuits, playing the organ and piano. When he was older, Eric struck out on his own and homesteaded in Saskatchewan, sixteen miles southwest of Watson, near Jansen Lake.

In a similar vein, John Evans said that he was raised in Ontario, but his parents were both from Radnorshire, Wales, where he was born in 1867.[15] His father's occupation was sheep farming as well as dog training. His mother enjoyed music and singing. As for himself, John moved to the area near Saskatoon, Saskatchewan, in 1892 in order to homestead. He learned the farming life from his parents, but as time went by he became interested in politics. In 1921, he was elected to the Canadian Parliament for the Saskatoon constituency and held this position until 1925.

Isabel Muirhead's family was also from Ontario, where they lived in Wellesley, Guelph County, until 1883.[16] This was when

Aron Johnson (who was of Swedish descent) plows his land with a team of horses. In 1910, Aron, his wife and son migrated from Gold Rock, Ontario (where Aron had worked in the gold mines), to homestead in Abbey, Saskatchewan. They travelled by rail in colonist cars, bringing all of their personal possessions with them. They landed in Swift Current, Saskatchewan, where Aron bought a pair of oxen and a wagon. Once the wagon was loaded, they made their way across the prairie, following buffalo trails until they reached their destination. Over time, Aron and his wife had a number of children. They worked to meet all of the homestead regulations and received the patent to their land in 1913. Eventually they expanded their farm with cattle. Aron's wife did all the milking and bottled the cooled milk, which she sold for eight cents a quart. She also sewed clothes for her family, knitted mittens and socks, and made house slippers out of old coats.[17]

her parents decided to make the trek west to homestead. Her father had been a farmer in Ontario, as well as a baseball player and a nature observer, while her mother was a "great knitter and dressmaker, fancy worker and quilter, practical nurse and midwife. She also made switches and wigs from real hair,[18] hooked rugs from rags or flour bag canvas, and she used herbs for medicinal purposes."

Albert Christianson also recalled the varied skills of his parents and their enjoyment of being homesteaders.[19] They were people who were very socially involved and were always willing to give a hand to their neighbours. Albert stated that his father was from Norway, while his mother was an American. Albert was born in the United States, in Minnesota. The family moved north to the province of Saskatchewan in 1912. While his father became a homesteader, he also worked as the local postmaster and storekeeper. Albert said that his father was a good leader and organizer in community projects. In fact, given that they were one of the first homesteaders in the vicinity, his father helped folks locate their homesteads when they arrived in the area. As for his mother, "she always believed that her place was keeping the home for her children and husband. Nothing was ever left undone." He also mentioned that she enjoyed sewing, knitting, crocheting and belonging to local women's clubs, where she could socialize with other women homesteaders.

Greenhorns, Snipe Hunters and Road Apples

While some settlers were farmers or had been raised to be farmers, others were novices or "greenhorns," completely unfamiliar with agriculture and the farming lifestyle. They lacked knowledge of the prairies, they did not understand how to work with animals and they did not know how to farm. With no previous experience to rely on, these new homesteaders would often make errors in judgment, risking harm to themselves, to others around them and to their farm animals. Until they learned the prevailing social norms and started fitting in with the homesteading populace, their lack of knowledge often made them victims of ridicule.

The naïveté of some of those immigrating to Canada was witnessed early on by one seasoned settler, Eric Neal.[1] He was travelling by ship from England when he encountered a group of young men who were planning to become homesteaders on the western prairies. Eric was surprised by their conversation. Rather than delving into deep discussions about building homes, seeding fields, purchasing farm machinery or animal husbandry, they were wondering which animal was the largest on the prairies, the buffalo or the gopher. When discussing the cold weather and what to wear, he overheard them ask each other, "Which is warmest? Snowshoes or moccasins?"

While these young men likely discovered the answers to their questions fairly quickly once they arrived on the prairies, the naïveté of others carried through to their first job as farm labourers, working for those homesteaders who had already gained title to their land. Homesteader Archie Althouse recounted, "When threshing time came, we hired a young Englishman, a former bookkeeper, to help. The first morning he came out in a bathrobe with a towel thrown over his arm and asked [in an upper-crust British accent], 'Will you please show me the way to the bawth room?' Everyone laughed, 'Ha, ha!'"[2] As Archie surmised, "He was a fine fellow, but new to the west" and didn't realize how rustic rural living was at that time. The Englishman was not aware that "washing up" on the homestead consisted of washing one's hands and face with water in a basin in the house, while toilet functions were done in the outhouse, a small building separate and apart from the house. Bathing occurred once a week, with water that was heated on the stove in a large pot and then poured into a large washtub.

Archie discovered that his new farm worker had never driven horses or oxen before, but he was willing to learn. The men hitched up the oxen and gave him the lines. He stood there a moment and then spoke to the team in a very gracious way, "Go on, please," with no result. The oxen continued to stand in place. By the next day he had learned to use the correct commands of "Gee" and "Haw" for the team to turn right or left; however, his penchant for proper etiquette continued when he said to them, "Gee, oh I beg your pardon, Haw!" As Archie said, "It sure was a scream for the men," who were all greatly amused by the young Englishman. As time went on, the men played jokes on their naive counterpart, but he took it in stride and, in the end, did make good in spite of it all.

Homesteader Charles Bray told another story of working with a greenhorn.[3] Sadly, the end result was not as successful as that experienced by Archie Althouse's Englishman. The situation was much more frustrating, and Charles ultimately had to admit defeat. "One spring," he said, "it was hard to pick up a man for summer work, so I hired an Englishman just newly arrived. He was physically developed, was educated and gentlemanly." After leaving college he had worked six years in a pork-packing plant in England. Charles was pleased with this particular skill, as he felt that it would come in handy when it was time for slaughtering. However, things did not work out as Charles had planned. Some days later, Charles said to the Englishman, "Well, this fall when we kill a couple of hogs, you will be able to cut them up and salt them down."

"Oh, by Jove," he replied, "I couldn't do that!"

Well, Charles asked, "What did you do in that pork factory?"

"Why, I put the hams in the vats and took them out when ready to wrap or smoke."

Charles then asked, "Who cut and trimmed them?"

Wide-eyed and shocked, the Englishman replied, "Why, the cutters did that!"

Even though his plans for slaughtering had gone awry, Charles was determined to teach the Englishman a skill.

> I tried to show him how to lift down the harness and put it on the horse. I told him, "Every horse has his own collar and harness and it hangs on these pegs right at [the back end of the stall]. You stand here and watch me harness this horse," which I did slowly and then took it off and hung it back on its peg. "Now," I said, "you do it." He took down the collar, put it on upside down up near the horse's ears. I never said a word, just waited till he got the now mixed-up harness on the horse's back. He was then completely stuck and didn't know how to proceed. I took off the collar and explained how collars were shaped to fit the horse's neck and showed him how the harness would fasten around it. "Now," I told him, "do it all over again." He took the collar, turned it around, studied it carefully and on it went upside down and inside out! Losing patience, I yelled, "Put that collar on right side up or I'll fasten it to *your* neck!"

Finally the collar and harness were successfully placed on the horse by the Englishman in the correct manner.

However, Charles continued to encounter problems with this new hire. "If I record all the funny things he did the next few weeks, it would fill a book, like when he was learning to back up a team on a wagon. He was pulling the lines and chirping directions at them at the same time and turning to the wrong side until the wheel upset the wagon box." Another time, Charles asked the man to drive the team and harrow in a field a little way away. He told him to stop working at 11:45 AM for dinner and 6:00 PM for supper. This would leave him ample time to get the team unhitched before the meal began. However, instead of driving the team to the house, the young fellow unhitched the team wherever he happened to stop, even if he was on the far side of a half-mile

Some young men who came west had no past experience with farming, particularly if they were from the major cities of Europe, where they may have been employed in offices or mercantile stores. The young man in this photograph, dated 1878, was from France and decided to travel to western Canada to try his hand at homesteading.
AUTHOR'S COLLECTION

field. He would then come walking up to the house. In frustration, Charles finally concluded that "his brain was so strained with book learning and learning to cure hams, it was not capable of further development," so he paid him off and "put him on a train headed further west towards the setting of the sun."

Other greenhorns came from Ontario, Quebec, the Maritimes and Newfoundland on harvest excursions. A harvest excursion was a seasonal working practice, where men would take a train to the western prairies to help homesteaders with threshing during the fall harvest. While this became an annual routine for many men, there were always some who were new to the practice. Because of their lack of agricultural knowledge, their youthfulness and their trusting nature, they tended to be gullible when they first arrived on the farm. A common prank that was played on newcomers involved an invitation to go snipe hunting with their new threshing crew friends, many of whom were seasoned harvesters. Wanting to become accepted members of the group, newcomers were more than pleased to go hunting with the gang after dark. With a kerosene lamp lighting their way, the threshing crew led the newcomer out into a field about a half mile away.

They then gave him a gunny sack and instructed him to wait quietly while the rest of the men herded the birds (i.e., the snipes) toward him. They told him to grab the birds and place them in the gunny sack, and they advised him to be patient as it might take some time. After they had the newcomer settled in place, and he had assured them that he would capture the birds, the crew returned to the bunkhouse, had a good laugh and went to bed. After sitting for hours waiting for the snipes, the newcomer, finally smelling a rat, would stumble back home in the wee hours of the morning. Facing his grinning comrades, he knew that he had been the brunt of their joke.

Lack of knowledge about local wildlife got other newcomers into trouble, especially those who came out to work on the harvest. In his family reminiscences, Gordon Stewart told of a German fellow hired to help bring in the crop.[4] On one bright moonlit night, the German looked out the bunkhouse window and saw a black and white animal. His mates told him that the animal could cause damage, and they encouraged him to take his rifle, pursue the animal and shoot it. While the men all knew that it was a skunk, they did not tell this young German about the possible repercussions if the animal was startled. "After firing a couple of shots, he got close enough to hit the animal with the rifle butt. The skunk's aim was better than the hunter's with the result that the poor fellow was temporarily blinded by musk.[5] He kept yelling for help till one of the men finally took pity on him and led him back to the bunkhouse. The smell was so pungent that they buried his clothes and made him sleep in the barn for a few nights until the smell dissipated."

Greenhornism was also evident among the men who decided to homestead on their own without any outside help or advice. As a result, they were sometimes at a loss when confronted with various problems. For instance, one veteran homesteader, Percy Thomson, recalled a greenhorn who did not know how to loosen the reins for his horse.[6] He said that a man just out from England was driving a horse and buggy. When fording a shallow stream, he wished to give the horse a drink, but as the reins (which were attached to the metal bit in the horse's mouth) were secured to the buggy, the horse had little opportunity to lower its head to the water. "So, after considering the situation for some time, he took off his boots, rolled up his pant legs, got out and went around to the back of the buggy and lifted it up, so as to tilt the outfit forward and so let the horse's head down so that it could drink." While Percy did not say whether this process was effective, it was likely humorous to watch, particularly as the new homesteader did not realize that he only had to loosen the reins so the horse could lower his head to drink.

In another case, two inexperienced young men settling in the Bowden district of Alberta bought a pair of oxen, a wagon and all the tools necessary for homesteading.[7] After purchasing their supplies from Bowden, they set out to their homestead a few miles to the east. Upon reaching a valley that they had to cross, the men had a difference of opinion on how to prepare the team and wagon for the steep downhill trek. One said he had been advised to tie the back wheels with a chain, which would give good braking power. The other young man suggested that they hobble the front legs of the oxen. Their argument became heated but they finally settled it by hobbling the oxen. They decided if hobbling did not prove satisfactory, they would then tie the chain on the back wheels. The oxen started down into the ravine. The full weight of the load immediately hit the oxen from behind.

Three farm horses with loose reins are drinking from a local stream, ca. 1920. NA-4548-3. COURTESY OF LIBRARIES AND CULTURAL RESOURCES DIGITAL COLLECTIONS, UNIVERSITY OF CALGARY

Because they were hobbled and unable to recover, "all arrived in a muddled condition at the bottom of the valley with injuries and damaged cargo and equipment." The two men were later ridiculed by other homesteaders for such a foolish performance.

Some stories focused on the dangers presented by those greenhorns who were too eager to prove themselves. As homesteader Eric Neal said, "Some of my neighbours were from a big city in the United States, never used an axe. One winter, we went to the bush for wood. Instructions were given as to how to chop down a tree in a safe fashion."[8] Everyone was told to watch out for trees that were leaning (as they would be more likely to fall in that direction) and to forewarn others by calling out when the tree that they were chopping down was about to fall. This was done to ensure that everyone got out of harm's way. Unfortunately, not everyone was ready to follow instructions. One young man in their group, whom everyone called "young Bill," was very enthusiastic and too excited to listen. When he chopped down his first tree, he let it fall where it may. It ended up falling on a team of horses. "When another tree almost fell on Eric's dad, he warned young Bill to watch what he was doing. Young Bill then dropped another tree and caught Eric's dad right on his head and knocked him down in the deep snow. His dad got up and severely reprimanded young Bill." Bill replied, "But, 'ow do I know where they're going to go?" In frustration, Eric's dad took the axe away from young Bill, as it was obvious he had not listened to the instructions and couldn't be trusted to do the job safely.

Eric Neal quickly came to realize that young Bill was also inexperienced with firearms. Bill owned a good supply of them, no doubt anticipating wild west scenarios with gunfighters and horse thieves. One day, young Bill visited his uncle's house and brought his pump-action gun with him. He always kept a shell in the chamber. He went into the house to show his uncle his gun. Bang! The charge went up through the ceiling and through a sofa on which his cousin was sitting (on the second floor of the house), barely missing him. Following a well-deserved tirade from his uncle and cousin, young Bill learned that guns should not be kept loaded in the house.

While one might assume that the careless handling of firearms was rare, Eric Neal recounted another experience with a greenhorn neighbour who fancied himself an impressive marksman and hunter. This neighbour came visiting one day and decided that he wanted to shoot at some ducks that he saw just outside the door of Eric's house. In his excitement, he grabbed his double-barrelled shotgun, which he always kept loaded and fully cocked, to take a crack at the ducks. Both barrels went off in the house. The shot went through the door and the walls. The ducks flew away unharmed. Eric did not elaborate on his reaction to his home being shot up or to the deafening sound of the shotgun blast, but one suspects the greenhorn's actions did not go over well. Eric would certainly have been aware that if a family member had been outside the house, coming up to the door or doing chores in the yard, they could have been seriously harmed or killed.

At the same time that some greenhorns were learning about guns and gun safety, others were facing a multitude of farm-related problems on their homesteads. For instance, many of them did not know how to work with a team of oxen or how to plow the land. Robert Wooff recalled how he and his father tried their hand at readying the fields for cropping.[9]

> I won't ever forget our first attempt at trying to break the land with a team of young, green oxen, a very green man, a very green boy, and a greener teaming of humans and oxen to the machinery. Father knew nothing about the bridle of a plow or how to gauge wheels which controlled the depth or width of the furrow. The oxen knew nothing about a furrow and I, at seven years old, did not know how to drive the team. In fact, I knew rather less about it [than] the oxen did. And therefore, between the furrow being far too deep for the oxen to navigate and the plow more than difficult for my father, the course that we took across the field was done in a zig-zag pattern. It was anything but what it should have been. I have looked back on it with a great deal of amusement over the years.

While many greenhorns lacked the skills that were needed in the field, others were not familiar with other aspects of the farm. For instance, many did not know how to raise poultry. Knowing that chickens were needed on their homesteads for their eggs and for future consumption, greenhorns found out how to purchase the birds from neighbours. They learned that the birds needed to be contained, and that a chicken coop needed to be built. While they found these tasks fairly easy to accomplish, they did not understand how to raise the birds. In particular, the chicken's eating habits left some inexperienced farmers in a real quandary. As reported by Lucy Johnson:

> We thought we were very well off to have a barn and a house to live in and a good well. Ours was the only frame house at the time. In the yard there was a conglomeration of chickens. Every breed seemed to be represented. Father thought they were "swell" but they rather worried mother and I. Not being used to chickens, we couldn't understand them eating all day, and the more we fed them, the more they seemed to eat. We just couldn't understand them always being hungry, so mother and I got tired of watching them peck and wanted father to get rid of them. Father didn't understand them either, but he said, "We have to have eggs, don't we?" That settled it—we kept them. Naturally, we laughed about it later when we learned that pecking was their nature.[10]

Mary Rogers Berkner also outlined her family's concerns with farming.[11] Her mother was a widow from South Wales who had six children. She decided to move herself and her children to Saskatchewan in 1910. Mary recognized that her mother had a lot of courage to be starting this new life, registering for her 160 acres and contracting for a home to be built on the land. Mary said that the "first year was extremely hard on all of us, especially my two brothers, George and Arthur." George, who was thirteen years old, and Arthur, who was eleven, were responsible for chopping down trees for firewood. They also had to haul the wood home, which was particularly difficult during the cold winter months. Her mother, being naive about farm life, bought chickens for the farm, even though the family did not know how to raise them. Unfortunately, the chickens were too old to be of use and would no longer lay eggs. She also ended up buying old cows, which turned out to be an economic loss. She purchased two horses, but they were not used to the cold winter climate and died. Then she bought two oxen and a small horse, with all three being hitched to the plow together. When her oxen became obstinate and headed for the slough and refused to work (a common character trait of oxen), Mary's mother thought they were dying. She went home and made them an oatmeal gruel, which she tried to force them to eat so they could regain their health.

Like the Berkner family, the Barr Colonists who settled in Lloydminster, Saskatchewan, were also greenhorns completely unfamiliar with agricultural pursuits.[12] They were a group of 2,000 people who had travelled from England in 1902 to start new lives as homesteaders on the Canadian prairies. They were initially led by Reverend Isaac Barr, followed by the Reverend George Lloyd (the settlement of Lloydminster was named in his honour). The Barr Colonists faced numerous challenges due to their lack of knowledge. For instance, one of the aspiring farmers, hearing that bran was likely to bring a high price, bought bran and scattered it on four acres of his newly broken land. Unfortunately, this was a costly endeavour as bran is not a seed. Rather, bran refers to the hard outer coating of a wheat kernel that is removed during the processing of white flour. Another Barr colonist tried to winter his pigs and piglets with hay. Unfortunately, pigs can not survive on hay alone. His fully grown pigs needed a more protein-based diet of chopped grain, milk and vegetables, while his piglets were unable to digest the hay and did not grow into healthy animals. One Barr colonist, who was scared to split wood for kindling, tried to protect himself in a haphazard fashion and actually ended up hurting himself. He adopted the policy of standing in a washtub to protect his toes. While he was splitting wood in this awkward position, a piece of wood rebounded from the axe and injured his eye. According to historian Grant MacEwan, "there were mistakes and needless hardships and the seasoned westerners were amused. Discouraged colonists went back to England. But the men and women who refused to surrender to reverses became the nucleus of a progressive farming community with good homes, good livestock, and advanced ideas about soil and crops."[13]

Rather than highlighting the experiences of those who came from England, John Singleton remembered American-born individuals who tried to make a living on their Canadian homesteads.[14] He stated that while some of those who came to Canada had years of farming under their belts, there were others who did not have any agricultural experience, and they ended up having a difficult time of it. They did not know how to handle farm stock, and they didn't know what to do when the crops suffered from an early frost. They also used weak poplar poles for building their log homes, and they didn't know how to chink the spaces between the poles with a mud plaster to keep out the snow and wind. They suffered horribly through severely cold winters and watched their horses freeze to death as they had not built any shelters for them. Those who had constructed barns saw their hogs become crippled with rheumatism because they were overheated when they were kept in the barn surrounded by straw stacks, then exposed to the harsh, cold weather when they were put outside.

Sometimes, rather than reflecting on the struggles endured by greenhorns, seasoned homesteaders decided to have some fun when they came across a newcomer. Ken Doolittle remembered a conversation he had with another experienced homesteader, Pat, and a newly arrived woman, Miss Good.[15] The two men started discussing road apples one day when they met in town. Knowing that Miss Good believed they were talking about fruit, they carried on with their conversation without the woman realizing that road apples were actually round balls of horse feces found on the road. Their conversation began with a discussion of the wildlife that was available in the vicinity:

> Pat said, "A man could usually find rabbits, prairie chickens and other small game if he could find time to go hunting for them. The same with fish; they were there if you could spare the time to go fishing. Some women did a lot of canning if they could afford the sealers and had anything to can." "There must be lots of wild fruit," said Miss Good. Pat answered, "In some areas there were lots of blueberries, most people called them huckleberries, and there were raspberries, wild strawberries, Saskatoon, highbush cranberries and a few other types of berries. But they were really not that plentiful sometimes as the frequent prairie fires often burnt the bushes, or the berries froze before they were right, or it was too dry, so you couldn't depend on a crop of them every year." "Were

there no larger fruits like apples or plums?" asked Miss Good. "About the only apples that grew in Saskatchewan in the early days were road apples," said Pat looking at me with a humorous twinkle in his Irish eyes. "By gosh, you're right," I quickly added. "You know I haven't seen a road apple for so long I had almost forgotten about them." Miss Good displayed immediate interest. "I never heard of that fruit before. What were they like?" "Well," said Pat, "They aren't of much account. They are about the size of lemons and are usually found along roads around farmyards and ranches. But, like many other natural things, civilization doesn't seem to agree with them. You might find a few around some of the ranches." "Were they edible?" asked the young lady. "Not really," I said, "although a few birds seem to find some food value in them. But they had other uses, particularly in winter when they were frozen solid. Being of a convenient size, they're handy for throwing at the cows if they didn't want to go back in the barn, and many a partridge or rabbit was knocked over by a well-aimed road apple." Pat added, "Yea, you remember how they would always be frozen down where they dropped? We usually wore moccasins in the winter and I got more than once a sore toe from trying to kick loose a frozen road apple to throw at something. They also made good pucks for the games of shinny we used to play on the frozen sloughs. Ken, did I ever tell you about the time I got a black eye from being hit with one? You remember how we used to build snow forts and have snowball fights? Only soft snowballs were allowed by the rules of war, but sometimes tempers got out of hand and illegal weapons were used. Well one time, my brother got mad and the first thing I knew I was hit smack in the eye with a frozen road apple. I will never admit how I got that black eye."

The conversation carried on with the woman never quite understanding what a road apple was. When she left, the two fellows had a good laugh at her expense.

While many greenhorns did not understand rural living and made numerous mistakes while they were learning their new vocation, and some became the brunt of jokes, there were others who did not appreciate the widely held negative stereotype associated with being a greenhorn. In fact, many of them were individuals who had extensive farming experience. One of those was John Potts, who took up homesteading in the Raymore area of Saskatchewan.[16] As he stated,

> Well, I would like to record that for the first few months I had to get pretty rough with some of my neighbors sometimes just to show them that the "Green Englishman" was not always as sappy as they apparently took him to be. That seemed to be the only language they would understand. But they soon understood and then we got along fine.

Travelling the Trails

Even though people came from a variety of different places and had their own interests, hobbies and occupational skills, a sense of community and shared experience developed as they travelled the trails across the western prairies. In the early years, the last major centre was Winnipeg, where many homesteaders would buy their wagons and oxen or horses, purchase their provisions, and buy necessary tools such as axes, hammers and nails, as well as agricultural implements such as plows and harrows. Once they were outfitted, they began their trek across the prairie trails to find their homestead. These are their stories.

A number of trails stretched across the prairies. Some were more frequently used than others. One path had been used by Hudson's Bay Company (HBC) and North West Company traders, the North-West Mounted Police (NWMP) and the Canadian military. Other well-worn trails had been created over the years by Indigenous Peoples or by buffalo herds and other wild animals, while some trails were little more than bush or grasses flattened by previous settlers blazing their own trails through the west.

The most common trail was known as the Saskatchewan Trail. It stretched over 1,200 miles between Winnipeg, Manitoba, and Edmonton, Alberta. Originally, it was used by employees of the North West Company in the early 1800s, followed by independent Métis freighters using horses and wagons that moved goods and provisions from fort to fort. The first part of the trail, which began in Winnipeg, diverged into two trails for a fair distance before the two converged in Minnedosa, Manitoba. The southerly route went west past Portage la Prairie, continuing through the settlements of Bagot and MacGregor. Travellers then turned

It was not unusual for traders and freighters to use three huge wagons (each weighing 2,000 to 2,500 pounds) to haul thousands of pounds of goods and materials from Winnipeg to the west. Eighteen to twenty oxen would be purchased to pull these loads. For security, they would often travel in large groups that included at least six of these outfits. Each team had "one driver with a very long and heavy whip which he used with great skill and appropriate language."[1] They would cover approximately twelve miles per day. A wagon boss to oversee the trip and a cook with a chuckwagon to dole out the meals would also accompany the oxen train. This photograph shows a couple of these oxen teams, ca. 1870. NA-98-23. COURTESY OF LIBRARIES AND CULTURAL RESOURCES DIGITAL COLLECTIONS, UNIVERSITY OF CALGARY

northwest and travelled on to Minnedosa. (This part of the trail was known as the Mission Trail due to the establishment of an Anglican mission in Minnedosa.) The northerly route went from Winnipeg to Portage la Prairie, northwest to Gladstone and continued west to Minnedosa.[2]

Those continuing farther west followed a trail from Minnedosa to Shoal Lake, and then went on to Birtle, where Fort Ellice was located. Fort Ellice had been constructed by the Hudson's Bay Company in 1831 to protect HBC trade with the Assiniboine and Cree Peoples from the Americans, who were seeking to expand their trading operations. From Fort Ellice, travellers continued northwest to Yorkton, Foam Lake, Wynyard, Humboldt and Wakaw,

▲ Settlers and their families who headed west tended to use Red River carts or wagons that were pulled by oxen or horses. The carts were made of wood, with "buffalo hide cut into tough strands and wrapped around the wheels. Because the two wooden wheels were mounted on wooden axles which could not be greased, the carts constantly squealed as they were dragged across the prairies. While some people travelled on their own, others journeyed in groups. They would form brigades often as long as railway trains. These columns created giant clouds of dust which made them visible for miles in every direction."[3] Here, a single ox pulls a cart, ca. 1898. NA-1709-35, BY W. PLAYLE. COURTESY OF LIBRARIES AND CULTURAL RESOURCES DIGITAL COLLECTIONS, UNIVERSITY OF CALGARY.

▼ Fort Carlton, Saskatchewan, 1871. NA-675-1 BY C. HORETZKY. COURTESY OF LIBRARIES AND CULTURAL RESOURCES DIGITAL COLLECTIONS, UNIVERSITY OF CALGARY.

finally reaching Fort Carlton near Batoche, Saskatchewan. (This part of the route became known as the Carlton Trail.) Fort Carlton was a major meeting place for HBC traders and became the central mail distribution point for the western region.

The Edmonton Trail began at Batoche, with people travelling northwest to Blaine Lake, Frenchman's Butte (which was close to Fort Pitt, an HBC post built in 1830) and Frog Lake, and then west to Elk Point. They then ventured northwest to Pakan, Alberta, and southwest to Fort Edmonton (another HBC post that was built in 1794).

Over time, some less-travelled routes diverged from these main trails, with some springing up between new towns that were developing. Homesteader Mary Kajewski told of the Wood Mountain Trail, which her family had used in the early years.[4] She said it was "a few miles south of Qu'Appelle and it had three forks. Travelling on one fork, one would come across a long log building on the crest of a hill, west of the town of Qu'Appelle." This was the NWMP barracks, with forty men stationed there.

▼ This photograph shows four NWMP officers standing outside of Fort Walsh's east stockade with a horse that is being readied for riding, ca. 1874–1880. *L–R:* Constable Alf Wilson, Adjutant Edmund Dalrymple Clark, Colonel James F. Macleod and Doctor John Kittson.
NA-52-1 BY W.E. HOOK. PHOTOGRAPHER. COURTESY OF LIBRARIES AND CULTURAL RESOURCES DIGITAL COLLECTIONS, UNIVERSITY OF CALGARY

Mary also mentioned that the commander of the fort, Major James Morrow Walsh, had his headquarters a quarter of a mile west on another hill, located on a farm that had previously been owned by Staff Sergeant Jerry Fyffe of the NWMP.

George Shepherd was also familiar with this route.[5] He said that "the Fort Walsh–Wood Mountain Trail crossed north of our place ... [and] about four miles south of Fort Walsh, the Wood Mountain–Fort Benton Trail was very plainly visible." Ella Otterson commented on a branch of the Wood Mountain Trail when she reported that there was an "old NWMP trail running from Maple Creek to Wood Mountain."[6] She also mentioned that

> there was an old Indigenous trail going from Battleford to Harlem, Montana, or the Belle Knap reservation when the Indigenous people travelled on their yearly visits back and forth for their annual pow-wows. It crossed the White Mud River at the 50-mile crossing. Lone Tree Lake was one of their points of celebration. While the river was shallow, it was hard to find places where it is possible to cross owing to the steep banks on both sides. However, the Indigenous people found a place and established a crossing.

William Affleck stated that he remembered the old Swift Current Trail, which was surveyed from Swift Current to Battleford in the late 1870s.[7] He noted that the trail was marked every mile with a land surveyor's wooden stake, with the distance in miles from Battleford inscribed on each one. William Gange recalled an old trail, called Lee Pine's Trail, which ran from the South Saskatchewan River to Prince Albert.[8] The trail was given this name because the ferry crossing was operated by a Mr. Lee Pine, who lived on a homestead on the south bank of the Saskatchewan River.

Other homesteaders, such as Eloise Anderson[9] and Harriet Stueck,[10] recalled a route that they and their families had travelled when they moved west. The Pelly Trail was named after Fort Pelly, a fur trading post, which was built in 1824 by the HBC. It was located north of Kamsack, Saskatchewan, near the Swan River. Sidney May, in particular, was quite familiar with this trail and those who travelled on it, as it was located close to his home.[11]

While many homesteaders could remember travelling from place to place on the various trails, others were quite taken with the deep ruts on the trails, which had been made by dozens of wagon wheels as they passed through on their way west. Percy Thomson commented on this phenomenon:

> The old Carlton–Fort Pitt trail ran northwest and southeast of here in the early days. We used to travel it all the way to North Battleford, and in some places, the wheel tracks were worn deeply into the sod. Some were so deep it would cause quite a dump when the plow passed over them when breaking [the land] with the old-time walking plow.[12]

John Laidlaw also referred to the ruts when he wrote in his memoirs, "One mile south of our farm was the Redrun Trail; rutted so deep [you] could scarcely cross over them. There were twelve ruts—a foot deep made by Red River carts and wagons. When the ruts were full of water, wagon drivers made a new trail alongside the old one. I have seen a string of carts a mile long—

Carts and wagons left deep ruts in the prairie turf, so the driving routine was to spread them out, with the right wheel of the cart behind following the left wheel of the cart immediately in front. Depending on the popularity of the trail, some of the trails could be more than twenty ruts wide (ca. 1879). NA-98-11 BY W.E. HOOK. COURTESY OF LIBRARIES AND CULTURAL RESOURCES DIGITAL COLLECTIONS, UNIVERSITY OF CALGARY

some with two horses on a wagon, some with one horse with a Red River cart going west."[13]

Instead of following well-beaten paths, some homesteaders pulled off from the established routes and crossed the prairie using buffalo trails. Mrs. J. Meredith,[14] for instance, said that her family often followed the buffalo trails, as did the families of John Hamer[15] and Norman McDonald.[16] These trails were rough, and travellers often needed to make improvements to the trails before they could proceed. Sometimes trees had to be felled, stripped of their branches and planed flat so that the logs could be laid over the muddy spots to form a solid base. Then the horses and oxen could pull the wagons through the area. In other cases, bridges had to be constructed over creeks in the same fashion.[17]

Albert Christianson remembered that his family had followed an Indigenous trail called the Nippi Trail, which ran by the Chagoness reserve (located southwest of Sylvania in Saskatchewan).[18] He said that his family used to trade with the Indigenous people on the reserve and had purchased grain from them, which his family used to seed their fields.

Flora Kennedy told how her family travelled across the western prairies in 1906 when she was only eleven years old.[19] She highlighted the day they left, the trails they followed, the distance they covered and the day-to-day work that was involved. She also marvelled at the beauty of the natural grasses and the never-ending blue sky.

> Finally, the day came for the start of the trip. It was early afternoon when we pulled away from Saskatoon, the wagon piled high, with the cow tied behind with a calf following. The beginning of a track of 150 to 160 miles, following the wagon tracks of others. We were headed in a southwesterly direction: Vanscoy, Delisle, Laura, Tessier, Harris, Zealandia, Rosetown, Brock and Netherhill. The foregoing names are given to the towns which sprang up as the railway line was built.
>
> Our trail stretched across miles and miles of unbroken prairie dotted here and there with settlers' shacks. The trail itself was in poor condition, often rutted, muddy, stony, and through numerous sloughs. It would take too long to skirt these sloughs, so usually an attempt was made to go

through them. If the wagon was overloaded, it inevitably became stuck. What to do? Unload some of the things and wade through to the dry land with them. Then a good slap of the reins on the horses' backs and with luck you reached dry land. Some were wiser and took some of their load off before the first try across. Then they would cross back over, load up and cross again. That spring of 1906 was a wet one so that every gully and pothole was full of water. Especially through the Eagle Hills around the Delisle-Harris Country.

But to go back to that first day on the trail, we made probably ten miles and then camped for the night. The tent had to be put up, stove, bed clothes, and food unpacked from the wagon. The horses were fed some oats and hobbled and put out to grass, and the cow tethered so that she could have some supper too. This evening routine was the same practically every night . . .

That two weeks on the trail was a wild adventure for a girl of eleven. The cow was tied behind the wagon and tended to pull back, so I had the job of giving her a prod once in a while to smarten up her step. We carried water from the sloughs for washing and drinking, we picked up buffalo chips and dried cow flaps for the fire, sage bush to make a smudge against the mosquitoes, and sometimes held the tethers while the horses ate the plentiful green grass. It wasn't a lonesome trail, for many others were going as far or further than we were.

After passing through the Eagle Hills with their scrubby trees and bushes, a new panorama stretched before us. A great expanse of prairie to the north, south and west as far as the eye could see covered with green grass and some sage bush and fluffy white clouds and blue sky overhead.

Like Flora, Tobias Lanegraff was enthralled with the beauty of the prairie and the wildlife that he saw as he and his family travelled the trails.[20] He stated that there were "lots of shelter and winding trails through the bush. We often saw a fox or coyote crossing a lake or meadow in winter and heading for the bush as fast as he could go. Further on, we saw a deer take a jump or two and stop and then walk on out of sight. I have often seen bears with their cubs. They were looking for fish along the streams and lakes."

Many homesteaders enjoyed the scenic beauty as they travelled across the prairies. In this photograph, dated 1912, a young man is having his lunch and enjoying the view. AUTHOR'S COLLECTION

Fred Baines offered a different account of his family's travels across the open prairies, one in which anxiety and fear prevailed.[21] His story began when he and his family reached Broadview, Saskatchewan, purchased a "prairie schooner" (a covered wagon) and headed west with others who were headed in the same direction.

> We struggled up over the Qu'Appelle Valley. Next day we camped for the night on the top of the hill. The mosquitoes, large and ferocious, assailed us, many of which would weigh a pound, and the large ones climbed up on the trees and bark. As darkness fell, the wolves' cry reverberated up the valley. My mother, becoming alarmed, inquired if they would attack us. She received the reassuring answer [from the group's driver] that they rarely did, but if they did, they always ate the horses first. Fortunately, the attack failed to materialize.

The next day the Baines family continued their travels west, hoping to reach their destination—Crescent City. Given its name, they expected to see a city, but when they arrived they saw only five tents and one log shanty with a sod roof. They wondered where the city was or whether they were having a bad dream.

When they turned to question the group's driver, he had already unhitched the horses for the day. Knowing that their planned stop for the night was Crescent City, they came to the disheartened conclusion that this place was their new home.

Sometimes people began their trek on trails that promised to be fairly easy to follow but turned out to be far less than desirable. In fact, some trails became so poor that they eventually petered out, and people became lost in the wilderness. Such was the case with a young Englishman named A.L. Brick, who decided to travel west with his parents in 1888.[22] Upon arriving in Edmonton, Alberta, his father and mother continued the journey on the river up to Athabasca, travelling by York boat with their provisions,[23] which included farm tools and equipment, machinery, poultry, pigs and a bull. Travelling by boat was an expensive endeavour—it cost A.L. Brick's father three cents a pound. Given this expenditure and the lack of space on the boat, the family decided that their three horses and two heifers they had purchased would be driven overland and through the bush in a reasonable amount of time. For this trip, A.L. Brick was accompanied by Richard, a Frenchman, who was taking two Oregon mares and thirty cayuse pack ponies to Athabasca. The trail that they decided to follow worked well for the first two days. On the third day, they were in trouble, as remembered by A.L. Brick:

> We came to realize there was no trail of any kind. [It had disappeared!] We could not see a single thing [through the trees]. We wandered around for days and eventually came out on the Athabasca River on the morning of the ninth day to what is now called Bald Hill. It is eighteen miles up from Athabasca on the north side of the river. We were five days without food with only berries to eat ... When we hit Bald Hill we went down to the river and some of the horses went over the bank into the water to drink. The little French Canadian mare [one of the horses which my father had purchased] got out into a soft place where there was quicksand, and could not get out. We took our pack ropes, twisted them together, got them around her girth and Richard got one of the big Oregon mares. Richard went behind the Oregon mare and she kicked him right on the back of the head and he fell down right beside the little French Canadian mare. I got him up on the bank

> somehow. He was unconscious for quite a while. [As we had reached the Athabasca River,] we knew we were only a short distance from the town of Athabasca but we laid there all that night and was undecided whether Richard would go on to Athabasca or not in the morning. He told me if anything happened to him to get a few logs, lash them together, leave all the horses, put him on the raft and go to Athabasca on the river. He warned me to tie up the raft to the bank at night or I would pass Athabasca in the dark. However, by morning he was feeling not too bad and we started on. If that horse had not kicked Richard, I believe we would have got the little mare out of the quicksand. She stayed there all night, so I shot her the next morning. Only her neck and one shoulder were out of the quicksand. I had a small caliber pistol and fired five shots into her ears and left her there.

While many people following the trails slept under their cart or wagon, in tents or in the open under the stars, every once in a while they would finish their day by lodging at a stopping place. Stopping places were private residences where travellers could obtain food and a place to sleep for the night. The cost for such an accommodation was twenty-five cents. It was also a resting spot for the horses or oxen who had laboured all day pulling the wagons. Feed was typically available, as was a barn where the animals could settle and relax. While some provisions were made available to guests,

> travelers usually carried their own bed rolls to use at the stopping places. The first arrivals got the use of the cots, the rest slept on the floor if there was room or in the barn on crowded nights. In summer, tents might be set up for the extra travelers. Sometimes these travelers ate their evening meal at the stopping house, at other times just a breakfast was included with the price of the bed. The porridge eaten at breakfast was very thick and was eaten with a little salt added but no milk or cream was usually available. Sometimes berries were added in season. Pieces of salt pork (fat belly) and tea might be included.[24]

Not surprisingly, many guests found that the amenities and the degree of comfort that they could expect at stopping places deteriorated the farther they ventured into undeveloped territory. One story, written by Ruth Upton,[25] described how these stopping places changed as she and her husband travelled in 1911 from Edmonton north to the Peace River country, where they wished to make their home:

> We had as our objective point Peace River Crossing, a small fur trading post on the Peace River, 500 miles from Edmonton, Alberta. Now the word, stopping place, is important to one traveling into the north land. To our eastern minds, [we believed that we would be stopping at] a small hotel or at least a comfortable place where accommodation could be had for the weary traveler. It was well for us that our initiation into the real mysteries of stopping places was very gradual indeed. For instance, our first night on the trip out of Edmonton was spent at Egges Halfway House,[26] the proverbial loghouse, quite spacious as I afterwards realized, and by spacious, I mean that it boasts of more than one room. The original one-roomed building had a series of additions indicating no doubt the prosperity of the farmer. Thus, it boasted a bedroom, a long dining room, which also served as a living room, kitchen, and a bunkhouse. Being such a tenderfoot, I regarded this place as really quite an institution and was greatly interested in the number of people we met there. There must have been about 20 men gathered the evening we were there. They were all on their way into the north land, or out of it, bent on all kinds of business, freighters, settlers, surveyors and many real estate men. This was my first intimation of a fact which I later came to realize, namely, that I had started on a journey into a man's land, for we encountered very few women on the whole trip. Since I was the only woman in this place, I was given the only bedroom in which was a real bed, a luxury not to be found in any other stopping place after leaving Athabasca Landing. Naturally, the memory of this first place made a very strong impression on me, not so much at the time for I thought it crude enough then, but in the days and weeks that followed it seemed so comfortable, even luxurious, by comparison.

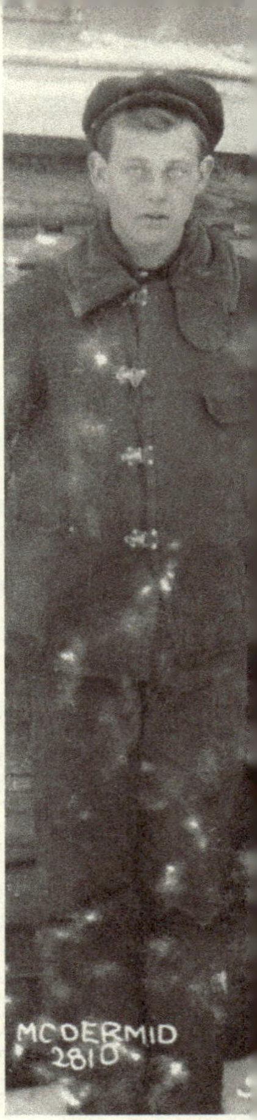

The second night brought us to Athabasca Landing, a flourishing little village of several hundred people. We were delayed here for several days getting some of our effects together, things which had been sent on ahead of us to this point. Here our real journey began. We learned that all stopping places beyond were homes of Indigenous and Metis, where the most you could get was shelter in some cases and feed for your horses. No amount of money could buy a meal or a bed in these places, for they were not to be had. Hence, we had of necessity to carry our bed and our meals with us. The traveler's bed is appropriately termed "a roll up." It consists of a thin mattress and a couple of pair of Hudson's Bay blankets. A canvas covering is attached to the bottom of the mattress and buckles over the blankets, resembling a sleeping bag when one is in it. In the daytime it can be conveniently rolled up and tied with ropes into a small bundle for carrying. I admit I regarded this bed rather skeptically at first, but in the course of our journey when I found out that the same bed was spread out ... beside a campfire or under a tree, I came to realize how very adaptable to the conditions of the country it was. It was necessary to remind oneself constantly that a good hard bed is healthier than a soft one, and I did have a good deal of difficulty in finding the soft side of the board. However, I learned to be thankful for even that kind of bed. The need of carrying one's own bedding on such a trip was made very impressive before we came to the end of our journey. The meals presented some difficulties at first when viewed from the standpoint of a very green pioneer.

However, at Athabasca Landing we bought our field supply, which we carried in the well-known grub box, equipped with granite dishes and necessary cooking utensils. The meals during the rest of the journey were cooked over a campfire, or on a camp stove when one was available. This we found to be quite an art when kept up from day to day. However, when one learns that the base of all meals on the trail consists of bacon, beans, bannock and tea—always tea—occasionally supplemented by some canned goods, the

A group of men, women and children pose outside a stopping place on Alberta's Grande Prairie–Edson Trail in 1912. NA-1328-2810 BY BYRON-MAY COMPANY LIMITED. COURTESY OF LIBRARIES AND CULTURAL RESOURCES DIGITAL COLLECTIONS, UNIVERSITY OF CALGARY

problem is simplified. So, we continued our journey for the remaining 400 miles. We followed the course of the Athabasca River for about 100 miles, then the Little Slave River for 75 miles and across Lesser Slave Lake for 100 miles. This trip from Edmonton to Peace River consumed six weeks of time due to disagreeable weather, the breaking up of ice and small rivers and many other difficulties which the traveler in those days had to face. Under normal conditions this trip would have been completed in two weeks.

Water, Water, Everywhere! Crossing Streams and Fording Creeks

Whether the homesteaders were travelling west or were making their weekly trip to town for supplies, many of them faced similar challenges associated with fast-flowing streams, deep rivers and lakes. While many tried to cross directly to the other side, expert manoeuvring was occasionally needed to avoid boulders and other obstacles. In some cases the water was so high and the current so strong that the wagon box would begin to float, and homesteaders lost their belongings as they flowed down the river. In other cases, homesteaders, family members, horses and even the family dog fought to keep their heads above water as they made treacherous crossings.

In his memoirs, homesteader John Fetsch highlighted the times he needed to make a trip to Saskatoon for provisions.[1] He remembered these trips well as he had to cross the South Saskatchewan, a deep river with a strong current and a rocky bottom. It was a treacherous undertaking and took a lot of skill to get across, as the horses needed to be steered in a particular direction. White rags were tied to trees on each side of the river to show travellers where they had to enter the river and where they should exit the river on the other side. However, crossing the river was not as simple as driving the horses straight across. Rather, once they had entered the river, they had to take a sharp turn north to avoid a large boulder under the water. After that, a quick southern turn was needed to avoid a big hole. In other words, to get to the other side, travellers had to follow a route resembling the letter "S." While navigating these curves, travellers also had to be aware of the increasing height of the water as they reached the centre point, and the strength of the current. After obtaining supplies from Saskatoon, John knew that he had to protect his goods. He said that the wagon had boards for a seat, so he would put his bags of flour on the boards, and then he sat on the flour. As for his box of groceries, he placed the box in his lap. In this way, the bags of flour and groceries would stay dry as the water never reached higher than the seat of the wagon. He used this method every time he crossed. Unfortunately, one of John's friends did not bother to protect his flour and groceries and just placed them in the back of the wagon. By the time he reached the other side, he had lost all of his groceries—they floated down the river—and his flour was ruined, soaked by river water.

Homesteader Frank Baines didn't have to cross a river, but he offered his account of how dangerous it could be when he and his wife crossed a deep, cold stream:

> The wife and I drove to Wolseley in the spring of 1901 with a team and buggy. Northeast of Grenfell, we came to a wide stream, just at dusk, that we had to ford. The water was well up in the buggy 'til we came to the creek bed, and then the horses had to swim. The current of the icy water [was so strong that it] took out the valise [small suitcase] from under our feet. The valise then struck the buggy wheel. Luckily, I was able to grab it and I swung it to the opposite side of the creek. When we reached dry land, we had to tip the water out of the buggy. We then drove another four miles which took us to an aunt of Mrs. Baines where we got dry clothing, hot tea, and real hospitality. We took no harm, but we heard of some people being drowned while crossing that same creek in a wagon.[2]

When Lillian Miles was a child, she went through a harrowing and dangerous experience with her mother, sisters and brothers when they tried to cross a creek in their wagon.[3] She remembered how her family was moving from Edenwold to Yellow Grass, Saskatchewan, and had to cross through Many Bones Creek near the town of Francis. While a number of men, including her uncle, rode alongside the wagon, others were driving a herd of cattle across the stream. One man took the reins of the family's

A woman crosses Loon Lake, Saskatchewan, on her horse, ca. 1885. NA-363-69, BY JAMES PETERS. COURTESY OF LIBRARIES AND CULTURAL RESOURCES DIGITAL COLLECTIONS, UNIVERSITY OF CALGARY

wagon to help drive the family's team through the water. Lillian described what happened next:

> The wagon was new, fortunately, and we had a canvass over the top. We had our bedding in this wagon box and all we children were in the wagon box. However, when we drove down into the water, our wagon box floated off the wheels and we floated down the creek. My Uncle Jack lassoed the little peg on the front of the wagon box and pulled us to shore from the other side. My mother was hanging onto the lines. The horses with the wheels were going one way and we were going the other. I can still see my mother crying. However, we managed to get across without mishap, and dried ourselves out by the fire that night.

Many other homesteaders told stories of stressful river crossings. Eric Neal, for example, reported arriving by train in Watson, Saskatchewan, in the spring of 1906 with a carload of settler effects.[4] He had to travel another sixteen miles to his homestead, and he set out with 600 pounds of supplies in his wagon, pulled by a team of horses. One mile out from Watson he found that he had to cross a river. As he said, there was "water, water, everywhere!" He began to cross, and as the water got deeper, the horses began to swim. They were also getting stuck in the mud whenever their hooves touched the river bottom. The wagon started floating. Everything ultimately arrived safely on the opposite bank, but Eric said that it took him sixteen hours to finally get to his homestead instead of the usual four.

Like Eric, Charley Johnston of Bowden, Alberta, faced some difficult and distressing moments when he, his horses and his dog tried crossing a river on their trip home from his friend Mack's place.[5] Charley had gone to Mack's to pick up ten bags of seed grain. To keep him company, Mack rode alongside Charley and his wagon to the riverbank. As recalled by Charley, this is where the problems began:

> It was almost dark and commencing to rain a little. The ford was somewhat difficult to follow[6] ... and was about one mile downriver and not far from Mack's farm. I rode in with the saddle horse to be sure that it was safe for a wagon and thus avoid having the grain get wet if the water was over the bottom of the wagon box. On the west side was a cutbank of gravel and clay to go down and come up, but as it was dark, we could not see it clearly. We had to go downstream to the end of a gravel bar and enter the water where it was most shallow and then head upstream at an angle of almost twenty degrees and follow the gravel bar until we were opposite the cut in the west bank. And I went, followed closely by my faithful dog. All went well as the horse took it quietly and carefully but when we reached the opposite side of the river. I found that I had missed the opening in the bank. The dog missed the outlet worse than we had and was carried down the stream with the current and evidently was in trouble by the howls he emitted. I took a moment off and studied the situation before making any further move. I figured that it was most unlikely my horse had overshot the outlet by going too far upstream, so petted the horse a little and talked to her a little and then we headed upstream. The

> water was halfway up the sides of the horse, so I made sure that my feet were not too far from the stirrups in case of a sudden drop into a hole. Some horses swim on their side if the water is deep. My horses had never been in deep water, so I did not know how they would react. Anyway, I made a silent prayer and set for it. So far as I can remember we were about thirty feet below the spring in the bank. The dog was still yipping for help. Mack and I shouted back and forth. He said, "Charley you had better see what is amiss with the dog first; one minute or two will not affect the situation." I slowly followed the bank along until I came opposite to where the dog was caught in the limb of a tree which had fallen into the river. I crawled out on the tree until I could reach him by the scruff of the neck and heaved him to safety. He did not show any more desire to go swimming that evening ... By the time we got home, it was well past the supper hour. As expected, mother was in a real dither. She had been outside when the dog was in trouble on the river. She said that in spite of the distance which was about one mile, she could distinctly hear the voice of the dog and therefore thought we were in trouble. However, all is well that ends well and the day's difficulties were soon out of mind.

J.H. Sand recalled the day when he tried crossing Swift Current Creek when it was flooded in the spring of 1912.[7] He was on his way home from town and only had a quarter of a mile left to travel when he found that he would not be able to cross the creek as the water was too deep and fast flowing. He stayed with a friend overnight and started out again the next morning. The only way that he could cross was to go twelve miles out of his way where a bridge was located. When he finally arrived at the bridge, he discovered that it was slowly being submerged. Realizing the precariousness of crossing, but at the same time anxious to get home, Sand decided to take the risk and nervously but quickly guided his horse and wagon across. Within fifteen minutes of his crossing the bridge was wiped out by the raging current and carried downstream.

Two other homesteaders, Charles Davis and his friend Sydney Morris, experienced a traumatic ordeal in the spring of 1907 when they were headed home after picking up supplies from North Battleford.[8]

On the return journey at Blackfoot Creek, we found the bridge was gone with the whirling stream. We searched blindly for landmarks. Even though we were so near home after our 120 mile trip, the night was overcast and intensely dark. We had no means of making the soundings for depth. I searched upstream. Syd searched downstream. At last he shouted, I've found a good place to ford. I slowly and cautiously arrived but in the darkness, it was impossible for me to agree with him. You can't hear the swirl of the water. That's not good, I replied, and according to the distance from the old staking pegs I found upstream, you're on or near the deep holes, but he's insisting. He knew he could ford it, right there, in a matter of minutes. He had the team and wagon. They were at the water's edge, asking if I was mounting the load. I said no! I'll ford it or swim, so with the order to get up, the team moved forward. The heel chains rattled, then came a terrific splash, the horses began blowing bubbling snorts and Syd began yelling and cursing. It was then I entered the water. The team and wagon caused an eddy, a little undertow in the stream, and as I approached the practically submerged wagon, I knew the horses would drown if the tugs [the leather straps that attached the horses' harness to the shafts or poles of the wagon] were not slashed. Syd wasn't a swimmer, so I shouted to him to keep on top of the load whilst I slashed the tugs. Luckily on journeys, I always carried my sheathed dirk. It was razor sharp. Now Syd, I shouted, keep a tight line so the horses can keep their nostrils up. I'll soon have them clear. Now I had the dirk and quickly submerged to cut the furthermost tug. My knife ripped through it quickly for I used all the power I had. The second tug was not so easy, but I kept the knife in the same cut and with a second supreme jerk, it too fell severed. My right leg was aching as it was hooked into the foremost upstream wheel and my bursting lungs were relieved as I guided towards the life-giving air. In a second or two, I was down fumbling with the tug near the pole. At last, I found it and without difficulty. It was so slack, I unhooked the heel chain and in a matter of seconds, the other was also slack and was so released. I was soon clear, breathing easily, and shouted to

Syd, slap your lines loosely in the water, and as he did, so did the tongue (or pole) fall. The horses were free and after swimming a little downstream, they made a safe landing for we could hear them shake themselves and snort. The wagon drifted downstream until it hit a bar of sandy soil. There it stopped, half submerged. I found the water shallow toward the east bank. Syd dismounted from the load and we waded ashore, like two shipwrecked mariners, one and a half miles away from another settler's home. He had heard us and came to our aid. There we dried out, drank hot coffee and dozed for a couple of hours. At dawn, we returned to salvage what we could of our supplies, one sack of flour had gone down stream, so had two sacks of rolled oats, two hundred pounds of sugar was saturated, and so was the other perishables. Making a summary of our losses, all that was left was some crude carbolic and some washed-out flour sacks.

Fording a river with horses and a wagon was particularly treacherous. The freezing temperatures, ice floes and river currents were hard on horses while they tried to navigate the rocky bottom with their hooves. Additionally, if anyone fell off the wagon and into the water, the weight of their winter clothes would drag them down into the frigid depths or at the very least make it difficult to fight the undertow (ca. 1912). PD-282-68. COURTESY OF LIBRARIES AND CULTURAL RESOURCES DIGITAL COLLECTIONS, UNIVERSITY OF CALGARY

From time to time, homesteaders found humour in their ordeals, or they tried to make light of the situation for the sake of others, especially if there were children in the group. For instance, Mrs. L.J. Adler of Emmaville, Saskatchewan, recounted the day her family was travelling to their homestead.[9] They were frightened as they crossed a fast-flowing creek, but they made it across safely—except for the loss of a box of dishes that had fallen off the wagon. Instead of expressing disappointment at losing her dishes or showing any signs of anxiety that would alarm her children, Mrs. Adler decided to put the event in a more amusing light by laughing and saying, "That was the last of the dishes at Little Red Deer Creek!"

The homesteader who had perhaps the most witty, funny and sarcastic statement about losing his wagon box and supplies down a creek was B.L. Tanner.[10] When he saw his purchases flowing downstream on Moose Mountain Creek when he tried to ford it in 1904, he remarked to those around him, "This experience was not foretold in the Immigration literature sent to me about the western prairies!"

"It's ta goombo. It wa' stick ta' y' teeth if't had the chance."

Along with the challenges of fording streams and rivers, homesteaders shared another common plight—getting their wagon wheels stuck in the gumbo whenever it rained or when the snow started to melt in the spring. Gumbo is thick, sticky, clay-based soil. It contains sodium bentonite, a component that enables soil to absorb water and swell up to three times its original volume. It is primarily found in an area extending from Regina to Weyburn, Saskatchewan; however, it can be found in other smaller areas around the province as well. Homesteaders also remembered sand spots in the road where wagon wheels would sink, while others remarked on the sloughs where horses and wagons would get bogged down. In all of these cases, homesteaders had to be prepared to unload their wagons to lighten the weight of the vehicle and then reload when the wagon was unstuck, or they had to search for assistance from local farmers in order to free their wagons so they could continue on their way.

In her memoirs, a young homesteader named Eloise Anderson recalled:

There were many stories every spring when one of the settlers would make the one mile trip to Yorkton, Saskatchewan, for supplies. It would always be, "Where did you get stuck with your load?" The answers would always be, "I got stuck near Whiskey Slough or near the Halfway Place."[1] One day, I came home from Yorkton with my father when he had a load on the wagon (bran, shorts [oats] and numerous other supplies). Of course, we got stuck and he had to remove his shoes and socks, roll up his pant legs and unload everything

> and carry it all to high ground, including myself. Then the horses were able to pull the wagon out and he reloaded. That seemed to be the main topic of conversation in the spring, how many times they had to unload and reload, and where they got stuck on the road to Yorkton.[2]

Homesteader John Ludlow had a similar story to tell.[3] He said that he and two other fellows left Moose Jaw, Saskatchewan, in May 1907. All three of them had yokes of oxen and large wagon-loads of supplies including lumber, plows, stoves, tools and food. After getting stuck many times in sloughs, unloading and reloading the wagons time and time again, they were all exhausted and relieved when they finally reached their homesteads by the end of the day.

Nine-year-old Henry Neufeld, whose family originally hailed from Winkler, Manitoba, recounted the many times they became stuck on their journey from Melfort to Lost River Valley, Saskatchewan, in 1906.[4] It took six days to cover sixty-five miles, and he remembered well the continuous frustration experienced by his family as they got stuck once for every mile they travelled. He explained that there were no roads to follow at that time, so no improvements had been made to any problem areas. Instead, Henry's family was blazing their own trail through the prairie, and each time they got stuck they would have to unload the wagon, pull it out of the mud and load it again.

Another young child, Isabel Muirhead,[5] told how her family's wagon got stuck, how an essential wagon part broke and how she was left alone on the prairie for hours.

> On our first trip to Estevan, my father got stuck in the gumbo about 2½ miles west of Estevan. Believe me, it was no joke as the horses tugged and pulled 'til they broke the whipple tree.[6] Dad had to unhitch a horse and go back to the Souris River about three miles east to get an ash pole to make another whipple tree. I was left sitting in the middle of the gumbo in the wagon. However, I soon got out and sat on the hills nearby so I could see Dad coming back. I was only twelve years old and believe me, it was rather lonely for there was not another soul around for miles.

"It's ta goombo. It wa' stick ta' y' teeth if't had the chance."

Kathleen Lennox Smith also remembered the challenges of getting stuck in the Weyburn area of Saskatchewan in 1904.[7] What is interesting about her story is how her family overcame these challenges, or at least tried to prepare for them. Her story begins with her Irish father registering for homestead land while she and her mother and two young siblings lived in Weyburn. Once her father had built them a home, Kathleen said, he returned to Weyburn in the spring, and her family purchased all the equipment and supplies they needed to settle comfortably on their homestead.

> We gathered together three big strong oxen, a pony, two wagons, a buggy, walking plow, disk, harrows, mower and rake, some oats and feed, potatoes for planting and garden seeds. One wagon had a hay rack on it and this was loaded with most of the machinery and drawn by the big black team of oxen. The other wagon, drawn by the pony and the extra oxen, was rigged up with canvas over hoops like a covered wagon. The buggy was fastened behind this wagon, which was loaded with our potatoes, feed, groceries, and clothing. It was necessary for Dad to make two trips to bring all of the equipment, so mother stayed behind [for the first trip] and Dad and we children started on our own trek around the 1st of June. It was a wet spring, and the roads had some very bad spots in the low places. We had only a prairie trail to follow. There were no graded roads west of Weyburn then. Dad kept his route by checking up on the section landmarks as we moved along. We could all read the numbers on these iron posts.[8] We made twelve miles the first day and camped for the night. The steer we had tied behind the big wagon got tangled in the wheel and we had difficulty releasing him. His nose bled so much we left him behind and Dad sold him later. With oxen, one must travel during the cold mornings and evenings and rest during the heat of the day. We rose bright and early the second morning and got on our way. We just got about a mile when we got stuck in a bad mud hole. We unloaded a good part of the heavy stuff on the ground but were unable to get out, so Dad went back to town and got a dray team to come out and help pull us out. After that experience we always drove the light wagon through the bad spots to test them before

> trying to drive through them with our big hay rack load. We would change teams to put the big ox team on the covered wagon and then when it was safely over, we put both teams on the big load. Our pony had a habit of baulking if pulling the heavy load, but if one of us got on his back he would pull fine, so it was my younger brother's job, as he was smaller and younger than my sister and I, to ride on his back through all the bad spots. There were a lot of caravans traveling west to new lands that spring and we always could find out what the roads ahead were like by inquiring as we went along.

Charles Davis offers an interesting account of how he and his friends, John and Jack, overcame the obstacles associated with less than desirable road conditions.[9] His story also gives a glimpse into how dangerous such conditions could be.

> There were gumbo and sand spots where men toiled and cursed and animals strained and groaned as only over burdened animals can. It's pitiful and indeed unmerciful and by carrying an extra or overload, we solved the problem and brought relief to animal and human. We simply carried four planks of wood, 14 feet by 2 inches by 12 inches. By using two at a time and rolling on to the next, we kept relaying until the sand or gumbo spot was crossed. We saved stress and strain and remained in good spirits. On one occasion, John was leading a wagon train of ten wagons of provisions. Each settler from the north-west knew well the spots on the west side of Jackfish Lake, Saskatchewan. Jack planked it and went to lead the oxen. He stepped off the planking onto the gumbo. His feet got balled up so badly, he was held as firm as the rock of ages. He was unseen and unknown to the driver of the wagon that was approaching. John, however, saw that Jack was stuck in the gumbo. Quick thinking, he told him to lay flat and sink into the gumbo and gradually, the wagon passed clearly over him. Jack was told that when the rear of the wagon came over him, to seize it and hang on to the protruding end of the reach. This is how Jack got dubbed "Gumbo Jack." The sight was amusing to onlookers and Jack said he dug gumbo out of his ears for ten years after.

"It's ta goombo. It wa' stick ta' y' teeth if't had the chance."

A wagon with a full load of groceries is stuck in a mud hole near the Springfield Ranch near Beynon, Alberta, in 1907. NC-43-28, BY H.B. BIGGS. COURTESY OF LIBRARIES AND CULTURAL RESOURCES DIGITAL COLLECTIONS, UNIVERSITY OF CALGARY

Many homesteaders presented a variety of stories associated with their experiences with gumbo. Ella Otterson, for instance, wrote about some neighbour boys who brought home her pet horse, who had become lost.[10] She said that he was covered with gumbo and that the boys told her he had been stuck in the mud. "I was very much excited for if I had lost that horse, I would have lost a very good friend." Mary Birkett remembered how her family's chickens suffered on their farm when they got into the gumbo.[11] She said the chickens' feet got so clogged they couldn't walk.

Charles Sargent recalled how he arrived at night in Kindersley, Saskatchewan, in April 1911 after rain and a snowstorm.[12] In the morning, when he went out to take a look at his wagon, he mistook the wheels on the wagon for solid wood. On investigating them more closely, he found that they had spokes, but the space between them was completely filled in with gumbo. James Tulloch also had a problem with gumbo, as it was stuck in his farm equipment.[13] He said, "We have lots of gumbo here. We do not enjoy it! Our land is flooded and what crop we had, we cannot save it, as the gumbo sticks to our machinery and prevents us from operating it." Felix Belliveau, after getting stuck in the mud a number of times, learned to pour water in beside the wheels and oxen's feet to break the suction of the gumbo,[14] while another homesteader recounted the story of a wedding party that got mired in the gumbo on their way to the church. Getting out of the wagon, they landed in the thick mud, ruining their shoes. They had to go into the church and go through the entire wedding ceremony in bare feet.

While most people highlighted the difficulties they faced with gumbo, there was one individual who tried to see its positive attributes. Clara Hoffer reported that her husband built their first house out of gumbo. She said that one day, he had it finished except for the roof. When he got up the next morning to finish the roof, all he found was a heap of earth. The dried gumbo had cracked and crumbled onto the ground.[15]

"It's ta goombo. It wa' stick ta' y' teeth if't had the chance."

Gumbo Quips

GUMBO WAS AN irritant for many homesteaders—so much so that certain phrases, expressions and stories describing this sticky mud became commonplace. When Elizabeth King reminisced about her earlier years on the prairies, she said, "I always remember one thing of concern always talked about by father and mother were the conditions of the roads. Were they in passable, impassable but we'll try, or just plain stayin' at home condition? Some of the mud holes certainly caused excitement. Father, in his Yorkshire brogue, used to say, 'It's ta goombo. It wa' stick ta y' teeth if't had the chance.'"[16]

Others indicated how hard it was to walk through gumbo when they said, "When you walk on the prairie grass, you can take one step ahead, but be two steps behind."[17] Others complained about carrying a homestead on one foot and a pre-emption on the other, while another said, "We always carried home our farm on our feet."[18]

There is also the tall tale of a man who got stuck in the gumbo. He had to leave his boots behind. When he went back to get them after a dry spell, they were so solidly cemented in the gumbo, he had to use a stick of dynamite to blast them out.[19]

Still others remembered how hard it was to work the land. John Thiessen said: "Our land was gumbo, very sticky when wet, but very hard when dry. People use to say that gumbo land could only be worked for one hour properly after a rain. Before that hour, it was too wet, after that, it was too dry."[20] Similarly, Harve Carson stated that there were odd spots of gumbo in his district.[21] One time he was asked why he wasn't breaking his land up with his plow. He responded, "If you try to go through there with your plow with all that gumbo, you would think the devil was there before you."●

Cypress Trees, Beaver Dams and Red Deer Antlers

For many people, distinctive landmarks like streams and coulees, or places where wildlife gathered, became important points of interest in their localities. The practical reasons for the names given these landmarks not only reveal the uniqueness of the area, but also led to a community spirit in the sense that everyone became familiar with those place names. People could use these names when providing directions for good hunting grounds, when they were finding other homesteads for a visit or when they travelled to local towns. The stories and events that led to the naming of such places also became part of the local folklore. In this chapter, people share their memories of the landmarks that were important during their homesteading years.

Fresh water was always important to homesteaders as they needed it to survive. Not only did they need the water for drinking, cooking and washing, but a significant amount of water was also needed for farm animals. As a result, watering holes were important locations. Where water was not readily available, it was not unusual for some homesteaders to travel up to six miles in search of water every other day and to haul barrels of it back to their farm. Mrs. E. Olmstead, for instance, remembered fellow homesteaders who would gather at Wolf Creek, a stream that passed one mile east of her family's farm.[1] She said that people not only collected water in barrels and transported them by stoneboat, but they also brought their stock with them to be watered. Mrs. Olmstead remembered how one farmer brought his cow with him, along with a goose who followed the cow everywhere. She reported seeing the three of them coming for water every day over the course of the winter months.

If settlers had a stream running through their land, the availability of water was of less concern, except when streams dried out and disappeared during years of drought. When that happened, being familiar with local streams and lakes was essential to daily living. One homesteader who exemplified this knowledge was Charles Davis.[2] He was well aware of the watersheds in his area. He also knew the tributaries from the local streams and which offshoots were drying up. In his memoirs, he described the stream that ran through his family's land. He said that it was situated at the bottom of a ravine that was 150 to 200 feet deep. In the spring, the stream "meandered in varying directions for a distance of eight to ten miles." He also stated that "many springs flowed chiefly from its south and easterly banks" and pointed out that Midnight, Long, Birch and Sibbald Lakes had creek connections with his spring. However, there was a concern among homesteaders at that time as other waterways near their homes like "Rousseau, Stinking and Lost Woman's Lakes were fast disappearing" due to drought.

Like Charles Davis, Harriet Stueck was also very familiar with her local waterways.[3]

> Our farmhouse was about two miles from Pheasant Creek, a tributary of the Qu'Appelle Valley. We were eleven miles from Fort Qu'Appelle. The creek, that runs along the bottom of the coulee, is about twenty or thirty miles long. It follows the same formation of hills and short runs as the valley. I think it was named Pheasant Creek because of the mound butte, or whatever the elevation might be called. It was the home of many pheasants. The whole plain in the early years was called Pheasant Plains. To this day, there are many pheasant and prairie chickens that make this mound their home.

Tobias Lanegraff mentioned how his local lake, Waterhen Lake (twenty-five miles north of the town of Meadow Lake), was also named after birds—in this case the waterfowl in the area.[4] He described the waterhen as a specific member of the duck family. While this lake was a landmark for him, he also said that he particularly liked the lake as it contained some "fine whitefish and jackfish." "Here," he says, "you find nature untouched." He was also interested in the area for its geological formations: "You can see how the ice brought sand and made these hills and sand ridges during the Glacier period."

Another landmark mentioned by early settlers was Turtle Lake, which was near North Battleford, Saskatchewan. Percy Thomson described this lake as being about fifteen miles long and five miles wide.[5] He thought that the reason for the lake's name was that the land around the lake was quite flat and stoney, with all the stones looking like a herd of turtles. Percy noted that the early settlers had a very hard time of it when they first settled in the 1910s and tried to live off the land. They were often on the verge of starvation. Luckily, the lake was "quite well supplied with good fish, and some of the settlers depended considerably on this fish for food."

Mary Ann McMurdo highlighted the waterways in her area of Tisdale, Saskatchewan, and recounted how they received their names.[6] When the area was being surveyed for the townsite, the chief surveyor's dog died. As a token of remembrance, he decided to tan the hide, so he and his fellow surveyors skinned the dog and hung the hide out to dry on the banks of a nearby creek. Afterward, the creek was known as Hanging Hide Creek. The river that intersected with this creek became known as Leather River. Mary Ann said that another landmark in her area was Presbyterian Creek, which was named after a Presbyterian minister who tried to walk across the creek on a log and fell in.

When Ella Otterson was reminiscing about the landmarks in her area, she made the point that their names were based on obvious features.[7] For instance, "Cypress Hills were named for the Cypress trees that were found there. White Mud River for the white clay in the hills. Lone Tree for the lone cottonwood tree on its east bank. Island Lake for the island in the lake and Shot Gun Coulee near Eastend, where a shotgun was found." She went on to exclaim, "It's a great mystery as to whom was in the country with a shotgun in those days!" She also mentioned the "War Holes, a deep canyon with high bluffs in which there were found trenches, shells, arrow heads and other signs of a big Indigenous battle being fought there."

In a similar vein, Mrs. W.H.S. Gange said that the Red Deer Hills in her area were named for the red deer antlers that were found on the local hills,[8] while Robert Shaw reported that the Bad

Hills in his region referred to the rocky terrain on a range of hills that was inhospitable for farming.[9] He also said that the Beaver River was named for the number of old beaver dams that had been built up on the creek that ran into the river. John Hamer mentioned that Echo Lake received its name because hunters and trappers always heard their echo when they hollered across the lake,[10] while Mrs. J. Meredith stated that the community of Willowmoor, located near the Saskatchewan River and Eight Mile Creek, was named for the number of willows growing there.[11]

Smoky Lake in Alberta was another distinctive landmark for those travelling across the prairies, particularly as the smoke rose high into the air. The early homesteaders, who "came to this community by way of the North Saskatchewan River, noticed a haze of smoke to the north of the river. They investigated and found a lake about seventeen miles long and a few miles wide. Smoke rose from its shore and hung over the lake in a thin blue haze."[12] They initially called the lake Smoking Lake, but this was soon changed to Smoky Lake.

Certain landmarks, like Goose Hunting Creek, were known for their proliferation of geese. In this photograph, two Alberta hunters are proudly posing with their dog in front of the birds they were able to shoot in one morning, ca. 1910. NA-5745-210. COURTESY OF LIBRARIES AND CULTURAL RESOURCES DIGITAL COLLECTIONS, UNIVERSITY OF CALGARY

Other key landmarks identified by homesteaders included Goose Hunting Creek, which according to Janet Downie was named for the large number of geese that used to land there.[13] She recounted how the men of her family and others in the community would gather their guns to see if they could bag a few birds. John Thiessen remembered one big lake, Red Lake, that was located near his family's farm near Morse, Saskatchewan.[14] What he found interesting was the creek that ran into Red Lake. It was called Lizard Creek on account of all the lizards that lived there.

Homesteader Dorothy Gush, highlighted how important landmarks were to her and her family.[15] As she said, "We had no roads to guide us to the other farms, but it was surprising how soon we could pick out our different shaped hills or bluffs. The hills were really very small rises, but we soon had names for them all. One I remember we called Coyote Hill because we always seemed to see several prairie wolves on it. They would watch us for miles but they never interfered with us."

Sometimes landmarks referred to the vegetation or types of trees that existed in particular areas. For instance, the Lone Pine district in Alberta was named for Lone Pine Creek, but how did the creek get its name? According to local folklore, there was a solitary pine tree that stood along one of the creek's banks.[16] However, many question whether it was in fact a pine tree. Some people from the area believe that it was actually a spruce tree. A cone could very well have travelled downstream on the crest of a flood, deposited itself in silt along the banks of the creek and grown in place. Regardless of whether it was pine or spruce, the solitary tree would have been an important landmark, easily identifiable to those travelling in the area.

People created landmarks using trees so that they would not become lost in the woods. The name of the Alberta town Lobstick is of Cree origin and refers to the tall, conspicuous spruce or pine trees that had all but the very top branches cut off. These nearly branchless trees were "used as guideposts by Indians, voyageurs and explorers; located on high ground they stood out as landmarks to wilderness travelers."[17]

Another interesting landmark to note was a geographical one called "Pointy Hill," which is a hill a quarter of a mile southeast of Irvine, Alberta.

The "pierced rock" at Roche Percée, Saskatchewan, twenty miles east of Estevan, was an important landmark for many. Mrs. Ed Wilson, a homesteader in the area, claimed that it was a site where Indigenous Peoples held gatherings and celebrations in the past.[18] The village of Roche Percée was also named after the rock. This photo is ca. 1890s. NC-22-44. COURTESY OF LIBRARIES AND CULTURAL RESOURCES DIGITAL COLLECTIONS, UNIVERSITY OF CALGARY

It got its name, Pointy Hill, because it looked like an ice cream cone turned upside down, very large at the bottom and tapered to the top. The hill is about 200 feet high, and anyone going to the top will find it about twenty feet in diameter, with a two to three foot depression that makes it look as though it may have been a small volcano at some time. The entire hill is covered with rocks.[19] According to Ella Mott, an important landmark to her family was Gooseberry Lake, named for the gooseberries found in the vicinity.[20] During the summer, her family would gather this fruit as it offered variety to their daily meals. In addition, gooseberries, when dried, could be stored for eating during the winter months. Similarly, James Tulloch noted how Carrot River became important to his community.[21] He said that edible wild carrots grew throughout the valley that ran along the river. These carrots, which were also known as Bishop's Lace or Queen Anne's Lace, were white flowering plants that were eaten when they first sprouted. Many homesteader meals were supplemented by all parts of the wild carrot (the root, leaves, seeds and flowers), which were eaten raw or cooked.

Lost Horse Hills

INTERESTINGLY, THE LOST Horse Hills (located near Forget, Saskatchewan) were not named for the number of horses that were lost in that area, but rather received their name from a young boy named Gerald Flood. He lived in the area at the time and felt that the name given to the hills by his father, Saskatchewan Hills, was a little dull and needed some flair, so he started calling them Lost Horse Hills.[22] •

Other landmarks were named for particular events that had occurred in the area. For example, Frank Kusch said, "When coming to Saskatoon from Moose Jaw, there were three Goodwin brothers, Charlie, James and Harry. They had a wickered jug of molasses or blackstrap on their wagon when fording a creek about forty miles south of Saskatoon. The jug fell out of the wagon into the creek and smashed open, so it was named Blackstrap Creek."[23]

Homesteader Charles Sargent also remembered a landmark that locals called "The Dip," which was located one mile south of Eyre, Saskatchewan:

> There was a magnificent spring which formed a small lake which was open all the year round and drained into Alsask Beach Lake. It was used to disinfect the herds of cattle. The cattle were penned in a corral at one end of a deep pit or trench filled with water from the spring into which the disinfectant was added. There was another corral at the other end of the trench where they were left to drain for a short time after being prodded through the water one at a time by the cowboys. It required considerable skill to handle the corral and was quite a dangerous performance. Accidents to the cowboys were quite numerous.[24]

Shirley Manary recounted an event that resulted in the creation of a community landmark.[25] On April 5, 1917, the Alberta government passed legislation, the *Livestock Encouragement Act*, to increase the amount of stock raised in the province. One homesteader, Berland Dressler, decided to take advantage of this act and brought a large herd of cattle into the Hattonford district in the fall of that year.

> The winter was long and cold and not enough feed had been put up for so many cattle. The cows grew thin and by early spring their numbers had started to diminish. Rather than suffer a complete loss, Berland decided to skin every animal that died and store the hides in the still icebound coulee that lay south of his farm. He relied on the ice and the salt that he sprinkled on the hides to preserve them until he could ship them. Alas, the hides rotted there and thus gave the coulee its name, "Cowhide Coulee."

Grain elevators were significant landmarks for many communities as they were tall, monumental buildings that were easily recognizable across the prairies. They were located at approximately seven-mile intervals to enable farmers to haul grain and return home the same day. These five grain elevators were in Wetaskiwin, Alberta, in 1906. NA-303-155. COURTESY OF LIBRARIES AND CULTURAL RESOURCES DIGITAL COLLECTIONS, UNIVERSITY OF CALGARY

Lucy Johnson also remembered a favourite landmark in her district, which she appreciated for a number of reasons.[26] As she eloquently stated:

> Slightly north-west due west ran the creek unseen from the house [near Saskatoon] winding in and out like a silver ribbon, gurgling merrily on its way. Hidden in a deep ravine, this wood and creek was really the greatest and most wonderful and valuable source of supply in all the country around. Words are inadequate to describe this beautiful creek. The deep woods, trees that flanked either side of the creek, supplied us and other settlers with fuel summer and winter, and we never ran short of wood. The creek itself supplied us with water until our wells were built, and always watered our horses on wood hauling days, and in the dry years that were to come, often replenished our water barrels on wash days, in the summer when our growing stock needed all the water. The creek also gave us fish and, in season, the bushes and trees on its banks gave berries of many kinds. Saskatoons, high and low cranberries, chokecherries, wild gooseberries, strawberries and raspberries, grew in great profusion and were free to all for the picking. As you stood at the top of the ravine looking down, a glorious sight met your eyes—especially in the autumn. It looked like a huge bowl scooped out of the earth, or rather, a number of bowls of various sizes, with the silver creek zigzagging in and out, deep down, sometimes seen, but more often not, unless you were right at the water's edge, so densely populated was it with bushes and trees. The creek proved to be the most popular place on the prairie for summer picnics. Sometimes people came for miles around, especially on Sundays, the more fortunate in their buggies, or democrats, but mostly in their wagons, and a few on horseback.

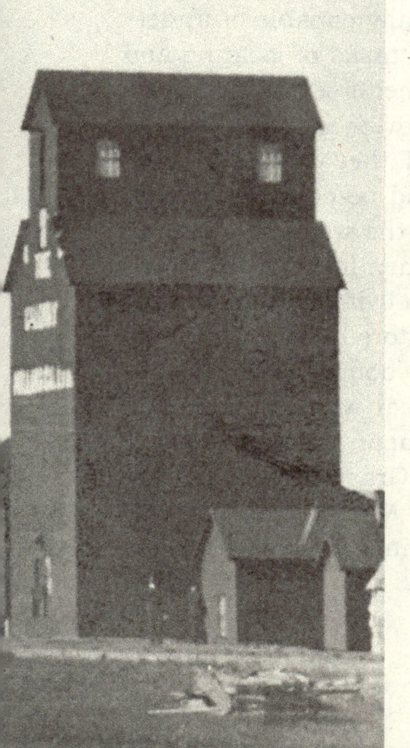

I Can Look as Far as My Eyes Will Carry and There Is Nothing to See

Many homesteaders, when they first moved onto the western prairies, found a vast wilderness with no amenities or social contacts. Outside of Winnipeg, Manitoba, which was the major centre for goods and services before the homesteaders began their trek west, there existed very few towns, villages or even small communities. Homesteaders found themselves completely isolated from others once they had settled on their 160 acres. Many found the remoteness very lonely; others tried to survive the quiet monotony of each day by keeping themselves busy. Still others saw the positive aspects of living alone, enjoying their own company and taking in the quietness and beauty of prairie life.

In the early years the prairies were primarily settled by male homesteaders, as men were physically capable of undertaking the arduous and hazardous tasks of locating and breaking homestead land and building shelters for themselves and their farm animals.[1] Few of those who were married brought their wives and children with them. Instead, they worked to ready their homestead for the day when it would be comfortable and safe enough for their families to move to the western prairies.[2] Given the substantially larger number of men in the west, it was not surprising to learn that the few women living on homesteads rarely saw other women, or even other visitors in general. Lillian Miles described how, when she took up homesteading duties with her husband, she became very familiar with loneliness on the prairies.[3] She especially missed the company of other women. She reported that her family lived in Yellow Grass, Saskatchewan, for three years. Their nearest centres were Milestone, which was fifteen miles away to the south, and Regina, which was many more miles away to the north. Their closest ranching neighbour was about fifteen miles away. As she stated, "We never saw another woman for years at a time in that territory."

Mrs. H. Teece highlighted how problematic it was to socialize with anyone outside of her family as her nearest town was over eighteen miles away.[4] And Lottie Meek reminisced about how her aunt, travelling by foot from the nearest town, carried her child fifteen miles to her homestead. Over all of those miles, she never came across another person. As Lottie said, "The loneliness of the new unknown country must have been terrible for her."[5]

John Fetsch realized how women suffered as they lived out their lives on the homestead.[6] Social norms of the day prescribed that women would stay at home to take care of the house and children while their husbands went to town for supplies. As John said,

> No written word could describe the loneliness. After many years, you can still feel it all over again. The women were nearly all from towns or cities and the terrible quietness [of homesteading life] was really awful. Men would be gone two days [to town] for groceries and supplies and women would spend many hours standing at the corner of the house waiting [for their men to return]. They listened for the rattle of the chains on the tugs [of the wagons]. The women never went to town.

He also indicated that it was particularly unfortunate for the women if the specific household items, material or groceries that they asked for were not available. It was heartbreaking for them. Their hopes would be raised again when their husbands set out for town the next month, but, once again, their hopes could be dashed if supplies were not available.

One young man, William Colby Reesor, saw first-hand how much his mother suffered during the early homesteading years.[7] Even when it was possible to attend a social event in the community, she ended up being disappointed. As he said, "In recalling the events of the first two or three years [of homesteading], I feel that Mother must have been very lonely for the companionship of other women as the only contact she had was in attending some dances in the winter, which meant a drive

A woman washes clothes outside her home, ca. 1916. While the men in the family went to town to purchase supplies, women often stayed on the homestead doing chores. Homesteader George Shepherd reported that the numbing monotony of women's lives could sometimes lead to sad situations. He knew of one woman who looked forward to hanging her wash out on the line, just so she could watch the clothes "dancing in the wind."[8]
NA-2041-1. COURTESY OF LIBRARIES AND CULTURAL RESOURCES DIGITAL COLLECTIONS, UNIVERSITY OF CALGARY

in the sleigh for anywhere up to ten to twenty miles each way." While his mother was able to chat with others at these events, his father didn't dance, which of course meant that his mother didn't dance. The children were too little to help out, as William indicated, "We youngsters were too young for such things at that time."

Arthur Stringer, in his memoirs, wrote about the drab, harsh, lonely life of the prairie woman, cutting notches in the window frame to note the passing of the days, especially the lunar cycle.[9] As he said,

> The picture is true. The Saskatchewan country is no cloying Eden of boundless ease and happiness. Women have gone mad, slowly, hopelessly, incurably mad because it was

stronger and bigger than they were. Men succumbed to its harshness too, as well as to its charms. The weak wilted, their moral and physical fiber not strong enough to struggle against loneliness, hardship, grasshoppers, early frost, hail, sawflies, rust, and drought. Slowly their bodies bent with the wind. Their hopes faded. Their eyes lost the sparkle of optimism.

Marion Anderson remembered different times when she experienced loneliness on the prairies: once when she was a child and another time when she was working as a schoolteacher.[10]

It was lonely enough on the prairies in the early days, but one good thing, members of a family stayed together as much as possible. My loneliest time as a child, was when mother would be called on and come for by a neighbor to act as a nurse, doctor, or housekeeper at someone's home ... We all missed mother then ... It was especially bad when wolves got to howling at night, although they never had a chance to harm us, unless it was when we were out bringing in the cows or out looking for nests of eggs. These fresh eggs were needed for food. We would always leave an egg in the nest so the bird won't be too much deprived and could fill up the nest again. [When I was older and became a teacher, I found that it] was lonely teaching in the one-room county school, although that is what I wanted to do and was going to stick with it. I would have company of some of the children on the walk in the mornings and coming from school in the evenings. There was nothing to do in the evenings except study or prepare for the next day's work. I didn't do any visiting in my first teaching district. I had no way to go. The last day at my first school, I was singing in my heart, I'm going home tomorrow.

Teenagers also suffered from a lack of fellowship with their peers. Some tried to visit others, especially during the long winter months, but in many cases the risk of travelling made socializing difficult, returning them to a life of loneliness at home. Mary Morrison, a homesteading wife with two daughters named Anne and Mary, recalled:

> Life was very monotonous in the winter, and very lonely. One year there were seven months that we never saw a woman or girl, outside of our own family circle. At times the loneliness grew almost unbearable to Anne and Mary as they craved the companionship of other young folk and made some desperate attempts to visit the neighbors. They started to walk through the snow, thinking that once outside the snowbanks piled up around the buildings, they could manage alright, but every step they took, they sank as deep as they could go, then with a mighty effort, would draw their limbs out of the deep snow, only to plunge in again. But the snow was too deep, even on the level of Prairie, to make any headway, and after a couple of hours of struggling, they managed to get back to the house, so completely tired out, they did not get over it for some time, though they had not gone more than a quarter of a mile away.[11]

Mary Morrison recounted another event where her third daughter, Margaret, was determined to go visiting others that were her same age at a neighbouring homestead. Her efforts could have easily led to her and her brother's demise.

> One winter when the snow was not very deep, Charlie [my son] hitched up his ponies to the sleigh and took Margaret to visit some friends who lived some eight or nine miles away to the West. The ponies traveled along briskly, the morning was quite mild, and they expected to reach her friend's home before noon. When they were two or three miles from home, a thick mist came up, and somehow the ponies got off the road. Presently, there was heard the sharp click of the horses' new shod feet on ice. At first Charlie thought that they were crossing a creek, but they kept on, the click click of the ice underfoot till the awful thought was borne to his mind, they must be on Lake Manitoba. The mist seemed to wrap them round like a pall, and well they knew how often such mists as that ended in a blizzard. Their chances seemed very slim indeed of ever seeing home again, for the country along the lakeshore, being marshy, no one lived there. After turning several times, they had the satisfaction of getting off the ice,

> and after traveling for a long time, they turned in through a gateway, then some buildings were seen through the mist and they found themselves at another friends, about a mile from their original goal. They were nearly perished, as it was late afternoon when they arrived, and as soon as they got warmed up, they started on their homeward way. They reached home just before the threatened blizzard broke loose and made up their minds they would have to be content at staying home during the winter months.

The isolating circumstances of living on a homestead were also experienced by a young girl, an only child, named Betty Iredale.[12] She tried to solve her problem of loneliness by constructing a doll to play with, but her mother Maude's overwhelming sadness and loneliness worked their way into her playtime stories.

> I sought out a tough and dependable playmate. Willie was a broom that had served its purpose. Worn-down bristles padded with flesh-toned cloth made a fine head. With crayons and paints, I daubed on eyes, brows, and mouth, improved upon by Father's gifted touch. Wool threaded into Willie's scalp was hair. He sported a man's felt hat. His shoulders, a length of lath, swaggered under a man's ragged suit jacket. His braided rag arm affectionately draped my shoulders or else flapped energetically when I grasped his broomstick body and together we raced across the prairie. Willie could talk. Into my mind he put thoughts which I then spoke aloud for him. "Crying makes you ugly. Stop it!" he would say. Or "Why, you ask, does your mother seem sad and often scold? Because instead of a sod shack, she would like to live in a palace, or maybe just a nice house like we look at in Christmas picture books." I spied her once, half hidden atop of mount of hay, still soft and spongy because not yet tramped and crowned against winter. She brushed her long, dark, freshly-washed hair that gleamed in the sun and fell over her face and blotted up tears. I crept away and then ran to find Willie. "Why does my mother cry?" I asked him. "Because she's lonely," he replied. "And the prairie makes her afraid." But about that, he indicated, we could

> do nothing. He was wise and loving but his appearance was raffish. Mother couldn't abide him nor did she allow him inside the shack. When we were apart, he lived on a shelf in the sod barn with the horses. Obedient to mother's commands, I quickly hid Willie if on the horizon a rider or wagon loomed; or maybe just an approach, as yet unseen, but heralded on the still and echoing prairie air. "A stranger would think you are out of your mind," Mother explained to me tartly. Father thought differently. "Willie is good for the child. Gives play to her imagination. Makes her less solitary. Leave them alone Maude."

Sometimes people could not handle long-term social deprivation and started displaying symptoms of "prairie madness," a form of insanity otherwise known as prairie fever or cabin fever. For those homesteaders who had emigrated from other countries or migrated from more populous and developed centres, the psychological toll of moving to the barren, undeveloped region of western Canada was overwhelming. Even though many of them were excited about the new opportunities available to them (such

Margaret Simpson, daughter of Dr. T.V. Simpson of Yorkton, Saskatchewan, plays with her doll in her home in 1903.
NA-2878-26. COURTESY OF LIBRARIES AND CULTURAL RESOURCES DIGITAL COLLECTIONS, UNIVERSITY OF CALGARY

as starting a new life in a new land and owning their own property), the reality of the situation was often far less than what they had expected. The culture shock of new surroundings, new people and new rules and regulations would have impacted them immediately, particularly if they were unfamiliar with the English language and British customs. They might have been disheartened when they realized the amount of hard work that waited for them when they reached their 160 acres of land. Building a home out of sod and living in dirt for the first few years was difficult, as was trying to construct a home out of logs or cut timber. Clearing acres and acres of land covered with brush and trees involved backbreaking labour, as did readying a plot for gardening or building barns, sheds, shelters and granaries. Trying to plow the hard, flattened earth was a tough endeavour for farm animals and homesteaders alike, and handling huge farm animals like oxen or horses was difficult for those who hadn't farmed before. Keeping starvation at bay was also a challenge. Undertaking all of these duties alone, with little or no social contact with others, heightened the negative effects associated with prairie madness.

John Fetsch said, "One man from our neighbourhood lost his mind through loneliness and wandered outside of his shack undressed at night and froze to death. His body was not found until the following spring."[13] Ella Mott stated, "I've known several people go insane through loneliness in the early days—especially before the railroad which came through in 1904."[14] John Ludlow also saw some of his neighbours experiencing prairie madness. Instead of going into detail, he succinctly said, "Loneliness on the prairie was no joke."[15]

Extreme loneliness, or prairie madness, can sometimes result in irrational thoughts and actions, as one homesteading family discovered when their mother was called by a neighbour to help with the birthing of a baby.

> Late one winter afternoon in 1904, a strange team and sleigh came into the yard. A man whom their mother had never seen before came to the door and begged for her assistance in helping his wife "have child." Enquiry established that it would be about a two hour trip to the south and after some deliberation she consented. She gathered up what she needed, dressed herself warmly and climbed

> into the sleigh box, setting herself on a stool provided and wrapping herself up in blankets. The stranger stood at the front of the box and drove without talking, behaviour which she found puzzling. Finally, they pulled into a yard and stopped in front of a shack. She was surprised that the place was in darkness. The man assisted her out of the sleigh, led her to the shack, pushed open the door, then made his way, in the dark, to a table where he lit a lamp. In the dim light my grandmother could see they were in a single room, completely alone. There was no pregnant wife! With a silent prayer that she would say and do the right thing, she convinced her deceiver that his best course of action was to return her to her home forthwith. The return trip was filled with suspense and eventually ended at her gate. Dismounting with great independence she lectured him about wasting her evening and sent him on his way with a warning that he should not pull off such a trick again. When asked why she didn't report the man, she said, "He did bring me back without harm and I guess I felt a little sorry for him. He probably did it out of loneliness. Living alone on a homestead can put notions in a man's head."[16]

This story highlights the lengths that some people would go to in order to have some company, even if it was just for a short period of time. Perhaps this man hoped the woman would stay for a while and visit, but either way, he was likely suffering from prairie madness. Fortunately, he still had the capacity to understand wrong from right. With the deception that was involved, the woman could have been kidnapped with no one from her family knowing her whereabouts.

Mary Morrison also experienced an act of desperation on the part of a single man.[17] Mary and her son, Charlie, went to Winnipeg one day to pick up some much-needed medicine and supplies. Her husband was sick at home as was her fourteen-month-old baby. Her daughter Anne, who was only twelve years old, was taking care of both of them. Mary felt bad about leaving them and was anxious to return home as quickly as possible, but shortly after they left Winnipeg, she realized a man on horseback was following them.

> With concern, she and Charlie urged the oxen to their best speed. The horseman behind them, who did not hurry himself [never took the opportunity to pass them], as she thought he might have done. [Rather, he kept his distance.] Whenever they had to stop, he found it necessary to rub down his horse, or fix his saddle. [For a while, they lost sight of him.] As night approached Mary sent Charlie to a house, to see if they could put them up for the night. When he returned he said, "Yes, but that man is there, who has been following us all day." As the roads were so bad and there was no other house in sight, they decided to go in, as she thought, "Well, he didn't bother us, so why should we care? He is only a traveler." When she went in, she found a splendid dinner awaiting them, and while she was trying to dry her clothes at the fire [as it had been raining all day], the hostess urged her to partake of it. But she was anxious, and as they had their own provisions, she did not wish to incur the additional expense, as it was shelter only they had expected. But the lady of the house informed her that dinner was ordered for her. In her weariness she wondered what that meant. Then the horseman [spoke to her and] urged her to at least take a cup of tea. While she was drinking it, he told her he had inquired of many in the city as to who she was, but no one knew her, and when he saw her starting out on her journey, he was determined to find out even if he had to follow her to the Rocky Mountains. This roused and startled Mary. With dismay and indignation, she told him she and her son were on their way home. "Your son?" he exclaimed in surprise. "Your brother, you mean." "No, he is my son," declared Mary, "and I cannot imagine what you mean by following us." "I mean this," he replied. "That I thought you were a young lady, and he was your brother, and I would have followed you anywhere, in order to have made your acquaintance."

While this story sounds like an innocent romantic flirtation (on the horseman's part), it had the potential to turn into a dangerous situation. It was not an acceptable practice for someone to follow others unless they were going in the same direction. The man's admission that nothing would stop him from meeting her and that he had made multiple inquiries about her in town suggested that he either was fervent in his desire for companionship or had questionable plans that may not have boded well for Mary or her son.

Others held a far more positive view of the wide-open spaces and the solitary life that they experienced as homesteaders on the prairies. As Harriet Stueck explained, "Some of the early settlers of course were very lonely and some just returned to where they came from, but I think most of the pioneers were interested enough in developing a new country they didn't have either time or desire to be lonely."[18] Mrs. Ed Wilson held a similar point of view: she and her family felt that the "loneliness of the early years was an altogether different feeling. We felt that we were here to build up and conquer the great open spaces."[19]

Still others found beauty and contentment in the quietness of the prairies, devoid of other people. For instance, Eric Neal stated that he lived sixteen hours in travelling distance by horse from his nearest neighbour but that he was never lonely.[20] He had good neighbours, he said, even if they were far apart. Likewise, John Hamer reported that he "never found the large open spaces

Bill Skilkow, a bachelor, sits in front of his one-room shack on the barren prairie near Medicine Hat, Alberta, in 1911. While some men appreciated their quiet time on their homesteads, others did become lonesome occasionally. Harry Martyn knew a man who became so lonesome when he was homesteading that he used to tell himself jokes and then laugh at them himself as there was no one but him to get the joke. Also, when he talked to himself, he always got the right answer![21] PD-132-2-25. COURTESY OF LIBRARIES AND CULTURAL RESOURCES DIGITAL COLLECTIONS, UNIVERSITY OF CALGARY

lonesome. He liked to travel over the open prairie in the early days of this settlement."[22] Albert Christianson admitted that his small family of three was a little lonely at first, but he said it "wasn't long until we were just one large happy family, working together and having fun together as well."[23]

Charles Davis also had some positive things to say about prairie living in the early years:

> There are so many things here to hold one's attention and occupy the mind. The first few years I spent alone away in a poplar log shack. My nearest neighbour was located only seven miles to the northwest in wintertime. If snow drifted badly, it became impossible to keep in touch. One diversion from loneliness was found in keeping diaries on different subjects, weather, general conditions, such as wind, cloud density, form, rain, graduated measure, first and last fall of snow dates, height, the number of wildlife—deer, coyote, lynx, grouse, other animals and birds over an area, stated times, accounting first migratory birds for arrival and departure dates. Only once did I feel that oppressive power of absolute loneliness, that was when I endured for two weeks that painful affliction of snow blindness.[24]

Similarly, John Henry Foerster admitted to feeling secluded and forlorn from time to time, but those feelings didn't last long.[25] As he said:

> [A] bachelor's life on the homestead, it's not the most enjoyable. I sometimes got very lonesome. Sometimes I felt like Robinson Crusoe. The daytime was alright, I had plenty of work to do. But the long winter evenings when I was out of reading material, I felt very lonesome. But then my thoughts would drift to my old friends and acquaintances back in Mornington, Ontario [and then I no longer felt lonely].

William Affleck reported that he and his family never felt lonely on their homestead, but there was a problem with distance—particularly when medical assistance was required.[26]

During the first year, there was no doctor or post office nearer than North Battleford, a distance of forty-five miles over the Swift Current Trail. We did not feel lonely and everyone was healthy, but one girl took typhoid and I went forty-five miles on a bicycle for a doctor in three hours over the Swift Current Trail. The girl recovered from the fever, however she only lived until three years of age.

FOLKLIFE AND SUPERSTITION

Everything from "Home on the Range" to Shakespeare

In order to pass the long, lonely evenings, many homesteading families turned to a variety of entertainments. They would sing songs or listen while others played familiar tunes on their mouth organs or violins. Some of the music reflected old ballads from their mother countries; some was more contemporary, focusing on the western way of life; other songs included lyrics that were humorous or romantic. Sometimes they sang hymns that were reverent and uplifting. They would also read books or listen to literary works being read aloud. Enthralling pieces of literature, like Shakespeare and Tennyson, Thackeray and Dickens, were always popular among the homesteading crowd. Whether they were singing together or gathered together for an evening visit to listen to a chapter reading, these activities helped to unite the homesteading community.

Marion Anderson recalled how her family was able to have music in their home even though they initially did not own any musical instruments.[1] Her mother and father would sing songs to her and her siblings, songs that they had learned while they were in school in Ontario. Her father, in particular, was adept at singing and teaching others how to sing. He was taught singing by the tonic sol-fa method, where each musical note on the scale was named (e.g., do, re, mi, fa, sol, la, ti, do), and he passed these techniques on to his children. The first musical instruments that Marion remembered seeing in her district of Moosomin, Saskatchewan, were the melodeons owned by their Baptist minister, Reverend Moylis.[2] The first organ she ever saw was owned by a neighbour, Mrs. Mary Struthers, who taught Marion how to play in the early 1880s. When another neighbour, a bachelor named J. McQueen, found out that she was taking lessons, he lent her his organ for a while. He had won the instrument when he entered a contest organized by the *Winnipeg Free Press*. Given that Mr. McQueen was busy working on his homestead, he had little spare time to play it himself. Soon after that, Marion said, her father was able to acquire some extra funds and purchased an organ for their family.

Over their homesteading years, Marion remembered her family singing a variety of songs. When she learned how to play the organ, they learned a few more. "I've Been Working on the Railroad" was one of their favourite American folk songs, while a cowboy tune, "Red River Valley," was one of their preferred Canadian ones. At Christmas they sang "Legend of the Mistletoe Bough," an English song that was written in the 1830s.[3]

John Evans also remembered the time when very few musical instruments could be found on the prairies.[4] Only two or three neighbours had some type of instrument, like a mouth organ or a fiddle. There wasn't even an organ in the church. However, this did not deter people, and at various times they tried to make music with what they had on hand. Washboards were employed as percussion instruments, with thimbles or brushes rubbed over the rough side of the board. Spoons were used to make "spoon music," where the backs of two spoons would be clacked together. Some people blew on the tops of jugs for a whistling sound, while others used a piece of paper and a hair comb to create a kazoo.[5] Others could carry a tune by simply whistling with their lips or through their teeth. While music in its various forms was often a welcome accompaniment, sometimes it was not needed. John Evans described how there were some wonderful singers living in their district between 1886 and 1899. They could sing duets, quartets and solos from *Il Trovatore* (an Italian opera) and other semi-dramatic oratorios and musical compositions. John mentioned that he and his wife were often asked to sing duets at community gatherings. They preferred romantic songs like "Tell Me Gentle Stranger" and "Pledge My Love, In Sparkling Waters." Other favourites included Scottish sea songs like "The Anchors Weigh'd," as well as songs of undying love like "When You and I Were Young, Maggie." Other Scottish favourites included "The Bonnie Banks o' Loch Lomond," "Huntingtower" and "Annie Laurie."

Mrs. Charles Archer recalled common sentimental songs like "Belle Mahone" being sung, as well as patriotic ones like "Our

A couple sing from a hymn book without the accompaniment of any musical instruments, ca. 1920. NA-5745-166. COURTESY OF LIBRARIES AND CULTURAL RESOURCES DIGITAL COLLECTIONS, UNIVERSITY OF CALGARY

Motherland: Song of America."[6] She said that there was an organ in their local schoolhouse, and when people in the vicinity congregated for a social event, her husband's family would bring out a piano to accompany the organ. Other neighbours brought their violins and guitars so they, too, could join in and play music for the crowd. Often, she said, the songs were so well-loved that people could sing the songs from memory.

In the Born family, the best singer of the group was their daughter Anna.[7] She would sing her way through each day with hymns, folk tunes and lullabies. Even though the rest of the family could not reach the singing standard set by Anna, they all took part in singalongs every Sunday. While most of the family were in harmony at these singalongs, sometimes Anna's father would

> slide off the melody to bumble around somewhere off-tune in the fond assumption that he was singing harmony. One year, the local teacher wanted the Born family to sing at the Christmas concert and undertook to teach Father the tenor line. He failed. Father simply could not learn it. One thing he

did possess, and that was a sense of time and rhythm which was a benefit to their small singing group. If they were singing too slow, her father would get them to pick up their pace. If they were too fast, he told them to slow down a bit.

Harriet Gerry also remembered how everyone in her family enjoyed their evenings of music and singing.[8] As she said, "The fun we had at that house! After the chores, and everyone had a chore to do, then it was a lamp lit evening and father would fiddle, and my brother had a mouth organ, and so there was music. Sometimes, mother took time out from the mending and sewing to chord on the piano. The rest of us enjoyed the performance or raised our voices in song."

According to Betty Iredale,[9] Leif Swengard, a young Swedish lad who was fair, slim and muscular, set out to work with a will, determined to achieve a producing farm and to make his parents

Entertainment for the Simpson family of Yorkton, Saskatchewan, in 1900 consisted of the mother playing the piano, while the father danced with their young daughter. NA-2878-23.
COURTESY OF LIBRARIES AND CULTURAL RESOURCES DIGITAL COLLECTIONS, UNIVERSITY OF CALGARY

in Sweden proud of him. She said that Leif's Swedish accent enchanted her. She also noticed that he carried a mouth organ in one pocket.

> When he stopped for a moment of rest from ploughing, hoeing, planting or raking, he put it to his lips. If the air was still, the tunes he blew and tongued tinkled across the prairie, bewitching as any piped in a fairy glade by the goat god, Pan. Leif's music far outdid any squeaks I could bring from my reed pipe, which Father had made by cutting notches in a hollow plant stem. Leif also turned his talents to more complex sounds that Father said were classical.

Leif persuaded his friends, along with Betty's parents, to teach each other the songs of their homelands. "When they met together and sang, Mother's high sweet voice mingled with those of the men. I think the bachelors worshipped her and, like Father, would have died to protect her."

Tobias Lanegraff recalled how much he enjoyed singing during his early homesteading days.[10] He often went to community dances and would work as the caller for square dances. During the breaks, he would entertain the crowd by singing to them. He was from the United States, so most of the songs he sang were American. He liked to sing the anti-slavery song "Oh, My Darling Nellie Gray," "The Wreck of the Old '97" (which was based on a railway accident that occurred in Virginia in 1903) and "Casey Jones" (about a railroad engineer who was killed in a railway accident in Mississippi). He also remembered singing "The Cowboy's Lament," as well as "When the Stars and Stripes are Waving" (a battlefield song). He sang an old family favourite religious tune that drew attention to his Norwegian roots. It was called "Broder og søster, som lider jo her."

Eloise Anderson, who also had American roots, recalled many songs that her family sang during their homesteading days.[11] They included "Silver Threads Among the Gold," which told a story about aging and immortal love; "Just Before the Battle, Mother," a Civil War tune about a dying Union soldier; and "Listen to the Mockingbird," about a sweetheart who passed away. Robert Shaw recounted the many American songs that his family sang, including "Minnesota State Fair," "Where Did You Get That Hat?" (a comical song), "Swanee River" (also known as "Old Folks at Home"), "My Old Kentucky Home," "Home Sweet Home," "Sweet Bunch of Daisies" and "Home on the Range" (a cowboy song).[12] Robert said that his family enjoyed one Irish song as well, "It's a Long Way to Tipperary."

Mary Kajewski of Cypress Hills, Saskatchewan, remembered how much the members of her community enjoyed singing.[13] Even though no one in the surrounding area had any musical instruments in the early years, when she was a small child she recalled how different neighbours eventually purchased organs and pianos. She also mentioned the travelling fiddlers or violinists who went from town to town in order to make some money, and she remembered the songs that were sung at the time. They included "Nelly Bly," "Far Away," "Billy Boy," "A Frog He Would A-Wooing Go" and "Tell Me Pretty Maiden."

To add some humour to the more popular songs or rhymes, and to keep his friends entertained, homesteader Harry Martyn would often switch the words.[14] For instance, instead of using the traditional lyrics for "Old Mother Hubbard," where a dog's owner was looking for food, he sang:

Old Mother Hubbard went to the cupboard
to get her daughter a dress,
but when she got there,
the cupboard was bare
and so was her daughter, I guess.

In a similar fashion, he changed the words to "Ruben and Rachel," a playground song, where the main character in the rhyme ends up drinking whiskey instead of turpentine:

Ruben, Ruben,
you been drinking whiskey,
whiskey I can smell.
If you don't stop this bad habit,
you will surely go the hell.[15]

He put together other ditties in his spare time. One that he sang most often was "I travelled east and I travelled west, most all over. If there is any old maid wants a beau, I'll be with her by the time this song is over."

It is not surprising to find that many homesteaders sang songs from the old country—wherever they had come from. For instance, Norman McDonald always sang Gaelic songs,[16] while George Williscroft became well acquainted with Scottish tunes when he homesteaded near a Scottish settlement in Manitoba in 1894.[17] He said that Robbie Burns's songs were very popular at community events—songs like "Auld Lang Syne" (sung New Year's Eve), "A Red, Red Rose," "A Man's a Man for a' That," "My Heart's in the Highlands" and "Ae Fond Kiss." George mentioned that the song "The Bonnie Banks o' Loch Lomond" was also particularly well-liked among the Scottish crowd. For those with an Irish background, the romantic song "My Wild Irish Rose" was popular, while those who wished to sing about shamrocks and leprechauns likely preferred "A Little Bit of Heaven."

A group of people from Calmar, Alberta, are singing in 1913, while two musicians play violin and guitar. *L–R:* Elvina Westlund, Fred Fladen, Louis Engberg (with violin), Selma Westlund (with guitar), Tillie Westlund, Alex Peterson. Adolf Engberg, front. NA-4174-3. COURTESY OF LIBRARIES AND CULTURAL RESOURCES DIGITAL COLLECTIONS, UNIVERSITY OF CALGARY

There were a number of ballads sung by those who hailed from England, including "Bonaparte," "The Isle of St. Helena," "Butter and Cheese and All," "Darby Ram," "Donnelly and Cooper," "Frog's Courtship," "Grace Darling," "Mush Mush, Off to Philadelphia," "Rosy," "Three English Blades," "Three Jolly Welshman," "The Fox Hunt" and "Will Ray."

In terms of Christian church music, many homesteaders remembered some of their familiar favourites being "A Shelter in the Time of Storm," "Bringing in the Sheaves," "Beulah Land," "Handwriting on the Wall," "Rock of Ages" and "Safe in the Arms of Jesus." Others remembered "Lead Kindly Light," "Abide with Me," "Nearer my God to Thee" and "Onward Christian Soldiers." For many, the highlight of each year was the Christmas season, when they sang hymns and carols like "Silent Night," "Jingle Bells," "Good King Wenceslas," "Angels We Have Heard on High," "It Came Upon a Midnight Clear" and "What Child Is This?"

Instead of an evening of music and singing, some families turned to reading aloud. This was not only for the benefit of the family, but it also meant an evening of enjoyment for anyone who stopped by for a visit. There were a number of homesteaders who had learned how to speak English but did not know how to read it. In some cases, owning a book was a luxury, as most of a homesteader's funds went into supplies, shelter and farm equipment. As a result, many found an invitation to hear a story from a book that would be read aloud hard to refuse. Family members who wished to read on their own found this pastime to be a fun and rewarding one, while others used their reading and writing skills to correspond with homesteading families across the prairies.

According to Grace Carr, both of her parents loved and cherished their books.[18] Her mother had brought books with her from England to the homestead and read and reread them throughout the years. Each night, after she had tucked Grace and her siblings into bed, she read to them. Sometimes she read single chapters from books, with her favourite being *Pilgrim's Progress* by John Bunyan; at other times she read poems like "Evangeline" and "The Song of Hiawatha," both written by Henry Wadsworth Longfellow. She also read the works of Tennyson, Whittier and Browning as well as selections from her own school books. As Grace said, "We listened, often spellbound, and a love of good literature was born in us. Often in the very cold weather, Father read aloud, while Mother sewed or knitted. I first heard Dickens in that manner. Father loved Dickens and would stop to laugh heartily at some apt phrase or description. Somehow, we got the idea that reading was a rare privilege."

Like Grace's mother, Dora Mitchell's father had brought books with him from Ontario, which he used for Dora's education.[19] There were no schools yet in the Blucher, Saskatchewan, vicinity, so she had to learn at home. Her father gave her "exercises to do in grammar and composition which she did for fun, little realizing that it was really homework she was doing." Eventually she "knew how to write and spent much of her free time writing stories and letters to the pen pal clubs in the 'Grain Growers' Guide,' the 'Winnipeg Free Press,' and other newspapers." As she said,

> I liked to see my letters in print, and to receive the membership buttons they sent to the young correspondents. I read many books, not many of them classics, but girl's books such as L.T. Meade's stories of life and girls boarding schools, series like the Bessie Books, the Elsie Books, the Mildred books, the Chautauqua Girls, the Anne books [*Anne of Green Gables* and its sequels by L.M. Montgomery], and later "Little Women," "Uncle Tom's Cabin," and "Robinson Crusoe." Sitting in a rocking chair behind the stove, eating an apple, and reading, was my idea of real pleasure!

Sue Harrigan remembered that her family didn't have very many books in their possession, but there were two that she was particularly fond of.[20] One was called *The Doctor*, while the other was *The Major*. Her sister, Julia, "read these books aloud and we enjoyed them very much. Then we all played cards and did some work and had company occasionally. I remember one evening that two young men drove thirty miles just to spend the evening at our house" to hear the readings. The family of Johann and Anna Paulson also enjoyed reading, so much so that Johann would walk nine miles to their local town of Kristnes, Saskatchewan, on Sunday mornings to borrow library books.[21] Evenings would then be spent reading a few chapters aloud to the family. They only had oil lamps to read by, but every day they looked forward to the continuation of the story in the evenings.

According to James Minifie, his family had an extraordinary number of books compared to other homesteading families, especially "considering their weight and bulk and our scanty resources in baggage" as they travelled from England to western Canada.[22] However, within a few months the number of books they owned doubled, as two boxes of books had been shipped to them from relatives back in the old country. The boxes were the size of military footlockers. They made cozy seats for reading beside the stove, and he spent many comfortable hours there, working through the books they contained. James built bookcases from salvaged lumber, with one bookcase nailed to the wall over the head of his bed. As he said, "They were not masterpieces of joinery, but they held books and they held together."

Folklife through Poetry

Along with singing, playing musical instruments and reading books, a common hobby among the homesteaders was to write poetry. This was not only a personal undertaking, allowing the writer to express his or her thoughts about life through verse; it was also a communal one, as many people wrote and shared their poetry with others. They would often write about the settlement process and their homesteading experiences, including the labour that was involved, the neighbours that they met, their children's lives on the farm, the farm animals they worked with and the beauty of the prairies. The poetry written during the homesteading era epitomized a new cultural landscape, a landscape reminiscent of the folklife of the time.

It is not surprising that when homesteaders found a desirous place to settle on the prairies, they put these thoughts down on paper. One such homesteader, who signed his poetry with his initials G.G.D., submitted his poem to the newspaper *Nor'-West Farmer*, where it was published in April 1886.[1] It is clear that he was impressed with the land available in Manitoba, as he encouraged others to emigrate and settle there.

Manitoba

This is the land, the famous land;
The land of great fertility;
Its prairies, too, are very grand
For men of good ability.

It is here the settler will find
Land of prairie, or of woods,

To please the most fastidious mind
So bring along your goods.

We will give you a welcome kind
On your arrival here,
So come along, make up your mind
You won't delay another year.

Other poems highlighted the long journeys families undertook as they sailed from their mother countries. Rena Roche described how her family travelled from Poland to the shores of eastern Canada.[2] They then had to travel by colonist car on the Canadian Pacific Railway until they reached their final destination of Prosperity, Alberta. She described the hard work that was involved with homesteading in her poem, as well as the kindness shown to her family by their new neighbours. And she wrote of her family's hope for a bright and prosperous future.

EXCERPT FROM <u>*From Poland to Prosperity*</u>

We were very anxious, with dreams of every kind,
looking towards a better life, our troubles left behind.
We settled at Prosperity, a lonely place but dear,
100 acres and 60, waiting for us to clear.
The axe came in handy, and a strong back too,
there was no need for jogging, after the day was through.
Exhausted sinews and muscles at dusk of every day
Hardy pioneers were we, in each and every way.
The little log cabin dad had built the year before,
leaking roof and tiny windows, four walls and nothing more.
Good neighbors on either side, would lend a helping hand,
their business brought much happiness in this
vast and lonely land.
Our hopes were a-soaring, our dreams were adoring,
north of Boyle.
Our home was there to be
at Prosperity for a $10 fee.

Some poems focused on the initial work that was needed on the homestead. The labour was gruelling, but it is clear that the anonymous author of this next poem recognized the level of perseverance required by individuals to continuously work the land day after day.[3] Obtaining title was important to homesteaders, and their drive and determination to accomplish this feat were qualities that were shared among all of those who homesteaded across the prairies.

<u>A Tribute to the Many Indomitable Men</u>

Pushing the frontiers further,
Back with relentless hands,
Blazing the trail with a plowshare,
Far in the hinterlands.
Holding fast to their birthright,
Born to the realm of toil,
Bearded grim and unconquered,
Ragged kings of the soil.

Building their lonely cabins,
Staking their homestead claims,
Beating a trail to somewhere,
Steady, fearless and fame.
Bounded by sky and muskeg,
Hedged by the vast unknown,
Earning their hundred and sixty,
Winning their fight alone.

Theirs is the dream eternal,
Hills that are rugged and green,
Lure of the far horizons,
Prairies windswept and clean.
Visiting towns in the making,
Faith in the untried lands,
Holding the country's future,
Safe in their calloused hands.

Many homesteaders had a great fondness for their horses, with many treating them as pets even though they were also workers on the farm. However, the mistreatment of horses was not unknown at the time. This poem, written by J.W. Riley and published in the *Nor'-West Farmer* in 1886, shows how he despised those who beat horses.[4] In his opinion, horses should be valued for their many qualities, respected and treasured.

The Hoss

I claim no hoss will harm a man,
Nor kick, or run away, cavort,
Stump, suck or balk, er 'catamaran'
Ef you'll jest treat 'em like you ort.

But when I see the beast abused,
And clubbed around, as I've see'd some,
I want to see his owner noosed,
And jest yanked up like Absolum!

Of course, there's difference in stock,
A hoss that has a little year,
And slender build, and shaller hock,
Kin beat his shadder, mighty near!

While one that's thick in neck and chist,
And big in leg, and full in flank,
That tries to race, I still insist,
He'll have to take the second rank.

And I have jist laid back and laughed,
And rolled and wallered in the grass,
At fairs, to see some heavy draft
Lead out at first and come in last!

Each hoss has his appointed place—
The heavy hoss should plow the soil—
The blooded racer, he must race,
And win big wages for his toil.

I never bet—nor never wrought
Upon my fellow men to bet—
And yet, at times, I've often thought
Of my convictions with regret.

I bless the hoss from hoof to head,
From head to hoof and tail to mane!

Homesteader Aron Johnson of Abbey, Saskatchewan, proudly displays his large team of horses.[5]

I bless the hoss, as I have said,
From head to hoof and back again!

I love my God the first of all,
Then Him who perished on the cross,
And next, my wife—and then I fall,
Down on my knees and love—the hoss.

Other homesteaders, like Robert Chase, were particularly fond of the fowl on their farms.[6] In Robert's case, he made sure his chickens were well taken care of and that they were safely secured in the henhouse before he called it a night. However, one of his chickens had a mind of her own. She refused to nest in the henhouse and would escape from the enclosure over the course of the day. Often Robert had to go on the hunt for her, sometimes late into the evening. This poem details his search and his success at finding his rebellious hen.

The Quest

I turned my steps down the wooded glade,
With thoughts on her who long had shunned my care.
And, gaining solace from the quiet shade,
It almost seemed that I might find her there.

'Twas eventide, the somber shadows fell,
And, faintly wafted from its far off tower.
Some slowly tolled and cadence-laden bell,
Paid out its tribute to the passing hour.

One low-hung cloud upon the western rim,
Showed gold and red the sun's receding light.
But, in the vale, the alder trees grew dim,
And tardy twilight kissed the brow of night.

I came upon her where glad flowers grew,
Like stars upshining in the cloistered glen.
My heartbeat quickened when at last I knew,
I'd found the hideout of that setting hen.

Children as young as four years old were expected to be farm labourers, helping their families on the homestead. Whether they were pulling weeds and picking stones out of the garden and fields when they were quite young or doing the work of an adult when they were fourteen years old, there was a social and familial expectation that all members of the family would contribute to the homesteading effort. For many children, work around the farm was endless. Like their adult counterparts, they did experience some good times throughout their lives, but some children were less enthused about the farming lifestyle. The following poem, written with tongue in cheek by an anonymous poet, exemplifies the life of a homesteading child—a life that many children of the homesteading era could likely identify with.[7]

I'd Like to be a Boy Again

I'd like to be a boy again
without a woe or care,
with freckles scattered on my face
and hayseed in my hair.

I'd like to rise at 4:00 o'clock
and do one hundred chores,
and saw the wood and feed the hogs
and lock the stable doors.

And herd the hens and watch the bees
and take the mules to drink,
and show the turkeys how to swim
so that they wouldn't sink.

And milk about a hundred cows
and bring the wood to burn,
and stand out in the sun all day
and churn and churn and churn.

And wear my brothers' castoff clothes
and walk four miles to school,
and get a licking every day
for breaking some old rule.

And then get home again at night
then do the chores once more,
and milk the cows and feed the hogs,
and curry mules galore.

And then crawl wearily upstairs
to seek my little bed,
and hear dad say that worthless boy
he isn't worth his bread.

I'd like to be a boy again
a boy has so much fun,
his life is just a round of mirth
from rise to set of sun.

I guess there's nothing pleasanter
than closing stable doors,
and herding hens and chasing bees
and doing evening chores.

While many discussed farm work, including animal husbandry, in their poetry, others reflected on the bitterly cold winters they had to endure. Not only was it dangerous for homesteaders to be caught out in a blizzard, but the length of the winter also left many wishing for a more hospitable climate. However, as set out in a poem by Archie Althouse, there were further problems that homesteaders had to contend with when spring arrived.[8]

Along the Battle Trail

The hardships that we did endure, from hunger and from cold.
Would take too long for me to tell, and never will be told,
To start from Battleford with a load, and face a blizzard gale,
T'would break your heart right from the start,
along the Battle Trail.

And then the blizzard would set in, one could choke with fear,
For we knew, t'would take two days, before the sky would clear.
And if you'd venture from your shack,
your death would tell the tale.
No more you'd see your old sod shack, along the Battle Trail.

The only fuel to know about, the twisted hay and straw
From November until April, we never had a thaw.
I'd rather be away back East, in some warm jail,
Than twisting hay both night and day, along the Battle Trail.

The rivers they were far apart, and a well was something new,
Sometimes it would take a week's travel to find water in a slough.
We sometimes carried a little jug, we called our ginger ale,
And once in a while we had a smile, along the Battle Trail.

And when the snow did disappear and gophers would begin.
They'd eat up everything you'd sow, and you'd have to sow again.
If I could get some good advice to kill those flicker tails,
I'd stand a chance to raise a crop, along the Battle Trail.

The flying ants were another pest, to drive a man back East,
They'd alight on you by the millions and upon you they'd feast.
Your clothes were no protection,
right through them they would sail
And sting and chew you black and blue, along the Battle Trail.

Sometimes the poems reflected the ongoing trials and tribulations faced by those who tried to eke out a living from the hard prairie soil. The stress and strain of life was soon etched on the faces of those who put their soul into their farm. Andrew Twedt wrote about a farmer who passed away and was welcomed wholeheartedly by St. Peter when he arrived at the pearly gates.[9]

<u>The Pearly Gates</u>

A farmer knocked at the pearly gates
his face was scarred and old,
he stood before the man of fate
for admission to the fold.
What have you done, St. Peter said
to gain admission here?
I've been a farmer, Sir, he said
for many and many a year.
The pearly gates swung open wide as Saint Peter
touched the bell,
Come in, he said, and choose your harp
You've had your share of hell.

Even though they experienced many hardships throughout their lives, many individuals were proud of their homesteading efforts. They appreciated their independent lifestyle, the fact that they could provide for themselves and their families, and the freedom of being able to own their own land. In an anonymously written poem, this pride is evident as the poet highlights the joy associated with farm life and the lack of envy felt for those who are wealthy.[10]

<u>The Farmer</u>

Let the wealthy and the great
roll in splendor and in state.
I envy them not, I declare it;
I eat my own lamb,
My chicken and ham,
I shear my own fleece, and I wear it;
I have lawns, I have bowers,
I have fruits, I have flowers,

The lark is my morning alarmer
So, jolly boys, now
Here's Godspeed the plow,
Long life and success to the farmer.

People living on the western prairies not only had pride in their abilities, but also took time out to enjoy nature and the beauty of the landscape. Some homesteaders wrote poems about their favourite sites, like the special wooded areas or lakes where they spent some time. Fourteen-year-old Julia Anna Asher wrote about the small lake that was located on her family's homestead.[11]

The Little Lake in the Wildwood

When in my sleep I am dreaming
I often behold a fair scene,
Where a lake of pure water lies gleaming,
Surrounded by emerald green.

All around it the willows are bending
Their boughs, its clear waters to meet,
While the shapes of their branches descending,
Are reflected in the pure deep.

In the far depths the fishes are gliding
Like streaks of silverly light,
Or 'mongst the mosses are hiding,
Their fantastic forms from my sight.

Its fair surface ripples so lightly
When the breezes are passing by,
Its sparkling face glistens as brightly,
As the distant deep blue sky.

That dear little lake in the wildwood
Will ever seem precious to me,
For there in the dear days of childhood,
On its banks I have played gay and free.

That fair spot I long will remember
As one of the haunts of my youth,

When my young heart was gentle and tender,
Filled with all virtue and truth.

Other homesteaders, like Margaret M. Stewart, highlighted the beauty of the vast, open prairies.[12] Her description is detailed and her love for the land, its birds, fish and animals is evident. She feels that there is no match for the richness of prairie life, and in the final line of her poem she states that the land is more wondrous than can "ever be dreamt in dreams."

<u>Our Western Prairie</u>

Have you seen our western prairie,
where the breeze blows soft and sweet,
and the flowers bloom by the million,
in the fields of grass and wheat.

Where the landscape spreads before you,
in ever changing scene,
hill and valley and green fields,
with river and lake between.

The sky is the purest Azure,
where the clouds float fleecy and slow,
and the sun rides by in splendour,
and sets in a crimson glow.

Then the moon comes out from her hiding,
with the stars in her silver train,
and their light is so clear and brilliant,
it seems like day again.

The robin sings in the bushes,
and the fireflies gleam at night,
and the cowboy rides his bronco,
as grand as an olden knight.

The wild ducks feed in the marshes,
and the fishes swarm in the streams,
And our country is fair and grander,
then must ever be dreamt in dreams.

Friendships and Good Times

In the early years of homesteading, few people had the time or opportunity to travel to the neighbours to visit and chat about the day's events. Most were concerned about building a home, clearing their land for seeding, planting a garden, constructing fences and taking care of livestock and poultry. Neighbours were few and far between, so it would take a fair amount of planning in order to go visiting. Once the area became populated, with more homesteaders settling in the area, visits became more frequent and a sense of community began to develop.

Homesteaders would often visit each other either during the hot summer months or during the winter when working times were slower on the farm. People would travel twenty miles or more in order to find some company. Florence Kenyon of Lemberg, Saskatchewan, described how she and her family travelled by horse team and wagon in the summer, but used different types of conveyance in the winter.[1] Sometimes they went by homemade cutter, while at other times they "would drive out on a stoneboat that consisted of a few logs tied together and a tongue attached to the team." Wrapping themselves in robes for warmth made the stoneboat a relatively comfortable form of travel. Problems could arise, however, and their plans for visiting might have to be delayed for a few days (or maybe even weeks) depending on the weather. Winter, especially, had to be viewed with a critical eye given the freezing temperatures and potential for blizzard conditions. However, when the family finally did decide to go, it was exciting. As Florence exclaimed, "It was quite an event to visit a neighbour!"

Others went visiting using their ox team with a wagon or stoneboat in the summer and a sleigh in the winter. Even though their oxen were slow, plodding along the trail, they were useful and reliable in hauling all family members to their destination. However, as Lillian Butler pointed out, oxen could also be ornery animals.[2] She recalled a time she and her family went to a neighbour's house about two miles away. When they arrived, they unhitched the oxen and turned them loose, then went into the house to begin chatting. The oxen decided that they didn't want to stay there and went home, leaving their owners stranded. In order to return home, Lillian and her family had to borrow the neighbour's horse and wagon.

Mrs. Thompson, from the Alliance district of Alberta, also experienced problems with her team of oxen when she went visiting a neighbour lady who had invited a number of women for afternoon tea.[3] Mrs. Thompson dressed carefully for the event and then went out to hitch up her team of oxen to the stoneboat.

> This was her only means of transportation, which she claimed she enjoyed as they could trot faster than any team of horses in the neighborhood. She called on the lady holding the "at home." A number of ladies were already there when she arrived. As the afternoon was very hot it was more comfortable visiting and having their tea outside in the shade of the house. [Time passed and] Mrs. Thompson had to leave early to prepare supper. Using a long, thin pole, with a sharp nail at the end of it, she prodded the oxen up on their feet. She gathered up the lines and dusted off the kitchen chair which was her seat on the stoneboat. Again using the pole she got her team started towards home. Unluckily she chose the wrong time of the day to go home. She had only gone a short distance when the heel flies made their attack. Running with their heads down and kicking frantically, tails high over their backs, the oxen unloaded all the green grass they had eaten during the past two days directly on Mrs. Thompson and the stoneboat. Bracing her feet she stood up and pulled on the lines. She could not stop or turn them. Somehow, they knew that the shade in the bushes across the newly planted field was the only salvation from the stinging bites of the heel flies and nothing could stop them from getting there. Heading across the garden, they hit the field and the runner hit a rock. Up went the stoneboat and Mrs. Thompson was thrown

into the dirt. The other women stood petrified until she stood up and they knew she was not hurt. Then when she turned towards them they could not hold back their laughter. The sight of her clothes and face was just too much. The laughter continued until a slight lull allowed them to hear her cussing that ox team. Her cuss words would put a mule driver from Arkansas to shame!

While some people relied on teams of horses or oxen and wagons for visiting, others, like Albert Elderton, a bachelor, usually walked wherever he wanted to go.[4] It was possible that Albert couldn't afford to buy a wagon or buggy, but he may have believed that horses or oxen, after working hard all week in the fields, needed rest on the weekends. Sometimes Albert walked four to five miles in order to visit friends. In the winter, he skied. He found it lonely living on his own, so he looked forward to a weekend of chatting, playing cards and singing songs.

When people went visiting, they travelled in a variety of ways. Some used a wagon or hayrack, some used a stoneboat, while others went by buggy or democrat. In this photograph, dated 1911, a family sits in a democrat that is being pulled by their two oxen on Royal Street in Coronation, Alberta. PA-696-18. COURTESY OF LIBRARIES AND CULTURAL RESOURCES DIGITAL COLLECTIONS, UNIVERSITY OF CALGARY

Other people did not venture out too often during the winter months. Kathleen Lennox Smith stated that long winter trips were a rarity for her family, but when they did decide to go visiting friends, they always planned on staying overnight.[5] Kathleen remembered those trips well and recounted many highlights:

> Usually for breakfast we had a big slice of toast with hot milk and butter and pepper over it, or perhaps pancakes and coffee. We always went in a big sleigh with a high box and hay in the bottom. Bricks were heated and put by our feet in the sleigh. Later we had foot warmers purchased from Eaton's catalogue. They had a small drawer and charcoal would be put in the range to get red and then put in the warmer. We were all bundled up in cowhides and heavy quilts. We had plenty of quilts made out of old overcoats, trousers and old denim overalls. We sat in the sleigh and took turns driving the horses.

Even during the warmer months of the year, some people planned on staying overnight when they went to visit, particularly if the trip covered many miles. Kathleen Keyser remembered that her family used to drive to Dundurn, Saskatchewan, two or three times every summer to visit an aunt and uncle (Mr. and Mrs. Robert McCordick).[7] It was an all-day trip to get there, and they would picnic halfway for a rest for themselves and their horses. When they arrived, the adults visited and had a game of cards, while the children would pull taffy. As Kathleen said, "This was truly an event for us children!"

Mrs. John Knaus and her family made long trips to visit neighbours and family members, but what she remembered was the beauty of the day, even though they had to suffer the ruggedness of the trail.[8] She recalled being jostled around when their family's huge oxen team took them over rough prairie and through deep sloughs, but at the same time she remembered the loveliness of the tall bulrushes, the muskrat houses, the flocks of ducks on the wing and the greenness of the poplar bluffs.

Instead of going to visit other people, a number of homesteaders remembered the times that neighbours came to visit them. Most of the time the visitors came unannounced, but they were

No One's Home

HOMESTEADER HOSPITALITY WAS always evident. When people came by to visit and the homesteader was not at home, it was expected that the visitors would enter the home (which was never locked), get themselves a drink or make a meal and rest before they returned home. Even if a person was not a visitor, but rather a stranded traveller, the same rule applied. If the owner was away, the traveller could help himself to a meal and stay the night. If the traveller could leave some kind of payment, it was appreciated but not expected. Sometimes homesteaders would leave signs on their doors, outlining a rule or two. For instance, a sign on one homesteader's door simply stated, "Eat when you come and eat when you go, but don't run off with anything!"[8] ●

always welcome. One homesteader, Etta Robinson, reminiscing about her childhood, remembered the day when a neighbour lady, Flora Biglow, came from a nearby farm to get acquainted with the Robinson family.[9] This was an exciting day for Etta, as the woman brought along her two young children, a boy and a girl. Meeting children her own age and being able to play with them for the afternoon was a thrilling event. Flora also brought two saskatoon berry pies with her to welcome Etta's family to the area. Everyone got along very well, especially when the women discovered that they had a Scottish background in common. Their chatting was non-stop as they recalled favourite places and stories from the old country.

Ellenor Merriken also remembered the day a new neighbour came to visit her family.[10] This first meeting led to many more visits, especially for the Merriken children.

> One day in early April of 1913, we saw a team of white horses hitched to a wagon coming over the hill heading toward our place. We could tell by the kind of load he had that he was a homesteader. He pulled up in the yard and asked if he could camp with us for the night. As soon as he opened his mouth to talk, we knew he was a Swede. His name he said was Nels Johnson and when he found that we were Norwegian he knew he was welcome and there was no more English spoken from then on that night. His homestead was one mile east of us; he was married and would send for his wife Ellen as soon as he could get a shack built. In about a month, he went for her and she was a grand person. We kids (three girls) got scolded for going over to their place so often. Every Sunday we pretended to be out hunting for crow eggs but instead we circled around and landed up at the Johnsons, playing whist. They would beg us to come, not that we needed much coaxing. We got so we could speak Swedish with a real skoning accent. This we had to keep a secret at home, for the folks were so intent on us learning perfect English and that accent is difficult to overcome once you acquire it.

Other homesteaders found that they became popular once people found out they owned a musical instrument. Elsie Campbell said that visitors used to come to their place after they got an organ, and talking soon turned to singing when her father started playing the instrument.[11] Similarly, Charles Kieper found that once he had learned to play the mouth organ, all the young folks in the surrounding area would congregate at his home, or else he was expected to bring along his mouth organ when they all went to another person's home for an evening or Sunday afternoon.[12] He became so proficient at playing the mouth organ that he could play and dance at the same time. Emily Millar's husband played the cello.[13] He would play familiar songs and hymns, which she sang along to. As she said, "If neighbours dropped in, so much the better, and there was always a cup of tea and a bite."

Instead of listening to music, some homesteaders invited their friends over for a night of card games. Patrick and Emelia Carson of Warspite, Alberta, claimed that they were avid card players.[14] They were never too busy for a game of Smear (a trick-taking card game) or Bidding Whist when visitors stopped by.[15]

Throwing horseshoes was another great pastime for them, particularly when Fletch Chambers, their neighbour on the adjoining homestead, joined them. On a hot summer day, he would tie his horses to the fence and come over for a game. They would pound a stake into the ground with a hammer, and then each person would pitch a horseshoe to see if they could get a ringer. The person who achieved the highest number of ringers in a set period of time would win the game.

Other homesteaders found that their home became a central locale in the district for the celebration of a variety of occasions. Whether it was due to their friendliness or to where their homestead was situated (i.e., an equal distance from everyone), they found themselves entertaining frequently. George Shepherd said his family's house in Girvin, Saskatchewan, was used for "every and any occasion. For funerals, weddings, birds,[16] meetings of all kinds."[17] George also mentioned that surprise and birthday parties were held in his home. "In our homestead shack when we had lots of visitors, the stove had to be moved to make space for everyone. There was always a lot of excitement with the aftermath of trying to put the stovepipes back into place correctly." Looking back at those busy times, George felt they were happy ones, especially when he compared his family's life to when they first arrived on

The McKinnon family poses outside their home, south of Foremost, Alberta, in 1910. NA-2604-32. COURTESY OF LIBRARIES AND CULTURAL RESOURCES DIGITAL COLLECTIONS, UNIVERSITY OF CALGARY

The Splash

ONE YOUNG GIRL named Grace Carr was excited when her family was invited to a splash at a fellow homesteader's house.[18] However, she did not understand that a "splash" was slang for a party and instead believed that it had something to do with splashing a rock into a slough. As she wrote:

> After we had lived in the district for two or three years, Walter Guthrie announced that he was going to have a "splash." It was in the fall, and the crops had all been harvested. When Mother announced that we would go, I was greatly excited. Walter's house was on a southern slope leading down to a slough. As the party progressed, my anticipation mounted. I saw several young teenage boys slip out into the darkness. I slipped out after them. They sauntered towards the slough, but none of them carried a rock. Still, I waited. After clowning around for a time, they went back into the house. Disappointed, I followed. After all, why had Walter mentioned a "splash" if he didn't intend to throw something into the slough? •

the western prairies from Canterbury, England. As he stated, "Our family made up of our father, mother, six boys and a girl landed at Girvin in 1908 with only the clothes we stood up in and hardly a dollar in resources except our willingness to work. Yet we made good and in an ordinary sort of way." He said that all of his family enjoyed the novelty of their new life on the prairies and the friendships and good times that they experienced.

Many settlers invited friends and acquaintances to join them in church services at their home. In the early years of homesteading, no churches existed as funds to build them would need to be raised by the local community. As a result, establishing a church took time and money. In the meantime, homesteaders who wished to follow a particular religious path would invite fellow homesteaders to their home on a Sunday afternoon or at any other prearranged time. One homesteader, Archie Althouse, fondly remembered how his family would attend church services in people's homes on a rotation, visiting a different home each week.[19] He and his family looked forward to the event and would all pile into their lumber wagon, which was drawn by a horse and an ox hitched together. Every once in a while a priest or reverend, if they were available in the district, were asked to attend these services. Marion Anderson remembered how the superintendent of Catholic Missions was invited to her church service one time.[20] She said that all members found it a little nerve-racking as they "had to be ready with catechism and Bible verses."

Eventually church services were held in the local school, once it was built. Mrs. Amanda Aikenhead remembered the unique way church services were conducted every Sunday in the Vaughn district of Saskatchewan.[21] Everyone in the community attended, representing all the different religious denominations, including

Poultry at the Church Service

ONE EVENING IN 1896, a preacher was invited to give a service at the home of Mrs. Pearson, who lived in the Water Glen area of Alberta. Initially, everything went well until the congregation turned to singing hymns. As soon as the music began, the congregation found that they were being accompanied by the clucking of chickens and the crowing of a rooster. It turned out that Mrs. Pearson had acquired a few chickens earlier in the week, and while she waited for the chicken house to be built out in the yard, she housed the chickens in the attic of her house. Every time they started singing, the poultry did as well, leaving the small children in the group unable to contain their giggles.[22] •

Catholics, Anglicans, Presbyterians and Methodists. Each week, she said, the preachers took turns speaking to the crowd. Alfred Mann recounted his experience going to the local school for church services in Lanigan, Saskatchewan.[23] They had a Baptist minister and a Presbyterian minister in their community, and both would arrive at the church at the same time. They would stand on either side of the teacher's desk, with people on one side of the room following the Baptist teachings while the other side followed the Presbyterian service. Both ministers tried to speak over the other when they were trying to conduct their service.

Sometimes Sunday school for children was held in the settlers' homes. Such was the situation for Susan Tucker and her family, who lived near the town of Craik, Saskatchewan.[24] She said, "We had Sunday school in our little shack, with as many as twenty-six in attendance. We also attended Sunday school in our neighbours' homes."

Some homesteaders hosted parties and dinners in their homes for their fellow settlers. Olive Phelps of Crescent Lake, Saskatchewan, remembered one lively event where the host, Hope Hay, wanted to hold a dinner in honour of all the bachelors

A group of Norwegians attend a church service in 1911 at the home of one of their members, Gilbert White of Seven Persons, Alberta. NA-3729-19. COURTESY OF LIBRARIES AND CULTURAL RESOURCES DIGITAL COLLECTIONS, UNIVERSITY OF CALGARY

in the area.[25] She asked another homesteader, Dick Medcalf, if they could use his home, a dugout, for the occasion. It was a fairly small home "as it was a hole dug about ten or twelve feet square and five feet deep with a pitch roof made of poles and covered with sods." According to Olive, Hope Hay

> sent to Winnipeg for supplies including cigars for after dinner. The ladies of the district kindly volunteered their services to unpack supplies, prepare dinner and set the table, after which they left, leaving the host to receive and entertain the guests. Imagine a room ten by twelve feet with a table extending down the centre, two benches, one on each side, and twelve bachelors . . . The little room was, to say the least, uncomfortably full. After these lusty boys had partaken of the generous repast, the host passed the cigars and when everyone got his "Havana" properly going, one could scarcely see across the room. Gordon Eakin, not being a smoker, did not remain. The last the boys saw of him he had his hat in hand and coat in the other, trying to make a hasty exit up the earthen stairway to the fresh cool evening air. The other guests remained until morning and some postposed their departure until the last crumb in the banquet hamper had been consumed.

It was not unusual for homesteading families to invite bachelor neighbours over for Sunday dinner. Many bachelors did not know how to cook, nor did they tend to be good housekeepers, so many were more than happy to accept an invitation for supper. They would often receive a hearty dinner of meat, potatoes, biscuits, vegetables and a cake or pie for dessert. Often these bachelors came so regularly on Sundays that they were considered one of the family. Ellenor Merriken said that her family looked forward to their company and would expect their bachelor neighbours every Sunday afternoon.[26] If they happened to miss supper, they were offered leftovers or coffee. When holidays like Christmas were coming up, her family made sure to invite them over for supper. The bachelors, Ellenor said, seemed to appreciate the meals, though sometimes they didn't express their thanks in words. Rather, some of them would bring a treat of candy or raisins for Ellenor and her siblings, while others brought along books to exchange. Given that all the members of her family were readers, they were always grateful for new reading material. Ellenor also indicated that the bachelors were energetic conversationalists and great storytellers. While most of the bachelors were welcome at their homestead, Ellenor remembered one time when her father was less than delighted with their behaviour. A man by the name of John Burgh got himself in trouble when a cultural misunderstanding arose from a joke. As Ellenor recounted:

> In the country where John Burgh came from, the custom was to barter for a wife. He had his eyes on my sisters and offered Papa the best horse he had in trade for either one of them. The girls were furious and refused to speak to him. Papa loved a joke and told John that he better wait until I grew up. John took it seriously and every six months or so he came for a visit, presumably to see how much I had grown. Each time Papa would joke with him and tell him he had to have a better house before he could expect to get married, or a new stove, anything he could think of at the time. When I was thirteen, he must have thought he had waited long enough. He stopped by our place on his way home from town one day with six hundred pounds of flour and a brand new cookstove in the wagon [all for trade]. When he came in the house, he looked straight at me and said, "You can come now." Mama put a stop to this foolishness once and for all right then, and poor John hit the trail as fast as he could, with his cookstove and all.

Emma Brydon of Shoal Lake, Manitoba, told the story of a young couple that had a more tragic ending.[27] In order to have a visit with Elizabeth (last name unknown), who lived on the far side of the lake, Ted Wainwright concluded that it would be more expedient to cross the lake by boat rather than circling the water by horse and buggy. So Neil Ryan (another homesteader) and Ted built a boat and smeared it with pitch to ensure that it was waterproof. It was one of the first flat-bottomed boats to be rowed on the lake. Over the course of the next few weeks, "the boat was moored as often on the east shore as on the west and this gave a very plausible excuse for a code of signals" between Elizabeth and Ted.

> Once a signal was sent for visiting, Elizabeth would wait for Ted's arrival in the boat. Sunday was always a very welcome relief from the week's loneliness for the young bachelor homesteaders, like Ted, in the district. It was the day to sally forth and hear one's own voice in more human and cheerful conversation than that addressed to the oxen during the week. One Sunday afternoon, neighbours Walter Lawrence and George Thompson were visiting Matt Thompson (another neighbour). From the hill where Matt's shack stood, the three young men looked down upon the rippling surface of the lake. As they sat on the hill slope, the wind blew over the lake in fitful gusts and a few white caps began to appear. The air became uncomfortably chilly and the three friends went indoors. Suddenly they were aware of someone shouting. Hurrying out they saw a figure on the road by the lake, who by his hands being used as a megaphone shouted to them, "Neil Ryan and Ted Wainwright are drowned!" Rushing down the hill at full speed, the same thought flashed through each mind. "Someone has been drowned, but not those two good swimmers, there is some mistake." But running down the west shore they came to a group of agitated people, busily searching the water with grappling irons. A passerby had noticed, some distance out, a capsized boat with someone clinging to it. He immediately rescued him. It was George Greta, who told his rescuer that his two companions, Neil and Ted, had gone down while attempting to swim to shore. A few hours later, both bodies were recovered. Ted with one big boot drawn off his foot and Neil with one shoe unlaced. Their clothing and heavy shoes had hampered their swimming. In the mind of each member of that sorrowful group was the thought of the stricken girl, Elizabeth. Two white tombstones on the west shore of the lake record for posterity this first tragedy of the Shoal Lake district.

Common Phrases and Casual Conversation

In casual conversation, people often relied on common phrases or idioms to make a point or to highlight some incident or event. With everyone comfortably using the same vocabulary, a sense of understanding and camaraderie is established that ties all members of the community together. Here are some of the common phrases used by those who lived during the homesteading era.[1]

A bird in the hand is worth two in the bush.

A stitch in time, saves nine.

A task well begun is half done.

A whistling girl and a crowing hen always come to a bad end.

As big as a balloon.

As black as night.

As blue as indigo.

As bold as brass.

As bright as a rainbow.

As bright as a silver dollar.

As busy as a bee.

As clumsy as an elephant.

As cold as ice.

As crazy as a bug.

As dark as a pocket.

As deep as a well.

As distant as the stars.

As dumb as an ox.

As easy as falling off a log.

As fresh as a daisy.

As fresh as a fish.

As fresh as a rose.

As green as grass.

As high as a kite.

As high as the mountains.

As large as life.

As low as a snake's belly.

As mad as a hornet.

As nimble as a cat.

As old as the hills.

As pale as death.

As playful as a kitten.

As quick as a dog.

As quick as a wink.

As quiet as a mouse.

As red as a beet.

As red as a rose.

As slippery as an eel.

As slow as a snail.

As slow as molasses in winter.

As sly as a fox.

As smart as a cricket.

As smart as a schoolteacher.

As smart as a whip.

As strong as a horse.

As strong as an ox.

As sweet as honey.

As welcome as the flowers in May.

Better come late than not at all.

Better half a loaf than none at all.

Birds of a feather, flock together.

Blind as a bat.

Clean as a whistle.

Cold enough to freeze the hair on a dog's back.

Curses are like chickens, they come home to roost.

Dark as pitch.

Early to bed and early to rise, makes a man healthy, wealthy and wise.

He would steal acorns from a blind sow.

Light as a feather.

Light as day.

Look before you leap.

Manners maketh the man, the loss of them the fellow.

Marry in haste and repent at leisure.

Meaner than poison.

Two younger members of the Johnson family of Abbey, Saskatchewan, work in the field with a harrow and team of horses in 1923.[2]

Patience is a virtue.

Poor as a church mouse.

Procrastination is the thief of time.

Scarcer than gold.

Scarcer than hen's teeth.

Sound as an apple.

Stiff as a poker.

Stubborn as a pig.

The grass looks greener on the other side.

Time and tide wait for no man.

Tough as a whale bone.

Up with the lark.

Waste not, want not.

When the cat's away, the mice will play.

White as snow.

Neighbours Helping Neighbours

Homesteaders always appreciated when a helping hand was offered. Whether neighbours picked up their mail or groceries when they went to town or helped out building homes and barns, the homesteader and his family always greatly valued their assistance. Everyone understood how trying it was to get the farm work done, so everyone tended to help each other out when assistance was needed. Getting together to work on various projects instilled a sense of companionship and community among the local residents—and typically, as they worked, a good time was had by all as they enjoyed each other's company.

The one form of communication that many people relied on was handwritten letters. Some homesteaders, like Herman Ehrlich, wrote letters to family and friends in the old country,[1] while others wrote to those who lived in Ontario, Quebec or the Maritimes. Herman described the wonder of the prairies and the beauty of wild roses in his letters, while others told of the homes they had built, the number of cows they had purchased and how their spouse and children were doing. Some used the mail for correspondence with the Dominion Lands Office regarding the homestead regulations, while many used it to order items from the mail-order catalogues. One hopeful suitor even tried to find himself a wife when he wrote a letter to the *Family Herald* newspaper. In his letter, he indicated that he was a "good looking man, thirty-five years old, a bachelor farmer with a dear old mother." He wished to correspond with a young woman who followed the Protestant faith and was less than twenty-six years old. He received twenty-one letters in return from women who lived in eastern Canada. One, in particular, caught his eye: a nineteen-year-old woman from Nova Scotia who had just completed high school. Things looked promising as they corresponded for over a year; however, when they met in person, the suitor was greatly disappointed. He was hoping for a full-bodied, fair-haired woman while the girl was petite, lean and brunette. They spent an afternoon together in Winnipeg, and that evening she proceeded on her journey west and he returned to his homestead. No further correspondence took place.[2]

While some homesteaders were prolific letter writers, it was not unusual for those letters to sit for weeks at a time. Many had trouble finding a period of time when they were not busy working on the farm and could take a day to travel to town to post mail. Having someone who would take their mail to post, and would deliver incoming mail, was not only a welcome relief but also a deed that the homesteader and his family were very grateful for. One such helpful neighbour was Ernest Ludlow.[3] Back in 1907, he often wrote letters to family and friends, but his nearest post office was in the town of Willow Bunch, Saskatchewan, which was twenty-five miles away. When he made the trip, about once a month, he often stopped in at the neighbours along the route to see if they had any mail to be posted. On the return trip, he handed them the letters that they had received. He usually ended up carrying up to twenty letters each way. What was remarkable about this feat is that Ernest walked the entire route, a total of fifty miles, which took him eighteen hours to complete.

Another helpful neighbour was Mrs. Sorine Franks' son Raymond, who was eight years old in 1917.[4] The family lived four miles away from the post office, so twice a week Raymond would make the trek to town. He took an empty flour sack with him so he could put the mail into it and carry it back home. He retrieved the mail not only for his family but also for all of his nearby neighbours. For the trip to town, he took his old dog Jack with him. Raymond put a rope around Jack's neck, and then he would merrily trot after the dog to the post office. On the return trip, Jack and Raymond, with his sackful of mail, headed directly home given the lateness of the day. The neighbours would then stop by from time to time over the course of the next week to pick up their mail. This was a more convenient system for them as they did not have to travel the extra miles into town, but instead could stop by for a visit with the family when they collected their mail.

Receiving a letter was a highlight in homesteaders' lives. In this photograph, dated 1904, one elderly lady named Bell is reading a letter she received to her sister Hildah. It is interesting to note that they are both sitting outside in the yard in rocking chairs. A portion of the house and the shed, as well as fencing, can be seen in the background. AUTHOR'S COLLECTION

John Milton Singleton of Morris, Saskatchewan, mentioned in his memoirs that the mail arrived in town weekly, but it took him weeks to find time to get to the post office as he was so busy with farm work.[5] In fact, he said, very few people ever went to town in those early years. If anyone did happen to go to town, they not only picked up outgoing mail from their neighbours, but also delivered incoming mail along with any groceries their neighbours needed. Likewise, Christopher Atkings indicated that his trips to the local town of Melfort, Saskatchewan, were few and far between because Melfort was over thirty-five miles away.[6] He would get to town once every two or three months, mostly travelling by oxen and wagon, though sometimes he used horses, and the odd time he walked. He also helped out with mail and grocery delivery, but he mentioned that it was a difficult chore as "quite often new trails had to be cut around sloughs or bad mud holes."

Herman Collingwood and his family, of the Qu'Appelle area of Saskatchewan, also went out of their way to help their fellow homesteaders:

> A small colony of Hungarians had settled around us and were busy building shacks. They were sure glad to see us ... You see, they knew very little English, so we took on the job of secretary for the bunch. They would bring all the mail over for us to interpret and answer, especially from the Government departments.[7] On Sunday, we would dig out the Stanley Mills catalogue and they would pick out things they wanted, mostly by the pictures.[8] We would make up the order. The trouble was the post office was ten miles away at the Hudson Bay post and we had the only horses so had to pick up the mail. We also had to make the trip to Lipton, to pick up the freight when it came in.[9] But it had its good side as we had good neighbours.[10]

While many homesteaders were reliant on their neighbours for mail pickup and delivery, Dorothy Gush and her family always received their mail quickly and efficiently as her father became the postmaster for the Strasbourg area of Saskatchewan in 1906.[11] The Gush family homestead became the central location for people to drop off their mail, and Dorothy remembered how she sold stamps to their neighbours, handled their money orders and registered letters. It was her father's job to drive the mail to and from Strasbourg, which was thirty-six miles away. He would leave on a Friday and come back home on Saturday. In the summer, he used a team of driving ponies and a buggy, while in the winter, he drove a cutter. As Dorothy said,

> It was a long cold drive for him in the winter. We put large stones in the oven overnight and by morning, they would be quite hot all through, and with straw thick on the floor of the cutter and the hot stones, a buffalo robe and coat, a fur cap with ear tabs and fur mittens, my father would start off whatever the weather. Unfortunately, he did not have the benefit of hot stones coming home. Father had a largeish moustache and the icicles would be hanging thick

on it when he got home and he would stand by the stove until they melted. The horses also had icicles around their mouths. Saturday, after he got home, the neighbours for as far as ten miles came to pick up their mail.

Harriet Gerry always remembered the excitement of receiving mail and the arrival of weekly newspapers:

> What excitement when the mail driver arrived on his weekly round [to the post office in town]! What a visiting took place when the homesteaders came to pick up their mail. There was mail from England, from the USA, from Scotland, from Germany and from Eastern Canada ... Also, the joy of a newspaper! The now firmly established Family Herald and Weekly Star would carry advice for the lovelorn, provide hints medical for the human and veterinarian for the stock, news of the world, and old favourites of song.[12]

When she and her family went to town to pick up their mail, they were thrilled to see other homesteaders. Since visiting was such a rare event, meeting friends in town was a joyful occasion.

Along with helping with the mail and groceries, many neighbours were more than happy to take part in building bees. These bees were arranged on a day when everyone could get together and meet at a particular homestead in order to help build a house, a barn and other farm structures. It was usually an event that people looked forward to, as it provided an opportunity for socializing, but at the same time they were helping out a fellow homesteader who needed their assistance. Often the womenfolk would bring along a picnic lunch with cookies and cakes for when the men needed a break. The atmosphere was upbeat, people were happy and it provided a warm feeling of camaraderie.

A number of homesteaders in their memoirs remembered how their family was helped out by neighbours. For instance, Frank Baines mentioned that his family had assistance in 1884 when they were building their first log house, twelve feet by fourteen feet in size.[13] It was built within a day. Brian and Eva Harris both recounted how neighbours came along and helped their parents with their first home:

> The neighbors cut down logs and raised a building for the family to live in for the winter. The next summer, another building was constructed and the first one we used for the barn. Later when the final house was built, the second building was put to good use as a chicken coop. This chicken coop, while the family lived in it, had no floor. Mrs. Harris [the mother] put down a canvas to cover the dirt. It served the purpose admirably. When it was time to sweep the floor, the canvas was taken out and given a shake![14]

Homesteader Charles Brong was also offered assistance in the summer when he was building his first home. As his daughter Edith Brong recalled:

> Several of the men of the Berwyn district formed the house building bee for us. The true pioneer spirit really showed then. The new house rose by leaps and bounds, or rather, I guess by rounds and rounds of logs. This house boasted a floor, crude though it was, made of poplar poles split and laid flat side up. This was a little improvement over the dirt floors that many of the pioneer women started out with. The roof was made of similar split poles with overlapping layers of sods. With chinks in between the wall logs, it proved to be a very snug house indeed ... This house was a site of a good many parties and Christmas celebrations.[15]

Harriet Gerry remembered the time that her family's barn was built.[16] As she said, "a barn raising was an eventful day. After the site was cleared and the logs cut, the neighbours gathered. The men worked on the barn and the women baked and brewed to feed the crowd." Later, when the barn was completed at the end of the day, there was a "celebration dance with the music of fiddles and the stomp of feet reaching the newly erected rafters. These men and women played as hard as they worked and the fun and laughter was the leavening toil and the sparking of romances."

Edith Stilborn, remembered how her family's barn burned down in the spring of 1886, and the neighbours came and helped build a stable for their horses in the fall, well before the freezing temperatures of winter set in.[17] Another homesteader, Arthur Tilford, recounted how helpful people were when a fellow homesteader became ill.[18] As he said, "The homesteaders always worked together and there were lots of bees to help someone out. Everybody was in the same boat and helped each other. Some farmer would be sick and there would be five or six neighbours helping out whenever and wherever they could." Emily Millar also remembered the kindness of her neighbours.[19] She felt blessed to have them as her family was completely dependent on them. Her husband suffered from inflammatory rheumatism and could not work, so neighbours would stop by with medicine, groceries and kerosene (for the lamps). They picked up mail for the family and chopped firewood for their stove.

Sometimes labour and farm equipment were exchanged for the benefit of both parties. According to Robert Widdess, there were a number of bachelors who lived close to his family's homestead.[20] They tended to lack farm equipment, while the Widdess family lacked labour power. So, Robert said, "the most popular method was for them to help my father for a time and then use

Women from the Czar area of Alberta hold a quilt that they all helped sew together at a quilting bee in 1910. *L–R:* Mrs. Joe McHenry, Mrs. Beck Senior, Mrs. George Johnstone, Mrs. Walter Brooks, Mrs. Florence Melcher, Opal Brooks, Lillie Johnstone, Mrs. J. Lundstrom, Mrs. Guy Roberts and Grace Melcher. NA-1534-10. COURTESY OF LIBRARIES AND CULTURAL RESOURCES DIGITAL COLLECTIONS, UNIVERSITY OF CALGARY

his machinery to prove up their own homesteads. That was the best thing that came out of that system. It helped my father but it also helped these young fellows get started. In many cases, they prospered and became the backbone of the country."

Threshing season was also a time for homesteaders to help each other out. Threshing teams would work from place to place, harvesting the wheat. According to Charles Bray, he became part of these threshing gangs and always assisted his fellow homesteaders, even if it took hours to complete the job.[21] He indicated that several of the local farmers supplied extra horses and oxen as well as additional men. Homesteader Edith Stilborn also remembered the threshing gang that stopped by her family's place each year in order to complete the harvest.[22] A dozen to twenty local men would arrive. The work would be intense for a few days, starting early in the morning and ending late in the evening. The men needed to be fed, so she, her sisters and her mother would cook and bake diligently over the course of each day to ensure that enough food was always available. They would also deliver the food and beverages, as well as utensils and plates, to the threshers in the field. When the men finished threshing, they (and her father) moved on to help out at the next homestead.

Men thresh a homesteader's crop in 1921. PA-115-13. COURTESY OF LIBRARIES AND CULTURAL RESOURCES DIGITAL COLLECTIONS, UNIVERSITY OF CALGARY

Feather-stripping Bees

SOMETIMES BEES WERE held to help women with their chores. A group of women would congregate at one woman's home and they would husk hundreds of ears of corn, shuck barrelfuls of peas or can dozens of jars of jam. They also sewed quilts and made soap and candles.

Feather-stripping bees were another common event as the work, if done alone, could be tedious and labour-intensive. Feather-stripping occurred in the fall when the geese were slaughtered with an axe. Their bodies would then be dipped for two or three minutes in boiling water. Once that was done, the feathers could be easily removed, grasped by the handfuls. The feathers would then be set out on long tables so they could dry. Neighbour women would sit at these tables and skillfully strip the quills from the down and the feathers. Eventually the down and feathers would be used by the farmwife when she made quilts or pillows for her family. (As for the meat, it did not go to waste as the bird would be canned, cured, smoked or dried for eating by the family over the long winter season.)

Feather-stripping bees, as well as all of the other bees that were organized, were favourite social pastimes for the women. Not only were they opportunities for everyone to chat and catch up on the daily news, but some of the women were storytellers who entertained the others with hair-raising tales as they worked. Once the work was done, tea and coffee, cookies, cakes or pies were set out by the farmwife for her friends to enjoy. ●

Not Being Neighbourly

SOME PEOPLE WEREN'T as sociable or helpful as they might have been. Emily Millar described how sometimes people could make life difficult, as her mother, Ellen, and her father, Sam, found out on a return trip to their homestead from Saskatoon, Saskatchewan.[23]

As more settlers moved in, better trails were broken during the winter to Saskatoon. As the winter wore on, these trails built up solid and high, while the snow on either side was deep and soft. Trips to Saskatoon were a major undertaking at any time but particularly hazardous in the winter, for a number of reasons. Settlers tried to stock up on enough staple foods in the early winter to last most of the way through the cold and stormy weather. There were occasions when a man was forced to make the trip before spring. On one such journey, Sam had bought some pigs. Besides the pigs, there were flour, sugar, tea, etc., as well as kerosene for the lamps. On the way home, Sam met a couple of young chaps in a light cutter. Both drivers stopped and waited. Sam was confident the strangers would pull off the trail because they were travelling light. When silence had no effect, Sam tried persuasion but the two men became verbally abusive. Rather than argue further, Sam pulled off and the sleigh promptly turned over, spilling pigs, flour, sugar, kerosene and Ellen into the deep snow. When Ellen spoke of this experience, she said Sam went after the pigs first and left her to disentangle herself as best she could. Sam's teasing reply to his wife was that he knew Ellen wouldn't go far but you could never tell about the pigs and they cost him good money. •

In some cases, organizing a bee was not required to help out fellow homesteaders who found themselves in dire straits. Rather, the offer of assistance from a special friend was all that was needed. Such was the experience of Mrs. Sorine Franks, who remembered a time when a fellow homesteader, who had a generous spirit, helped her and her family:

> One spring, we did not have any money to get garden seeds and were talking about selling a nice heifer to get some money. Well, our neighbor, Mrs. Barton, came along one morning and put a dollar bill in my hand and said, "Get your garden seeds with that" and we did. It does a person good to think back to times like that and there were many like that in those days. Neighbors helping neighbors.[24]

Mail-Order Catalogues

In the early years of homesteading, many depended on the town's mercantile store. However, their product choice was limited, focusing primarily on the essentials. If homesteaders wished to add diversity to their lifestyle, and they could afford it, they often turned to mail-order catalogues. Clothing could be purchased for children and adults, as well as shoes, boots and hats. Furniture, including wood stoves, were included in these catalogues, as were utensils, tools, books and other dry goods. Dried fruits could also be purchased, to add to the homesteading diet. Given the prevalence of mail-order catalogues, and the reliance that many homesteaders placed on them, the catalogue business became a common feature across the prairies.

The primary mail-order catalogue for many homesteaders across the western prairies was the one that was distributed by the T. Eaton Company in the spring and fall of each year.[1] Many people waited with great anticipation for the catalogue to arrive in the mail and were thrilled when it finally found its way to them. Andrew Salamon remembered that "the ladies spent quite some time looking through these catalogues, selecting goods generally in the clothing line. These catalogs were often called the Women's Bible, the Prairie Bible or the Farmer's Bible. I think I am safe to say that mail order purchasing especially in the line of clothing would be about 50% of total purchases in the rural areas."[2] Kathleen Keyser also remembered the excitement associated with the catalogues.[3] She said that her mother used to send in an order twice a year "for a full complement of clothing for the coming season. Coats, shoes and other necessary clothing. If I remember correctly, the order usually came by freight, being quite a sizable one for a large family. It was also an event to see what we had got. It was almost as if there were three Christmases in the year!"

Mrs. Florence Kenyon commented on the importance of the Eaton's catalogue to her family.[4] They first came to Canada in 1895, and in the beginning they had plenty of clothing that they had brought from England. Over time, however, they began to purchase items from the catalogue. "We would try to get a bulk order with neighbors to cut down on freight expenses. It was mostly wearing apparel. As money became more plentiful, we ordered furniture and hardware." Similarly, Lena May Purdy and her family, who moved to Saskatchewan in 1896, also came to rely on the Eaton's catalogue for a variety of items.[5] Like others, she sent in orders for cottons and prints for dresses and aprons and table linen, but she also ordered tea, raisins, currents, rice, barley, spices and toilet soap. Lena Bacon remembered ordering wallpaper for her home as well as sturdy material to cover a homemade lounge.[6] She also ordered lace to make collars on clothes for Christmas presents. Other homesteaders placed orders depending on their particular needs. For instance, the Eaton's catalogue included medicine and medical devices, such as canes and wheelchairs and bindings for broken ribs. For those who needed farm equipment, they were able to purchase seeders, plows, rakers and threshers, while those who wanted to build a home and barn could purchase the plans and all the materials that they needed as a package. In the early years, all of the orders were filled by the Eaton's company, located in Toronto. By 1905, a subsidiary department store was built in Winnipeg to serve western customers.

The prospect of receiving the catalogue was exciting, as was looking through the pages at the vast amount and variety of goods that were available, but a number of homesteaders soon realized that they would not be able to buy many of those items. They had to be selective given their lack of funds and the need for practicality. Pearl Stone noted:

> The T. Eaton Catalog was truly an introduction to a world of magical things. The fabulous feathered hats were awe inspiring, the fancy, embroidered petticoats, the shoes which buttoned high above the ankle, and the coats trimmed with

This is the cover of the T. Eaton Company fall and winter catalogue in 1903–04. These catalogues were distributed across the west, with many homesteaders ordering clothing, household supplies, food and other essential items.[7]
AUTHOR'S COLLECTION

fur delighted us. But, no, these gorgeous things were not for farm kids. The underwear, plain everyday shoes, yard goods, wool for knitting and men's socks were some of the more practical things to be chosen. Once in a while, a new coat was purchased. We girls, my older sister and I, turned sadly from the pretty to the practical. Our choice was not always what was ordered. Mother, with so many to buy for and not too much to buy with, often substituted something cheaper than our choice. Anyway, after a couple of weeks, it arrived. What excitement prevailed when it was opened and examined. Maybe the shoes pinched a bit, but we were sure that they would stretch and be comfortable. The adults felt our shoe-encased foot and would say firmly, "No, they must be returned." Crestfallen, we had to wait another two or three weeks. Eventually, they arrived and happiness prevailed, having new shoes that squeaked.[8]

Annie Norris and her family shared a similar experience.[9] While they tried to find enough money to place an order, they were often forced to rely on alternative methods to ensure that each family member was fully clothed. Clothes were mended and re-mended, while other household items were made from flour, sugar and oat sacks.

> Money was something we or our neighbors had not much of. We didn't mind too much; we never went naked or starved and we made our own fun. Lack of money hurt most at Christmas when trying to make out an order from the Eaton's catalog for much needed wearing apparel for the husband and children and a small toy for each child. The preschoolers wore hand-me-downs and made-overs until they literally fell apart, but back to the Eaton's order. I learned later that I was not the only mother who made a list, added up the amount, tore it up and made a smaller list with the same result, until through tears secretly shed, I made the order fit the little money I had to spend. More patches went on the underwear, even Dad's were patched on patch until they must have been doubly warm. It was an era of make do, make over, or do without. Women took pride in making neat patches since they were a must. Cotton flannelette, even though only $0.15 and $0.20 a yard, was hard to buy, so we used flour, sugar and rolled oat sacks. The latter two were of soft fine cotton that could be used for baby clothes, tea towels and curtains or children's underwear. Flour sacks were made of a strong and sturdy material. I couldn't have kept house without them. Ripped open after every last speck of flour had been shaken into the bread pan, they were then washed and bleached. They were made into pillow slips or sheets. It took five 100 pound bags to make a large sheet, two to make a crib sheet, one to make a pillow slip or two tea towels. A spare one or two could be made into tablecloths, touched up with rickrack or embroidery or an edge of lace crocheted from the string that had been ripped out of the seams. Dyed, they made up into men's shirts; my husband wore two for three summers. Of course I had to patch elbows and shoulders, and renew collars and cuffs. I made

dresses for myself and the little girls, swimsuits for the children, and the patches left over were made into quilt tops and horses' hats. Horses' hats were made to cover the horses' ears because on hot summer days the sand flies were so bad they nearly drove the horses crazy by getting into their nostrils and ears.

Nannie Walker also remembered the days of flour sack clothing.[10] She said, "Life was very hard in those days, so mother would use the material from the flour bags to make our school dresses. Later she would send orders to Eaton's catalogue for material, printed cotton would cost about $0.15 per yard. Many times, Eaton's did not have exactly as mother had ordered. Instead, they would send a substitute of equal or better value."

Theresa McDonough recalled the time her mother studiously perused the pages of women's fashions.[11] As Theresa said, the "Eaton's Catalogue, based in Winnipeg, was a boon to women although there was never money for much more than necessities." But "women still had to have corsets, and there was a great variety of yard goods of fine quality for sale. Women wore gingham dresses and aprons for work in the summer, serge in the winter, and perhaps a factory-made coat, which was expected to last for years." Sometimes these items were too expensive to purchase, particularly if family funds were low. When this happened, her mother would look at the new fashions in the catalogue, use newspapers to cut out a pattern, and sew the dress within two days. She reused items saved from old clothes, including trimming, buttons, braid, buckles, hooks, lace or binding, when she sewed her new creations.

While many spent their money on basic clothing or other necessary practical items, every once in a while someone would order clothes from Eaton's for a special occasion. For instance, one fifty-five-year-old bachelor named George decided that he wanted to court a woman who was working at a neighbouring farm.[12] He visited her every Sunday. One day he ordered a suit from the Eaton's catalogue, likely in the hope that it would impress her. When the suit arrived in the mail, he put it on and everything fit perfectly. Very proudly, he stood in front of the mirror and then decided to head out on his weekly visit. In order to get to her place, he had to take a shortcut through A.J. Riley's farm. This shortcut entailed crossing a creek. Large stones were strategically placed so a person could hop from one stone to the next to get to the other side without getting wet. According to A.J. Riley, he caught a glimpse of George coming down the hill one Sunday, all dolled up in his new Eaton's suit, heading toward the creek. Quite a bit of time elapsed, and there was no sign of George. A.J. started to get concerned. Eventually, he saw George retreating back up the hill to his shack, so A.J. decided to go and pay him a visit. When he saw George, he was a mess. "He with his new suit had fallen into the Creek. No cleaners them days. We had to do it ourselves. I helped him. He went over this time [to visit his lady] just in his overalls." In the end, A.J. said, everything turned out all right. Trying to impress the lady with a new suit of clothes did not seem to matter as George ended up marrying the woman and they were very happy together.

Another young man had romance on his mind when he sent in his order to Eaton's. He was getting married so he decided to buy some wedding clothes from the catalogue in 1913. His suit

Along with summer dresses, women could order a variety of items, including corsets, chemises, aprons, skirts, shirt waists, nightgowns, woolen underwear, shawls, hats and coats.[13]
AUTHOR'S COLLECTION

The Eaton's catalogue offered men a variety of clothing items, such as trousers, vests, shirts, ties, collars and cuffs, socks, underwear, sweaters, overcoats and hats.[14]
AUTHOR'S COLLECTION

cost $15, one shirt was $1.50, two linen collars were $0.25, one pair of suspenders was $0.50, one silk tie was $0.25, two pairs of socks were $0.54, and one pair of patent shoes was $3.50. The wedding ring cost him $5, four handkerchiefs were $0.25, and oil for his hair was $0.20. The total came to $26.99, a princely sum at that time.[15]

While the general consensus among homesteaders was that the mail-order catalogue was an essential service, and many were happy to receive it, there were a few who were not as enamoured of the intrusion of this business into their community. In fact, they felt that having such a business in operation was damaging. As Alexander Cameron stated, he and his family did not believe in "mail order buying as it was detrimental to the progress of the community in which you live. Every dollar expended in your own community helps every member of that community and helps your community to grow and every good citizen should be anxious to see the district in which he lives flourish."[16] Members of Stephen Hall's family were of a similar mind, saying, "We regarded the mail order house as an octopus that prospered by not paying taxes in the areas from which they got much of their business."[17] Joseph Hammerschmidt also held a strong opinion about the mail-order catalogue business: "We didn't have so much money then, to throw around for mail orders. We called these catalogues, the Devil's Bible. They were a great temptation for women. The cause of domestic trouble."[18]

Other homesteaders, instead of emphasizing the detriment to the local economy or to family life, indicated that they preferred to shop at the mercantile in town. They appreciated the personal touch when visiting with the shopkeeper and staff, they enjoyed looking at the goods that were available for purchase and they were grateful for the generosity they experienced from time to time when they did not have the money to cover their purchases. Alfred Riley said, "Our local merchant was better than a bank because if you tried to borrow from the bank most likely you would get turned down, if you did not have enough security. My credit was always good with Mr. C. Beach Craven at the Laidlaw mercantile store at Lumsden."[19] Alfred went on to explain why he and his wife, shortly after they were married, thought of turning to the Eaton's catalogue in order to buy "several extra things their local store did not keep in stock." As he said, they wrote an order out for Eaton's for around $75. They both felt bad about placing the order, and before they mailed it, Alfred decided to check with his local merchant to see if he would be able to find all of the items that he had listed on his Eaton's order. To the Rileys' surprise, the merchant was able to track down everything they wanted. They were especially pleased that they were able to save the freight cost (which they would have paid if they had sent their order to Eaton's). They received their items quickly, paid for them and thanked the merchant. The merchant was happy as well, as he told them that he was making 10 percent on their order and that he had the use of their money for thirty days before he had to pay his own bill for the goods. As he said to them, it was "good business all around. I wish all my customers were as thoughtful."

Wear-Forever Suits

EVERY ONCE IN a while, travelling salesmen would visit. In the following story, a salesman is selling men's suits, but his sales pitch turns out to be less than honest with regard to the quality of the cloth. Given these types of stories, it is not a surprise that many people came to depend on mail-order catalogues for their clothing, particularly as they could return items if they were not satisfied with them. Returning items to a travelling salesman was next to impossible, as the salesman never stayed in one area long enough to be tracked down for an exchange or refund.

> One settler was named John Ash. One day while in our village, Mr. Ash was accosted by a traveling salesman who was selling men's "Wear-Forever Suits." Actually, a coat and pants made of tough, hard material similar to overall denim and brown in color, and suitable for any occasion—dress or work. To impress a prospective customer the salesman always produced a swatch of cloth and asked the other party to hold it tightly between their two hands. Then the salesman opened a pocket knife and ran the pointed blade end across the cloth a few times. Then he had the prospective customer examine the cloth which would be unharmed; no doubt the point of the knife blade was always very, very dull. However, John Ash was completely sold and ordered a coat and pants at a fabulous price right on the spot. He obtained a swatch of the cloth to take home. Arriving home, he hastened to pull up his team of horses, and hurried to the house to tell Mrs. Ash of his wonderful purchase to arrive soon. He produced the cloth sample, requested Mrs. Ash to hold it and stretch it tightly between her two hands. She did as requested, albeit with some suspicion. Mr. Ash then took out his pocket knife, which was razor sharp, opened the long blade and with a proud flourish applied the point of the knife across the cloth. The cloth parted down the center, cut like a piece of cheese. Mrs. Ash stood there with a piece of cloth in each hand and looking blankly at her husband John, and said, "So what?" John Ash just stood there speechless and flabbergasted while he sheepishly closed his knife and put it away.[20] •

Toilet Paper

WHETHER THEY APPROVED of the Eaton's mail-order catalogue or not, many homesteaders indicated that the out-of-date catalogues came in handy as toilet paper in the outhouses. Gladys Holmes mentioned that, in the winter, children as young as six years waded "through snow sometimes two feet deep or more to go to the bathroom in the outhouse. The catalogues were very much in evidence in this building."[21] William Colby Reesor also wrote in his memoirs that the catalogues were put to good use by his family: "The catalogues were not wasted. As the new one came in, the old one served a very useful purpose in the outhouse."[22] He highlighted how they were useful in another interesting way. If a farmer started using each page from the beginning, by the time he got to the hardware section in July, he knew it was time to start putting up hay for the coming winter. Claude Hellekson also offered his opinion about the catalogue:

> Every homestead had a little log house, later frame, known by various names—outhouse, throne, little house—a real part of the so called "good old days" back then. These one or two holers always had an Eaton's catalog hanging handy. I think a law should have been passed making mail order companies use only soft pages, no shiny, slick ones. Any politician making this law surely would have won all homesteader votes![23] ●

Childhood Friends, Games and Toys

Like their parents, children enjoyed socializing with each other. Whenever they had the opportunity, they would play games or construct toys with their friends. Meeting children their own age was exciting, and being able to play for a time was a special moment that many homesteaders remembered. Such friendships reveal the community spirit that thrived at the time, even among the smallest individuals in the district.

Many young homesteaders remembered the new settlers passing by their home on their way to their own homestead. Grace Carr said, "They were people just like ourselves, who had decided to go homesteading. Some came in wagons drawn by horses, some came in oxen-pulled wagons. Sometimes there was a woman and some children among the settlers. Mother always welcomed them and tried to make them comfortable."[1] Grace played with these children, especially if their parents had stopped at her family's place for the night, but unfortunately, after they left the next morning, she rarely saw any of them again. For Grace, it was difficult to make any long-standing friendships when their acquaintance was so fleeting, and it was disappointing to see these children leave, especially after they had experienced a wonderful playtime together.

Others were able to create bonds of friendship. Dora Mitchell, for example, remembered the delightful times that she had with other children, even if there was an age and sex difference.[2] She had been an only child for the first six and a half years of her life and never had any companions of her own. Eventually her parents took her visiting with them, and over time they called on a number of different families. Their nearest neighbour, the one they visited with most often, had a son who was four years older than she was. Given that he was a boy, she had to adapt to the types of games that he enjoyed playing. When they got together, she said, their activities "took the form of building things with scraps of wood, playing with wagons and sleds, playing horse and other such male oriented occupations."

Peter and Pauline Kozdrowski remembered the pleasant way they passed the time with new friends they found in Warspite, Alberta, after emigrating from Poland in the late 1890s.[3]

> Although we all had work to do, tending livestock and milking cows morning and night, getting firewood during winter and farm work during the summer, there was also time for play. We made skates using two heavy wires under each skateboard along with a pole with a nail at one end to propel ourselves on the pond ice. In summer there was baseball with homemade bats and balls, soccer and even volleyball. On Sunday afternoons after church, whenever and wherever a group of boys and girls gathered, they would sing, play ball or dance in some empty granary. There were always musicians with a harmonica or violin to provide the music.

If children wanted to visit their neighbour friends, they either walked over from their homestead, rode their own horses or were dropped off by parents in order that they might have an afternoon to play with other children. The children of the Jardine family of the Redpath district of Alberta remembered some of their favourite times when other children came over to visit. In fact, they often thought up a variety of entertainments to keep their visitors happy. They would run and explore every corner of the homestead, chatting along the way. They would ride stick horses, and they dared each other to take off their shoes or boots and run barefoot to the barn in a race. They even fished off the roof of the house. The older children climbed up on the roof, while the younger ones stayed below. The older ones would have a string tied to the end of a long stick and cast the string down to the children, who found something strange or unusual around the farmyard and tied it to the end of the string so that the older

Smoking Out Behind the Barn

SMOKING WAS A popular pastime among the men, so it was not a surprise to find boys who wanted to emulate them. As recalled by August Roenspies, Sr. of Annaheim, Saskatchewan, a group of three friends—Charlie Schreiner, Jr., Gracian Miller and Ed Roenspies—decided to try smoking.[4] They gathered together some fireweed stems (a herbal plant), rolled them in a paper and proceeded to smoke their homemade cigarette. Unfortunately, their time as smoking connoisseurs was limited as they all became incredibly ill. •

In this photograph from 1912, both young men are holding cigars. It was quite fashionable at the time to be a cigar smoker. In addition, smoking was seen as a rite of passage to adulthood for young men. AUTHOR'S COLLECTION

ones could pull it up. Great fun was had, particularly if something unusual was caught when they fished. Another time, the older boys built a log raft that they wanted to try out on one of the deeper sloughs. All of the children who were there got on the raft at the same time. "The boys dived off the edge, shoving it as they vaulted over the edge, and caused one of the little girls to fall into the water. Fortunately for all, the boys were strong and quick, and managed to have her out and carefully dried off in the sun before returning home."

If it was a miserable day out, children played inside the house. Sometimes they made a game of picking out odd bits and pieces of stuff that had been mixed into the plasterboard that covered the walls of the shack, while others tried to read the newspapers or magazine pages that had been used as wallpaper. They had contests to see who could eat the most boiled eggs, while other homesteader children remembered playing board games like checkers, crokinole, snakes and ladders, and *Parcheesi*, as well

Two brothers play checkers while their two sisters look on in 1910. Children often had to stay indoors during the cold winter months. To pass the time, they played board games.
AUTHOR'S COLLECTION

as card games like Snap, Old Maid and Fish. There was also a gossip game that many children enjoyed, especially when friends came to visit. Everyone sat in a circle, and the first person whispered a secret into the second child's ear. This child would then whisper into the next child's ear and so on. There were always lots of giggles when it was learned what the first child whispered and how differently it was heard by the end.

Visiting children often found themselves happily playing in the hayloft, bouncing through the loose piles of hay, while others played hide-and-seek. The hayloft was a great place to hide because it was easy to get into the loose hay and burrow down deep. Sometimes the older children would pretend that they didn't know where the younger ones were hiding, especially if a foot was sticking out or a piece of clothing was not completely hidden. However, if older children were hiding, their friends had no problem pouncing on them and scaring them. Children also liked to hike out in the woods. They would build forts or tree houses and make mud pies, or would make screeching noises with a blade of grass. They also used their imaginations and made up stories, often playing house or playing school.

Pearl Stone and her sisters, in the Carstairs district of Alberta, built their own playhouse out of whatever material was available and then furnished it with scraps and baubles.[5] They placed sticks on the ground to identify the various rooms, including the kitchen, the bedroom and the dining room. They retrieved broken dishes from the junk pile, and when they "rummaged through a neighbour's garbage heap, an old electric lightshade of pink and green glass was found." Pearl said that they "were absolutely delighted as that was something that we never found at home. These friends had come from eastern Canada and no doubt the shade was broken on the way out. What difference did it make to us if it was cracked or broken? Of course it was dirty, but soap and hot water made it brilliantly beautiful."

Dora Mitchell recalled how many childhood activities required the extensive use of imagination: "While bouncing a ball, rolling a hoop, or even pulling weeds in the garden, I told myself endless stories, stories without a plot or an ending, describing characters at great length."[6] She learned how to skip a rope up to 100 times, played tug-of-war with the dog and piled loads of hay onto her toy wagon. Her father made her a toboggan from a round cheese box. She used it to slide down the hill on their farm in the winter. Dora also mentioned that she had quite a collection of dolls and enjoyed playing with them. "There was a homemade rag doll, an Eskimo doll, a small doll with a painted China head named Daisy, and then the Eaton's Catalogue Beauty Doll,[7] with real hair and eyes that closed, whom I called Hattie. She had a set of tiny China dishes and some small doll furniture and set out tea parties for the dolls." However, Dora spent most of her time playing with paper dolls. She said that her interest in paper dolls began with the *Ladies' Home Journal* feature for children called "Letty Lanes' Paper Family." "It had pictures of people for cutting out, and clothes for them with tabs for fastening them on." After being introduced to those paper dolls, Dora decided to make her own paper dolls using the Eaton's catalogue. She would cut out pictures of men, women and children from the underwear pages, and then draw and colour clothes for them. She also

> collected any scraps of colored paper [she] could find, such as envelope linings, to make costumes for [her] paper dolls. There were whole families, each one had a name written on its back, and each family had an envelope for its home. The catalogue also provided furniture for the paper houses [she] made for the paper dolls. Tin foil from packages of tea was used for dishes and cutlery.

Instead of using the Eaton's catalogue for paper dolls, some children would make scrapbooks with pictures from the catalogue and any other newspapers or magazines that were available. They would make a paste of flour and water, then glue the pictures onto pieces of paper. This activity kept children busy for hours. Often mothers saved old catalogues for the days when their children were at home sick from school. The children could look at them or play with them, depending on how they felt.

Sometimes parents got involved with their children's playtime. One homesteading mother demonstrated her creativity when she made a hammock out of flour sacks and binder twine. She sewed the sacks together and then used the twine to tie each end of the hammock to a strong tree fairly low on its trunk. This novel contraption entertained her children for

Children play on a homemade merry-go-round in the Pine Lake district of Alberta in 1915.
NA-2727-14. COURTESY OF LIBRARIES AND CULTURAL RESOURCES DIGITAL COLLECTIONS, UNIVERSITY OF CALGARY

hours as they fell in and out of the hammock and swung back and forth.

Ella Dickie remembered the time her father built a merry-go-round for her and her friends.[8] He sank a post into the ground, leaving two feet of the post exposed above ground. He attached two crossed planks and made seats on the ends. Four children were able to ride the merry-go-round while others pushed. The merry-go-round kept Ella and her friends entertained for quite a while. She said that her father also made a hammock out of page wire and hung it up between two trees in the backyard. However, the most exciting undertaking was when he took the running gears out of an old wagon, "removed the tongue, and tied a rope on each side of the front axle to steer it by. All of [the children] piled on and down the hill we would go!" She said that there were enough children living nearby that they were able to play ball games and kick the can.

The Old Swimming Hole

ELIZABETH E. ROBINSON reflected on her childhood days on her family's homestead in the Boyle district of Alberta.[9] She remembered how happy she was when she was with family and friends or just enjoying the beauty of the land.

> Social events, mostly revolving around the school in the earlier days, as well as the beauty of the trees and rolling countryside, all were a big part of my growing up in Boyle. Of the farm, I loved the Creek, it being the site of many, many hours of play. The old swimmin' hole was the center of many summer activities, wiener roasts, swimming and just a little quiet place to reflect. I'll let you in on a little secret: the boys swam in the nude and if I ventured near to them when they were indulging in this "for boys only" activity, the "thunder of the gods would rent the air," said my mother. •

Four boys swim in their local swimming hole in southern Alberta, ca. 1920. Their horses are waiting for them in the bush. NA-2579-5. COURTESY OF LIBRARIES AND CULTURAL RESOURCES DIGITAL COLLECTIONS, UNIVERSITY OF CALGARY

Three children play on a homemade see-saw in the Homeglen area of Alberta in 1927. They likely made the see-saw themselves with a two-foot by six-foot length of wood placed on a cut tree trunk. NA-4181-33. COURTESY OF LIBRARIES AND CULTURAL RESOURCES DIGITAL COLLECTIONS, UNIVERSITY OF CALGARY

Children in the Elnora district of Alberta enjoyed playing together, but their play was more organized, forming teams and playing baseball. They laughed and enjoyed their time together as they tried to improve their skills by throwing the ball and playing the various positions. Even on the hottest summer days they were not deterred, as they would endlessly pitch to each other. They were determined to fine-tune their curveballs, their fastballs and their control over the game. As for their equipment, the "tools, in the beginning, were primitive; a catcher's mitt was made from old overalls and horsehair," and "bats were fashioned with a jackknife from Poplar saplings."[10] Early baseballs were created by wrapping string or yarn around a small rubber ball until it approached correct baseball size. Then it was covered with a piece of old leather that was sewn on. Once they were ready to play, the children would be divided up into two teams, with the smaller children playing in the outfield.

Children play baseball in the field behind Fairyvale School in Hussar, Alberta, 1926. NA-2968-93. COURTESY OF LIBRARIES AND CULTURAL RESOURCES DIGITAL COLLECTIONS, UNIVERSITY OF CALGARY

Some children, instead of focusing on the fun they had during the summer months, remembered the great times they had during the winter. Florence Allen, for example, remembered how her father made a big bobsled that held seven people. As Florence explained, it was a lot of fun and really exciting going down the hill on the sled, but it wasn't much of a thrill pulling the heavy sled back up.[11] Like Florence, Anna Born remembered the various games that were played during the winters; however, the games that she described were all played indoors.[12]

> The backs of old calendars were used to draw game boards, such as checkers or parcheesi. Buttons from Mother's collection made the game pieces. Blind Man's Bluff was a game even the parents joined in. One person was blindfolded and had to try to catch someone else who was running by and, calling out, identify who had been caught. If you guessed right, that person received the blindfold and was "it" in turn. It was a very noisy game, but everyone enjoyed it. Quiet games, some of them used to while away the tedium of picking wool, included "I Spy." The leader would look around

FOR MANY CHILDREN, playtime began when they were babies. One homesteading mother, Lena May Purdy, described how parents and siblings would sing cradle songs, play finger and toe games, or sing alphabet rhymes with the newest member of the family.[13] Popular ditties included "This Little Piggy Went to Market," "Humpty Dumpty," "Pat-a-Cake," "Row, Row, Row Your Boat," "Rock-a-Bye Baby," "Jack and Jill," "Baa, Baa, Black Sheep" and "I'm a Little Teapot." •

the room, find something interesting, then say, "I spy, with my ghost eye, something that begins with '__'" and give the letter of the alphabet that started the name of the chosen object. The first one to guess what was "spied" was the next leader. Or one person would imagine hiding somewhere in the room and the others had to guess where "it" was hiding. Whoever guessed right was the next to "hide."

Some homesteader children reminisced about how they had to make their own toys, especially during the long winter months. Empty spools of thread could become caterpillars or snakes after a piece of twine was threaded through the middle of the spools and tied off at the ends. Slingshots could be made out of jar rings, with beans from the cupboard becoming the ammunition. When shot, the beans could fly a fair distance through the air, but few children attempted to perfect their target practice while they were indoors. George Gunn from the Red River Settlement in Manitoba remembered how children "had to rely on their own resources and ingenuity for the childish amusements that they enjoyed."[14] As he said:

> In my childhood days on the banks of the old Red River, there were no beautiful factory-made Express wagons and sleighs,

resplendent in paint and varnish ... A rude, home-made box of unpainted boards, with wheels sawed off of the end of a stick of firewood, was the proudest possession of that kind that a country boy, at any rate, had any conception of. His Express sleigh was of the same rude, home-made manufacture—three or four wooden bars nailed across a couple of boards roughly shaped to the form of runners, with no hint—outside of the nails—of metal in its construction, the boy himself generally being, in both the above cases, his own designer and manufacturer. Such vehicles, it may be added, were not wholly for pleasure purposes either. They were used for pulling the night's firewood into the house, during the winter, when large quantities of that commodity had to be supplied to keep Jack Frost at a respectful distance, and for various other utilitarian purposes around the place. The main use of the sleigh's being, of course, for hitching a dog to or sliding downhill.

The few indoor toys that we had were simple affairs, entirely of home manufacture. For the girls, a potato or a ball of yarn, tied in the middle of a handkerchief, with eyes, nose and mouth of charcoal, and a roll of rags for a body, served the purpose of a doll ... Happy the little girl who could get hold of some small ordinary box to do duty as a cradle or bed ... Tops, we had, of course, a plenty, but they were not the gay, geegaw kind, resplendent in gold, silver and many colors ... The top of the average child was a much simpler affair, and much more easily made. It was made out of the end of a wooden spool, or reel as we used to call them. In our household, the emptying of a J & P Coates reel of thread was an event to be hailed by us youngsters with rejoicing! For every one of these empty spools could be quickly and easily manufactured into serviceable tops. All that was necessary was to saw the spool into two across the middle of the barrel, whittle down each of these sawed ends to the shape of a cone, drive in a proper wooden spindle to whirl it by and for it to dance on, and the thing was done. Every such spool yielded two serviceable tops.

The younger ones were confined almost continuously indoors in the winter. In such cases, they had to find their own amusement or do without. There were no railroad trains, no kiddy-cars, not even a set of cheap picture blocks. Under such conditions, I have seen children stand for hours at a window thickly coated with rime [frost] (for there were not storm sashes on the windows in those days to keep the rime from gathering), amusing themselves by printing circles in the rime on the panes with a thimble, the modus operandi, in doing this, being to hold the thimble in the mouth until it was warm, then pressing the open end against the rime on the pane until it penetrated to the glass; the result being a clear cut circle of light. These circles could be worked into intricate geometrical patterns, according to the skill of the individual artist, the possibilities of variation accounting largely for the charm of the performance. As a little child, I often solaced myself with this pastime.

I can well remember on the opening of spring, when such games of make-believe were largely transferred to the outdoors, with what zest we hunted for treasures ... A few rods from the kitchen door ... was a piece of ground especially rich in such relics. This particular piece of ground, formerly the site of a neighbour's dwelling, but then part of a cultivated field belonging to my father, always yielded a plentiful crop after each plowing, making it a veritable happy hunting ground for us kids. Just as soon as it was dry enough to go on in the spring, we were out there picking up what we could find and oh the thrills when a glass bead, or a button or a broken fragment of china with a bright colored flower or pattern on it, was found. Such finds were all packed over to where we had our "house" (imaginary of course) and made to do duty as the furnishings. Large clam shells as might be picked up on the river's bank complete the layout; those having a rosey, mother of pearly inside being especially prized ... An upturned packing box was our table, and we did without chairs. A few short boards ... constituted our cupboard, where the glories of our broken dinner dishes were displayed. And oh, what happy times we used to have in there!

Two boys on a wooden sled slide down a hill in Edmonton, Alberta, in 1913. NA-1328-1016. COURTESY OF LIBRARIES AND CULTURAL RESOURCES DIGITAL COLLECTIONS, UNIVERSITY OF CALGARY

The Weigl boys of the Boyle district of Alberta were very creative and ready to get into mischief, especially if others were around.[15] One time, they decided to fill a forty-five-gallon barrel half full of water and then light a fire under it. They placed rocks at the bottom of the barrel so that when they got into it, they wouldn't burn their feet. They did not elaborate on how long they were able to stay in the barrel before they started jumping out of it when it got too hot. They also decided to experiment with the ten-foot toboggan that they owned. It was typically used in the winter, when the horse would pull the toboggan load of children to and from school. The boys decided that they wanted to see if the horse could pull them in the summer through the water holes in the fields. Unfortunately, as soon as they hit the water, the toboggan started to tip. They tried to balance it, shifting their weight from side to side, but they ended up completely upside down, absolutely drenched with muddy water. They decided that it was best to forego tobogganing in the summer.

One day, two of the Weigl brothers, Hubert and Ewald, decided to saddle up a four-year-old cow. Hubert said to Ewald, "You get on." When he did, "the cow took off on the run, she lit out under the shed and stopped, turned right and went through the gate. But where was Ewald? His head, feet and hands were planted in the chicken manure where he landed in the shed. That was the last ride on that cow." Another time, Ewald took Allen up to the roof of the barn. They each had a piece of cardboard to sit on, and the plan was to slide down to the roof of the shed, which was attached to the barn. As Ewald recounted, his pants were well worn, with holes in them, so when he came off the cardboard, one of the holes in his pants caught on a large sliver of wood, making the hole bigger. As a result, he went down the rest of the way on his bare backside. "Thousands of cedars slivers went in. Did I ever burn! Fun over."

The Wedge boys, who lived on a neighbouring homestead one mile to the south, came over one day to visit the Weigl brothers. The afternoon activities included a manure fight. The boys put a soft cow pie on the end of a board and then flipped it at the others. There was always great excitement when someone was hit. The Weigl brothers must have lost this particular fight, because they prepared for their retaliation if the Wedge brothers ever came over for another visit. The Weigl boys made a trap door in the barn over the bullpen below so if the Wedge boys came up to the barn loft, they would fall through to the bulls. The Weigl boys felt that this would scare those Wedge boys good! Unfortunately, the Weigl memoir never mentioned if the Wedge boys ever came over again or what the outcome was. One also wonders how the boys' father reacted when he saw the trap door that had been cut into the floor of his loft.

Allen Weigl remembered the day that he and his brothers Hubert and Ewald made some crossbows and arrow guns. Once they had finished constructing them, they tried them out, standing 300 to 400 feet away from each other. They made sure to use dull arrows so that when they hit a person, they did not break the skin. A few years later, when Allen was twelve years old, he and another brother, Frank, pushed up the dirt in the summerfallow to make a berm and then shot at each other to see how close they could get to shooting one another. The arrows that they used were far sharper than the ones Allen's brothers had previously made. It was at that moment that Gary Knoblock, an older boy from a neighbouring homestead, came over for a visit. Allen

Children could often be found playing in the yard with their siblings when they were not helping with chores. In this photograph, four sisters and their brother pose in front of a fence in 1912. Note the two tree limbs on either side of the children. They were likely used as goal posts or as safe spaces in games of chase. AUTHOR'S COLLECTION

shot an arrow about thirty feet from Frank, and Gary ran over to retrieve it. As part of their game, Allen yelled at Gary in warning, "Don't get out in the open or I will shoot!" But Gary continued to run and then bent over to pull the arrow out of the ground. Allen shot his crossbow. When his arrow hit Gary in the bum, it stuck there. "He hollered and pulled it out. He was so mad, he chased Allen across the field. Allen swam the creek and got away."

While this shooting was intentional, there were other dangers that existed where children played. A girl named Clary recalled the time she and her sister Nannie Walker, of the Boyle district of Alberta, were playing

> on the sloping roof of a log chicken coop. The roof was made with poles with straw on top. Some poles were broken. I slipped into a long narrow opening and couldn't get back up. But my head wouldn't go through so Nannie held my hands to relieve the pain in my neck. Then she said, "I'll slip down

Chickens and Piglets

GLORIA KOLMATYCKI, A homesteader child, remembered the times she got herself in trouble around the farm.[16] Everyone else had chores to do, including all of her older brothers and sisters, but she was too young, so she had to find things to amuse herself. As she said,

> I loved to watch chickens fly. Swinging a willow branch across their legs seemed to give them enough incentive to do so. My mother happened to be passing by the chicken coop one day and saw feathers and chickens spewing from the door. She mistook me for a skunk after her precious eggs. Upon seeing me in the midst of flying feathers, with weapon in hand, a short chase ensued before I bolted through the door and hid in the woodpile until her anger subsided.

Another time, her mother gave her a small chore to do. She was sent to check on the newborn piglets in the pig hut.

> Walking into the hut and finding the little ones alone, I stood a while admiring them, not realizing that the sow, returning from her stroll, stood behind me, blocking the only doorway. Thinking me an intruder she proceeded to attack. I leapt for the window, my only means of escape, to find that I couldn't completely squeeze through. That is how my father found me—half in, half out of the window, laryngitis setting in, having screamed a good ten minutes before being rescued. ●

> and stand under you so you can put your weight on me." She was just disappearing when I yelled, "Nannie, Nannie, come back, my head's coming off." She came with all speed. Then our little sister Jennie came along. I tried standing on her shoulders but she was like a willow wand. After a while

> Nannie saw mother up by the house and wanted to call for help. "No, no, no, don't call mother," I said, [fearing that I would get in trouble for playing on the roof]. I don't know how much longer I hung there until my head finally slipped through.[17]

Homesteading children remembered the wonderful times they had playing with other children when they went to school. This was when they were able to make new friends with children of all ages. Recess and lunch times were highlights for many as they had the chance to chat with each other or play various games.

One popular game was Four Sticks or Prisoner's Base. It could be played in either the winter or the summer. When the game started up, everyone wanted to play, and it only stopped when the school bell rang. Two or three children would be It.

> All the rest ran from one base to the next in either direction. If a player was caught between bases by a person who was "It," he was put inside the "pen" formed by the four sticks in the middle. The prisoner's feet had to stay in the pen, but his arms could be stuck out as far as he could. If someone running between bases touched the prisoner's hand, he was then free to run to a safe base. If he was caught on the way he became "It," and his catcher became free. When the "Its" were quick, and the rest daring, the Pen could get pretty full.

While they were playing the game, the bigger children would give the smaller children a pretend chase every once in a while, but with all ages playing there were plenty of challenges as to who could keep the jail the fullest and who could get away.[18]

Another popular game was Ante Over Pigtail. This game required a ball and a schoolhouse that had an A-frame roof. The children were divided up with an equal number of children on each side of the school. The team with the ball threw it up over the roof. At the same time, they would yell, "Ante Over." If the ball didn't make it over the roof and came bouncing back down, they would yell "Pigtail" and try throwing it again. If the ball did make it over and it was caught, the player with the ball could run around the school to tag the children of the opposing team, and they would have to join the team with the ball. When the last child was tagged, the game was over. At times, the rules were not followed so stringently. Sometimes the children would throw the ball over the roof so that the other side could have fun chasing it. Once the ball was caught, they would throw it back so that the other children could race for the ball.

Other schoolyard games included playing Tarzan by swinging from tree to tree, hide-and-seek, Pom Pom Pullaway, Red Light Green Light, and Farmer in the Dell. Both boys and girls played London Bridge Is Falling Down, tug-of-war and various foot and sack races. They also played cricket, croquet and Pig in the Hole.

Football was popular among the boys, and those who were more daring and owned a pocketknife could play mumblety-peg, which involved two players. They would stand opposite each other and throw the pocketknife so that it stuck into the ground as close to their own feet as possible. Whoever stuck the knife closest to their foot won.[19]

Girls enjoyed skipping. One child would bring a few feet of rope that would be used as the skipping rope. The older children would turn the skipping rope for the others to skip to. At the same time, everyone would sing a rhyme, such as “Isabella, dressed in yellow, went to town to meet her fella. How many kisses did she get?” Each girl would skip as many times as she could, as the number of times that she successfully jumped over the rope determined the number of kisses. When she tripped, that was the end of the count, and then it was another girl’s turn. The girl who lasted the longest was the winner of the game. There were other variations to this game such as Salt, Vinegar, Mustard, Pepper, which tested the skipper’s ability. While the rope was turned at a normal rate throughout much of the rhyme, there would be a double turn done when certain words like pepper, supper, heron and pudding were sung. In other words, when these words were uttered, the skipper had to skip once while the rope went under their feet twice. If they tripped, their turn was over.

Salt, mustard, vinegar, pepper,
French almond rock.
Bread and butter for our supper,

That's all mother's got.
Eggs and bacon, salted heron,
Pease pudding in a pot,
Pickled onions, apple pudding,
We will eat the lot.
Mabel, Mabel, lay the table
Don't forget the
Salt, mustard, vinegar, pepper.[20]

More skilled skippers would try out Double Dutch, where they would skip with two ropes in play, each going the opposite direction.

Open ditches with water were also places where children played. During the warmer months of the year, the younger ones would play with the minnows and try to catch them, and older children would try to throw stones so that they would skip across the water. Those who had pieces of paper would make paper boats and float them on the water, while others tried to sink them with pebbles. Every so often, an older boy would "accidentally" push an unsuspecting girl into the water. When this occurred, the teacher would cordon off a drying area in the school for the clothes of the soaked victim.

In the winter, boys and girls would take part in skateless hockey. No one could afford to buy skates, and they did not have a flat hockey rink to play on, so the children adapted. They played hockey on a frozen field or slough and they carried wooden sticks or stripped branches rather than hockey sticks. Dividing into teams, they would all chase a can, a small block of wood or a similar object around the field. The goal at each end of their rink was identified with two sticks of wood. The team to get the most goals, by sending the "puck" between the two sticks of wood, won the game.

Another winter game that the children loved to play was Fox and Geese. A large area of untrampled snow was needed for this game. Children would create the playing field by shuffling through the snow to make a fairly large circle with spokes extending from the outer circumference of the circle to the centre. In the centre, snow was trampled down to make enough room for the geese (five or six children) to wait. One child, the fox, ran around the outside wheel and attempted to catch any of the geese as they ventured

Throwing Snakes at the Girls

SOMETIMES THE BOYS would tease the girls while they walked to school. Wasylena Hellum of the Warspite district of Alberta remembered well the times that she and her girlfriends encountered these mischievous fellows.

> Wasylena attended the Lobstick school, walking four miles to and from school each day. In the summertime, she walked to school barefooted as [her family] didn't have the money to buy shoes. When walking to school they were joined with other boys and girls. Garter snakes at that time were plentiful and when the sun came up, they would come out of the tall grasses and sun themselves along the roadside. The boys had fun catching these snakes and throwing them at the girls trying to wrap them around their necks. Wasylena said sometimes they would run all the way to school screaming.[21] •

down the spokes of the wheel. If they were touched by the fox before they could retreat back up a spoke, they were out of the game. The game continued until all of the geese were caught. The last goose standing in the centre was the fox for the next game.

If it was too cold to play outside, the children were kept indoors. Some teachers were very creative when entertainment was needed. For instance, one teacher set up the classroom so the students could bowl. Desks and chairs were moved to the sides to clear the centre area. At the front of the room beneath the blackboard, the bowling pins (made out of pieces of wood) were set up. The students chose teams and then, one by one, they rolled a baseball toward the bowling pins. When their three throws were over, the pins that were still standing were counted for their score. Then it was the next student's turn.

In other cases, teachers might turn to indoor games like Our Old Sow. In this game, the students formed lines a couple of feet apart and held hands with the students beside them. One student was chosen to be the farmer, and one was the sow. They were placed at opposite ends of the classroom. During the singing of the "Old Sow" song, the farmer would start chasing the sow, but the farmer could not break through the line of students. Throughout the song, the teacher would give a signal for the students to switch hands so they were holding the hand of the student across from them instead of the one beside them. If the farmer could catch the sow through the maze of children, he or she won the game. If the sow made it through to the farmer's starting position, then the sow won the game.

The Christmas concert, held at the school, was a highlight for children and parents alike. People would come from miles around with their horses and sleighs, wrapped in their furs and

These children attended school at Bowsman, Manitoba, in 1904. Their teacher is seated in the second row on the far right. NA-3154-12. COURTESY OF LIBRARIES AND CULTURAL RESOURCES DIGITAL COLLECTIONS, UNIVERSITY OF CALGARY

blankets, to attend this social event. For many, it was the focal point of entertainment for the year. Months in advance, teachers would start preparing for this big day. In fact, the Christmas concerts were a source of rivalry among the teachers in the district and surrounding areas, with each trying to outdo the others in terms of the length and excellence of their programs.

Teachers worked tirelessly to see that every child in the school took part in the concert. One student, Katherine Schurko of Zbaraz, Manitoba, remembered the extraordinary effort and energy that her teacher, Miss Ellen Lee, put in, particularly when she had to devise their annual Christmas program.[22] Times were difficult for Miss Lee, as none of her students knew any English. They were all immigrants from various European communities, with many originally from Poland and Ukraine. Several never made it past the first grade. Instead of focusing on learning, many of the older boys in class were more interested in chasing the girls, while many of the older girls wanted to get married before they reached the age of sixteen (which they saw as the cut-off point for being an old maid). Even with these distractions, Miss Lee was able to teach them how to act out scenes from the birth of Christ and how to square dance, do the heel-and-toe polka and sing the song "Pop Goes the Weasel." The day of the concert, all of the students in her class met her expectations; they were proud of their accomplishments, and they performed for their admiring parents, "who packed the school to the rafters." While this teacher was remembered with fondness for her Christmas program, Katherine also remembered another instance of her teacher's thoughtfulness. "Just before Christmas, she would pack boxes of food and clothing for the most needy in the district and send word over that they could come and pick up the gifts. I remember seeing one such person kissing her feet, and she just stood there, tears streaming down her face."

Another student, Frances Crawford of Carstairs, Alberta, remembered how the students, their parents and the teacher worked together in preparation for the evening's festivities.[23] Decorations were made so that the schoolroom was transformed into a wondrous Christmas display. Colourful crepe paper was made into streamers that were hung across the room. A Christmas tree was set up in the corner and was trimmed with strings of popcorn and dried cranberries and coloured pieces of paper.

Blackboards were cleaned and decorated with stencils of Santa and his reindeer, while other Christmas scenes were drawn on with chalk. Bedsheet curtains were hung so they could be pulled open and closed with each performance. "Mothers made Angel wings [for their children] out of wire outlined with tinsel and covered with cheese cloth; crowns were made out of cardboard and painted gold," and footlights were fashioned out of old cans lined with cellophane.

After much planning and organizing, the evening of the Christmas concert finally arrived. With great anticipation, people came from miles around with their horses and sleighs. Once everyone was settled in their seats in the schoolroom, the concert would begin with the small children who were in Grades One and Two singing a welcome to all those in attendance. Then older students who had written impressive stories or poems in class presented their work, while others showed off their dramatic skills in modified plays such as Dickens' *A Christmas Carol*. Nativity scenes were a part of the concert, with children wearing bathrobes as their costumes. Sometimes unique skits were performed, like when the Grade Nine boys put their arms into long black stockings and placed shoes on their hands. Then they stood behind a short curtain and placed their arms in front of the curtain. To the audience's great amusement, it looked like their legs (which were dancing and kicking) were attached to their heads. For the next performance, all the children formed a pyramid and sang a variety of Christmas carols, including "Away in a Manger," "Silent Night" and "Star of the East," with their teacher accompanying them on the upright piano. Parents glowed with pride as each of their children recited or sang their part. At the end of the concert, the children were delighted with the surprise appearance of Santa Claus. He distributed his bag of goodies to all the children in the school. Each child received a gift as well as some homemade candy and an orange. No homesteader ever forgot the shining eyes of their children on this biggest night of the year.

A Paradise of Pets

A common feature on every homestead was the family pet. While typical companions were cats and dogs, the homesteading life offered the opportunity for families to acquire a wide variety of pets. What many homesteaders and their families discovered was that almost any living thing, domestic or wild, could be made into a pet. Whether it was a calf or a horse, a goose or a pig, a bear or an owl, a fondness developed between these animals and birds and their owners—a fondness so great that these pets were remembered for years after their passing.

Each homesteading family had their own favourite animals. For instance, when Fred Baines was a child on his family's homestead, he remembered collecting a number of different pets.[1] He said that he had cats and dogs, two foxes and two sandhill cranes. He also mentioned that there were other game birds that could be captured as pets, such as ducks, geese, crows and prairie chickens. Clarissa Bean had two wild coyotes, which were given to her as puppies.[2] They were very tame and became her best pals: "Just like two dogs, I would cuddle and play with them." Harriet Stueck said that she and her siblings made pets out of everything they could capture.[3] At one time they had a muskrat named Jennie as well as a garter snake. She said that her father also made pets out of a team of horses, Biddy and Pat, that he had brought from Ontario with him, while her mother preferred her driving horse, named Lady. Mary Rogers Berkner recalled how she would go out exploring to find new pets or play with the wild animals of the prairie.[4] She said, "I spotted a coyote which I took to be a dog; gophers were lots of fun too, you chased them down a hole, and waited for them to pop up again. Then there were grey squirrels around the bluffs, which would dart into the underbrush if you got too close. This open prairie seemed like a paradise of pets to someone who had just come from a small Ontario town."

Marion Anderson's family pets included a cat named Pussy that killed the mice, a dog named Buster that was used for duck hunting, and two oxen, Buck and Bright, that helped with plowing.[5] She said that they also owned five horses, Daisy, Maizy, Billy, Maud and Monty, as well as a colt, a dog, a cat and a batch of kittens. One calf in particular became a favoured pet as she was easy to play with. Marion could dress the calf up in a coat and bonnet, and she and her siblings played "chase," with either the calf chasing them, or the children chasing the calf.

Instead of mentioning the variety of animals they owned, some homesteaders would highlight particular animals and the stories surrounding them. For example, many of them favoured horses, as they provided a number of benefits to the homesteader and his family. Grant MacEwan, who wrote several books on agriculture and the history of western Canada, had this to say about the importance of horses on the prairies:

> In almost all the work performed by a farmer, his horses were his helpers and partners. When he plowed, harrowed, disked, drilled, and harvested, his horses were the power. When he went to town for supplies, the trip was with his horses hitched to the buggy or to the wagon, and he knew his team would be scrutinized by critical horsemen along the way. When he went to a picnic, the entertainment was likely to take the form of a horse race or a game of horseshoes. When he visited neighbors, conversation would be about horses and when he went to the weekly prayer meeting with horse hairs on his clothes, he felt no embarrassment because every other person present would be similarly marked.[6]

Elias Parmlee St. John, in his memoirs, mentioned how important horses were to his family and noted how one became his personal favourite.[7] "We had many horses in the early days and if I told you all their names, I wouldn't have room for anything else. There was one in particular that was a Hamiltonian mare. I brought her [to the west] with me as a colt and named her

Jessie. She turned out to be a wonderful horse." She would work in the fields with the big horses or could be driven in a harness or ridden under saddle. She worked harder than a dozen horses, and at her death, Elias "preserved her height" by taking a rope, measuring her from her hoof to her back and cutting it. In this way, the piece of rope became a memento, something that he could always remember her by whenever he used it.

Robert Eckel recalled, "Horses were treated much like one of the family" in that they were very well taken care of.[8] For instance, after trips to town, they were often covered in blankets, lightweight ones in summer to ward off flies and mosquitoes, and heavier ones in winter to protect them from the cold. Before spring work, they would be fed oats, and their teeth were checked. Some were clipped to get rid of their thick winter coat.

> When working, they had lots of prairie wool and oats, three times a day. They were curried in the morning before harnessing, and their shoulders were washed off at night with salt and water. After working all day in the field, they were

Jessie Burk, from Milo, Alberta, poses with her two horses in 1911. NA-1367-66. COURTESY OF LIBRARIES AND CULTURAL RESOURCES DIGITAL COLLECTIONS, UNIVERSITY OF CALGARY

usually turned out for the night. They usually had a good roll on the ground and would roll around from side to side from one to six times before getting on their feet.

Sue Harrigan's family had a soft spot for one of their horses, a fellow named Barney.[9] As she said,

> We kept one horse, Barney, in the barn in the winter. He was our driving horse and the only thing Barney couldn't do well was talk. I think he understood everything that was said to him. This one winter, my Dad decided that he would turn Barney out [of the barn] with the other horses, so he did turn him out, but Barney had other ideas. He came up to the window and looked in at us. He looked so cold and miserable and if he had been able to talk he would have said, "Don't you know that I am out here in the cold?" Barney was getting old and he felt the cold and he did love his nice warm barn. My Dad let him stand there about half an hour. Then he couldn't stand watching the poor horse looking so cold and miserable, so he went out and put him in the barn, and that ended Barny being turned out in the winter to rustle for himself.

The Walter Rector family of Westlock, Alberta, also owned a horse named Barney, who seemed to be just as smart as the horse owned by the Harrigans.[10] The Rectors' Barney, who was a cute colt, was the family's favourite animal on the homestead; however, he could cause trouble from time to time. For instance, he learned how to open the oat box with his nose when he wanted something to eat. It was difficult to keep him away from it until they locked it. He never objected to having three or four children climbing on his back at one time, but once they were aboard, "he had the habit of running from the barn to the spring, and the riders had to hang on for dear life or go flying when he cleared the three-pole fence."

A young homesteading boy named Bill Sanders got more than he bargained for when he was playing with a colt one day.[11] He was one of a set of twins, and when people asked how to tell them apart, the answer was that one of Bill's fingers was shorter than the other. When questioners wondered how this happened, the

The Outlaw

LULU WILKEN REMEMBERED a horse that her family owned when she was young.[12] This horse had a mind of its own, and most of the time it did not appreciate being bothered. In fact, most of Lulu's family was scared of this horse given its uneven temperament. One day the horse surprised them when Lulu's little sister decided to go out and play with him. Lulu recalled the incident:

> One horse was an outlaw, refusing to adjust quietly to civilized ways. He was a fine horse but very nervous. No one, not even father, dared to go into his stall wearing anything different from the usual clothing. One glance at a new hat or jacket would send him into a frenzy of kicking and rearing that would send terror to the heart of the bravest. It was this outlaw that attracted my little sister Margaret. She slipped out of the house one day, while everyone was eating dinner, headed straight for the stable, and marched right into the outlaw's stall. Father found her there, swinging happily on the horse's leg. The animal was just as happy and munching hay as if they were the best of pals who did this all the time. My father was aghast. How could he remove her from danger without precipitating an in-stable stampede? When my sister would not respond to father's "Come to Daddy" request, with an unspoken prayer on his lips, and a gentle "whoa whoa," he gently took her little arms from the horse's leg, picked her up and softly tiptoed away. Once out of the reach of those wicked hooves he ran, clutching her in his arms, to the house. Depositing her on the floor, he slammed the door and sank into a chair. Margaret ran gleefully to mother to tell her all about the lovely horse. After that incident, the barn door was kept shut. •

family told the following story: Bill had been teasing a colt who was outside the barn. Bill put his finger into a hole in the barn wall. Each time he stuck his finger out, the colt tried to nip it, and Bill would pull his finger back in. This game continued on for quite a while, until finally "the colt was quicker. The result—one finger partially missing!"

Homesteaders also had tales to tell about other farm animals like calves, steers, bulls and oxen that were treated favorably. Children, in particular, tried to make playmates out of many of these animals. The Jones family, who lived in the Alliance district of Alberta, related their story about a calf named Fred.[13] Fred was so beloved that he became a family pet. He was "a joy and playfellow to all the kids that came around. Like a friendly dog, he liked attention, and to get it he would keep butting their rear end until they took hold of his stubby horns." This began the pushing and pulling game, where the children would try to pull him one way and he pushed back. When Fred tired of the game, he would throw his head sideways. This sent all of the children sprawling on the ground. Then he would take off at a run, expecting the children to chase him. The children loved him. Fred had not tried his playful tactics on anyone but children until one hot afternoon when Leo Thompson, a neighbour, came for a pail of fresh water from the well. He had to jiggle the pail to make it fall into the well, and he had to bend over and raise and lower his arm to work the windlass.

> This caused your rear end to move back and forth. Fred, lying in the shade a short distance away noted the unusual movement. He got up and strolled over to investigate. Neil got the pail full and was pulling it up with the windlass, extending his rear end motion. Fred's movement towards the well had attracted the attention of some others standing in the shade of the building. That rear end motion was a dare to Fred. He lowered his head and trotted forward. Too late to shout a warning of the impending clash, they watched as Neil bent over further to pull the pail out. At that second, contact was made. Down went Leo and the pail of water to the bottom of the well. Luckily, the well was not deep as the water was only eight feet from the top. Before any of the onlookers could get

> to him, he pulled himself up the rope and out of the well. Leo looked like a drowned rat! The surprise and stunned look on his face added to the comical spectacle he presented for the amusement of the hilarious onlookers.

The children of the Roberts family enjoyed playing with the calves in their farmyard, but one summer day they went a bit too far with one calf, and their mother doled out a punishment that she felt was suitable.[14] Their mother found that they had hitched a calf to a sled that was usually used in the winter. They had not hitched the calf up in the usual way, with a harness and reins, but rather had tied a string to the hair of the calf's tail. When their mother arrived to check on them, the hair on the tail had just pulled off in a big chunk. Their mother was not impressed, and she created a punishment that was comparable to their crime: the children had to haul their mother around the yard on the sled with prickly binder twine tied to their bare wrists. By the time their punishment was over, they had likely learned never to interfere with the calf in that fashion again. As one child said, their "tears didn't alleviate the pain in our wrists or the hurt in our pride!"

In another case, a lost and sickly calf became a pet to the local church superintendent, Harold Burningham.[15] One cold day, Harold came across a calf who was suffering from pneumonia. He felt sorry for the calf and decided that he would try to alleviate its misery. He took the calf into his warm shack and set up a pen for it in the corner. By using poles, he was able to fence it in. Every few hours he gave the calf a cough remedy called Pinex (which contained chloroform and alcohol). In a few days, the calf recovered. While "keeping a small calf in a little shack ... is not exactly the utmost to gracious living conditions, the calf grew to be a fine mature animal and always bore the name which it had been given, namely Pinex."

George and Maggie McMillan's children had a pet steer.[16] The boys of the family had trained it so that it would pull a sleigh in the winter. The problem was that the steer only pulled the sleigh when he felt like it. If he didn't feel like pulling the sleigh on any particular day, he wouldn't. However, the boys soon found a remedy for this problem. They knew that the steer did not like their brother Alex, and Alex held no great fondness for the steer. So to make the steer pull the sleigh, they persuaded Alex to run ahead of the steer. The steer would take off in pursuit of Alex, and the boys then had a wonderful ride on the sleigh.

Ellenor Merriken recalled hitching up their milk cow Guro one day so she could help them with their chore of collecting barrels of water.[17] However, like the McMillans' steer,

> Guro was inclined to be temperamental. This we knew but did not realize to what extent until we got the harness on her and were ready to hitch her to the stoneboat to haul a barrel for water from the well in the pasture. Papa was away plowing with the oxen at the time and we were tired of having to make several trips to the well every day with a bucket to get water for the house. It was a quarter of a mile and we could see no reason why the cow could not be put into service and save us that much work. We did not consult Mama as to the feasibility of the idea, for we were somewhat dubious as to her reaction. However, we thought we could manage without her finding out. Guro did not like the arrangement. To be on the safe side, we put two ropes around her horns with one of us on each side holding on. In that way we kept her between us in case she got the notion to attack. [However,] she already had that notion and we had a wild west show all by ourselves. The only time that we made any headway was when she took off after one of us that happened to be in front of her. The barrel rolled off the stoneboat and almost hit me and from then on her sole idea was to get even with us. We finally got close enough to a fence post to get a hitch around it and tied her tight. We managed to get the harness off her and carry it back to the barn. We retrieved the water barrel and got our buckets and started for the well. We made two trips before we dared to turn her loose. At milking time, Mama was wondering why the cow acted so strange and she gave only half the usual amount of milk. None of us said a word.

Annie Condon remembered her favourite cow when she was a girl on her family's homestead.[18] She described her as a "fine cow." Given that there were no fences in the early years of homesteading, the cow was allowed to amble freely over the prairie, where she would meet up with neighbouring cows. In the evening she headed home for a feed of oats with all the other cows tagging along behind her. The cows, as a herd, developed a social hierarchy, and Annie's cow became the boss cow, the one to be followed. Each of the cows had a bell around her neck, so homesteaders could find them when they went out searching for them. Annie said that all of these bells were musical and made a welcoming sound as the cows plodded along together. Given this daily routine, neighbouring homesteaders did not have to search too far for their cows, as they knew where the cows would be at the end of the day. Unfortunately for Annie, her favourite cow did not have much time to live. A neighbour had an ox that developed tuberculosis, and instead of mercifully killing it, he tied it to a bush where he fed and watered it. It broke loose and had placed its nose against their cow's nose. Her father was so afraid the cow would contract the disease that he sold her to the butcher. Annie "cried nearly all night, [as she] was so attached to that gentle creature."

Ellenor Merriken recalled how she and her two siblings delighted in playing with the oxen during the summer months.[19] She said, "As soon as the folks gained enough confidence in our ability to handle the oxen and some assurance that the oxen were not aiming to kill us (given that they were unpredictable and ornery), we amused ourselves immensely by practising different kinds of stunts on them. We noticed that one of the oxen, named Bill, had a back that was broad and flat, so he became the main object of our experiments." One day, when Bill was relaxing in the water hole, they decided to pretend that he was a three-masted prairie schooner. "All three of us climbed on Bill's back and standing straight up and holding onto each other, we sang 'Over the Bounding Main' at the top of our voices." They kept singing as Bill got out of the water hole and headed home. "What we lacked in harmony we made up in volume, to the annoyance of the ox, as he kept flapping his ears back and forth and shaking his head."

In other situations, animals showed their preference for their own homes and the routines and customs of the family that owned them. They would rebel if they knew that they were to be taken away to live elsewhere. Such was the case with a purebred bull named Burnside. This story was told by the homesteader who wished to purchase Burnside from a neighbour. After negotiating a price, he started off for the neighbour's place to pick up the bull early one day. However, instead of returning within a reasonable time, hours passed, and it was late in the evening before he finally returned home with the bull. His wife asked about the delay, and he related the day's events to her:

> I arrived safely at the ranch and after a chat and a meal with the genial foreman, we got the bull rounded up and I started for home. The foreman said, "You'll have no trouble with him; he's quiet and gentle as a kitten." I got along fine for a couple of miles. Then he began to lay down, and I had to urge him on. He still lagged and then he seemed to be played out, and finally in spite of all my urging, he laid down. I tried to get him up but he stretched out, apparently dead as a doornail. I rode quickly back to the ranch. The foreman hearing my predicament was soon in the saddle saying, "It's queer. He was all right, but you know, he is a bit foxy." As we came over a little rise, we were astonished to see a herd of range cattle (none in sight when I left) encircling the dead bull, bellowing and piling up the earth. We rode quietly nearer and the herd advanced nearer and nearer to old Burnside stretched out as when I had left him. "I guess he's dead all right," said the foreman, "and these fellows have come to hold a wake." As the cattle kept creeping closer, I thought I saw old Burnside slowly open one of his eyes. Calling this to the foreman's attention, sure enough he opened it again. In a minute or two, he slowly raised his head as if taking in the situation. With a puff and a snort and a bound, he was on his feet in an instant, and charging left and right putting all the other cattle to rout, and did they stampede! We leaned back in our saddles and laughed long and loud at the sudden coming to life of the old bull. "I thought it queer," said the foreman. "He is sure foxy and I guess played possum so he would not have to leave the home range."[20]

Other homesteading families, like the Dennings of the Boyle district of Alberta, had pigs for pets.[21] One of their pigs, a boar, would follow the children around the farmyard, and the children used to play with him just as they would with a dog. He never seemed to mind, even when all four of the Denning children climbed onto his back at one time. One day their mother unintentionally ended up getting a ride, but instead of riding on the boar, she had a ride on a sow. One of her daughters, Ethel, recalled how this happened. Her mother was checking on her hens, which were laying eggs in the barn. It was a bright sunny day, so she could not see clearly when she went into the dimly lit barn, but the sow could see her. The sow ran between her mother's legs, got caught up in her mother's long dress and ended up giving her mother "a brisk ride around the barnyard, backwards on the pig's back!"

Mr. Salisbury of Crescent Lake, Saskatchewan, was fond of telling the story of an incident that happened to his young son Archie.[22] They owned a big sow, which the young boy had broken in to ride.

> One day, Mr. Salisbury, taking out some swill and not seeing the pig anywhere around, began calling her in the time-honored fashion. In a very few minutes, she came into view on the run with Archie on her back. Several feet away the sow stopped short, but the rider kept on going until he landed headfirst into that overflowing pail of swill! It was never related just what happened when Archie was taken to his mother, a dejected and dripping little boy.

A child rides on the back of a pig in Bowell, Alberta, ca. 1920. NA-2637-18. COURTESY OF LIBRARIES AND CULTURAL RESOURCES DIGITAL COLLECTIONS, UNIVERSITY OF CALGARY

Roosters with an Attitude

HOMESTEADERS HAD A variety of pets, but roosters were not often seen as amiable, playful birds. They were very territorial and aggressively protective of their brood of hens. The stories told about roosters tend to show the fiendish side of their personalities.

According to a story by Glen Carmichael of Stony Plain, Alberta, the rooster they had in their farmyard used to follow them whenever they went outside.[23] When they walked toward a doorway or a gate, the rooster would leap up at them and try to drive his spurs into their legs. Even though the spurs were over an inch long, Glen said, "They seldom hurt through the heavy overalls worn in those days, though the attacks always gave one quite a start." He also mentioned that their rooster was "really sneaky about the way he pretended he was busy scratching, and eating, or just going somewhere, until one's back was turned, then he would race silently with neck outstretched toward his intended victim." Often their dog, seeing the intent of the rooster, rushed at him and foiled his attack. Interestingly, the rooster seldom tried to attack women or girls. His victims were always male.

In another rooster story, the bird would not attack the boys but would attack their sister Maisie. According to Nick Sherwin of Westlock, Alberta, his family owned an old red rooster.[24] The boys in the family had tormented it so much that it had developed a vile temper. "He was mean and ambitious, and just waited to attack when least expected." Instead of retaliating on his tormentors, he went after young Maisie when she left for school in the morning. When she returned later in the afternoon, he would meet her on the lane and charge her. He could outrun her at every instance. Often, "he would keep her cornered in the outhouse or any other building where she took refuge. She wondered why he didn't get into the stewpot, but of course, his services were needed to increase the brood in the hen house." •

Mrs. W.T. Billing remembered people having pet pigs.[25] She recounted how a man in her local town of Regina, Saskatchewan, enjoyed the company of his pig so much that he constantly discussed his pig with friends and acquaintances. Eventually, everyone became tired of the topic, with someone stating that if the pig was so special, it should be exhibited in the agricultural show in Moose Jaw. While this statement was meant to ridicule the pig's owner, he took the suggestion seriously. He started to pamper the pig by washing it, polishing it with an old shirt, scrubbing out its sty (so that no smell lingered) and putting it to bed each night.

Gust Wallin of the White Swan district of Alberta remembered a time when his litter of pet pigs enjoyed going to bed.[26] He began his story by describing how he and his family lived in a tent when they were first homesteading. They had brought a litter of pigs with them, but they lost track of them one evening. They hunted for the pigs until it was too dark to see, and returned home to their tent with plans to continue their hunt in the morning. When they got into the tent, they found the little pigs. They were all lined up on the blankets on the bed, sound asleep.

Cats were common pets on the family homestead. They served a number of different functions. Cats could be playmates with children, but they also had an important duty to rid the

A young girl plays with her pet lamb on a farm in the Alderson area of Alberta, 1921.
NA-2083-7. COURTESY OF LIBRARIES AND CULTURAL RESOURCES DIGITAL COLLECTIONS, UNIVERSITY OF CALGARY

home and farmyard of mice and other rodents. Ellenor Merriken remembered well the special bond that she had with her pet cat when she was young.[27] As she said,

> I was real fond of Old Puss, a big, black tomcat. As long as I stayed home, he wouldn't leave the place. If I happened to go away for any length of time, he moved up to the neighbours and made himself at home there and seemed perfectly contented. As soon as I was back home, here came Puss, just as if someone had told him. It puzzled all of us, and we wondered how he could sense it from a mile away. When I got married, I brought my cat with me and he lived to the ripe old age of twenty-one.

One homesteader child had a cat that let her dress him in doll clothes. He was such an agreeable soul that she was able to lie him down in a baby buggy, and then she would push him around the farmyard like a mother with her child. Eloise Anderson recalled how her pet cat, while friendly most of the time, was ferocious when he was protecting his friend, the family dog.[28] When the neighbour dog came over to pick a fight with the dog, the cat would tear off after the intruder and attack him. The punishment the cat doled out ensured that the other dog never came around their homestead again. D.H. Maginnes remembered how his homestead was overrun with mice.[29] When he went to town, he came across a little girl who had a kitten in her arms. He offered to buy it from her for a dollar, but she didn't want to part with it. He told her that he would be good to it. She finally relented and let him have her kitten, who helped solve his rodent problem.

Alfred Mann of Lanigan, Saskatchewan, recounted how desperately he wanted to own a cat when he was a boy.[30] He not only wanted one for its mousing abilities, but also desired its companionship. One day he heard that a homesteader who lived quite a ways away had a cat that he no longer wanted. Alfred immediately made a cage for the cat and walked twenty miles one way to get the feline, then made the return trip with her. It was a long trek, but Alfred was incredibly happy with his cat and felt that all of that walking was well worth it. Dennis Kirkham,

A young French girl holds her pet cat in this photograph, dated 1917.
AUTHOR'S COLLECTION

a boy from the Saltcoats district of Saskatchewan, was also incredibly anxious to own a cat for the same reasons.[31] "After many futile inquiries near home, he learned that Mr. Partridge at Crescent City had some kittens, so early one morning he set forth to walk a distance of thirty-two miles, to try to obtain one. His perseverance was rewarded, Mr. Partridge gave him two, and it was a tired but happy boy who arrived home late the following day with his much-prized pussies."

James Minifie also yearned to own a cat or two.[32] One day he was inadvertently given the opportunity to own two kittens. He and his father had been making a trek to town when they were caught in a thunderstorm. Seeking immediate shelter, they happened across Ted Lewis and his bachelor shack just outside Vanguard, Saskatchewan.

> Inside it was the customary bachelor muddle of unpainted bare boards, unmade beds, unwashed dishes, and old porridge-pots and newspapers. Among this refuse played two of the prettiest kittens we had ever seen. One of them was pure tortoise-shell with solid patches of black, white and orange; the other displayed a pattern of stripes ... Both were bright and sparkling ... Lewis wanted to get rid of the kittens which he felt only added to the overwhelming burden of bachelor housekeeping. We did not need much persuading. I put them in a bag and threw them into the back of the buggy. My father succumbed to their charms ...

> and immediately called them Bubble and Squeak, after an Old Country dish of fried cabbage and potatoes which he liked. They were too young to mind the change [of moving to our place]; they soon settled down to the routine of the barn, became friendly with the horses and learned to be on hand at milking time to get an old tobacco can full of warm, foamy milk, into which they could plunge their muzzles, their tails straight up, their whiskers pointing forward, their whole existence concentrated on milk ... One fine morning when father went to milk, he found the stable crawling with kittens—ginger, tabby and tortoise. Bubble and Squeak were going out of their cat minds salvaging their babies from too close association with horses' hooves, carrying them like dead mice back to their birthplace beneath the manger. Marvellously, they survived, all eleven. Soon they learned to sit in a semicircle behind the cow while father milked, waiting for him to direct a stream of milk at them.

Like cats, dogs were favoured companions on the homestead. Not only were they eager and amiable when children wanted to play, but they also guarded the home and protected all members of the family.

The Minifie boys always enjoyed playing with their dog Scottie.[33] Many times they tried to make him into a draft animal so that he could pull them around the farmyard, but in the end Scottie got the best of them as he was the one that was being pulled around the yard. James recalled:

> I built a simple harness for Scottie out of old reins, pieced together with copper rivets. He objected at first, but ultimately gave in when for a heavy four-wheeled "express wagon," we substituted a light two-wheeled dog cart, which my mother and I built. It was not too successful, however, as the wheels squealed like a Red River Cart—and for the same reason, that there was neither grease nor roller-bearings between wheels and axle. We had simply scored a hole through a board with a red-hot poker and rounded it off as well as we could. However, by the time Scottie was properly broken in, we had given up on the dog cart. Scottie's real

Kitten in the Well

DANGERS LURKED ON the farm, as Betty Iredale found out when she nearly lost her beloved pet kitten when she was a young girl.[34] Her father had bought the kitten for her and she treasured it. However, one day when her father was watering his horse at the well, Betty let her kitten get too close to the well cribbing and it lost its balance.

> Legs splayed out, tiny claws helplessly clutching, it plummeted into the well. I howled at Dad, "My kitten! You must rescue my kitten!" Leaning over, looking into the blackness, he shuddered. "Down there? No, impossible. You shouldn't have let it fall in." He was furious with me. "The rope ladder!" I shrieked. "It's somewhere about. Get the rope ladder." Scowling, he did as bidden. Night drew on as he fastened hooks attached at one end of the ladder to the top of the cribbing. Slinging a leg over the parapet, he found footing on the wobbling rungs. I heard him cursing all the way down into the inky depths. At water level, he clung with one hand to the ladder, his other captured the still paddling kitten. When he handed the poor little thing to me, I shoved it under my clothes where it shivered wetly against my skin as I ran with it to the shack. ●

> triumph came with winter when he was hitched to a handmade sled. He galloped over the snow with this at great speed, until it occurred to him that it would be easier if he rode and we pulled. Thereafter he never missed a ride on a sled, cutter, or stoneboat and we were willing enough to tow him about.

Evelyn Olson of Bladworth, Saskatchewan, remembered the playful qualities of their family dog, Bob, but she also mentioned

Dogs were great playmates for children. In this photograph, dated 1913, two dogs pull a child in a wagon in Millarville, Alberta. NA-2520-12. COURTESY OF LIBRARIES AND CULTURAL RESOURCES DIGITAL COLLECTIONS, UNIVERSITY OF CALGARY

how helpful and intelligent he was when given instructions, especially at milking time.[35] As she said,

> I recall playing hide-and-seek with Bob. Two or three of us children would tell Bob to stand still in a secluded spot while we quickly and quietly hid. Then someone would call out "Ready" and Bob would search for us, pretending to look many places before he found us. He barked joyfully to let us know he found us and we would pat him and tell him what a good dog he was. It was now Bob's turn to hide and we would attempt to find him. Even though at times he was quite visible, we would pretend to look everywhere. He would bark excitedly when we found him where he was hiding.

At milking time, when her mother went out to see to the cows in the barn, she would whistle for Bob. He would come running and whining for instructions, and when mom told him to "Go get Betsy," Bob, knowing the names of the cows, would find Betsy

A child pulls a dog who is sitting in a wagon, near Yorkton, Saskatchewan, ca. 1913. NA-2878-71. COURTESY OF LIBRARIES AND CULTURAL RESOURCES DIGITAL COLLECTIONS, UNIVERSITY OF CALGARY

and bring her to Evelyn's mother for milking. Once Betsy was finished, Evelyn's mother repeated the command for each of the other cows, and "Bob never made a mistake and brought the wrong cow." As Evelyn said, when thinking back to their dog Bob, the entire family loved him.

Much like Evelyn Olson's mother, William Donner trained his dog Teddy to understand commands.[36] Instead of asking the dog to herd a particular cow into the barn, William trained Teddy to retrieve a number of different items, whether they were farm tools or personal objects. One time, when William was working with a threshing crew, he told the men on the crew that his dog could retrieve whatever item he happened to ask for. They laughed at him as they thought it was a joke. However, when William asked Teddy for the hammer, the dog ran off, found the hammer and brought it to William. Next, he asked Teddy for a saw, and Teddy retrieved the saw. The men on the threshing crew were amazed. When William went home for supper at the end of the day, he asked Teddy to bring Mac (William's wife) her slippers. The dog immediately ran for the slippers. Finally, William asked Teddy to bring his supper dish. This is when Teddy finally received a reward for all the work he had done that day: a real hearty thresherman's dinner!

The Johnson family also owned a dog who earned her keep through her hard work around the homestead.[37] This little dog's name was Pinky, and she was a black water spaniel. Her expertise was hunting gophers, but she also sought out other prey that she would bring home as an offering for the family. In the spring, the gophers

> began popping up their heads from the awakening sod, after sleeping all winter. This excited little Pinky. If she could only catch one of those pesky things! How it would please her! What a feast! She would gaze longingly from the top of the woodpile until she could stand it no longer, and then riveting her gaze on a certain mound that she had been watching for so long, would slink away, body low, in the buffalo trail, creeping, creeping and then, when she thought she was near enough, would crouch, waiting for the gopher's head to pop up—the signal to spring. She would catch it, too!

Every day the Johnsons found that she would bring home something from her hunting trips. Sometimes she would catch a bird; at other times she would bring home a rabbit, with the head hanging out of one side of her mouth and the legs out the other. Once she brought home a huge gopher that was almost larger than she was. It was a hot day and she had a terrible time trying to bring it home. She had to keep dropping the gopher and resting. When she arrived, she was exhausted and panting from all her exertions, and the Johnsons feared she might be on the brink of death. However, she was out hunting again the next day as usual. Pinky, with all of her hunting skills, was a valued member of the family. She even had a "special place at the table, with her own little blue tin saucer." She sat between two family members "on a high stool and would place her front paws on the table, waiting patiently until we put something in her saucer. If it didn't come quick enough to please her, she would nudge an arm gently with her paw and if that didn't work, she would nudge an arm on her other side." The Johnsons were sad at her passing, as they all dearly loved Pinky and remembered all of her qualities and her good nature.

Instead of spending the day hunting, one homesteader's dog liked playing with the rabbits in the field.[38] The dog seemed to enjoy a close affinity with one rabbit in particular. They had created a game that they played, which the dog's owner, Arthur Wheeler, found confounding when he was out walking with his dog. As Arthur recalled, he and the dog spotted the rabbit one day. The rabbit ran a wide circle with the dog in pursuit, then came back to Arthur and dropped, apparently dead. The dog did not touch it at any time, and Arthur and the dog proceeded to walk away. "As we did so, the rabbit got up and ran again with the dog in pursuit, once more returning to me and dropping again. The dog never touched it. There seemed no life to it, so we continued on." The game continued until the rabbit suddenly ran off in a different direction. As Arthur said, "I looked back and the rabbit was gone."

Other dogs took on the role of a babysitter when parents were away working in the fields during seeding in the spring and harvesting in the fall. Parents relied on these family pets to ensure that their children were well taken care of. Martha Todd said that their family dog, Collie, would act like their grandmother when she knew she was responsible for the children.[39] The dog would boss them around and made sure they didn't misbehave in any way. The family dog also babysat Rena Michael when she was a two-year-old.[40] The family homesteaded fifty miles north of North Battleford, Saskatchewan, in the late 1800s. Her parents were out working in the fields, and they needed someone to look after Rena. They decided to let the dog undertake this task as they trusted their pet. Rena told a story about how the dog helped her one day when she got herself in trouble:

> I kept my babysitter on the run. Mother still reminds me of the time she came home after stooking all day in the field. She couldn't see neither me or the dog. She called us and ran up a cattle trail searching for us. She crawled up on the barn but couldn't see anything because of the dense brush. Mother climbed down, then she saw the dog coming without me. The dog's head was hanging low and his eyes were

melancholy. "Where is she?" mother asked the babysitter. The dog turned and started walking towards the pasture. When he saw mother was following him, he moved swiftly ahead, over the prairie. Mother followed in fast pursuit. Soon mother saw me lying on the ground so still she thought I must be dead. I was covered with dust. She grabbed me up in her arms. She then noticed I had both my hands in a gopher trap. Dad had set the trap down into a badger hole. She could tell by looking at me that the dog had pulled me out, then went for help.

Willie Becker was also left alone as a young boy with only the dog and the cat to mind him and keep him company while his father worked in the fields and his mother went to fetch the cow from the pasture for milking.[41] His mother did not finish up until after dark. To her bewilderment, when she returned to the house her boy was gone, as were the dog and cat. She began to search in the house and out in the yard. His father returned from the fields, and together his parents started looking and calling everywhere for the trio. They were reaching the end of their search when they decided to take the lantern and walk up and down the rows of the potato patch in the garden. "Finally in the last row of potatoes they found the boy, cat and dog, all asleep in a nice huddle under the leaves of a potato plant." Their relief at finding them was profound, and in the end they realized that the dog and cat had been responsible babysitters and had taken care of Willie throughout the day.

Some dogs made themselves useful on the farm in other ways. A dog named Tweed, owned by Mary Morrison's family, enjoyed rounding up the cattle, which was of great benefit when Mary and her sister Margaret were charged with the chore of bringing the cattle home from the pasture.[42] The dog "seemed to know which direction to go even though the cattle had strayed away several miles. If there were other cattle with them, Tweed would separate them, and was not satisfied until every strange animal was out of their herd. He would then trot along with the girls quite pleased with himself." While his herding abilities were exemplary, there were times when this skill caused a problem. One day, a neighbour who was suffering from rheumatism stopped by to visit the Morrisons, as Mary's father was a doctor. He had been confined

Saving a Collie Pup

ALFRED ESTLIN AND his brother Frank were making the rounds one day, going from homestead to homestead in southern Manitoba looking for cattle that were for sale.[43] At one place, Alfred says,

> We saw a nice collie with a litter of pups lying in one of the stable mangers ... We found one of the pups had gotten out and been trampled on by a horse and all its four legs were broken. The owner was much perturbed as good collies like these were valuable. We asked him what he was going to do with it and he replied that he would drown it as it would never be of any use. We asked him if we could have it and he said, "Sure, but I don't think it will ever walk." With great glee we took it home and made some wooden splints for its legs, bound them up and kept the pup tied up. It kept us busy putting the bandages on, for the pup kept gnawing them off, but with patience was finally rewarded and the legs gradually set. We found we had saved a collie with a fine intellect who learned to do everything we told her and many things we did not. •

to his home for two weeks because of the pain, and he needed a prescription. In desperation, he had ridden over on the back of one of his oxen as he did not own a horse and wagon. He had a pleasant visit with Mary's father, but when he said his good-byes and went to get on his ox for the journey home, the animal had disappeared. Tweed, knowing that this ox was not part of his family's herd, had quietly guided the ox back home. Mary's mother offered to hitch up her pony to their Red River cart, and she delivered the gentleman back to his home.

Gordon Stewart reminisced about a special dog that he had in his life during his homesteading years.[44] Her name was Dimple and she was a registered Irish water spaniel. Gordon said she was as fond of him as he was of her. One time when Gordon had suffered a serious farm injury (he was cut up from forehead to ankle when a disc ran over him in the field), Dimple stayed under his bed for days, except for a short run outside every morning.

> Dimple was the most intelligent dog I ever owned, and a wonderful retriever. I had trained her to bring things back to me, and she would get my shoes but she would not work under a gun as she was supposed to, and was no good duck hunting. And she was a notorious thief. One day I walked into the kitchen where Mother had a roast beef on the oven door to cool and found Dimple pulling the roast towards the door with her teeth bared and lips curled up so she would not get burnt. I caught her, got a small stick and gave her a trimming. She howled and after I let her go, she ran away. When I threw the stick after her, she brought it back to me! Dimple never got another spanking from me as long as she lived. A few years after that incident, I walked into the kitchen one night and found Dimple stretched out on the floor, front paws stretched out in front of her and hind paws stretched out at her rear end and suffering untold agony. I had no idea what could be wrong, but she looked quite pitiful, as if asking for help. I got my horse and drove to town twelve miles away, where there was a doctor and he sold me a little chloroform. When I got home, Dimple was lying there, but did not notice me. In a few minutes, she was only a memory, and while I did not shed a tear, I very nearly did.

While many homesteaders had domesticated animals as pets, others were more adventurous and tried to make pets out of wild birds or animals. John Evans found an injured young eagle on the trail one day when he and his father were returning from town.[45] It was weak from a lack of food. John gathered up the bird and brought him home. He nursed the eagle back to health. Eventually, he let the eagle go so that it could live in the wild, but after six weeks it returned for a visit. John's sons fed him a generous helping of salt pork, but it was obvious the eagle was unwell. He died shortly after returning, and they buried him. As John said, "We all mourned his death as of a great friend."

Elsie Campbell and her family also adopted a small feathered bird who required assistance.[46] In their case, they came across a baby owl. They kept it contained by attaching a string to its leg as they nurtured it back to health. The children hunted for gophers, chopped them up and fed pieces of gopher to the baby owl. Over time it grew to a healthy size, and even though they released it into the wild, it stayed nearby and would often visit the family. Annie Gamroth Strachan's family also adopted a bird: a sandhill crane.[47] Her father first found him in the coulee behind their home. He had a broken wing, so her father picked him up, brought him home and nursed him back to health. Annie said, "We called him 'Dick.' He became a family pet. The first spring when my mother was out planting onion sets in the garden, Dick was right behind her pulling them out." Another time, her mother had just finished baking a carrot pie and put it on the table for dinner. When her back was turned, Dick, "who had the run of the house, spied the pie, and reached over with his long neck and plucked the center right out!"

Ellenor Merriken mentioned that her family raised and tamed wild geese.[48] They became favoured pets of the family, with each goose having its own name. However, it was difficult to protect the geese, especially when hunters were around and willing to trespass on their land. Ellenor described this sorrowful event in her memoirs:

> Two hunters came by and we heard two shots in rapid succession just south of the house in the slough where our geese had the habit of swimming. We ran as fast as we could to see and there lay Nels and Mr. Young, floating and dead. The hunters, now realizing what they had done, got away as fast as they could. It was a sad day for us. We buried the ganders, and Ellen walked around honking and honking; it was easy to see that she was a lonesome goose ... She stayed with us until one day late in the fall when a flock of geese coaxed her along on their flight south. The next spring, I watched a big flock of geese winging their way north, one lone goose left the formation and settled down in our yard. It was Ellen for sure. She stood a moment, her neck outstretched, glup-glupping at me. Then, all of a sudden, she flew back and joined the rest. That was the last time we saw her.

Other people were more daring and desired dangerous animals like brown bears for pets. One such individual, Ed Price, was the proprietor of the pool hall in Nipawin, Saskatchewan.[49] He decided to add an extra attraction to his business by finding and raising two bear cubs. He tamed them so effectively that they were allowed to mingle with the patrons in the pool hall. "Often a patron, about to drink a bottle of pop, would feel a paw on his shoulder, and looking around, would find himself face to face with a huge brown bear who would put out his paw, take the bottle and drink it, while the stunned customer looked on." The two bears became a well-known curiosity across the district and were revered as great entertainers.

In some cases, bears that had been caught were not as tame as people thought they were. One homesteader named Raymond (a neighbour of Cecil and Nona White of Hattonford), had a bear that he kept on a long chain in his farmyard.[50] Raymond and his family were not at home one day, so Cecil and Nona's children (a boy and a girl), believing that the bear was tame, decided to go and visit him. They planned on feeding him and had brought a treat for him—a loaf of bread. However, while they were there, the bear got loose. The children ran into Raymond's house to escape. The bear kept walking around outside looking for them, so one of the children, Florence, threw the loaf of bread out a back window. The two children then quickly left out the front door. When they got a ways down the road, they saw the bear coming. They ran so fast that the bear gave up. The boy was so out of breath that he had to sit behind a bush. Afterward, he said that he "couldn't have run another step even if that bear had kept coming."

Dave Koelln, who lived in Grouard in the Peace River Country of Alberta, remembered an encounter that he had with a bear.[51] A man by the name of Mr. Griffin delivered the mail from Grouard to Dunvegan. On one of his trips he came across a black bear, captured it and decided to bring it home. He had it tied to a tree with a long rope. Dave, who had never seen a bear before, had heard that they liked to eat candy. So he went and got some candy from town to feed to the bear. When he visited the bear, he thought he was far enough away from it to be safe, but soon found out that he was not. To his great consternation, the bear put his front legs around him and hugged him. He said, "I didn't much plan to give him all the candy, but was glad to do so in

This pet bear, placed in a pen behind the Merchants Bank in Vegreville, Alberta, in 1905, is drinking out of a bottle. NA-884-3. COURTESY OF LIBRARIES AND CULTURAL RESOURCES DIGITAL COLLECTIONS, UNIVERSITY OF CALGARY

order to get away from him. Since that day I've seen and been near many bears, but I make sure I have no sweets with me."

Julia Asher also recalled close encounters with her uncle's pet bears.[52] She and her family had travelled to Manitoba in 1881. They decided to spend the winter on her uncle Richard Short's homestead at Kildonan before they homesteaded on their own in the spring. It was their first experience with country life, so everything was new and exciting, especially the bears. She said:

> Uncle had two bears, chained to oak trees, a jet black one called Dora and a cinnamon brown one named Jemima. How we loved to watch and cheer on the dog as he circled, barking, about Dora, while she rose on her hind feet and endeavored to strike him. Once he inadvertently came within reach of Jemima, who dealt him such a cuff that he was flung several yards away and barely escaped with his life. Our four year old brother Willie, had a narrow escape too,

> when May [our sister], caught hold of him just in time to drag him from the claws of Dora, who resented the attempt to interfere with her dinner.

Some children opted for gophers as pets. This was not a surprise as gophers were the most prolific creatures across the prairies. They could be caught with little effort, and they were small and manageable. One young homesteader remembered how his father found a half-grown gopher in the field during a rainstorm and brought him home as a pet for his son.[53] However, it did not last long in the house. As he said,

> It was very tame but always under foot so one day when I was away at school, Ma stepped on it and killed it. I felt so bad about it that we went out into the barn and while I watched, she just went over to a corner and picked up a wild one (how she did it I will never know). We took it back to the house where a few days later when my mother pushed it out of her way, it bit her, so she picked it up and took it to the door where she threw it just as far as she could. That was the end of the pet gopher era!

Other children caught gophers and kept them for a time as pets, but more often they caught them so that they could make money from the gopher bounty. Gophers were very destructive rodents that not only ate crops in the field and vegetables in the garden, but also dug holes everywhere across the prairies. These holes were a menace to all farm animals, especially horses, because if they stepped into one of these holes, they could break a leg. As Evelyn Slater said, "There were always gophers to catch, which not only was a pastime for all the boys, but it brought them money as well. The Canadian Government offered a bounty of one cent for each gopher tail turned in."[54] Her brothers, Clarence and Lawrence, were both diligent gopher hunters.

> Usually, they snared the gophers with a slipknot at the end of a length of binder twine. After a gopher ran into his burrow, the loop was placed around the entrance to the hole and

top: Three men from Nanton, Alberta, pose for the photographer, with two of them holding their pet coyotes, 1908. NA-390-8. COURTESY OF LIBRARIES AND CULTURAL RESOURCES DIGITAL COLLECTIONS, UNIVERSITY OF CALGARY

bottom: A man stands and strokes his two pet moose, ca. 1885. NA-239-24. COURTESY OF LIBRARIES AND CULTURAL RESOURCES DIGITAL COLLECTIONS, UNIVERSITY OF CALGARY

> the boys flattened themselves about twelve feet back. In only a few minutes, they had their prize. One day Clarence caught an albino gopher. He skinned it and proudly approached his father who was drawing water from the well. The albino skin called for some examination on the part of Dad, who accidentally dropped it in their 90 foot well. It could not be recovered, and they never did tell mother [about the tainted water].

The Dozorec family of the Calhoun district in Alberta tried their hand at raising minks.[55] One of their daughters, Annie, told how her father caught a wild mink in a trap on their homestead. It was only slightly injured so he decided to build a cage for it and raise it as a pet. However, the mink refused to eat even though her father tried to coax it with tasty bits of food.

> One day he put his hand in a bit too far and the mink grabbed his thumb. Dad tried to pull away but it held on, coming out of the cage still clinging to his thumb. Dad swung his arm around and round and still it hung on so he gave it a slap on the head. Then it let go and scampered off, leaving dad with a very painful thumb. So that ended mink raising at our place.

A Badger Pandemonium

RETA EVANS SIMONS offered a detailed account of how her family tried to keep a badger as a pet.[56] She discussed the experiences they had with him, particularly as he seemed to get more ferocious over time, and she highlights the day that she and her siblings unintentionally ended up taking him to school.

> One summer's day, Dad came home with a baby badger and let us have it. The animal was pretty heavy but we carried him around and soon he followed us everywhere. He slept in the house, under our beds, on the beds, or anywhere he pleased. He was built low and looked rather clumsy but could ripple along when he ran. We had never seen a creature who could dig so fast! Badgers live in deep burrows in the ground and we often climb down them, feet first, up to our armpits. We'd seen our dog, Purp, dig after the wild ones. They could dig out fresh sod faster than he could keep up on the soft dirt left behind. Face to face in a fight, a dog wouldn't stand a chance as badgers are so strong and quick. While out playing with us, we watched Badger dig numerous holes around the house, which our parents didn't like. He ate only raw meat and looked very vicious while about it. He could take good sized bites. However, he never bit us and Purp gave him a wide berth. As he grew older, he played rough and we didn't quite trust him ... We became dubious as to whether he was following us or chasing us. He growled when crossed but there were times we preferred him out of the way at play. He had to be shut in the house. One day, halfway to school, we discovered him rushing to catch up with us. Taking him back would mean being late. After standing still till he caught up, we tried jumping at him, scaring him away. He stood still and watched. He was picked up and put down facing home and we ran on. He turned around just as fast. We tried running a piece toward home so's he'd get the idea. Nothing worked so we gave up and went on to school, hoping he'd leave on his own. But no. When we

tried slipping in the door, he was in the cloakroom with us. The other children were already seated and quietly working. We quickly pushed him under a handy wooden box of slates and hope for the best. Soon the teacher asked if anyone knew what all the strange noises were about ... I put up my hand to be excused. What to do? Badger was happy to see a familiar, friendly face and stopped his noise. My next idea was to get him outside. I carefully raised one side of the box. My hand reached for him. Out he rushed. He had never been penned before. Around the corner [of the cloakroom] and into the schoolroom he ran. The teacher went into a panic, shrieked, climbed up on her chair and then onto her desk, wringing her hands. That's where she was when I came in. I'd heard her shriek before reaching the room; maybe he had bitten her. My sakes, what a state of affairs! There was pandemonium among the kids. Of course, there was trouble all around. Badger had to be caught and taken home. Mom decided something had to be done about him. He wasn't trustworthy and he was an awful nuisance to her with his insistence on being with us kids every waking hour. Dad's idea was the quickest solution but we set up such a howl, he relented. We couldn't think of our beloved pet being killed. There must be some way we could still see him once in a while. Any number of kids had wanted the unusual pet so he was given to one of the older neighbor boys, whom he promptly bit. That was the end of him. For a time, we sorely missed him. ●

"A Wonderful Social Spirit in the Community"

Throughout the late 1800s and early 1900s a large number of towns were created across the western prairies with enough amenities to service the local homesteaders and increasing numbers of townfolk. Post offices were built, as were barbershops, hotels, hardware stores, implement shops, butcher shops, laundries, banks, schools, drugstores, grocery stores and lumberyards. As larger numbers of people congregated in and around these centres, residents started creating social clubs catering to a diversity of interests and offering a variety of venues for entertainment.

George Harris offered details on how his town of Heward, Saskatchewan, developed numerous recreational activities for adults and children between 1900 and 1914.[1] As he recalled,

> an ice rink was erected and surely was a splendid gesture for winter skating and curling, for sometimes in the long winter, time dragged rather slowly. A baseball club was formed together with several other towns who had baseball clubs; made it very pleasant for all on Saturday afternoons during summer when games were played. A brass band was organized also at that time, I believe by Newton Krish, who himself played the bass tuba, [and it] was added to our functions especially during the baseball games. A civilian Rifle Association was organized in 1909. The first captain was George Jackson and the secretary was myself. We got permission from the Federal Government to have the range on vacant school land. We had ranges of 200 yards, 300 yards

Rifle associations became commonplace across the prairies. Here, members of the Innisfail Rifle Association hold a shooting contest with the Lindastall club in 1905. *L–R:* Mr. Stevenson, Mr. Douglas, Mr. Fisher, Mr. Curry, Mr. Stevenson, J. Beggs, W. Lundy, Captain F. Archer, R. Archer, Mr. Holgate and Mr. Mundson. NA-103-87. COURTESY OF LIBRARIES AND CULTURAL RESOURCES DIGITAL COLLECTIONS, UNIVERSITY OF CALGARY

> and 600 yards and practiced Saturday afternoons and occasionally had a contest with other associations. They were very interesting. The rifles we used at first were Lee-Enfields, but when the Ross rifle came out, we exchanged our rifles for the Ross.[2] We had thirty-two members but when World War I was declared in 1914,[3] they called the "Rifles,"[4] and of course the club was disbanded.[5]

Another rifle club was formed in Winlaw, Saskatchewan, in 1886. According to homesteader Ernest Bishop,[6] his father joined the club, and he and his friend Will Richardson sent an order to Massachusetts for a Maynard Creedmoor target rifle.[7] Ernest said:

> It was a wonderful gun and would carry over a mile. It was a .44 caliber with both open and peep sights. Mr. Halliday of Winlaw put up a silver medal for the winner of a summer shooting competition. Dad and Will Richardson were contestants and Will won the medal, scoring 49 points out of a possible 50 ... They had regular rifle pits and revolving targets set at 200, 501, and 1,000 yards, with men in the pits

to mark the shots made. This contest was an annual event for years.

Nell Williams remembered the fun social events that her community of Griffin Creek, Alberta, initiated.[8] She said that the men had created baseball teams and played against each other, but what was really exciting were the two basketball teams. One team was made up of married women, while the other was a team of single girls. The two teams played against each other on special occasions, such as the annual sports day that was held on May 24 each year and also at the annual fair. "The married men cheered for their wives, while the younger swains cheered for their girlfriends. We made our own fun and what fun it was!"

Baseball games were also a highlight for the homesteaders in the Argyle district of Alberta. The sport became so popular that people quit work early on Saturdays during the warmer months of the year and gathered together a half mile north of the local school to practise their baseball skills. More than enough people always showed up to form teams, so they were able to have a game. A great time was enjoyed by everyone who attended.[9]

The residents of Rimbey, Alberta, also enjoyed their baseball games.[10] In the early 1900s, some members of the community who were interested in the sport (Bert Saunders, H. Eckhardt, the Uhl brothers, and Frank Peabody) decided to combine their efforts to create a baseball club. The problem they faced was that they needed to find nine good men for the team among a sparse population that lacked talent.

> This was definitely the case with a lot of small towns and districts until all at once it seemed Rimbey and the surrounding country began to boom in a big way and settlers from almost all over the world started to pour into the country. Among these were J. Lethbridge, the first manager of the First Bank of Rimbey. As a boy, he had been a real ballplayer, and with his coming it seemed to open the doors to a tide of talent that included the Connellys fresh from Illinois High School and semi-pro ball, followed by the Kutinas, semi-pro and professional ballplayers from Minnesota. Joe Kutina, hav-

ing suffered a stomach injury, had been released by the Saint Louis Browns, and having his career cut short decided to homestead in western Canada and his choice became Rimbey. Along with him came Bill and George, two of his brothers, both high-class semi-pros. These boys had been preceded a few months by Floyd Little and Cyde Ely from the Nebraska state league, and already here were some boys showing great promise, namely Alfred and Gilbert Lloyd and Carl Cox. Little did all these immigrants know that they were to form one of the best if not the best ball club in Alberta.

While many of the baseball teams consisted of male players, there was a team from Arrow River, Manitoba, that included only female players. Known as the Arrow River Ladies' Baseball Team, they travelled to different venues to play against other female teams. In 1904, they were set to play against the Crandall

The baseball team from Rimbey, Alberta, ca. 1900–35. ND-2-187, BY B.S. CAMERON. COURTESY OF LIBRARIES AND CULTURAL RESOURCES DIGITAL COLLECTIONS, UNIVERSITY OF CALGARY

Nine (a women's team from Crandall, Manitoba) for a $10 prize. Unfortunately, the Crandall Nine did not appear on the day of the game. Nine men from Hamiota, Manitoba, stepped in so that the game could begin. One spectator said, "The game proved very interesting and from the minute the horsehide was placed in the pitcher's box, the greatest excitement prevailed."[11] When the game was over the score was 19 to 12 in the Arrow River Ladies' favour. The women beat the men and enjoyed their winnings![12]

The choice of sport for the Anwoth, Shoal Lake and Ancrum areas of Manitoba in the late 1890s was football.[13] It was viewed as a "natural game for the early pioneers to turn to for recreation. It was a game that was a part of the background of the English, Irish, and Scottish stock that pioneered in the district. All that was needed for the game was a ball, a reasonably level piece of ground (which the prairie abounded in) and eleven eager young men."[14] Intense rivalries developed between the teams, and their games became highly anticipated and attended by hundreds, especially as prize money was involved. Injuries such as wrenched knees, sprains and broken bones were not uncommon among the players. Football was also the preferred sport in the Carstairs area of Alberta. In April 1908, members of the community got together for a meeting to discuss the organization of a football club. Their first game occurred in Bowden, with the Carstairs team winning by a 4 to 0 score. However, they lost their second game against Olds with a 1 to 0 score.[15]

The community of Sheho, Saskatchewan, was also very proud of its football team especially as the team won the Provincial Football Championship in 1907.[16] Over the years, the team often had to travel by horse and democrat over rough trails in order to play against other teams in the district. Most of these games were played with spectators watching, as games were exciting social events that many in the community looked forward to attending. Typically, spectators would cheer for their teams and everyone would have a good time. However, in one instance the crowd became too involved. This game was played in Humboldt, Saskatchewan. "During the course of the football game, some of the crowd got into an argument and fists began to fly. Jim Enright, an Invermay merchant and, formerly, a livery barn operator in Sheho around 1904, was one of the spectators. In the fray, the new Christie (stiff brim) hat that he was sporting, was

Ernest R. "Jake" Fullerton, light heavyweight boxing champion of western Canada, was born in a covered wagon while his parents were on their way to Calgary, Alberta, from Marquette, Michigan, in 1882.[17] Jake, his parents and his three older siblings settled in Springbank, Alberta, in 1883. Jake was prominent in sports from a young age, taking part in bicycle races, rugby, and lacrosse. His greatest passion, however, was for boxing, and he was the winner of the Western Canada Amateur Light Heavyweight Championship for years. Eventually he married, had children and moved his family to Bragg Creek, Alberta, to take up homesteading in 1913. According to his daughter,

> Jake never tired of promoting or participating in sports, organizing skating parties, a catch as catch can hockey team, lacrosse matches, softball teams and of course the inevitable boxing bouts. In the early days when Mounties stayed overnight with us, after eating a good meal of illegal venison, Jake would produce a set of boxing gloves and ask the Mountie to have a little workout. After riding horseback all day, I cannot imagine a man being too enthused about this idea, but not one ever refused and I can never remember one leaving without a black eye or several inches of skin missing. I have often wondered how these men explained their battered appearance to their superiors.

The photograph shows Jake ca. 1906–07. NA-265-10. COURTESY OF LIBRARIES AND CULTURAL RESOURCES DIGITAL COLLECTIONS, UNIVERSITY OF CALGARY knocked off his head and the crowd had a grand time kicking it around the grounds." By the time everyone had their fill of fighting and hat kicking, the football game had been forgotten. The outcome of the game was never mentioned, nor was the ultimate condition of the hat or the feelings of the hat owner.

Instead of football, the community of Roland, Manitoba, became enamoured with the game of lacrosse.

> It was a running game and took great stamina on the part of the players. Eleven men spaced the field, and a stick about the size of a broom handle supported a triangular basket of woven rawhide or catgut. The stick was bent at the end into the form of an inverted "L" which allowed the player to pick up and throw a rubber ball with speed and dexterity.[18]

The point of the game was to throw the ball through the opponent's goal post at the end of the field. This game became so important to Roland that crowds of people would gather to watch their hometown team practice. Homesteaders who were on the team would hire others to do their farm work so they could get ready for an upcoming game. Practice was usually six hours each day and included running up and down the town's main street or running out of town on the country roads. In 1900, their efforts came to fruition as the town won the Lacrosse Provincial Championship of Manitoba.

Two young men play lacrosse in 1907. ND-392-1-1C. COURTESY OF LIBRARIES AND CULTURAL RESOURCES DIGITAL COLLECTIONS, UNIVERSITY OF CALGARY

The residents of Pine Lake, Alberta, preferred playing cricket and formed a club in 1900.[19] They primarily played against clubs from Calgary, Edmonton, Red Deer and Strathcona. In 1906, the Red Deer club donated a Challenge Cup that was to be competed for annually, but which was won outright by Pine Lake each year. The last match was played in Edmonton in 1912. It was a two-day event. One day Pine Lake played against Strathcona and the next against Edmonton. The club disbanded between 1914 and 1918 (the war years) but was revived after the war, with many members playing in the club until 1930. Pine Lake residents also built a tennis court, which became a popular attraction, as were their tennis parties. The residents also established a rifle club (which was a branch of the Innisfail Club). The rifle club held an annual shooting competition every fall up to the First World War, as well as a shoot every Boxing Day. The community organized a militia in 1909, appointing a Lieutenant and holding weekly drills.[20] It was disbanded in 1914 when most of the members enlisted for overseas service. Many of them died in the war. As for other social activities, the community held an ice boat race on Pine Lake every winter, and areas of the lake were made available to the general public for ice skating.

The people of Basswood, Manitoba, also took part in winter activities, skating and playing hockey on the local sloughs once they had frozen over.[21] In 1906, the community wanted to expand on these outdoor activities by building an enclosed curling rink. A large frozen slough was chosen and the snow was cleared away. Six long wooden poles were frozen into the ice, three on each side the slough. These poles were to be the studs of the structure. The owner of the local lumberyard donated 10-inch shiplap for the walls and roof, which were nailed in, just well enough to keep the snow out. Inside the building, the rings were scratched into the ice at each end, and gas lanterns were hung for light. Curling rocks were purchased from Winnipeg, and the membership fee for the season was four to five dollars. Excitement over the new curling club was high, with many men looking forward to the curling matches. However, that enthusiasm soon waned. As homesteader Dave Rose said, "I can remember me and my dad, just driving down there, puttin' the horse in the livery barn, then goin' down there, curlin' for a little while. I can remember two or three times it was so cold we couldn't stay there. We just curled a few ends, then quit and got out." Unfortunately, many members likely felt the same way, as the rink only lasted one year. In the spring, the building was torn down before the ice melted, and the wooden poles were fished out of the water after the spring break-up.

While many districts were involved with sports clubs, other communities had an interest in developing freemasonry associations. Freemasonry was a secret fraternal social club with a religious and historical base.[22] Members joined voluntarily, held meetings bi-monthly and strove to do charitable work in their areas. Through their rituals and beliefs, they sought to make "good men better men," who would lead exemplary personal and public lives. A number of Masonic Lodges began appearing on the western prairies, beginning with the creation of the Northern Light Lodge in 1864 at the Red River Settlement in Manitoba. By 1880, there were eleven lodges in Manitoba, with more being created over time. A lodge was eventually established in Regina, Saskatchewan, in 1882, and in Moose Jaw, Saskatchewan, by

Eight officers of the Masonic Lodge at Innisfail, Alberta, pose in their official regalia, 1895. Each of the members wears an apron that was bestowed on him when he was initiated into the organization. The aprons were so revered by the members that they would be buried with them when they passed away. *L–R back row:* W. Playle, R. Archer and S.P. Fream. *L–R front row:* W. Richards, L. Wilson, J. Simpson, H.M. Douglas and C.G. Ross. NA-103-42. COURTESY OF LIBRARIES AND CULTURAL RESOURCES DIGITAL COLLECTIONS, UNIVERSITY OF CALGARY

1883. Men in Calgary, Alberta, created a lodge in 1884, with Medicine Hat and Lethbridge following suit in 1885 and 1887 respectively. Lodges were created in other towns once there were enough members to take part.[23]

While men were involved with freemasonry, women joined the Order of the Eastern Star. By 1912, approximately forty chapters of this organization had been established across the western prairies, with more being organized as time went by. In order to join, a woman had to be at least eighteen years of age and had to prove that she was related to a member of the Masonic Lodge.[24] Following in the tradition of freemasonry, members of the Order of the Eastern Star also had to go through an initiation ceremony; follow rituals; learn lessons relating to fidelity, charity, purity and hope; and attend monthly meetings. They also had to have a belief in a supreme being.[25]

Other fraternal and social groups began organizing across the western prairies. For instance, Loyal Orange Lodges (Protestant fraternal organizations with roots in eighteenth-century Ireland) were involved with many benevolent activities in their communities. They also helped Protestant immigrants settle in areas across Canada. The first Orange Lodge in the west was established at Red River Valley, Manitoba, in 1870, followed by a lodge at Hamiota, Manitoba, in 1882, the Turtle Mountain district in 1884 and Holmfield in 1885. Members met once a month to discuss important matters of the day (including political and economic issues) and worked for the good of the community. Larger community events included Orangemen's Day, when the town would be decorated, Orangemen from nearby locales would be invited to attend and they would all parade up and down the main street led by a drum and fife. Celebrations were held over the course of the day, with meals being served and drinks being offered.[26]

Another community-minded social group was the Canadian Order of Foresters. In Hamiota, Manitoba, this group organized a chapter in 1892 and, over time, became the third-largest Forester group in the province. "The purpose of the organization was fashioned after the idea of Robin Hood and the Forest of Sherwood, namely to band together for the purpose of helping those in need. The three main principles of the [group] were liberty, benevolence, and concord, meaning freedom, kindness, and agreement."[27] They developed an insurance policy for their members, which proved to be a great help to beneficiaries. They also created a funeral benefit fund that paid members who were on the sick list up to $28, and $30 to any beneficiary of a deceased member. In addition, they organized social events such as debates, card parties, lunches, community performances and dances, and they took part in the town's annual parade.

The Independent Order of Oddfellows, along with its sister group, the Rebekah Lodge, also did its part in helping out with community service. The Oddfellows, which was created in the early 1900s by an American named Thomas Wildey, was a non-sectarian and non-partisan group that welcomed all individuals regardless of national origin or background. Its primary purpose was to encourage personal and social development and promote truth, charity, justice and friendship. The organization spread across the United States and into Canada, as did the Rebekah Lodges. Groups appeared in many cities in Ontario and Quebec and made inroads into new communities on the western Canadian prairies. For instance, an Order of Oddfellows was created in Foam Lake in 1910, while a Rebekah Lodge was organized a number of years later.[28] The Oddfellows and members of the Rebekah Lodge took part in money-making projects such as euchre drives (i.e., card parties), dances, teas, banquets and social get-togethers in order to raise funds for those in need or for community projects.[29] Other service clubs and groups such as the Lions Club, Cub Scouts, Girl Guides, Royal Canadian Legion, 4-H Clubs, Garden Clubs and Canasta Clubs were not organized until the 1920s and later.

Women of the various prairie communities were also involved with Women's Institutes or Ladies' Aid societies. Audrey Kulak, in her reminiscences of Stony Plain, Alberta, described how the first Women's Institute was organized in Ontario by Adelaide Hunter-Hoodless.[30] The aim of the organization was "to improve the knowledge of rural women in areas of homemaking and childcare." This type of organization appealed to many women across the western prairies, and many attended presentations that described how such an institute worked, who was involved and how it should be organized. In Stony Plain, for instance, on the afternoon of December 8, 1913, fifteen local women attended a presentation at the Town Hall given by Miss Stiven from the federal Department of Agriculture, who discussed the aims and benefits of creating a Women's Institute in their area. The women were impressed with the presentation and decided to organize a branch. Over time, they invited a number of speakers who presented on a variety of different subjects, including first aid and home nursing, planning and caring for a garden, and making toys for Christmas. They also shared their ideas for hooking rugs, recipes, household hints, school lunches and carding wool. The group became involved with the Red Cross in 1916.

Evelyn Olson of Bladworth, Saskatchewan, mentioned the benefits of having a Women's Institute in her area in 1911.[31] This group of women strove to improve the community by organizing events like bake sales, where the money collected (or donated) went toward the building of a church and other important community structures. (Evelyn mentioned that it took three years of tireless effort collecting funds before the church could be built.) Lena Purdy described a "Lady's Aid" organization that was created in Condie, Saskatchewan.[32] She indicated that it worked as a missionary society. Members would "sew and do needlework, take part in devotional exercises, and enjoy the social hour that they had when they visited different women's homes" each month. Lena Morin of Pickardville, Alberta, highlighted the work of the Ladies' Aid Society, which was organized in her area on February 17, 1909.[33] Over the years, Lena reported, "It would be difficult to estimate the number of socials, suppers, bazaars and picnics that have been held. Besides doing a large share of helping out financially, they have created a wonderful social spirit in the community."

Lena said that the first Ladies' Aid social function was held at Stanton's Hall in Pickardville. It involved a "pie contest where the most popular bachelor was to receive a pie. The financial result was $29 which was given to the trustees to help pay for the lumber for the church."

> At this time, Mr. McKinney, the Liberal member for this constituency, donated $150 and Mrs. Edwards of Eastburg donated $10 towards the purchase of an organ for the church. In June, the organ was hauled by Andrew Telfer from Morinville, Alberta to Pickardville with a freight bill of $125. The organ was installed in the church and plans were made for the opening and dedication of the church on August 1st,

This is a gathering of the members of the Ladies' Aid Society from Mayton, Alberta, in 1915. *L–R back row:* Edith Smellt, Mrs. Louisa Campbell and Mamie McLean. *L–R third row:* Elizabeth Reid, Cora Berkely, Agnes Phillips, Huldah Holmes, Mrs. Empye, Harriet Stirton, Elizabeth Reid, Kate Pretty, Margaret Rands and Mrs. Pell. *L–R second row:* Janie Buckton, unknown, Grace Adair, holding baby Emily Adair, and Violet Fox, in back, seated. *L–R front row:* Mary Berkely, Charles Buckton and Jack Aldridge. NA-1946-5. COURTESY OF LIBRARIES AND CULTURAL RESOURCES DIGITAL COLLECTIONS, UNIVERSITY OF CALGARY

1909. On October 10th, 1909, the first Thanksgiving service was held at the church, followed by a chicken supper on the following Monday. The first bazaar was held on November 30th, 1909. It was a decided success both socially and financially, realizing $70 for the church.

A Ladies' Aid Society, officially called the Hamiota Hospital Ladies' Aid, was created in April 1908 in Hamiota, Manitoba.[34] At that time, the main concern of many women in the community was the number of ill people who could not be adequately cared for in their own homes. They recognized that a hospital was needed for these suffering individuals, where their needs could be taken care of by those with medical expertise. The women sought approval for their project from Hamiota's mayor and then proceeded to raise funds by "sponsoring concerts, catering to sports and citizen's days and serving meals at the local annual Agricultural Fair." Their efforts paid off when a hospital was built in 1913.[35] The women were also called on whenever a medical emergency arose. Such was the case in 1908 when a family lost their home to fire. The women rented a partially furnished house in Hamiota from a local resident, and immediately donated chairs, tables and bedding as well as clothing, dishes and groceries. The Ladies' Aid also agreed to pay $100 a month for one year to cover maintenance on the house.

Other social groups that were formed in communities included debating and literary clubs. Events put on by these organizations always attracted a number of people, not only for their entertainment value, but also because the debates and discussions allowed them to gain knowledge about a variety of subjects. Aaron Biehn indicated that in his community of Lanigan, Saskatchewan, two men were chosen each month to debate a political issue.[36] When two men could not be found, someone was invited to give a recitation from a book that they were currently reading or from a story or set of poems that they had written. At other times, someone might get up and entertain the crowd by singing a song like "Sweet and Low"[37] or "Down by the Old Mill Stream,"[38] or by playing a musical instrument like a mouth organ or violin. In Carstairs, Alberta, the debating club held a very lively discussion in 1914 on the question of "Who makes a better wife, the home girl or a business girl?" After the debate, thirteen people voted in favour of the home girl while ten voted for the business girl.[39] Lena May Purdy, described the literary club in Pense, Saskatchewan, and how it was used to integrate the young people into the community.[40] Its primary purpose was to teach them how to serve on committees. As she said, "Boys who could hardly stand up in school to answer a question gained experience by acting as chairman, committee members and secretaries and they learned how to take their turns speaking without embarrassment." They also held debates. At the end of the evening refreshments were served.

Drama clubs were popular during the early homesteading years, and the plays that they presented were seen as a great form of entertainment. In the Waskatenau area of Alberta, for example, dramatic presentations were given by a few groups of people once every few months. They would compete against each other for the honour of being the best acting group in the area.[41] In Carstairs, Alberta, one of the first plays put on in their community with local talent was "Irish Assurance and Yankee Modesty." It was a two-act farcical play written by James Pilgrim in 1864, and everyone who attended enjoyed the performance. The drama club also presented the play "A Farmer's Daughter," which was also remembered by the community with great fondness.[42]

Box socials were organized by community groups for their entertainment value, but also to raise money for worthy causes. Mrs. W.T. Billing of Regina, Saskatchewan, noted that a lot of money could be collected.[43] When her community held a box social, they made $156. This money would often be used to purchase teaching materials that were needed for the school, like textbooks, maps, a globe, slates, chalk and chalkboard, or it would go toward the building of a church.

For a box social, the young women in the community were asked to decorate a box and place a lunch for two inside it. Lunches would typically include sandwiches, and cakes or cookies for dessert. The owner of each box was kept a secret, but the young woman who had decorated and assembled it would put a slip of paper with her name inside the box. When the time came, the boxes were put up for auction, and the young men in the crowd would bid on them. The man who bid the highest on a particular box was the winner of the box, and when he opened the box, he would learn who he was to share his lunch with. Box socials tended to be happy and lively events, with men trying to outbid each other for particular boxes. Sometimes the young men in the crowd would try to deceive a friend if they found out that he was sweet on a particular girl. "It was quite a game to ride him with all kinds of false clues as to which box was hers, and rivals, real or pretended, would attempt to outbid him. It was considered quite a triumph of deception if he could be called into paying a high price for the wrong one." If this played out as his friends intended, the young man was faced with "smurks and grins" from his fellow mates while he ate his lunch with a young woman who had not caught his eye.[44]

While this situation may have been a source of amusement for the young men, it wasn't so enjoyable for the young women who realized that the fellow had been duped into bidding on their box by mistake. Seeing the disappointment on their partner's face would have been extremely embarrassing for the young woman, and the time spent eating together would have been uncomfortable, if not unbearable. Unless both could overcome the awkward situation and laugh about their shared experience, their conversation would likely have been very stilted. While most people made the best of it, there were times when a young man became angry at the deception. Nellie Anderson of Erskine, Alberta, recounted such a situation where a man who was very determined to get a certain girl bid highly on what he thought was her box.[45] When he discovered that the box was owned by another young woman, he was so disappointed and irate that he kicked the box he had purchased all over the hall until it was destroyed.

Some girls who attended box socials ended up being hurt and embarrassed for other reasons. While some girls from the community could afford to make fancy sandwiches, cookies and cakes, and could decorate their boxes with fancy crepe paper and ribbons, there were others who did not have access to these luxuries. They came from poorer farming families who had little to spare. While these girls looked forward to the event, they knew that their plain wrapped boxes, with plain jam sandwiches

Many communities held pie socials. About twenty-five to thirty home-baked pies—strawberry, raspberry, blueberry, raisin and lemon meringue—would be auctioned off to the highest bidders. The money raised from these events would go toward the construction of churches and schools. Unlike the box socials, there was no expectation of couples sitting together and visiting as they ate their pie. Instead, those who bought the pie could take it home and enjoy it at their leisure. In this photograph, people are gathered for a pie social in Okotoks, Alberta in 1895. NA-2702-1. COURTESY OF LIBRARIES AND CULTURAL RESOURCES DIGITAL COLLECTIONS, UNIVERSITY OF CALGARY (sometimes made with day-old bread) accompanied by a simple cookie or two for dessert, would be found lacking in comparison to others. The disappointment on the face of the young man who bid on their box was disheartening for those young women. As well, the beautifully designed boxes tended to be put up for auction first, while the more poorly constructed plain boxes were auctioned off last. Being one of the last ones was always humiliating.

More clubs were created as the population increased. Some invited performers and travelling shows (or chautauquas) to come to their district to entertain the residents. The show would stop in town for a couple of days and perform each afternoon and evening. There might be comedic acts, plays, singing, dancing and every once in a while a magician would appear. These shows were a highlight for people; they would leave their work in the fields and in their homes, and children would be excused from school, in order to attend. Other clubs arranged for silent pictures like *The Great Train Robbery*, *A Trip to the Moon* or *Cabiria* to be shown at the community centre. Local dances and plays were organized.

In the community of Carstairs, Alberta, the entertainment club (otherwise known as the Friday Night Club) not only offered a variety of amusements, but also built structural amenities like Lusk's Dance Hall and the Opera House, where these events could take place. Beginning in 1906, the women of the Friday Night Club held weekly dances at Lusk's Dance Hall. At other times, moving pictures were shown in the hall earlier in the evening, followed by a dance where lemonade and ice cream were served. Eventually, residents of Carstairs formed their own orchestra. One time, twenty-five couples danced to the music of this orchestra, with one resident, A. Whyte, on the piano and another, S. Dugdale, on the drums. On December 7, 1907, the Friday Night Club organized a grand ball for the community, while at another time the Frasier Pierrots, a company of fine musicians, entertained at Lusk's Dance Hall. The Claman Stock Company, a group of actors, stopped by and performed for three nights, while Nellie Watkin's Australian Bird Circus also came to town for a few days. A Thanksgiving supper was held in conjunction with the Thanksgiving Ball in 1908, and in 1909 the Carstairs Orchestra held an open-air performance in the lot west of the harness shop. Also in 1909, the community held a Valentine

Men stand around the tables, waiting to play pool, at Horace Jennings' Pool Hall in Foremost, Alberta, in 1915. NA-2044-1. COURTESY OF LIBRARIES AND CULTURAL RESOURCES DIGITAL COLLECTIONS, UNIVERSITY OF CALGARY

social with lunch, and in the same year an entertaining group of Swiss bell ringers stopped in town. McPhee's Big Company held a variety show under tents on a vacant lot, and in 1910, local resident H.F. Griffiths held a country club dance in his granary south of town. To raise funds, the baseball club sponsored the play *Managing Mildred*, which was held in the town's Opera House, while the Quadrille Club offered private dances where people could learn to dance. A concert was held on May 19, 1910, with advertisements stating "Come ye bachelors and bring your best girls to the Opera House." Yon Yossen came to town with the Swedish Comedy Traveling Show in 1913. Apparently the show had everyone laughing so hard that their sides hurt. In 1914, Carstairs had a big show from Broadway, in New York, called *50 Miles From Broadway*. It was reportedly a big hit.[46]

The Evils of Gambling

SOMETIMES SOCIAL GROUPS formed that others in the community were not too fond of—for example, those associated with certain entertainments like gambling. Even though many residents, particularly those on the town council, made strong arguments for such practices to stop, there were members of the police force and the business community who enjoyed gambling and refused to bend to any political will.

> In 1909, in the village of Carstairs, Alberta, village councilors Simon Downie, R. Scott and J.W. Biggs bulleted poster notices that all gambling and dice throwing in the village of Carstairs, whether for money or merchandise, should be stopped at once. They also ordered that the pool and billiard tables were to be closed at 11:00 p.m. [Another councilor], W.R. Seeley wrote to the Carstairs newspaper in 1909 ... that when any personal gain, whether it be a cigar, $0.10 or $1,000 becomes a consideration in a game, with the possibility of one person by chance securing it from the other without giving equal value in return, it is gambling [and should be halted immediately] ... What is necessary is an institution [like a YMCA] where healthy recreation, without the cultivation of such evil habits, can be enjoyed [by young men].
>
> Many times, village citizens pressed the local constable to use his best efforts to put down gambling and dice throwing. However, often the local constable was one of those people who enjoyed gambling. Counselors Downie and R. Scott then ordered that the law against gambling must be strictly conformed to. They wanted all gambling in Carstairs to stop. They blamed much of the gambling on the pool and billiard halls, because they were an easy place for men to assemble and gamble. They also felt that it was too easy for participants and non-participants of a pool game to bet on the outcome of a game, or even on certain billiard shots. However, several businessmen over the years held their daily card or dice games at noon [and also held all-night card games on a frequent basis throughout the years. So gambling, including betting in the pool and billiard halls, continued in Carstairs regardless of those who were against the practice].[47] •

Winning Prizes at the Country Fairs

Along with clubs and organizations that developed over time, annual country fairs and exhibitions soon became a social norm. People looked forward to these events with great anticipation, making plans to enter the various competitions months in advance of the big day. Men prepared their stock for show, hoping to win first prize, while women crocheted or knitted and baked pies and cakes in the hope that they would also beat their competitors. Horse and oxen races took place, as did wood-chopping competitions and plowing matches.

Edith Stilborn remembered the first agricultural fair in Pheasant Forks, Saskatchewan, which occurred in 1886.[1] It was memorable for her as she won one of the first prizes. She said that there were

> exhibits of horses, cattle, sheep, and swine, grain and garden produce, dairy products such as butter, cheese and eggs, as well as bread ... Then there was sewing, quilting and rug making, also plain sewing and fancy work of all kinds, knitting and crocheting and embroidery. I remember as a very young girl taking first prize for embroidered pillow shams, which articles were very much used in those days.

Joseph Wilson of Lashburn, Saskatchewan, remembered with great fondness the local agricultural fair in his area in 1908.[2] He and his family were successful, winning prizes for many of their agricultural efforts. Joseph won first prize for the auction race (a race where two- and three-year-old horses harness-walked for half a mile and then ran for the last half

For the first agricultural fair in Griffin Creek, Alberta, in 1914, the cattle and horses were all tethered to a fence so they could each be evaluated by the judges. NA-1865-1. COURTESY OF LIBRARIES AND CULTURAL RESOURCES DIGITAL COLLECTIONS, UNIVERSITY OF CALGARY

mile). He also won second prize for his general-purpose team of horses, where he had to show how well he could manage his team while he sat in the wagon, how the horses followed his directions and how well they all worked together. His family won third prize for their brood sow. In this competition, judges evaluated the body of the sow (which had to be long, broad and compact), the legs (which were to be short and straight) and the feet (which were to have erect pasterns).[3] Finally, Joseph's mother won first prize for her butter-making skills. In this category, judges evaluated, by taste, the amount of salt that had been added to the butter and the dryness and firmness of the block.

Charles Bray and his wife, from Wolseley, Saskatchewan, did well at their local fairs.[4] Their vegetables always took a lot of prizes, as did their dairy cows and calves, and sows. His wife also won prizes for her baking, particularly her bread. When they entered the various competitions one year at the Regina fair, Charles said that they "cleaned up all of the top prizes with their Toulouse geese and their gander, which weighed 52 pounds alive."[5] They also won top prize for their dressed poultry.[6]

These vegetables, grown by J.A. McDonald in 1914, were exhibited at the first fair in Hanna, Alberta. NA-3596-175. COURTESY OF LIBRARIES AND CULTURAL RESOURCES DIGITAL COLLECTIONS, UNIVERSITY OF CALGARY

The first fair held in the Carmangay district of Alberta occurred on September 14 and 15, 1911 (the same year the local Agricultural Society was formed).[7] Everything did not initially go as planned at the fair, as the "large tent erected for the grains, grasses, vegetables, and home industries was blown down by a strong wind. Not to be outdone by the wind, the exhibits were immediately moved to the new brick school and the fair was a success." The prize list was extensive and included everything

from horses to four lines of writing by school children. Some years there was even prizes for the most gopher tails. That turned out to be a smelly business for those who did the counting! Prizes were awarded for the best bread baked, the best agricultural team, the best Shorthorn heifer, a pen of bacon hogs,[8] a pen of mutton sheep, and a pen of chickens. There were also various horse classes as well as cattle classes. Prizes were also given for the best sheaf of Marquis wheat and pound of butter.

A Curiosity

IN STONY PLAIN, Alberta, local people had a chance to compete when the annual fair was held.[9] They brought in their cows, pigs, horses, sheep, chickens and turkeys. One year a man brought in a chicken that was unusual. It was a four-legged chicken and caused quite a stir among the locals. "A second pair of legs grew out a little behind the regular legs, straight back along the body, ending up without feet."[10] •

People also came to the Carmangay fair to see all sorts of sports including ball games, foot races, horse races, horseshoe tournaments and bucking contests. Over time the fair became larger as more people from distant locations began attending. For many, "it wasn't only a matter of winning prizes, but it was also a chance to meet up with friends they had not seen in a long time."

Annual fairs were held in the Griffin Creek district of Alberta beginning in the fall of 1915.[11] At the 1915 fair, the class that attracted the most attention "was the fine display of ladies' work and domestic products which alone spoke volumes for the type of lady pioneers in the Peace River Country." Another class that was watched with a great deal of interest was the Hudson's Bay Baby Contest.[12] The judge for the baby contest was the local doctor, Dr. Grimshaw, who had to choose the cutest baby. One wonders how the "losing" mothers reacted when their babies were not chosen by their family doctor.

There were numerous other prize winners at this fair. One person won a silver cup for a bushel of wheat. A Canadian Bank of Commerce silver medal was given for the most prizes won in the stock show, five dollars was given by the *Peace River Record Gazette* for the best dual-purpose cow, and a horse scuffler was given by the W. Age Wilson Hardware Company for the best display of vegetables.[13]

Sometimes problems arose at these annual agricultural fairs, particularly if one person suspected another person of cheating. Such was the case in 1909 at the third annual fair in Irvine, Alberta, as "there seemed to be some protest about the wheat grown by a farmer who entered it in the fair. The fellow who protested claimed the wheat was grown by another person."[14] Whether the claim was true or not, it seemed to have a detrimental effect on attendance the next year, as far fewer people showed up to take part in the grain competition. As recounted by those who attended, "There was $180 in prize money but only $80 of that was handed out for prizes."

Over time, with greater numbers of people attending and competing, fall fairs became more complex and more expensive to organize. Costs needed to be covered, so they began to charge a fee for admission. The Bowden, Alberta, fair that took place on October 3, 1913, is a good example of how everything became standardized, with more rigid rules being created. All specifics were outlined in a twenty-page pamphlet that included a wealth of information about the type of products, items, animals and fowl that could be shown at the fair. It highlighted the

> relative importance of farm livestock, poultry, vegetable raising, school work and even showed a class for the greatest number of gopher tails caught by an individual ... Among the general rules and regulations, the first item said that the price of admission to the grounds for adults was $0.25 each time of entering and for children under 14 years of age, the price was to be $0.15, members and their wives and families under eighteen years of age were to be admitted free. There was a great long list of rules in regard to entries, how they should be made, what registration papers were needed, and the making of declaration or affidavit under certain circumstances. Showing the great importance of the horse in those days, there were thirty-two different sections for showing the various classes of heavy draft horses and lighter animals used for saddle ponies or driving horses. The beef and dairy cow groups were just as extensive. In the poultry class there were some eight or ten breeds ranging from Brahmas to White Leghorns. Dairy products, roots and vegetables,

School Fairs

THE CHILDREN FROM Stony Plain, Alberta, learned at an early age how to participate in a fair as a school fair was set up for them. According to local resident George Spady,

> The children were given vegetables and flower seeds in the spring and encouraged to grow a small garden of their own. The products of these gardens as well as their schoolwork, were then shown at the school fair in September. The girls also showed their sewing and knitting. By going through this experience and learning the rules of competition, the children would be ready to take part in the town's fairs when they were older.[15] •

> grains and grasses, ladies' work, nature study, baking, flowers and several specialty items were also included. Generally speaking, the prizes ran from a low of $0.50 for a third prize to a high of $6 for a first prize.[16]

There were some instances where a community held a public event during the summer months instead of in the fall. They were listed as Summer Fairs, Sports Days or Stampedes, or they were held in recognition of a special occasion like Dominion Day.[17] A variety of events were planned in each community depending on the local preferences. Olive Phelps of Crescent Lake, Saskatchewan, remembered that in 1884 her community sought to raise money to build a school.[18] They decided to organize a summer fair, which offered a variety of competitions and races and ended with a concert. It was a full day's entertainment:

> There was a chopping competition in which [four men] competed. A log was laid on the ground and each contestant

had to make three cuts, two of which were one in clear wood and one in a knot. One local man, John Atkey, seems to have been a "dark horse" as it was believed the contest would rest between the two Thompson boys. Before many minutes elapsed, it was very evident Atkey was out to try to win as he and J. Thompson soon forged ahead of the other contestants. Excitement ran high and it was a very much surprised crowd that watched Atkey, who was rather a short stocky built man, knocking out chips as big and as fast as John Thompson, who was nearly six feet tall and built in proportion. When the chips ceased to fly, J. Thompson was declared the winner with Atkey so close a second that it was considered a tie by many onlookers.

In the milch cow class, it is not known whether Mr. Eakins with Muley or Mr. Phelps with Rosey took first place. The big event of the day was an ox race. Some of the teams lined up belonged to C. Partridge, Willard Eckardt, W. Switzer, Harry Maddaford with Bob Maddaford driving the latter's team. The course started from what was known as "Eighteen House," otherwise known as the two-storey house on Section 18, went west to a small bush a quarter of a mile away and return. Bob Maddaford had his roans away on the crack of the gun. The oxen, believing that they were just "pulling off" another runaway, soon outdistanced the others. In fact, such a good time was made, that after circling the bush and returning, Bob and his roans met the balance of the racers still on the outgoing lap. The day was concluded by a concert in the evening which was held in the newly erected mill building. A few of the items on the program worthy of mention were a bass solo by Robert Garvin, entitled "The Swell of the Alpine Hat," concertina solos by Mr. Nelson, whistling by Joe Crow, banjo solos by A. Moore, and step dancing by Duncan Fummerton and George Phelps. After this, there was a dance with Messrs. Nelson and Moore supplying the music. This music was worthy of great appreciation and many of the present residents often recall delightful hours [being entertained]. The funds raised from this entertainment were used to start the first school ... with Mr. Middleton as the teacher.

In the summer of 1899, the Agricultural Society of Hamiota, Manitoba, decided to hold a plowing match. They believed that this match would not only be an exciting social event but would also be an incentive for everyone in the community to learn the fine art of plowing. The first match was held on the farm of William Pedlow, and a large number of people attended. Competitions were broken down into categories. Boys under the age of sixteen competed against each other, as did boys from sixteen to nineteen years of age. Men twenty years and older competed in the Walking Sulky Plow and Gang Plow competitions. There was also a match for men over the age of fifty-five.[19]

In order to encourage farmers to "strive for good crops and to maintain attractive well-managed farms," Hamiota's Agricultural Society also created another match—the Good Farming Competition. Judges would travel from homestead to homestead and assign points for the farm's general appearance (i.e., the house and surroundings), the system of crop rotation that was implemented, the condition and purity of the farm crops, the variety of livestock that the farmer owned as well as the type of machinery that was used. By 1917, another competition, the Field Crop Competition of Standing Grain, was introduced by

Marvin Heck of Hanna, Alberta, rides on a two-bottom plow using a three-horse team, 1918.
NA-3596-197. COURTESY OF LIBRARIES AND CULTURAL RESOURCES DIGITAL COLLECTIONS, UNIVERSITY OF CALGARY

A Greased Pig

MANY OF THOSE who settled in the Bowville area of Alberta were American, so instead of acknowledging Dominion Day, they decided to continue celebrating their national holiday, Independence Day, on July 4. They all gathered each year in Bowville, beginning in 1907, with a variety of races making up the day's events. There were children's races where children ran from one point to another to see who was the fastest. They also took part in sack races where they would put their legs into a burlap or flour bag, hang onto the sides of the bag, and hop along until they reached the finish line. Another race that caused a great deal of excitement among children and adults alike was the hog race. "A greased hog, real nice and slippery with grease was let loose. The first one to catch and hold it was the winner, the prize being the fat hog." For the smaller children, there was a peanut scramble, where peanuts were thrown across a small field and the children had to race to find as many as they could. For adults, there were the horse races where locals would compete against each other to find out who had the fastest horse in the district. The racetrack was a half-mile prairie trail that ran between the Bowville Hall and the cemetery. After a few years, the residents of Bowville decided to forego their American holiday and instead started celebrating Canada's national holiday, Dominion Day on July 1.[20] ●

the Agricultural Society. Judges for these competitions evaluated the wheat and oat fields of the local farmers and allocated points for yield, growth, uniformity and cleanliness (i.e., freedom from weeds, smut and other varieties of grains).

The Carstairs community in Alberta decided to celebrate Dominion Day in 1906. The event took place on the vacant grounds west of the Presbyterian Church in town, where a racetrack had been prepared for the running events. The ladies of the church set up a tent and sold lemonade and ice cream. Over the course of the day, "J.M. Johnston's little running horse, 'Billy Fisher' won first money in the free-for-all race and in the ladies' race."[21] They also had horse bucking events and held a soccer game. The people of Montmartre, Saskatchewan (a community of French immigrants), organized a celebratory day in 1893 with horse races and athletic events. Instead of holding the celebration in town, it was held outside of town, where a large slough with a sandy bottom had dried up for the summer. The events progressed smoothly, but there was one incident that people remembered for years afterward. As told by Dan Kennedy:

> Jim Smith, a Scotchman, was there with his bagpipe to liven things up for the occasion. He was the chief attraction. People crowded around him to listen to his lively music. When the horse race started, one of the horses broke away and ran amok among the spectators. He knocked down the poor Scotchman, head over heels, tumbling in one direction with the bagpipe tumbling the other way. The pipe was still emitting a mournful dying note, even though it was parted from its player.[22]

A Scottish bagpiper in 1915. NA-3596-33. COURTESY OF LIBRARIES AND CULTURAL RESOURCES DIGITAL COLLECTIONS, UNIVERSITY OF CALGARY

The residents of Carmangay, Alberta, remembered an incident that occurred while they were celebrating their Stampede in 1909. Up to that time, stampede events were quite common in the area as it was ranch country, where big summer roundups occurred annually. On this particular date, a bucking contest was held on the main street of the town.

> Bert Talbot, a local resident, came to town leading a horse called Badger [a bucking bronco who was blindfolded]. A cowboy by the name of Ed Williams from Havre, Montana, agreed to ride the horse for a collection.[23] When the rider mounted, and the blindfold was removed, Badger went into action. He bucked down the street right into the side of a buggy, tipping it over. Fortunately, the two lady occupants were not injured. Williams successfully stayed on the horse and collected the money.[24]

Flossie Boice of Elnora, Alberta, recalled a memorable event that occurred in 1910 on one of their sports days.[25] She said that homesteaders had a lot of work to do on their farms, but from time to time they took a day off to have some fun. A day of horse racing in the summer was always something to look forward to. These races were set up as professionally as possible, with jockeys who would ride the horses. However, as Flossie mentioned, sometimes the horses had a mind of their own.

> Frank [her father] was quite a horseman and raised quite a few horses. He enjoyed horse trading, and horse racing was a favorite sport. Krokane, Flying Dutchman, Flaxie, and Prince were some of his race horses. Some of the jockeys of that time were Marian Wyndham, Goldie Lauder, and Babe Woods ... [On racing day], Frank and [his friend] Albert Dye led two of the horses (Krokane and the Dutchman) around the track so that they could become familiar with it before they raced. Frank stopped to talk to a friend, and dropped the halter and shank so the horse could graze. Albert came along with the other horse and he too dropped the halter and shank. At this point, Krokane and the Dutchman couldn't miss a chance for a race so away they ran. The gate was

Bloomers and Button-hole Shoes

IN ORDER TO take part in sports, girls sometimes exchanged their long skirts for bloomers, baggy pants that were gathered around their waist and extended below their knees. Many of the ladies also wore above-the-ankle-length shoes that buttoned instead of lacing up. They had to use an old-fashioned button hook to get the button into the buttonhole. The shoes had to fit snugly so that they would not sprain their ankles. While it took some time to get their shoes on, they had a pleasing appearance as the shoes made their feet look dainty. Occasionally the women's shoes went higher up their leg, sometimes reaching half-way to their knees. As one homesteader exclaimed, "That must have taken some work to button up and unbutton!"[26] •

open, leading to the road and the open prairie beyond. A gentleman with an early vintage car, told Frank to jump in and they would catch the horses. Frank sat on the hood of the car, with his lariat, but roads weren't built for cars at that time, so the horses ran merrily away. The horses never did return to the racetrack that day.

According to Laura Matz, the homesteaders of the Prince Albert district of Saskatchewan got together each summer to try out their athletic skills.[27] Various sports were organized for the day's events, including footraces, sack races and tug-of-war. A pig was greased up for the pig-catching contest, and a fast-running rooster was found for the rooster-catching contest. "Sometimes a daring young lad would perch loftily on the back of a bucking bronco and he was forced to bite the dust, no doubt in order to show off for the benefit of some young lady he had met."

The annual event in Rimbey, Alberta, Celebration Day commemorating Dominion Day, was considered the beginning of the

The women of Beaverlodge, Alberta, play a game of tug-of-war, with the men cheering them on, 1915. NB-15-38. COURTESY OF LIBRARIES AND CULTURAL RESOURCES DIGITAL COLLECTIONS, UNIVERSITY OF CALGARY

horse racing season. Many family-related events took place, with prize money being raised through a collection.

> There were children's races, also foot races for the ladies as well as the men, and each event usually brought out a large number of contestants. Purses for the horse races were usually $10 for the first place, and five for the second. The purse for the pony race was usually $8.00 divided by $5 and $3. In the footraces, the money was $2 and $1 for the adults and 50 cents and 25 cents for the children. In the summer of 1913, the first match race of any importance in the Rimbey district occurred. This was between Perry Bunch with his stallion Buck Winks and Joe Montgomery with Sportsman. The half mile heat took place southeast of Rimbey. The first heat was won quite easily by Sportsman, who was also leading by a good margin in the second heat, but who bolted ... This heat was awarded to Buck Winks. Sportsman seemed to injure himself when he flew the track and ran a very dull race the third heat, being easily outdistanced by Buck Winks, so the race and the $100 side money was awarded to Perry Bunch.[28]

Hot Arguments

GIVEN THAT HORSES were used so often by the homesteaders and townfolk, whether they were working with horses on the farm, travelling from one place to another, riding on horseback or driving a team with a buggy, it was not uncommon for hot arguments to arise as to who owned the fastest horse in the district. These arguments usually ended up with a bet and a race for as much money as the contestants or onlookers could afford. Usually bets ranged from one dollar to twenty-five dollars, though it was not unheard of for higher bets to be placed. •

Horse races could occur at any time of the year. In this photograph, dated 1906, the members of the Elbow River community in Alberta decided to have a horse race on ice. *L–R:* J. Twobey with horse Six Bits; W.M. Parslow with horse Clearwater; J. Hamilton with horse Minnie; I.G. Ruttle with horse Queenie Wildmont; H.B. Sommerville with horse The Kid; and W. Stewart with horse Babe. NB-15-38. COURTESY OF LIBRARIES AND CULTURAL RESOURCES DIGITAL COLLECTIONS, UNIVERSITY OF CALGARY

Some communities were more involved with ox races rather than horse races. As many people came to realize, oxen possessed a hidden talent in that they could move far faster than expected. When working, oxen typically set a speed of a slow walk, but when motivated by the sound of mosquitoes or the bite of a heel fly, bee or wasp, or when they got too hot, they would race for the nearest slough. As historian Grant MacEwan exclaimed, they would change "into galloping fiends ... Adding to the reputation for cussedness and unpredictability, the normally placid oxen would occasionally stage a runaway. Winnipeg papers in 1874 made record of a runaway ox team which hit some guy ropes and wrecked some property, including the Customs House flagpole."[29] MacEwan pointed out another example of excessive speed when a pair of oxen broke the law by exceeding the speed limit on a local bridge. They ran instead of walked, and their owner was charged a dollar in fines and costs.

One ox became famous across the prairies for his racing abilities. In 1893, a large ox, a cross between a highland bull and a Mexican Longhorn cow,

> was raised on the range near Walsh, Saskatchewan and it was there that George Nugent, a manager of the local CPR saw him. Strange as it seemed, the steer's usual gate was a trot and when he was being pursued, a cowboy and a horse had to travel at a fast gallop to overtake him ... Named Evader, the ox was raced in Medicine Hat and on nearby tracks where he humiliated some of the most highly rated trotting horses ... He was picturesque, with longhorns, a long tail, and an unfriendly face. The ox seemed to enjoy a race, and like a good horse, he knew how to keep a bit of extra speed for the homestretch.[30]

When ox races were part of the country fair's activities, the prizes for oxen were larger than those for horses. At Saskatoon's annual fair in 1886, a prize of one dollar was offered for the best trotting ox hitched to a buckboard, while another prize was offered for the best walking team. In another race, a homesteader named Stanley King entered his oxen team to compete against horse teams. "The horsemen protested the entry of oxen, contending that horses had exclusive claim to the term 'team' and two oxen could be nothing more than a pair or a yoke. The executive committee of the fair was called to adjudicate and ruled that two oxen constituted a legitimate team and surprisingly, King's oxen won the first prize."[31]

Typically, winning first, second or third prize for the fastest ox did not appeal to most homesteaders. Rather, competition surrounded the issue of weight. Regardless of quality, the weight of an ox is its most important feature, and when there was a dispute, the animal's weight could be confirmed by using the grain elevator scales. Arguments would then be settled by the elevator agent. Over time, a number of oxen of tremendous weight were discovered across the prairies. In 1886, at the Manitoba Provincial Exhibition in Saint Boniface, an older ox named Big Band weighed in at 2,650 pounds.[32] An ox from Pibroch, Alberta, who was only five years old, weighed in at 3,170 pounds. His weight was so impressive that he was sent to the exhibition at Brandon, Manitoba, where people paid 25 cents each to view him. He was also put on display at the Calgary and Edmonton exhibitions, as well as the British Empire Exhibition in Wembley, England, in 1924. By this time, a few years had passed and he weighed over 4,000 pounds. He was a "sensation of the cattle world" and was sold for $350, a staggering amount of money at the time.[33]

Dancing the Night Away

Dancing was a favourite pastime for many homesteaders. When dances were advertised, or when news of a dance was spread by word of mouth, people would come from miles around to attend. A dance promised a night of revelry, filled with good times, laughter and music until the wee hours of the morning. Neighbours became reacquainted, conversation was lively, everyone was dressed in their best clothes and thoughts of farm work were temporarily put aside.

According to Bertha Shaw Myer, her community of Gainsborough, Saskatchewan, held dances in their one-room schoolhouse, as it was the only building in town with a large open space.[1] The music was supplied by local violinists. She remembered how the excitement rose among her family members as plans were made to attend this event. They lived miles from the schoolhouse, and she described how everyone piled into the sleigh that was being pulled by their horses. The sleigh had been filled with hay so everyone would be able to sit comfortably as they travelled to the dance. There were also plenty of horse blankets and buffalo robes that they covered themselves with for protection from the subzero weather. Bertha mentioned how the dance usually lasted all night, with a break at midnight when coffee, tea, sandwiches and desserts were set out on a table for everyone to enjoy. When the small children and babies fell asleep during the evening's entertainment, they were put to bed with blankets on top of the school desks alongside the wall.

Patrick O'Toole remembered how thrilled and happy people were when they heard that a dance was being organized in town.[2] Plans were made for travelling, and each person ensured that they wore their best clothes and cleaned up to get rid of the dirt and smells of the farmyard. In one of his poems, "A Story in Rhyme," Patrick detailed the preparations each person went through in order to look their best. His neighbour, Mrs. Fred, put curling pins in her hair and gave her husband a haircut. Another neighbour, Mr. McKreary, planned on wearing his best Sunday "going-to-church" shirt, but found it in a corner, all dirty and wadded up in a crumpled ball. In desperation, he tried to wash it at the last minute and even boiled it, but to his great consternation, he couldn't get it back to its original white colour. Another acquaintance hurriedly tried to patch up a pair of pants where some mice had chewed some holes. Once everyone was ready and dressed in all their finery, they gathered together and headed off by horse and sleigh to town for an evening of revelry. Excitement rose among the homesteaders the closer they got to town. As Patrick recalled in his poem, they soon saw the ballroom all bright with lights, they could hear a ragtime tune being played and, through the windows, they could see dozens of people all dancing and spinning around the room. "Well," he wrote, "we headed for the ballroom, and joined the dancing lot, whirling around to beat the band in the farmer's old green trot. This was none of your fancy glides, no pussy-footing thing, but a real old rattling rounder, where you hear the rafters ring."

People in the Berwyn district of Alberta also enjoyed their dances, with music supplied by those with musical talent. Two people in the community knew how to play the violin, while another could play the guitar. From time to time, someone would bring a harmonica and play a song or two. Eventually Charlie Klenk and his son took on the job of playing music all night long until 4:00 or 5:00 AM. Given their efforts, a collection was taken up for these two players, which typically amounted to $1.50—a lot of money at that time.[3]

Harry Bell, a homesteader from the Gladmar district of Alberta, remembered the dances that were held in his area.[4] Albi Barnes, a local man who knew how to play the violin, usually supplied the music. The dances were so popular that they always filled the schoolhouse. Nobody wanted to miss out on the evening's events, and it was a great disappointment if they did. One time, Harry says, a notice was placed on the coal mine dump (a local gathering spot for those who collected coal to use in their stoves) two days in advance of the dance. At this particular dance, people noticed that two young women from the community, who usually attended dances, were not there. It was determined that the two women

White Handkerchiefs

IN THE WASKATENAU district of Alberta, an open-air dance in the evening was sometimes held on a platform that had been built, as dancers could dance more easily on wooden boards rather than on prairie dirt. Waltzes, quadrilles and square dances were ably called. The whole family went to the dance, and a girl was lucky if she didn't wear out her shoes by dancing all night. In the early years, when there was a shortage of women in the district, "some of the men would tie white handkerchiefs on their arms and take the place of the missing women." This ensured that everyone could have a partner and no one would be a wallflower. A good time was had by all![5] ●

Sometimes platforms were built, as people could dance more easily on the wooden boards than in the dirt. In this photograph from 1921, a group of people from Oakburn, Manitoba, are dancing on a platform while two musicians are sitting on a bench. One musician is playing a violin while the other is playing a dulcimer (a stringed instrument). NA-2394-1. COURTESY OF LIBRARIES AND CULTURAL RESOURCES DIGITAL COLLECTIONS, UNIVERSITY OF CALGARY

had likely not seen the notice, so a couple of people went to their home, roused them out of bed at 10:30 PM and brought them to the dance. Once they were there, Harry says, everyone was happy.

Residents of Alberta's Stony Plain district recalled the dances in their vicinity that were held on Friday nights and tended to attract the younger people. In particular, they gave young men an opportunity to ask young women to accompany them to the dance with their horses and cutters. A highlight of the evening was when the "ladies of the neighborhood brought sandwiches, cakes and cookies for the midnight lunch. Coffee was usually boiled in a wash boiler atop the school stove or brought from home in a cream can."[6] Mrs. W.T. Billing highlighted how exciting the local dances could be in Regina, Saskatchewan.[7] As she said,

> Dances were often held in the winter when there was little to be done on the farms. The dances usually were very jolly. They were [usually] held in a barn. Whole families arrived in sleighs ... Warmth came from a huge stove at one end. Close to it stood the fiddler and the caller. The dance always started out with a rollicking square dance, the caller's voice ringing out, "Take yer partner, swing her round, over and under, away yer go," and so on. They ended with a waltz to the tune of "Home Sweet Home." Sometimes dancers danced to a song, thus relieving the caller. The favourites were "By the Banks of Saskatchewan" and "The Moon Shines Bright on Red Wing Sighing." [One time], a new barn was built and its opening celebrated with a dance. The roof was not finished, so snow fell on the dancers. The men wore their sheep skin coats and boots and the women the warmest clothes they possessed, and all clustered around the stove between dances.

Julia Asher offered her account of the dances in her district of Alberta.[8] When she attended her first dance as a young girl, she remembered that it was less than successful because the musicians never showed up. It was a particularly cold winter evening, and luckily for the crowd, one person had brought their mouth organ with them, while her uncle happened to have his accordion in the sleigh. The two both played a few tunes, and people were able to dance. Julia said that she danced her first four dances that evening. The next time she went to a dance, it was for New Year's and she was asked to dance fourteen times. However, the dance she remembered most of all was a Valentine's Day dance, which was held at a stopping place on Mosquito Creek. She had a fifteen-mile trip to get there, but she said many people travelled a lot farther than her family, some coming from over fifty miles away. This dance ended up being a "most successful affair," where she was able to dance over twenty-six times. She mentioned that there were no wallflowers among the girls as there were so few ladies compared to the larger number of young men. "The dances were mostly quadrilles, with the changes called off by someone with a good strong voice. An occasional polka or schottische was thrown in and, once in a while, a waltz, but most of those present preferred the quadrilles, which, toward morning, became more like boisterous games set to music than real dancing." Dances usually began at 8:00 PM and lasted until daylight. As Julia recalled, the dances were enjoyable, but not frequently indulged in as everyone was exhausted for days afterward.

Sue Harrigan remembered the dances in her community.[9] She did not elaborate on how many dances she was able to dance, but she remembered how fun the event was for everyone, regardless of ethnicity. As she said,

> We heard that there was going to be dance in the school (Kingsview district). We all went to it, there wasn't much else to do, so young, old, and the in-between, or as they say from one to ninety years went there. You would think that there weren't any girls or very few until you went to a dance and then you would find some very nice-looking young people. Every nationality under the sun was represented and mixed and had a good time. Each household took either cake or sandwiches, and each man put a quarter on the plate to pay the musicians. There was no drinking and the dance was carried on in an orderly manner and with good taste. The music was extremely good, violin, organ and banjo. There proved to be considerable talent in that crowd. Two men with lovely voices sang. They were just a nice sociable crowd of people that wanted to better themselves in a new country. If a storm came up, we didn't go home until daylight.

Stealing His Gal

WHILE MOST PEOPLE had a wonderful time at the local dances, sometimes their good times could go awry, particularly if jealousy was involved.

> On one memorable occasion, a huge crowd was enjoying a dance in Rimbey's first dance hall, which was built by Woos and Peabody. In fact, the crowd was so large that a numbering system was adopted. Everyone was given a number, and the odds and the evens took turns standing outside while the other half danced. The orchestra, composed of Clarence Platt as organist and Mike Donovon, Bert Saunder and Al Preston as fiddlers, was in the midst of a hoedown, with eleven sets on the floor. Suddenly, the merriment was interrupted by Fred Hayes, described as a wild and wooly hombre from way out west. Stamping and shouting and brandishing a .30-.30 rifle, he demanded revenge on the guy who had stolen his gal. He really broke up that square dance. Those forty-four people were said to have cleared the floor in mighty short order. Hayes virtually had the floor to himself. How he did it isn't clear, but he got his girl back—and later married her.[10] ●

Herman Collingwood of Qu'Appelle, Saskatchewan, offered his unique perspective regarding the dances that were held in his community.[11] He said that as soon as the homesteaders in his area found out that he could play the fiddle, he became very popular. Sometimes this popularity was not something that Herman desired. As he reminisced:

> The new settlers found out that I had a fiddle . . . I have often thought that the fiddle was the greatest blessing to come in with the settlers. It was all you needed and you had yourself

> a ball. However, I always hated the fiddle since Dad made me practice every day for three years, and now I bet I travelled a thousand miles and played in every little schoolhouse for a hundred miles around, for the next twenty years, including 25 towns. The first three years, there were no towns. I and my brother would be sitting in our shack on a cold night and we would hear a racket and I would say, "Damn!" and brother would laugh. [And then I would hear a holler], "Bring out the fiddle!" I'd climb into a sleigh load of people and I was stuck for the night. I never asked where we were going but it would be some house with a room big enough to dance in. Having taken music lessons, I could play any dance you ever heard of, but we had one standing rule—every third dance was a square dance. And if you want to see one wild dance, just watch one of these, in the early days. Even the ground shook. I soon switched to steel strings on the fiddle as no gut string could make enough racket to be heard over that gang. Many times, we would travel ten or twelve miles behind a team of broncos to find a house big enough to dance in. When the little schoolhouses started to go up, it was worse. I'd get word to be at some place and another team would be there to meet me and we'd go another eight or ten miles and step into a school full of happy folks and we were off for the night, and they wouldn't quit until daylight. I think that they only thing that kept me going was the home brew. Just about the time I was falling asleep someone at the door would crook his finger and I would drop the fiddle and head for the door. Of course, everyone knew what it meant but they weren't squeamish in those days. Outside, in the snow-bank, was a jug. If you haven't drunk home brew dug out of snowbank, try it sometime. It goes down like milk but about ten minutes later, you would swear you swallowed the stove.

Even though Herman's story relates to his life as a reluctant musician, it's interesting to note that he felt a responsibility to help entertain the community. In fact, even though it seems he didn't like playing the fiddle, he had some pride in playing the instrument for others. As he said, "I got myself a name for being reliable and never letting a crowd down."

According to John Fetsch, he and his companions often drove twenty-five or thirty miles in order to go to a dance.[12] When it was winter, they heated rocks and put them under the covers in the sleigh. However, not everyone stayed warm. One man's feet got so cold, he kept kicking the sleigh box, like this one from 1907, to keep his circulation going. When they got home, they discovered that he had been kicking a violin case and had broken it to bits. PA-2650-15. COURTESY OF LIBRARIES AND CULTURAL RESOURCES DIGITAL COLLECTIONS, UNIVERSITY OF CALGARY

Patrick O'Toole, who was mentioned earlier, also reminisced about the wonderful times he had when he attended local dances as a young single man in Vegreville, Alberta.[13] He was so fond of those good times dancing with the Ukrainian girls from the area that he once again put down his thoughts in poetry. His verses highlighted their winsome smiles, their "lovely dark brown eyes," their raven black hair, their pearl-white teeth and their blithe, jovial air of youth. He said that even though he had travelled through Britain, France and Spain and met Europe's fanciest belles, no girls could compare to the Ukrainian girls of Vegreville.

Over time, as communities grew larger with a greater population, more amenities became available. No longer did people rely on the local schoolhouses for their dances as halls were built for social activities. For instance, a hall was built in 1907 in Bowville, Alberta, financed by a man named A.T. Root. "The hall was made available to anyone desiring to make use of its facilities. Concerts, dances, boxing matches, and funerals were held there. Dances were sponsored by a number of individuals. Homemade donuts and coffee were served at the midnight break. Admission charges were $0.50 a couple. Numerous wedding dances were held through the years, the hall being filled to capacity."[14]

Annie Norris from the Calahoo district in Alberta remembered the good times that she and others had in their community's dance hall.[15] The music was supplied by the Calahoo brothers, John, Jimmy and Dick. All three played their violins, accompanied by the postmistress, Mrs. McDonald, who would play either the organ or the piano. Admission to the hall was 25 cents for men, while the women were asked to bring a cake. Sometimes, instead of collecting money at the door, a hat was passed around to everyone who attended, and this collection of money was given to the musicians. Meat sandwiches were brought by the social club that sponsored the dance and were served at the midnight lunch, along with the cakes. While people were taking a break and eating their lunch, a few step dancers would take to the floor and entertain the crowd. In terms of the types of dances that were popular, very few people could resist dancing to a polka or a schottische, but Annie believed the square dances were everyone's favourite. The crowd also liked dancing to waltzes, the one-step and two-step, and the foxtrot, with the least favourite being the French minuet. The minuet was difficult to dance to, and few attempted it. Dances lasted until 3:00 or 4:00 in the morning, when everyone would head for home, exhausted but happy.

Taking the Family to the Picnic

Less formal get-togethers occurred during the warmer months of the year. Families and neighbours arranged picnics where they would gather for an afternoon. Whether they met at the local slough, at a special place by a lake or at a homesteader's home, they all looked forward to the event with great excitement and enjoyed the day. They ate the lunch that had been prepared by the womenfolk, chatted with each other, played games and enjoyed each other's company.

Everyone had different places where they would meet for a picnic, whether it was by a river or a stream or in a clearing in a forest. Some even met by the nearby slough. Mabel Hawthorne of Saskatoon, Saskatchewan, said that the slough was the choice spot for picnics in her vicinity.[1] "Everyone and their families would meet beside this nice big slough, and as long as the young fry could find a level piece of ground to play ball on, they were happy. The parents and smaller children just visited beside the water and the women got lunch for everyone. When the mosquitoes got bad, they would make smudges, but if the wind was blowing, they never bothered. It was generally a perfect day for all." Afterward, everyone made their way home to get their chores done. Farm animals needed to be fed and cows needed to be milked. Happy but exhausted children were put to bed.

Instead of meeting at a slough, Archie Althouse of Handel, Saskatchewan, remembered the effort that was needed to create a welcoming picnic spot in his area for all the people who wanted to attend.[2] Given the lack of trees or streams, the young men in his community "got together and built up a shelter with

A group of people from Fort MacLeod, Alberta, wade in the river, cooling off during a hot afternoon of picnicking in 1913. NA-5051-86. COURTESY OF LIBRARIES AND CULTURAL RESOURCES DIGITAL COLLECTIONS, UNIVERSITY OF CALGARY

boughs brought from a ravine." Archie noted that "it made a delightful place to have our picnic lunch." He was also amazed at how many people showed up for the picnic: five women, two girls and sixty-five men attended. He wondered how the news spread, as people came from miles around. Along with the picnic lunch, Archie mentioned that they played a game of baseball and had horse races, foot races and tug-of-wars, which all enjoyed. Everyone pronounced the day an overwhelming success.

Picnics were also held at Manitou Beach in Saskatchewan. To ensure that all of the people who wanted to attend the picnic could get there, everyone who wanted to go gathered at a local farmer's place. Some came with their horses and buggies or wagons and offered rides to those who did not have any kind of transportation. Aaron Biehn said that once everyone was arranged into the buggies and wagons, they travelled to the north side of the lake, where they settled in for their picnic.[3] One buggy-load of young people drove around to the south side of the lake, where a boatman was located. They went to his boathouse and asked him if he could bring his boat over to the north side and take people for rides in his boat. He agreed, and everyone had a fun afternoon relaxing on the lake. As for the horses, they also had a restful afternoon, as they were tied to a tree, their harnesses were taken off and they were fed oats and hay. Then the girls spread a tablecloth on the grass and set out all the lunch items they had prepared. As Biehn stated, "We all sat around and ate our good things. In the evenings, some boys would play ball, while those that could not play ball would have a sing song with the girls. After it started to get dark, we would hitch our horses up and go home tired, but we had lots of fun."

Annie Norris of the Calahoo district of Alberta highlighted how wonderful it was to have a picnic and be able to visit the neighbours after a long spring of seeding and getting the farm work started after the winter.[4] July was her district's picnic month, and everyone looked forward to it with excitement. Men would play tug-of-war, while the children competed in sack races, three-legged races and egg-on-spoon races. The ladies enjoyed chatting with each other and caught up on all the news, while teenagers visited together and carved their initials into the tree trunks. Everyone brought food with them—sandwiches, cakes, cookies and pies that would be shared amongst the group when they all sat down for a bite to eat. Real lemonade had been made by the crockful, and for a special treat, ice cream had also been prepared.

> Ten-pound Rogers syrup pails were filled about two-thirds full of a mixture of milk, cream, sugar and vanilla. Most people cut ice out of the Sturgeon River or a nearby lake during the winter and packed the blocks in sawdust in a shed, so when picnic time arrived each family broke a block into pieces in a gunny sack and brought them to the picnic. A mixture of ice and salt was packed about three or four inches deep around the syrup pail [all contained within a larger pail], then the pail was turned back and forth by its handle. Periodically, the lid was removed and the frozen mixture round the inside of the pail was scraped into the center until it was evenly frozen. Clean towels were placed over the lid and more ice and salt packed on top, then the pail was set in the

A group of people from York Lake, Saskatchewan, enjoy a picnic in 1904. NA-2878-64. COURTESY OF LIBRARIES AND CULTURAL RESOURCES DIGITAL COLLECTIONS, UNIVERSITY OF CALGARY

> shade to ripen the ice cream. After lunch, huge dishes were served to everyone with extra helpings available. Good! ... After a rest and more talk everything was cleared away and home to chores and bed we went.

Rose Feist, whose parents homesteaded in the Clyde district of Alberta, remembered how her father prepared for a community picnic on his homestead.[5] To make sure everyone had a good time, he put a lot of effort into making the picnic area as hospitable as possible. She recalled that her father cleared a large area in the yard for games like cricket for the adults and races for the children. He put basketball hoops on two tall spruce trees the right distance apart so people could play basketball. He also cut off tree limbs that could get in the way of a game. He sawed wood and built tables where lunch and drinks could be served, and made benches for sitting. On the day of the event, farmers and their families came from miles around. Lunch was prepared, and Rose's mother made ice cream, which was a real treat for everyone.

An Odd Refreshment

ONE BACHELOR DECIDED to have a community picnic on his homestead. He invited everyone for miles around. For lunch they had sandwiches and tea. One of the ladies remarked that the tea had a "rather peculiar flavour." Some of the men looked in the bachelor's well and noticed that a number of gophers had fallen in and drowned. It was not mentioned whether this bachelor ever offered to have another community picnic at his place.[6] •

Instead of inviting the community for a picnic, sometimes the gathering was just for close family members. They would congregate at a local picnic spot or spend the day at their aunt or uncle's, grandparents' or parents' homestead. Samuel Jackson of Kinistino, Saskatchewan, told how his family would have a family picnic, and his two sisters and a brother, who all homesteaded in the vicinity, would be invited for the day.[7] While the usual games were held for the adults and children, Samuel reminisced about one picnic where a neighbour had also been invited. This neighbour rode over on his horse. Samuel said, "I well remember my dad betting that he could run a half mile [in one direction] and then walk backwards to the starting point before his neighbour could on the horse. Needless to say, the horse beat him the half mile going ahead, but he never did get back again, even with Dad just backing along leisurely."

For many homesteaders, picnics were enjoyable fun-filled days. Claude Hellekson of Hattonford, Alberta, said that his whole family attended community picnics at Beta Lake and looked forward to them.[8] However, one time they returned home and were

A Funeral, a Rodeo, a Picnic, a Dance, a Fist Fight and a Roundup

WHILE THE COURSE of a homesteader's day was fairly routine, sometimes a series of events occurred that were well worth remembering. Aubrey "Jack" Davies and others in the community of Huxley, Alberta, had a very eventful day that began with a funeral (the first one in the district), included a picnic and ended with a roundup.[9]

> A Scotsman named McKay was a wild Highlander, as wild as a crane, and crazy as a coot. He had brought his mother-in-law out with him [to homestead] and the old lady died. All the settlers decided to go to this social event . . . The hearse was a wagon, the coffin was loaded on, and the mourners all rode horseback, seven women and a group of men. They had followed the hearse to the church at Pine Lake but not without some excitement. Just south of the church, one of the ladies decided it was improper to ride a horse into the churchyard, so they all dismounted, except McKay, and proceeded on foot. One of them thought it would be fitting to sing a hymn and she started off in a high-pitched soprano. It was too much for the wild Scotsman's bronco. He began to buck and gave everyone the opportunity to see a wonderful display of horsemanship. It was a beautiful June day and after the lady was laid to rest, it seemed a shame to waste the day, so they all decided to have a picnic. Everyone was famished so they invaded Spencer Wyndham's log store at Sandy Cove. They took his whole stock of crackers, cheese crackers, and canned tomatoes to feed the crowd. Manly Downing, a rancher, was there with some of his riders. One of them was a Mexican who never rode without his banjo. After lunch, he struck up a lively tune and the group started dancing on the soft green grass. All went merrily along until two men claimed the same partner. A fist fight developed and everyone sat down to watch the best man win. By now the day was getting on, so they thought it was time to go

home but the fun wasn't over yet. Somebody, by accident or design, had left the corral gate open and half the saddle horses were missing. "So," said Jack, "it was a marvelous day. It began with a funeral. They'd had a rodeo, a picnic, a dance, a fist fight, and ended up with a round up. Who could possibly ask for more?" ●

startled to find that the front door of their home was wide open. Not knowing what had happened, or what they might find in the house, they approached the door cautiously. His mother was the first who looked in, and she "nearly passed out, just moaning, 'My God!'" It turned out that the cows had been in there all day. As Claude said,

> You can imagine what the inside of the house looked like—loose cow manure all over the dirt floor, some even on the walls, the table upset, 100 pounds of flour and oatmeal scattered all over. The cows had eaten a box of Royal Crown laundry soap, which thinned down the manure even more. Some mess to clean up! It seemed as though the cows had enjoyed their picnic as much, or more, than we had. Dad had to hitch up the team the next morning and make the long trip to McLeod Valley with the wagon to replenish all of their groceries.

Shopowners, Strong Men, Justice-Keepers and Criminals

For some homesteaders, the notable people in their district were the ones who helped build up their local town with small businesses. Others pointed to the interesting characters who resided in the community, and some were impressed by the unique skill sets various people had acquired. Still others identified those who had a belief in justice and enforced the law, while some remembered the criminals who passed through the area and how they were dealt with. People who had a positive influence on the community, especially those who had a caring and nurturing personality, were also noted with fondness.

Homesteaders were excited by the idea of progress. For those homesteaders who registered for land in the early years, amenities were few and far between. They had to travel many miles in order to purchase food items and dry goods, agricultural tools and farm equipment, as well as the horses, oxen and chickens that were needed on the farms. Personal services such as banks, barbershops, drugstores, dentists and doctors were also rarities across the prairies until population increased and towns began to develop.

Given this reality, it was not a surprise to find that many homesteaders remembered the rise of their local towns. In fact, they could not only recall the first businesses to set up shop and the people who owned them, but they remembered how stores and services were built one by one until they finally had a full-service community that offered a full range of amenities. For instance, people of Carmangay, Alberta, recalled the building of the barbershop, jewellery store, hotel, Chinese restaurant, pool hall, hardware store, implement shop, butcher shop, laundry shop, clothing store, bank, drugstore, grocery store, lumberyard, and real estate and insurance companies. They also recalled when the Mounted Police station and jail were built, and the first men who manned them—Constable Frere and Sgt. A.S. Cooper.[1]

Those who lived in the Carnduff district of Saskatchewan recounted the first arrivals in their area by name. There was James B. Preston and his brother Andrew Preston, John Preston and his son Dan, who all arrived early in 1882. William Barker, Robert Barker, Jim Barker, William Rowen and John and Richard Carnduff followed soon after. In the fall, the women arrived, with Mrs. Andrew Preston noted as the first white woman in the district. In 1884, the Prestons opened a small store and brought in supplies by pony and buckboard from the closest town, Deloraine. Residents also remembered the building of their first stopping house, run by John Carnduff (who was also the first postmaster); the first missionary, Mr. Hay, a Presbyterian; and the first school (which also served as a log granary during harvest), along with the first teacher, Mr. T.R. Preston (who eventually became a local storekeeper).[2]

Those from Busby, Alberta, recalled the first homesteaders who settled in their area in the early 1900s (the Pickerings, Owens, Colinses, Lauries, Grafs and Shovellers). They came in with oxen, horses and mules. Many came by wagon while others came alone on foot. Some travelled north from Montana, others came from England and still others migrated from Ontario. Once they had built their log homes and started raising children (with the Shovellers having the first baby in the community in 1901—a girl), the residents of Busby turned to building a log schoolhouse in 1905. This schoolhouse served double duty as a place of learning for their children and also the community's entertainment venue for concerts and dances. In the same year, James McConaghy, a blacksmith, came to Busby with his wife, Mabel, who was a trained nurse. These two new residents became valuable members of the community, as did Mrs. May, a talented pianist, who arrived with her piano in tow. In 1906, two homesteaders named Hough and Graf purchased a horse-powered threshing machine, the first threshing machine in the area! Local homesteaders vividly remembered working with the new threshing machine, the long, arduous hours that were involved, and eventually the exciting transition to using a steam engine instead of horses for power.[3]

Mercantiles were important to the local community and were often one of the first buildings to be constructed. They offered a variety of essential provisions including hardware and clothing as well as dry and canned goods. This photo is dated 1914. AUTHOR'S COLLECTION

The people of Sheho, Saskatchewan, remembered the first house that was built (a two-storey stone structure that was eventually transformed into their first hotel), the first railway station and station agent, the building of a mercantile and post office, the first Mounted Policeman to live in town, and the first church to be built. They also mentioned the first doctor who resided in town (he had come out from Ontario), and the first bank to be built (the Northern Crown Bank), as well as the election of their first town council.[4]

Lena May Purdy recalled the increasing community spirit in Condie, Saskatchewan, when all the farmers worked together to build their first grain elevator.[5]

> Sometime about 1896, the farmers of the Condie neighborhood formed a company and during the summer of 1897 they built a grain elevator at Condie. This was ready for the harvest that year. I'm not sure how it was financed. I believe a good deal of negotiation with the railroad was necessary before a

siding was built to serve the elevator. This was probably one of the earliest farmer-owned elevators in the territory.

Residents also remembered the country of origin of many of the first families to homestead in their district. For instance, in the Ponoka area of Alberta, a number of people had travelled north from the American states of Minnesota, Nebraska, Iowa, Illinois, North Dakota, South Dakota and Wisconsin, while others had come from eastern Canada. A smaller number emigrated from overseas. Within two years, in 1900, 309 more people, mostly Americans, had decided to homestead in the area, bringing with them thirty carloads of belongings. In no time at all, Ponoka "grew from a whistle-stop into a settlement, from a settlement into a village, and from a village into a thriving energetic town."[6] In southern Saskatchewan, a colony of Hungarians moved into the Esterhazy area, while homesteaders with a British background settled in Yorkton. Germans migrated into the Langenburg, Neudorf and Lemberg districts, while Doukhobors settled around Verigin, and Icelanders settled in Thingvalla, Foam Lake, Holar, Walhalla and Kristnes. Kelvingrove was primarily Scottish, while Edmore and an area east of Sheho were predominantly settled by those of Polish and Ukrainian origin.[7]

Other homesteaders focused on their own accomplishments. Albert Edward Elderton, for example, stated that he was "the first and probably the only one to walk all the way to Swift Current from his homestead, one day somewhere about 1912 and all the way back the next day. About 90 miles. I had urgent business to attend to in Swift Current and having no horses of my own, I started out walking, fully expecting to meet someone driving in. I didn't! I made it, but oh boy, was I ever a tired boy!"[8] Joseph Bonas and his family mentioned that in 1904 they were the first brick manufacturers in Muenster, Saskatchewan, as well as the first contractors and builders,[9] while Lena Bacon indicated that she was the first professional nurse in Girvin, Saskatchewan.[10] She worked from 1904 to 1908 and "cared for thirty-four obstetrical cases without a doctor. Also, one case of pneumonia. One case of typhoid." She also set a dislocated shoulder for a man who worked with a threshing crew.

Other homesteaders were so impressed by the unique abilities of neighbours that they always remembered these people and their skills. Lila Pope of Borden, Saskatchewan, for example,

Chinese Residents

AS MANY SMALL towns grew in size, enterprising individuals who were interested in investing in the communities set up Chinese restaurants and laundry businesses, while others purchased or built hotels. For instance, in Alliance, Alberta, in 1916, the first person of Chinese descent in the area, Wong Jim, purchased and operated a café. Harry Lee, who arrived in 1917, opened a laundry to serve the clothes-washing needs of the community, while M.R. Lee, Mah Him and Hop Hing purchased the town's hotel, renamed it the Alberta Hotel and operated it until it burned down in 1922.[11] Similarly, in Ponoka, Alberta, the Mah Chung Laundry was established in 1906. Not only did this business offer to wash and iron clothes, but it also had a delivery service, all for just 25 cents per load. James Mah Poy opened the first Chinese restaurant in town in 1918, called it the Union Café and managed it for decades.[12] ●

◄ The Union Café in Ponoka, Alberta, 1939. NA-5683-16. COURTESY OF LIBRARIES AND CULTURAL RESOURCES DIGITAL COLLECTIONS, UNIVERSITY OF CALGARY

◄ Glen, Song and James Mah Poy stand inside the Union Café in Ponoka, Alberta, 1940. NA-5683-17. COURTESY OF LIBRARIES AND CULTURAL RESOURCES DIGITAL COLLECTIONS, UNIVERSITY OF CALGARY

recalled a family of three brothers who lived in the vicinity.[13] She said that they were unusually tall and strong and "could lift things easily that other men couldn't." She also remembered another man, a Russian named Big John, who "could readily lift a barrel of water into a wagon at threshing time." That would be about 160 pounds. Mary Kajewski told a story about how her husband had to prove that he was the strongest man in the Cypress Hills area.[14] As she said, "I was told that my husband and another young man argued as to which one was strongest. It was settled when one picked the other up by the seat of his pants and placed him on the ranch house roof. He then had the reputation as being the strongest man in southern Alberta." Percy Thomson said that in 1905 there was a man by the name of George Findlay, known as "the Moose," who lived in the Cavalier district of Saskatchewan.[15] He had a powerful build and knew how to wrestle even though he had never been formally trained. "A professional wrestler once came to the district and offered $100 to anyone who could throw him. Findlay threw him and won the money." Percy mentioned another powerful man in the Vacon district, an Italian named Vicario, who could do as much work as any other three men. He impressed everyone in the district as he was able to drive and control fourteen oxen all at one time. Harry Martyn also remembered a strong man who lived in his area.[16] His name was John Nyman and he was of Finnish descent. Harry mentioned that John could lift a forty-five-gallon drum and place it in a triple-deckered grain wagon. This was quite a feat given the high sides of the wagon. He went on to say that John could also drink a twenty-six-ounce bottle of booze in one drink, "never taking it away from his mouth." Unfortunately, John did not repeat these feats for too many years as he passed away from tuberculosis when he was only fifty-five.

While strength was an impressive quality to have, other homesteaders remembered neighbours who had other types of skills. Lena May Purdy recalled how Anthony Neville and Robert Kernon Sr., two gentlemen from Balcarres, Saskatchewan, who were both over the age of seventy, would "vie with each other doing gymnastic tricks to the wonder of boys and younger men."[17] Anthony could also perform a few sleight-of-hand tricks and swallow knives or table silver. Lena May said that no one ever found out how he did these tricks.

Monsieur Legal did not have any kind of magical ability, but he became known as the Wolseley district's local minstrel. "On clear days, he could be heard half a mile away. Whenever he made his periodic trips to Wolseley for supplies, everybody within hearing distance knew of his whereabouts."[18] Monsieur Legal was also known for how his ox carried his supplies. Rather than taking a wagon or riding on the ox, he would walk alongside the animal to Wolseley, a trek of twenty miles one way. Once he picked up his supplies in Wolseley, he bundled them all together with string and then secured them between the ox's horns. Then he led the ox home.

Another fellow who became well known among all the homesteaders in his community was John Bartlovich, nicknamed "Jumping Jonnie." Little was known of John's past history, but many suspected that he came to Canada from Czechoslovakia in a search for the land of milk and honey. He decided to

> set down his roots in the Sandhills area of the Bowden district where he made his home for a number of years in a very poor shack indeed. He worked for farmers in the Hillcrest and Red Lodge areas, stooking and looking after livestock for them. He did no one any harm ... and he was honest. John was a happy go lucky sort. The Jumping Johnny name was affixed to him when his neighbors started noticing one of his peculiarities in walking. John usually walked wherever he went and was reasonably fast paced. Swinging his way to town he would be whistling or singing to himself, probably dreaming about the one or two glasses of beer he allowed himself to have, and then at periodic intervals, he would jump high in the air. Whether the jump was from sheer exuberance or a sudden twist of pain no one ever found out.[19]

Lila Pope wrote about an interesting character in her memoirs.[20] He was known as a remittance man—that is, he was a recent immigrant from England, who was paid a regular stipend by his family to ensure that he would not return home. His return would have been an embarrassment to the family, as it would mean that he had not succeeded in his venture to the Canadian west. Those who came in contact with him and offered him a meal found him to be a "prodigious eater," and he would often mix his food together before he ate it. They also found him to be somewhat irritating and condescending. As Lila said, his hobby was words. He always "used them in odd meanings to confound others." For example, if he came across a woman who was wringing out her clothes while she was doing her wash, he would exclaim, "Oh, Mrs., I see that you are expressing the moisture from the cloth."

Lena May Purdy recalled a schoolteacher named Mr. Ward who had a significant impact on her community.[21] He was hired by the local school board in the early 1900s, and when he arrived, residents soon learned that he was a music enthusiast. Given the community's eagerness for music, everyone became immediately enchanted with this newcomer. Not only did Mr. Ward teach music in the school, but he also organized a church choir that included the local farmers and their hired men. He was a very hard-working, community-minded individual and everyone appreciated his special skill of bringing people together.

In a similar vein, Mrs. Tom Guy of Ogema, Saskatchewan, was highly respected in the community given her kind nature, friendliness and generosity. As homesteader Murdock Matheson wrote:

> Of all the names I have written and of the others that could be written, no name stands out in the hearts and memories of the early residents of Ogema as that of Mrs. Tom Guy. I must speak of her in particular. Tom and Mrs. Guy and their family (three children) came to Ogema among the very first families. They came from Maxwell, some ten miles east of Flesherton, Ontario. They came, as others had come, and were coming to make a fresh start in the west and also for the sake of change and adventure. Mrs. Guy was, I judge, in her early forties. She was an extraordinary woman. She became known in Ogema immediately for her kindliness, hospitality, and readiness to be of help to anybody in need. She kept a boarding table at her house and men of every description were to be found among her guests. The meals she gave were bounteous, nourishing, palatable. Soups, meats, pastries were there in abundance. Even vegetables were there in a new locality where vegetables were hard to obtain. Everything was there on the table, and

guests had only to reach for it. No guest went hungry, and the hungriest guests had more than he could eat. Conversation at table was jolly and lively, but the jolliest and liveliest of all the group was Mrs. Guy herself. She would be in and out from the kitchen to the dining room and from the dining room to the kitchen, but she could take part in the general discussions as she went about. Her voice had a singular vitality, yet it was melodious and sweet, and graciously feminine. Her laughter was contagious, her jocularity a boon to depressed spirits.[22]

In the Ponoka district of Alberta, a number of people were remembered for the kindness that they extended to others as well as for their generosity. Tim Russell, for example, was always full of fun and quick with a joke due to his witty nature. However, his sense of fun was eclipsed by his sense of duty when work needed to be done in the community. His wife was also highly regarded as she always helped whenever and wherever she was needed. Will Cerveny, another member of the community, always welcomed those who stopped by his home. "When boys of the neighbourhood had a few hours to spare, the Cerveny home was always their rendezvous as it was the atmosphere of friendliness and welcome which always prevailed that drew them." Similarly, Dan Morrow welcomed people to his home, where he would regale his visitors with stories and songs. He became well known in the district as he kept a record of all the local happenings. His fondness for his neighbours and community was recognized by all, and he was held in high esteem for his efforts.[23]

Nell Williams highlighted a number of people who resided in her community of Griffin Creek, Alberta.[24] For instance, she mentioned that she had "one neighbor, a bachelor, who was a very nice fellow. Another one was a real likeable fellow but a bit strange." She remembered a nurse named Miss Conlin who lived in the district. A bachelor named Sam Hill, who lived fairly close by, was infatuated with the nurse. One day, the preacher invited her out for a buggy ride. During their ride, the horses became spooked, they bucked, and Miss Conlin was thrown out of the buggy. She broke her leg when she landed. The horses ran away. Sam never did forgive the preacher for Miss Conlin getting hurt. Nell recalled a man by the name of Scotty Grieves. "Whenever there was a gathering, they could always depend on Scotty for a

A Strange Coincidence

CHARLES SARGENT NOTED a peculiarity of the district he lived in, which gave the old-timers a sense of pride.[25] The names of the original homesteaders of Golden Valley (renamed Eyre, Saskatchewan) were such a coincidence that they were authenticated by the original assessment role of the municipality. As Charles stated:

> On the south side were stabled a very fine team of mares (F. Mares), on the west side a lion and lioness (F. Lyons), while on the north was a Bengal tiger (A.H. Tigar). On the east was a hunter (W. Hunter) and next to him if you followed the right (C. Wright) trail, you would land safely in Paradise (Paul Paradise). In the centre to keep order among the humans and wild and domestic animals was the sergeant (C.E. Sargent) and if it became necessary to enforce it, he had only to go a little further to procure a couple of guns (Chas and Alex Gunn). ●

song. The song was always the same, the "Yellow Rose of Texas" even though he was from Scotland." She also mentioned Herb Clark, the community fiddler who played for the dancers, and Mrs. Bill Evans, who accompanied Herb on the guitar. Nell mentioned Art and George Dixon, who owned the first combine harvester in the district, as well as Ed Laverington, who was always smoking O.P.T. (other people's tobacco). Finally, Nell couldn't forget the Lund brothers, who came from Norway and were identical twins. Everyone in the community had a problem telling them apart and never knew which one they were talking to.

Other homesteaders took note of the lawmen who imparted their own brand of justice or the criminals who were passing through the district and causing problems. The residents of Nipawin, Saskatchewan, remembered two men, Ed Price and

Wes McTavish, who both enforced the law with their knuckles. In Nipawin's early years there was no North-West Mounted Police detachment close by, so individuals like Ed and Wes were left to their own devices. A fellow homesteader told the story:

> Cash was in short supply and there was very little in the way of trouble that could not be settled without much ado. After all, as long as we had Ed Price around, there wasn't much need for a policeman. Few policemen could put the fear into wrongdoers the way Price could. He had a keen sense of justice, was an ex-prize fighter and now the proprietor, along with partner Wes McTavish, of the pool hall on 1st Ave . . . The peaceful village was somewhat aroused twice a year, in the spring and fall, when the lumberjacks from the Pas Lumber Company descended upon the town. After a long winter of hard work without a break, the young fellows at the camps were bent on celebrating a bit with pool, poker and possibly some bootleg liquor before moving on out to their respective homes. During this time, the occasional fight would occur. As long as the fight was fair and no one was getting hurt very badly, Mr. Price didn't interfere, but if you saw anyone hitting the man when his back was turned or using anything other than his fists in the fight, one of Price's blows to the jaw usually put him down for the count. One evening, he and his son Don were lunching in a local cafe when a fight broke out. They noticed that one of the two had severe cuts to the head and face, and upon looking closely discovered that the other fellow had brass knuckles. One blow from Price, and the assailant went down. Don removed the knuckledusters. The victim, with lacerations to his head and face, was a sorry sight . . . Though Price and McTavish were often accused of taking the law into their own hands, they still had the respect of the community.[26]

Sam Vickar, who lived near Star City, Saskatchewan, recalled the early times when policemen were scarce.[27] In his story, he highlights a community of settlers who got the best of a criminal who was trying to steal logs and make a raft in his attempt to escape from the jail.

In 1912, on a Saturday afternoon just before harvest, we were having tea and I decided to go for the cows. The tea was being enjoyed by my brothers David and Louis and their wives, as well as my sisters. I went down to the Carrot River and noticed a man making a raft from logs which belonged to the settlers which we had hauled from away north as the community had an idea of erecting a Turkish bath. I stopped and asked the stranger what he was doing with our logs, when another settler who was just coming from Star City drew my attention and notified me that a telegram had arrived in Star City that a fugitive had escaped from the Prince Albert jail and was last seen heading east of Kinistino on the Carrot River. This aroused our suspicion, but caution had to be used not to alert the suspected fellow who continued to erect his raft. I therefore mentioned out loud to the other settler to go up the hill to my home and put your team in the barn and stay for supper. He agreed and alerted the entire settlement. The women became panicky and were rather nervous. Since I had already spoken to him, it was decided I would return and invite him for supper. I went after and after lots of persuasion he decided to come along. When he arrived at the home and noticed a fairly large group of settlers, he refused to go further and commenced to return, I advised that this was all one family. He submitted to my request. Settlers were posted all around behind bushes as he made the proper turn. One courageous settler, my late brother-in-law, put his arms around him and infected a scissor hold on him. The remaining settlers became braver and assisted, he was wrestled down, his gun which he carried on his shoulder and his axe were removed. My brother Louis, claimed, "You are arrested in the name of the king!" He was requested to behave, and he was given supper. After supper, we bound him. One of the settlers struck out to contact the police, to tell them that we had a suspect. His description was of the fugitive wanted. The police requested we start out to meet them with this convict [as they were five miles away]. We complied and tied him to a chair, lifted him into a wagon, and started out. We met the police near Star City, Saskatchewan.

A family of homesteaders in the Carievale district of Saskatchewan came in contact with some horse thieves in 1885. Ernest Bishop described the encounter:

A band of four passed through the district on their way to Brandon. I heard afterwards they had stolen a bunch of horses south of Moose Jaw. They had a team and wagon with horses tied beside the team and behind the wagon, and two thieves rode on horseback driving several loose horses following behind the wagon. They were armed to the teeth with Winchester rifles and pistols and belts of loaded cartridges around their waist. They stopped at our place and tried to sell dad some horses but he suspected they were thieves and didn't buy. They went on traveling east. The chief of police, Mr. McMillan, got wind of them, and with three other policemen disguised themselves as hunters. They rode out south of Brandon and met the thieves. Pretending to buy horses from them, they caught them off guard and made them prisoners.[28]

Another colourful individual who acquired local celebrity status was homesteader John F. Grant of Carman, Manitoba. He enjoyed "borrowing" horses from others. He would travel up from the state of Montana and bring with him "some of the most

Main Street in Lang, Saskatchewan, ca. 1919. In 1912 the town experienced an attempted bank robbery one night. The following morning, the residents noticed that the front window of the bank was shattered and the door of the bank safe was resting on the porch of the hotel, which was across the street. Dynamite had been used, but in such an inefficient manner that money was strewn all over. It was impossible for the bank robbers to collect the money quickly as it was no longer tied into neat bundles that could easily be carried away. So they left the money behind, got out of town quickly and never returned. When the money was collected by the townfolk, it was "revealed that not one cent was missing."[29] NA-3229-21. COURTESY OF LIBRARIES AND CULTURAL RESOURCES DIGITAL COLLECTIONS, UNIVERSITY OF CALGARY

beautiful horses that were seen in the Carman district." He was something of a "freebooter,"[30] so it was no surprise that he made a return trip to Montana. In 1869 he hired a gang of men and they made the trip north, but this time he arrived in Carman driving a large herd of cattle and horses. Local residents of Carman asked him how he got all of those hundreds of animals. He replied that he "borrowed" them as he headed north. He did acknowledge, however, that he and the men almost got in trouble as a posse (including the owners of the animals) nearly caught up to them.[31] Fortunately, he said, they had already crossed the international border into Canada, where the posse couldn't touch them. Knowing that their pursuers were frustrated and extremely angry, he stated that he bowed and waved them a "grandiose adieu" before he and his men continued on their way to his homestead northeast of Carman.[32]

In the district of Rimbey, Alberta, Joe Montgomery stood out from all the other residents, not only because of his background, jovial personality and unique characteristics, but also because of his illegal moonshine-making abilities.

> He was without a doubt the most remarkable and colorful character of his day. Reputed to be an Irish nobleman in straitened circumstances, he came to New York City as a

Horse thieves from the Crowsnest Pass at Fish Creek, Alberta, 1884. They were all captured by the North-West Mounted Police. PD-262-37. COURTESY OF LIBRARIES AND CULTURAL RESOURCES DIGITAL COLLECTIONS, UNIVERSITY OF CALGARY

young man, where he was employed as head coachman for the wealthy Vanderbilt family for a number of years. But Joe had a lot of pioneer spirit in his blood and tiring of the effete east, he came west to Alberta about the turn of the century and settled on a quarter-section about half a mile north of where the Forshee elevator now stands.[33] He remained a bachelor, his only loves being his horses and his moonshine whiskey. He was really remarkable in appearance, 6 foot in height, broad of shoulder, and erect in carriage. He let his hair grow long and braided. Somewhere in his travels he suffered the loss of an eye, and a glass one was substituted for the real one, and when in conversation he constantly wiped the good eye while the other one naturally remained in a glassy stare, leaving his audience, especially strangers, in a somewhat bewildered state of mind. He also possessed a very peculiar voice, usually starting to speak in a moderate baritone, but gradually rising until he ended in a high tenor.

He was convicted on three occasions of operating a still and selling moonshine whiskey. Joe had his still concealed in a cave about ten feet underground, and the police were never able to actually locate his still and Joe was convicted mostly on circumstantial evidence. He called his still "Old King Tut" and of course, the "Cave" was King Tut's tomb. He paid a stiff fine on the first conviction, but served time in Fort Saskatchewan for the last two offences. Each time he returned from prison he informed all and sundry that he had learned more up at college, which was his name for the penitentiary, then he knew before about whiskey making. Joe also claimed to be possessed of supernatural powers which allowed him to converse with ghostly but friendly spirits, who warned him on several occasions of impending raids by the police, and Joe immediately concealed all incriminating evidence. One cold bitter day with a thermometer hovering at a nice cool 50 below 0, one of his neighbors found Joe lying in

Two men on a wagon being pulled by a horse, 1910. In the wagon are barrels full of moonshine, beer and whiskey. NA-3903-91. COURTESY OF LIBRARIES AND CULTURAL RESOURCES DIGITAL COLLECTIONS, UNIVERSITY OF CALGARY

a shack in a semiconscious condition. He was immediately taken to hospital where his feet were found to be badly frozen and the doctors advised immediate amputation, but Joe strenuously objected to such a silly proceeding saying that they were going to remain on his legs where they belonged, and be buried with him, and so they were. For Joe passed away a few days later and thus ended the amazing career of the wildest, wooly Irishman to ever invade the wild and wooly West. Joe was buried in a dress suit which was found in an old trunk which he had brought all the way from old Erin.[34]

Jokes, Anecdotes and Halloween Tricks

All homesteaders enjoyed a good joke or a humorous story. Not only could they relate to many of the amusing tales and scenarios, but the telling and retelling of these stories brought the community together. People commonly played jokes on family members, friends, teachers, preachers and even storekeepers, and Halloween pranks were popular. Sometimes humour could be found in daily occurrences that inadvertently resulted in a funny situation, while at other times humour was used purposely to send a message to a fellow homesteader or a child about their less than desirable behaviour. Most of the time the humour was playful, with many people laughing at the antics of those involved, but sometimes it could unintentionally lead to hurtful and disastrous consequences.

When he was reminiscing, John Alexander from Boyle, Alberta, indicated that even "though times were hard, they were still laced with plenty of humour."[1] He remembered when homesteaders, like his father, would offer advice to neighbours, but sometimes this advice did not play out as expected. One time a neighbour told John's father about the trouble he had trying to get his cows to come home. Mr. Alexander told the neighbour to buy a cowbell the next time he was in town. John's father did not elaborate on how to use the cowbell as he assumed it was a well-known method: the cowbell would be placed around the neck of one of the cows and it would ring every time the cow took a step. Homesteaders were able to track down their cows by the sound of the bell. "A few days later my father saw the neighbor and asked him how things were going. The neighbor replied, 'The bell might work for you, but it sure doesn't work for us. I stood on the doorstep and we rang and rang that bell and those cows still never came home.'"

Sometimes advice was offered that was not meant to be followed—in other words, homesteaders liked to "pull the leg" of their neighbours. According to Nell Williams, a homesteader named Harry Wyckoff (more commonly known as Slim) lived in the Griffin Creek area of Alberta.[2] Nobody knew how he acquired the nickname Slim, as he was tall and heavyset. He enjoyed playing jokes on others and on one person in particular, Mrs. Lampley, who was a novice at farming.

> Once, her chickens had something wrong with them. They would stagger around and finally fall down. Slim happened along one day so she asked if he knew what was wrong with the chickens. He said that they had the "Dizzie." All you have to do is throw them up in the air. He grabbed one and threw it up high. It came down to earth with a jolt and ran off to the bush. When her husband came in from work that night, there was Mrs. Lampley throwing chickens up into the air. He asked her what in the world she was doing. She told him that the veterinarian [aka Slim] had come by and told her what to do for the chickens. Her husband just grinned, he knew who had been along [and he wasn't a veterinarian]. Another time, the cow had freshened and had a caked bag.[3] Slim was on his way to the post office, so Mrs. Lampley asked him in to ask his advice. They were standing out in the yard. Slim looked down and saw a jawbone from a pig. Right away his fertile mind went to work. He said, "All you have to do is to take this jawbone, put it in the fire and when it has burned enough that you can pound it into a powder, make a cone out of a piece of paper and blow the powder into the cow's ear." Mrs. Lampley followed his advice. You can guess how much got into that cow's ear. When Mr. Lampley went out to check the cow, he found that her head was white with powder. He knew right away that the veterinarian had been along again.

Betty Iredale's father pulled the leg of their neighbour Mike when Mike told him that his boots were too tight and needed to be stretched.[4] Betty recalled that she saw Mike's boots when she stopped by for a cup of tea. Mike was typically a good-natured fellow, but on that day he was not happy. As she said,

> In one dark corner, I saw a pair of high boots, laced to the top. From them sprouted some six inches of growing oats. In places, their roots had burst the boot's leather uppers from the soles. I was entranced. But, for once, Mike was not. Momentarily, he was gruff. "The boots were too tight," he growled. "It was your father's idea that they be filled with oats and water poured on to make the oats swell and stretch the leather." He glowered at the forgotten splitting boots and their lush greenery.

When Betty returned home, she told her father the story about the boots and "he roared with laughter."

Another time, three friends went on a fishing trip to catch some western jackfish (also known as northern pike).[5] Two of them decided to try their luck at fishing one morning. George Phelps, who brought the tackle, went with his friend M. McBean to the creek, while the third friend, Mr. Evans, stayed at their camp. After a few hours of fishing, they had not felt even a nibble on their line. However, they were determined to have fresh fish for supper, so they tried a different method. They backed up the wagon into the creek. M. McBean grabbed a pail, and when the fish swam by, he leaned over the side of the wagon and scooped the fish into the pail and put them in the wagon. They repeated this process a number of times until they had all the fish they needed. They then decided to return to camp. When Mr. Evans saw how many fish they had caught, he got excited and wanted to try his luck at fishing. When they got back to the creek, George and M. McBean decided to play a joke on Mr. Evans. Instead of telling him how they actually caught the fish, they devised a new way for him to fish.

> M. McBean showed Mr. Evans a couple of big stones and handed him a pail with orders to stand on one of the stones and when he saw a fish coming, "just scoop him in." Mr. Evans carefully followed instructions and took up his position.

> Before long, he saw a nice big one coming towards him, and seizing his pail, made ready to bail him out, but before his pail touched the water, the wary fish had disappeared. The two jokers on the bank were getting considerable amusement out of this exhibition, and kept encouraging Mr. Evans to try again and again, and "just dip a little faster." After five or six vain attempts, he became suspicious and looking up caught the twinkle in the others' eyes. His ambition then was to trim them individually, collectively, or in fact, any way. However, he eventually admitted the joke was on him and the three friends returned to camp and enjoyed their first meal of western jackfish.

Another humorous story involved a homesteader by the name of John Bender.[6] He was well liked in the community of Didsbury, Alberta, and was known to have a good sense of humour. So one day his neighbour decided to play a joke on him. Everyone knew that John had a great affection for his hens. He had twelve of them and was quite pleased that they would each lay an egg every day without fail. His next-door neighbour, who also raised chickens, snuck over to Mr. Bender's chicken house and put an egg in one of the nests, so when Mr. Bender went to gather his eggs, he found thirteen eggs instead of twelve. When Mr. Bender realized that he had one extra egg, he couldn't figure it out. He was completely mystified and told everyone about this rare occurrence. Laughing at his joke, it was some time before his neighbour let him know that he had added an egg to one of the nests.

Another chicken joke was played on a woman who carefully ministered to her twenty-five chickens and collected the eggs from them every morning. When she went out one morning to feed the chickens and gather their eggs, there were no chickens to be found. She was quite upset at the disappearance of her chickens. When she told her son about it, he became angry, as he had a good idea as to who had taken the chickens. "He turned on his heel and walked into town and just happened to stop at the pool hall where many of the local pranksters gathered. One of the more observant noticed that the 'Son' didn't look too happy." Son agreed that he wasn't and went on to say that the people who had borrowed his mother's chickens wouldn't be looking too happy either, because he knew who was responsible for taking them. "The next morning his mother was awakened by the crowing of a cock. She couldn't believe her eyes when she opened the henhouse door." There was the weirdest assortment of chickens ever. "There were red ones, white ones, big ones and little ones and a few barred-rocks, but there were twenty-five chickens!"[7]

Harve Carson remembered a joke that his two sons played on a young man who had come courting a hired girl on their farm.[8] While the young man was being entertained with a cup of tea and cookies inside the house, the two boys changed the wheels on the buggy so the smaller ones were on the back and the larger ones on the front. The boys laughed uproariously after the young man left, as he would have had to travel ten miles in an uncomfortable fashion, tilted backward. Also, the wagon would have been difficult to steer, as there wouvd have been less flexibility for turning.

Charles Davis remembered a joke that was played on a fellow homesteader, Mr. Nelson, by a man named Sam Blower.[9] Mr. Nelson had a team of moose named Book and Bright that he would hitch to his wagon. He was very proud of the fact that he had

Sometimes jokes were played on people who rode in buggies. The front wheels would be switched with the back wheels. The wheels are in the correct position for Ernest Allen and his horse in 1924. NA-1534-13. COURTESY OF LIBRARIES AND CULTURAL RESOURCES DIGITAL COLLECTIONS, UNIVERSITY OF CALGARY

tamed them and boasted about how proficient they were at listening to his commands. They were also very quick at getting him from place to place.

> All went well, until a prankster, like all pranksters do, got ideas. So it happened one beautiful balmy evening late in the month of August, Mr. Nelson was setting forth for his mail in town, a distance of 18 miles, when a call of a bull moose ... abruptly changed the direction [of his team] from west to north, dragging his prairie schooner, which most of the time sallied forth in mid-air. Then, like a flash from the blue, it happened. Book went to one side and Bright the other of a solitary standing tree. Mr. Nelson had only time to shout "Whoaaaah" and all the stars in the universe fell about him ... till he was awakened by Sam Blower who had already untangled Book and Bright and released them [from the tree]. Nelson asked him how he just happened to have been there when the accident occurred. He also asked him, "What's that slung over your shoulder?" "Oh, that's my moose call," Sam replied.

Mr. Nelson jumped up, ready to exact revenge, but Sam, realizing what was going to occur, turned and outran the enraged Mr. Nelson.

Another comical situation occurred when Heinrich decided to play a joke on his brother Abe when he was out searching for the family's milk cow. Anna Born, their sister, recounted the joke in her memoirs:

> In the fall, the cattle were turned loose to graze along the roadside and the edges of the fields where the grass was still long. The milk cow was included with the rest of the herd, and when milking time came, it was sometimes a bit of a chore to find her and bring her home to be relieved of her milk. One evening, young Abe was dispatched to find the cow. He took a long time coming back in the gathering dusk, so Father sent Heinrich to find and hurry him up. Walking along the outside furrow on the field, Heinrich presently spied two shadowy shapes coming to meet him, the cow with Abe behind to keep her moving.

> Heinrich lay down in the furrow. As the cow and her herder neared, Heinrich raised one leg in the air, and held it there. The cow, astonished, stopped. Abe tried to urge her on, peering around her to see what was stopping her. Heinrich kicked both legs up. Frightened by this strange apparition, the cow began to bawl and stampeded off across the field, Abe in pursuit, yelling at her to stop. Heinrich got up and started after her, trying to call his brother, but laughing so hard he had no breath for anything but running. The terrified cow headed for home, followed by Abe, who was nearly as scared by the creature that was chasing them in the dark. Heinrich caught up just as the procession wheeled into the yard under the waiting eyes of Father. Henrich grabbed his brother, who grappled with him in return, half crying, "You scared me nearly to death!" At this, Heinrich ended up rolling on the ground in an ecstasy of laughter. Father caught the cow, knowing there would be no point in trying to milk her, but he couldn't resist Heinrich's laughter and ended up joining in.[10]

A couple of jokesters from Bowden, Alberta, who hung around the town's hotel, Brewster House, decided to have some fun with the hotel's porter. They noticed that when the train arrived in town, it was the porter's responsibility to meet the trains, welcome the guests, direct the guests to the hotel, and carry their valises to the hotel and up the stairs to their rooms.

> One evening, they took one of their number down to Olds [a previous stop before Bowden], dressed him up in a beautiful array of women's finery and loaded him on the midnight train bound for Bowden. Two valises being carried were filled with 80 to 100 pounds each of old horseshoes, plowshares and pieces of iron. On arrival at Bowden, the "lady" indicated that she would stay at Brewster House and that the Porter should carry her bags the block or so to the hotel. The poor old Porter struggled and panted and perspired and wondered what milady had in her bags.[11]

The story did not mention if the porter was ever told about the joke or his reaction, but the tricksters likely had fun at his expense.

The Widowmaker

CHARLES KIEPER HAD an interesting, but terrifying experience.[12] Over a summer, he worked as a farm hand for a fellow homesteader. One evening, after a long day of working, he began his trek back to the farmhouse from the field, travelling by horse and wagon. The mare that he was working with was "switchy" in that she was ornery and irritable. When they were near the farmhouse, she kicked over the shaft of the wagon and got the line under her tail. She went running down the road, kicking as she went. Charles, who had now lost all control over the horse, slid down off his seat as he felt that he would be safer down in the wagon. His boss saw them coming and tried to stop her, but she just dodged him and ran on. However, the wagon clipped him before he could get out of the way. He was thrown to the ground with a "terrific force." His wife and some of the other farmhands rushed to help him up and carry him into the house. Meanwhile, the mare had finally worn herself out, and Charles was able to steer her toward the barn and stopped her there. The boss saw the humour in the situation, so rather than punishing Charles for not controlling the horse and for putting his boss into jeopardy, he made a joke out of it by saying that Charles probably wanted to kill him so that he could marry his widow. •

Pranks were sometimes played on guests who arrived at a hotel, particularly on those who were going into the tavern. During the harvesting season one year, five boys from Bruderheim, Alberta, decided to fill paper bags with water and then drop them from the roof of the hotel onto the heads of unsuspecting guests. One guest, a local farmer, turned out to be less than impressed with the antics of these young fellows and gave chase so that he could teach them a lesson. "The boys fled down the pitch black alley, with the angry and wet farmer in pursuit." When they came

Chivaree'ing the Newlyweds

GOOD-SPIRITED JOKES WERE often played on newlyweds after their wedding service. For instance, newlyweds often found that old shoes, empty cans and chains had been tied to the back of their buggies. During the wedding dance in the evening, it was not unheard of for friends to good-naturedly kidnap the bride or take a part of her attire, like her shoe. The groom was expected to buy back his bride or her shoe for an outrageous sum, typically around $5. If friends had access to the newlyweds' home sometime during the day, they would cause mischief by untying the ropes that held the bedframe together so that the bed would collapse once the couple decided to lie down on it, or they would hang a cowbell under the bed. Sheets on the bed were shorted (i.e., folded in half on the bed), or they were sewn together. In other cases, pigs or some other small farm animal might be placed in the house so that a bit of havoc would occur.

Typically, after a couple had settled back into their home after a day or two, neighbours would "chivaree" the newlyweds. They would band together late at night, bringing with them any noise-making device that they could think of. Some brought pots and pans that they would bang together, others brought horns and cowbells, while others brought guns. Once the couple had retired for the evening, the friends would gather around the house, whooping and hollering, making noise and shooting their guns. The newlyweds would then get out of bed, meet their friends at the door and invite them in for a midnight lunch and drinks. Sometimes the revelry ended at this point, while at other times the friends would stay and party and dance until early the next morning. When the visiting was done, the neighbours left with good wishes and good feelings all around, with the newlyweds assuring everyone to visit again.

Every once in a while, the tables were turned on the chivaree revellers. In Bruderheim,

Alberta, a newly wedded couple, the mayor and his wife, knew that a large number of well-wishers would be stopping by their home. (They lived on the second storey of the local hardware store.) Just before the revellers came by, they left their home and positioned themselves at a vantage point where they could see the hardware store and, at the same time, watch the approaching revellers. Given that it was dark outside, the revellers passed them by and did not notice them. When the chivaree began, with whoops and hollers and the banging of pots and pans, the couple sauntered over to the crowd and asked if they could also join in to honour the new couple. They were enthusiastically welcomed. The mayor and his wife then proceeded to have a wonderful time chivaree'ing themselves. Before long, however, the crowd began to realize that the couple that they were supposed to be chivaree'ing in their home was actually standing alongside them. The mayor and his wife had caught all of them by surprise! The crowd realized that the joke was on them.[13]

If newlyweds refused to take part in the chivaree, bad feelings could occur. Charles Sargent knew of one case where neighbours continued making noise until 5:00 AM but were still not welcomed into the couple's home. Because of this response, he said, "There was a bad feeling in the community for months after."[14] John McChesney, in his discussion of chivarees, mentioned the same problem. If the couple was not amenable to the efforts of their neighbours, it took a long time for the couple to regain their standing in the community.[15] ●

This decorated shack on a sleigh was used as a joke by the Beiseker, Alberta, community to greet Bill and Tillie Schissel at the railway station after they returned home from their wedding in 1914. As it says on the door, this was "Bill's Country Home," the house that the couple was supposedly going to live in. NA-4079-34. COURTESY OF LIBRARIES AND CULTURAL RESOURCES DIGITAL COLLECTIONS, UNIVERSITY OF CALGARY

across a friend (an adult), he told them to hide out in a potato patch and proceeded to misdirect the farmer when he was asked if he saw in which direction the boys had fled. As the farmer took off, still seeking revenge, the friend said to the boys, "Get the hell out of here if you want to stay alive." Each of them then went his own way.[16]

At times, jokes were used to teach people a lesson or to make a point about what others saw as their irritating character flaws or negative behaviour. Mrs. Charles Archer remembered some of these jokes, some of which she felt were on the nasty side.[17] For instance, if people assumed that someone was "light-fingered" and stole a particular item, then a replica of that item would be given to them as a gift at Christmas. Similarly, if one person in the community was gossipy, they might receive a megaphone or some other broadcasting device with their name printed on it.

Other homesteaders recalled instances where people received their just desserts. William Boyle told a story about three boys who were planning to steal some food from two bachelors, Joe and Hugh.[18] These two bachelor friends had been out hunting and had successfully shot two ducks for their dinner, which they planned on eating the next day. Three neighbour boys heard about the ducks and decided that they would steal them as they were cooking on a pot on the stove. Joe and Hugh were forewarned of the thieves' plans,

> so they cooked the ducks early in the morning and took them off the stove and put them away safely. Then they filled the pot up with buffalo bones and tied the lid down and left the pot on the stove. It wasn't long until one of the boys came along and asked Joe and Hugh to take a walk down to the road to look at something. So they went along. While they were gone, two other fellows came in from the back of the house, took the pot off the stove and ran about 100 rod down through the field. When they opened the pot, they hadn't anything but old bones, so the joke was on them.

Joe and Hugh ended up inviting the three boys in for dinner, as they had learned their lesson. They all had a share of the ducks.

Another story that was retold among homesteaders was about a man who received his comeuppance after he scared a settler who was on the road looking for his registered homestead. This man was a cowboy who went into Claresholm and got very drunk at the local bar. He passed out, awakened the next day around noon and headed for home, feeling sick and ill-tempered from a hangover. Six miles out he met the settler with his team and wagon on the road.

> The cowboy, in his unpleasant frame of mind decided to throw a scare into the settler, so he stopped him at gunpoint and told him get down from his wagon and dance. The man, in very broken English, said he couldn't dance and pleaded with the cowboy to leave him alone. The cowboy threatened to shoot him if he did not dance in the dirt, and finally the man, in fear of his life, did so. After the cowboy felt he had had enough of this fun, he holstered his gun and rode on. Before he had traveled a few hundred feet, the settler called

> out to him and when he turned the settler was standing in his wagon with his rifle trained on the cowboy. He ordered the cowboy to turn around and then demanded that he get off his horse and dance. The cowboy protested but soon realized he had better do as he was told or else he was going to be shot, so he got off the horse and in the heat of the noonday sun he danced. Then the settler told him to ride away, and every time the cowboy looked back he could see the man still standing with the gun trained on him.[19]

After considering the confrontation, the cowboy found some humour in it and told others about what had happened to him on the road. He knew that "he got what was coming to him," likely learned from the experience and never repeated it.

Family members would sometimes take revenge on others in the family who they felt were not treating them properly or who they wanted to teach a lesson. Such was the case with a small boy named Don. He was about ten years younger than his brother and his brother's friends, who saw Don as a pest who was too young to take part in their activities. They often left him behind, even when he would come running with his arms raised, shouting, "Hey, wait for me!" One Sunday the group of boys decided that they were going to travel by horseback to a nearby lake. When Don came up to them, they said that he couldn't come along as he did not have a horse and no one was willing to take him double. "He stood there watching crestfallen, then he spoke quietly to his constant companion, the old farm dog. 'Sic 'em!' he commanded." The dog heeled (nipped the heels of) his brother's horse, and the horse reared and threw his brother off. Don took off into the house, seeking the protection of his mother from his angry brother, who was dealing with a sore backside. The storyteller did not indicate whether the boys took Don along with them in the future.[20]

Sometimes the farming community took revenge on fellow homesteaders, particularly if community members did not take kindly to a homesteader abusing his farm animals. In one case, local farmers took action to rectify the situation by playing a joke on the farmer in the hope that he would learn from the experience. The farmer's name was Mike and he owned a bull named Horace.

He Sings Now Instead

EVERY ONCE IN a while a small child misbehaved. While some parents might take action and discipline the child, Marion Anderson found a more effective and humorous way to change her son Harvie's bad behaviour.[21] Marion remembered how she and her children spent one summer on a farm near Sintaluta, Saskatchewan. Harvie started howling and crying over every little thing that didn't suit him. They all tried to break him of this bad habit, but Harvie's bad behaviour continued. One evening when it started to get really dark outside, her young son "struck up his tune when suddenly a howl set up in the bluff beside the door." Stunned, Harvie stopped his howling, ran scared to Marion and hid his face in her lap. She explained to him that the wolf was responding to his howling; he thought it was a companion he had heard, and the wolf was coming for him. Harvie was scared of wolves—so much so that Marion said, "We never had trouble with Harvie after that. He sings now instead." •

Mike caused great consternation in the community as he would team Horace with a beautiful horse named Murrin. "She, poor beast, after each step, had to endure the nerve-strain of being forced to hesitate so as to match her faster stride to Horace's plodding gait. Perhaps lost in thought behind his mismatched team, Mike didn't recognize the torture to which he put Murrin. Nor did he listen to criticism."[22] Betty Iredale's father, who was a fine horseman, strongly protested to Mike about his treatment of Murrin. Mike refused to listen; he disregarded Murrin's misery and continued to yoke the pair together, even though Horace was a mean-tempered brute. One winter day, Mike returned to his shack on horseback, took off Murrin's saddle and let her roam free. Eventually, when he went in search of her, he could not find her. "The alarm went out that Murrin had disappeared. Mike was beside himself. A horseless man had to walk. Apart from the loss, that meant work. He borrowed a mount and for days scoured the prairie. But Murrin, her sorrel fur in sharp contrast with the snow-covered plains, was not seen. For that matter, no horse was found." After the spring melted most of the snow, her father's friend brought word that a white horse had been spotted grazing on the prairie. Unusual! A party of men set out to investigate, Mike included. The horse was sighted as her white winter coat had started to shed. Murrin had been made invisible because she had been painted white by Betty's prankster father. "Mike, in his relief to regain his horse, promised never again to team Murrin and Horace together." In the end, Mike was invited to join the men and her father in an evening of revelry so that no hard feelings lingered. As Betty recounted, her "father's tomfoolery was effective in gaining the desired result!"

Sometimes farm animals took their own revenge on unsuspecting individuals, like the ram on the Born homestead.

> The ram was a fine animal with a beautiful set of curling horns. One year, the hired man of the season got into the habit of teasing the ram by catching it by the horns and forcing it to walk where it did not want to or pushing its nose into a snowbank or a mud puddle. One time he force-fed it a wad of chewing tobacco. The ram bitterly resented its tormentor but was helpless when the man grabbed it by the horns. One early spring day, Mr. Born and Jake, the hired man, were starting to get ready for seeding. There was still a sizeable snowbank in front of the barn, but there was a clear patch around the door, and there they had set up the machine for winnowing and cleaning the seed grain. The livestock were all out exploring the thawing yard for last year's seeds and grasses. After dinner, the ram saw Jake come out of the house and head back to work. Very quietly the ram snuck around the snowbank and came up behind Jake. It got itself nicely lined up, tucked in its legs, lowered its heavy head and charged. It caught the hired man precisely at the bottom of the spine and drove him hard against the barn wall. Then the ram strutted off with an air of having accomplished a

job well done. Jake got very little sympathy from the family. Rather they likely felt that he got what he deserved.[23]

Many people remembered funny anecdotes about events that occurred on the homestead, particularly between family members. For instance, Rusty Roberts of Noyes Crossing remembered the time when a farmer's wife named Ma Flynn was sitting on a stool with her legs spread around a washtub full of potatoes and water.[24] She was busy peeling the spuds when her fifteen-year-old daughter came up behind her and pushed her head into the water. As the daughter ran away, yelling ensued. "Catch her, catch her!" Two people finally caught up with the girl. One took her by her hands and the other by her feet. They hauled her over to the boat landing and then heaved her into the lake. A good laugh was had by everyone.

Marion Anderson remembered how her mother played a joke on her uncle when he was visiting them.[25] He had gone out for the evening to court a young woman. When he returned to their house late at night, he entered quietly, "not wanting to waken the sleepers of the house." He started climbing the stairs "when all of sudden, there was a great clatter. Her mother had put tin pans on the steps and with no lamp lit, her uncle did not see them." Everyone got out of bed and had a good laugh at the startled uncle.

The Alexander boys from Boyle, Alberta, found themselves in a funny situation one day when their dad was out cutting grain in the field. When he came home at noon for dinner, he found a pig in the yard. He told his two sons to take the pig back to the neighbours, as he assumed that it had escaped from its pen. They started herding the pig back to the neighbours' farm, but every time they got about halfway there, the pig would turn around and run back to their place. This happened time and time again. They couldn't convince the pig to continue on. Finally, the two brothers gave up and followed the pig back to their home. It turned out that it wasn't the neighbours' pig at all! It was one of their own.[26]

Elias Parmlee St. John remembered a time when he played a joke on his wife.[27] She asked him and their son Howard to go berry picking, so she would have enough berries for canning. Rather than getting an early start, it was approaching midafternoon when father and son finally got going. His wife was skeptical as to how much they would pick, as she believed that they would just end up having an afternoon nap in the bush. He and Howard arrived at the berry-picking site and set about picking berries for a couple of hours. They had picked enough to fill two large milk pails. Still stinging from his wife's skepticism, he told his son on their way home, that they were going to make their berry-picking efforts "look good" to his mother. They stopped by the shed and found a ten-gallon can. They stuffed a thick blanket into the bottom of the can and poured the berries on top. Then they went to the house and knocked on the door. The husband told his wife that they did have a nap in the bush but that they also managed to get her a few berries. She couldn't believe that the pail was so full, but then became suspicious and said, "You didn't pick that many. You bought them, that is what you did." Her son replied that they hadn't bought any of the berries. She knew that he wouldn't lie to her, so she got excited about how successful they were at picking so many berries—until the moment that she shook out a few berries from the can and saw the blanket. Knowing that they played a joke on her, she said that she knew they hadn't picked so many!

Instead of playing a joke on a parent, Marion Anderson tried to play a joke on her children.[28] The usual fare each morning was to eat prepared porridge for breakfast, using oatmeal that had been soaked in water and heated on the stove. A bit of salt was also added. By the time it was done, it was like a thick gumbo paste. One day, Marion decided to put a "big bowl of dry rolled oats on the table, along with a jug of milk,

Children often had their own sense of humour and enjoyed telling each other jokes. Two children pose for this 1912 photograph. AUTHOR'S COLLECTION

Children's Riddles

WHETHER CHILDREN WERE playing at home or gathering with friends at school, they had their own brand of humour. They would tell each other jokes and riddles where the listener would have to guess the answer. Here are a few examples:

> *Thirty-two white horses upon a red hill, now they dance, now they prance, now they stand still. What am I?* Teeth.
>
> *Little Ann Netticoat in a white petticoat. The longer she stands, the shorter she grows. What am I?* A candle.
>
> *I am big at the bottom and small at the top and have a thing in the middle that goes flippity-flop. What am I?* A butter churn. ●

thinking they would be surprised and fooled." To Marion's great surprise, the big bowl was passed around and all were pleased with the change, so the joke turned out to be on Marion.

In another case, a dog played a joke on an unsuspecting farm family, the Schermanns of Arvilla, Alberta. Ernie Jenkins, a homesteading neighbour, had a team of white horses called Barney and Jess, of whom he was inordinately proud. He was also very fond of his big dog Mick, who accompanied him wherever he went. One day, Mrs. Schermann had put a pan of filling for raisin pies outside to cool. At that moment, Ernie came to the Schermanns with his team and buggy and Mick, and they visited for a short while before he continued on to Busby. During their stop, and while everyone was chatting, Mick found the filling and ate all of it . . . except for one raisin.[29]

A Chamber Pot Story

ONE TIME AN uncle came to visit his sister and her family. Given the lack of space, he had to share a bedroom with his six-year-old nephew, Johnnie. In addition, given that there was no indoor plumbing, one had to use the outhouse during the day and a chamber pot at night. Chamber pots were typically placed under the bed, and if they were used during the night, they would be dumped out in the outhouse in the morning. As the story goes,

> Bob was not a particularly religious man, but he decided, when he saw Johnnie kneeling at the side of the bed as if in prayer, he should do likewise. He got down on his knees on his side of the bed and bowed his head. A moment later Johnnie looked up and said, "Say, Uncle Bob, what are you doing down there?" To which Uncle Bob replied, "Exactly what you are doing, Johnnie." "Gee whiz, Uncle, you'll catch it from mom then. I've got the chamber pot over on this side of the bed!"[30] ●

One farmer liked to tease his fellow single homesteaders, particularly after visiting a woman in the vicinity named Albertina who could not speak English very well. He recalled that he was bringing home a load of seed wheat from town one day. As he passed her house, he was invited in for dinner. During the meal, he said that Albertina

> confided to me that she put out traps to catch badgers. There are a lot of badgers, she said, and was excited over her prospective catch. Being French and the English language alien to her, she had difficulty in pronouncing the word "badgers" and instead she said "bachelors." There were a number of bachelors in her vicinity so I warned them that Albertina,

their new neighbour, had set out traps to catch bachelors and to keep away from the toils of her snares if they valued their freedom.[31]

In her memoir, Viola Cameron reminisced about a funny incident that happened when she was a young girl on her Uncle Joe's homestead.[32] She stated that her uncle had planted his crops and was quite happy with how they were growing compared to other years, when the crops had been so poor. Viola, who was six years old at the time, along with six other young children, went into her uncle's wheatfield one day. For fun, they lay down on the ground, one after the other, and rolled through the crops. When her uncle went out to see his crops the next day, he couldn't believe what he saw. Six acres were ruined, just flattened and broken off at the ground. He did not know that the children were the cause of the crop destruction as they were too frightened to tell him, given that he was so upset. Instead, he believed that his Russian neighbour, Mr. Manchi, was to blame. Mr. Manchi had a team of oxen and a stoneboat that he had used to clear his own land. It was obvious to Uncle Joe that Mr. Manchi's team of oxen got loose with the stoneboat and ran through his field. He was going to sue him! When Mr. Manchi heard about the problem, he swore up and down that his oxen were never loose, but her uncle didn't believe him. He never ended up suing him, but there were bad feelings for years. Viola finished her story by stating that it took over thirty years before she could tell her uncle the truth. When she finally told him, he burst out laughing. As she said, "I've never known anyone to laugh so hard. It was awful. Well, you get seven, eight kids rolling, you see. And we rolled one after the other. We just kept going and going. Oh, crazy!"

While various humorous incidents occurred on the homestead, funny things also happened to schoolteachers, shopkeepers, preachers and members of the North-West Mounted Police (NWMP). While jokes may have tickled the funny bone of those who were playing pranks, sometimes they were not well received by those who bore the brunt of them.

Allen Weigl and his brothers, Hubert and Ewald, decided to add some excitement to their school day by playing a practical joke on the teacher, but their joke went too far and could easily have led to a grave outcome.[33] They made a bomb using a rifle

Potential for Tragedy

ACCORDING TO LENA MAY PURDY, there was one joke played on a homesteader that was the worst thing she had ever heard of.[34] "A man used a trail, also used by others, but had to turn off to his own little trail. He stuck up a branch at the turn, so he would know when to leave the main trail. One very cold night, someone had moved the branch and the settler was a long time out in the cold before he found his way home." As Lena May said, this joke could easily have turned into a tragedy. ●

shell and filling it full of match heads. They snuck into the teacherage and placed the bomb in the wood cookstove when there was a fire burning in it.[35] The boys ran for cover and waited. The bomb blew the top off the stove, driving it into the ceiling. They all felt that the bomb worked really well and were satisfied and happy with the results. The story did not include the terror the teacher must have felt when her cookstove exploded. It is highly unlikely that she saw the humour in their joke.

Another time, the Weigl brothers were playing ball at recess. The teacher came out and rang the bell so all the children would gather and return to the classroom. She turned around and went into the school. At this point one brother said to the other, "'See if you can throw the softball through one of those three little windows above the door.' The ball went through the middle one with the red cross, spraying the teacher's hair with glass." This time Allen did note the reaction of the teacher, as he was called up to the teacher's desk. In an angry tone, the teacher told him to bring ten cents for the window. However, the anger of the teacher was lost on Allen as he found the request ludicrous. As he said, "How could I get ten cents? I was only eleven years old at the time."

Other students reported playing jokes on their teachers, but their jokes were much milder than those instigated by the Weigl brothers. Teachers would find some kind of harmless animal in their desk drawer, usually a gopher, lizard, garter snake or frog. While a few teachers played along with the joke (depending on if they had grown up in a rural area and were aware of such pranks), many were offended by this type of classroom behaviour, especially if finding the animal had startled them. They would try to track down the culprits so they could dole out punishment, such as a switch across the student's backside or a strap across their hands.

Sometimes when students wanted a day off, one or two mischievous pupils would create some havoc so school would be cancelled. David Stammen, who lived in the Annaheim district of Saskatchewan, told how some boys got together one evening and set some traps for the skunks who lived under the schoolhouse.[36] The following morning their teacher, Mr. Strueby, was forced to cancel school until the fumes cleared. Another time someone toppled the outhouse over, so they had to spend school time putting the outhouse back into its upright position. The teacher asked the larger boys in the class to help out, but the boys made sure the process took longer than necessary. While boys on one side of the outhouse tried to pull it up, the boys on the other side worked to keep it down. The teacher, not understanding why the outhouse was so difficult to fix, was greatly exasperated by the whole affair, while the boys likely felt that the time was well spent.[37]

Sometimes students didn't appreciate their teacher's behaviour and decided to do something about it. Frank Roenspies of the Annaheim district recalled that their male schoolteacher took a shine to the girls in the classroom. At that time, it was not unusual for male teachers to date their older female students, given that they were close in age. (Individuals could obtain a teaching certificate if they had a Grade 10 education, which could make teachers as young as fifteen or sixteen years old.) Typically, this teacher would be outside with the students during recess, spending time on the swings with the girls. The boys, who noticed their teacher's enchanting ways, decided to play a joke on him. Before the school opened one morning, they cut the ropes on the swing almost all the way through. "When the young debonair was in the midst of displaying his boldness for the benefit of the girls [showing how high he could go], the rope broke and sent the embarrassed young man into the bushes."[38]

Sometimes the students didn't set up a joke on the teacher, but a humorous incident would occur while the teacher was giving a lesson. A.J. Riley was a farm worker in Lumsden, Saskatchewan, when he heard this story.[39] He had been invited for dinner with his employer's family, and this is where the story begins.

> The farmer had three girls and three boys, the two younger at fifteen and sixteen years still going to school ... Now this farmer was a very strict man with his family especially at the meal table. We were sitting at supper and the two boys started to laugh. One would set the other off. Father got cross. They were not to laugh at the table when the others did not know what they were laughing at. So finally he said, boys if there is anything to laugh at tell me or you go upstairs to bed without your supper. So the younger boy said it was something that had happened in school. Well, what was it? The teacher was quite a young lady from a good Methodist family, very modest. She had the older children all down to their lessons and called four little ones up to the blackboard and wrote the word "feet" on it. Now what does that spell? she asked. They did not know. Well now, she said, you have to use your thinker and I will help you. I have two and you two have four altogether. One little boy put up his hand. Very well, Johnny, what's the answer? He said "tits." It took her over an hour to stop the others from laughing. What a shock for teacher!

Sometimes the prank happened while students were making their way to the schoolhouse. Vernon Seibert of Vermillion Springs, Alberta, recalled how some of the boys took the notion, as they were walking along the train tracks, that they should try and stop the train.[40] They felt that this would be a good joke to play on the train's crew. Finding a pile of railway ties that were set off to the side, they decided to pile them up high on the tracks. They then proceeded to walk to school. They had just settled down to the day's lessons when there was a knock on the school door. Two railway men began questioning the class about who had tried to block the train. The boys owned up to their misdeed and got quite a scolding. As Vernon concluded, "It was a good thing the trains were slower in those days and the section crew spotted the blockage in time, otherwise there could have been a serious accident."

Shopkeepers were not immune to the tactics of jokesters and ended up being the brunt of their jokes from time to time. Cox's Mercantile Store was the only business in Rimbey, Alberta, in the early years and became the local meeting place for everyone. A humorous incident occurred one day involving Jim Cloverdale's dog, Curly. Someone tied the end of a string, that was wound up in a cast-iron string holder, to Curly's tail. Jim opened the door and ordered his dog to go home. Curly was well trained and set off at a mad pace, unwinding quite a length of string before Mr. Cox realized what was going on and cut the string before he lost any more.[41]

J. Beeley, a storekeeper in Lacombe, Alberta, in 1902, was the target of a joke that could have turned out quite badly. "He clerked in the store and used to use the edge of the counter as a cutting board for his tobacco, which he shaved from a plug. Sometimes if he wasn't too busy, he would shave off enough for two pipe fulls, and leave half until he was ready for it. One day a small quantity of gunpowder was slyly slipped into the waiting tobacco." The jokester felt that it was a great trick. As he said, "When Mr B lit up, he really did, no foolin'!" As for Mr. B, the story did not elaborate on his response to the joke, but the flare-up so close to this face likely caused him some distress and could have caused serious injuries.[42]

John Fetsch told a few stories of two practical jokers who lived in his district and played tricks on the local preacher.[43] One time they hid the church organ in a wheatfield. Another time they put a pail of water on top of a door. It was balanced precariously, so as soon as someone pushed the door open, the pail of water fell on their head. In a third story, John said the jokers were digging a well on their homestead when the church minister called. The minister was curious about the well and asked the two men if he could go down the well and take a look. They set him on a pail and let him down into the well. It was at this point that a desire to pull a joke on the minister overwhelmed the two men, and they left him there for an hour. When they pulled him back up out of the well, he found that they had played another joke on him by sticking his cane through his hat. According to John, the minister never called there again.

Members of the NWMP also faced a practical joker or two. Isabel Muirhead remembered "a joke that was played on a Mountie who aways sang *Little Brown Jug* at every party until we got tired of it."[44] At the end of the song, he always lifted up an empty jug and pretended to drink from it. One evening "someone thought it would be a good idea to put some water into the jug that he always used to demonstrate with. That night when he tipped the jug up he got all wet and never sang *Little Brown Jug* again."

Dorothy White Gladwin recalled another humorous event that involved a member of the NWMP.

> In the winter, [her brother] David and some of the Bruner boys used to fish through the ice on Chip Lake. They had a small cabin on the ice to keep warm, and mother had a bright awning she let them have to cover their supplies. One weekend when they were home, some of the young boys from up at Anselmo came by with a sleigh full of things covered with mother's bright awning. Mother spotted it, so David went down to Chip Lake and all their fish and everything in the cabin was gone. They sent for a Mountie and in a couple of days he got to our place ... He had ridden his horse all the way from Junkins (Wildwood) ... and he was just frozen. The next day he went on north to find the boys and made them bring all the stuff back. The awning had given them away. The Mountie stayed at our place for a couple of days. One morning, [Dorothy's young sister] Florence thought it would be fun to try his boots on before he got up. With her own boots already on, she put his on too, but she couldn't get them off. We all tried but couldn't move them, so everyone went to the barn to do their chores and left Florence sitting there. She had to wait until the Mountie got up and took his boots back. We all thought it was funny except Florence.[45]

Halloween was one time of year when people expected jokes and pranks would be played on them. Therefore, it came as no surprise when they woke up in the morning to find something amiss in their farmyard or something awry at their business in town. While many took it with good humour, some people were likely not too happy with the night's shenanigans. Gates would

A typical Halloween trick was to place buggies on top of haystacks. This prank was pulled in 1930. NA-598-12. COURTESY OF LIBRARIES AND CULTURAL RESOURCES DIGITAL COLLECTIONS, UNIVERSITY OF CALGARY

be removed from fences, cream cans would be hung on the horns of cows, and buffalo horns would be attached to the heads of oxen. Syrup would be poured on doorknobs, saddles would be exchanged on the horses that had been ridden into town, and farm implements and tools would be hidden in the bush. White sheets were hung in the trees or were placed over horses so they would look like ghosts at night and scare the local inhabitants (especially if they happened to be near the cemetery).

Some pranksters would take wagons or buggies, dismantle them and then place them on top of barns or town buildings. The farmer or owner would have to get the neighbours to come and help them get the wagon or buggy off the roof the next day. Alternatively, an owner could wait until the Halloween tricksters came back to fix what they had done. Such was the case described by Ernie Sanders of Alberta's Alliance district. He remembered how some tricksters had "carried off a wagon and pulled it to town. There it was dismantled and reassembled on top of the livery barn. Mr. Stanbridge [the owner of the wagon] said that whoever put it up there could take it down, so there it remained for a whole year until the next Halloween."[46]

It was not unheard of for outhouses to be moved to the main street from behind local businesses. Sometimes only one would appear, while at other times a number of outhouses would be

As a Halloween prank, outhouses were sometimes placed on the main street of a town, as happened here in 1920. NA-3903-21. COURTESY OF LIBRARIES AND CULTURAL RESOURCES DIGITAL COLLECTIONS, UNIVERSITY OF CALGARY

moved. After they were set out in a row, the signs were taken off the businesses and placed on the outhouses. One outhouse would be the candy store, another would be a mercantile, while a third might be a hotel. In Carstairs, Alberta, "a small outhouse was moved to the street between the Union Bank and the post office and decorated with real estate dealers' signs."[47] In other cases, an animal was placed in the outhouse in the hope that a ruckus would occur when the door was opened. The Roy Misner family of Saskatchewan's Grainland district told the story of an Angora goat named Billy, who was taken from his pen and placed in an outhouse that was positioned with its door facing the entrance of a mercantile on the main street. The clerk came in the next morning through the back door of the store. When he opened the front door and then the outhouse door, he came face-to-face with Billy, who had no intention of leaving. As the Misner family remembered, the clerk tried to remove the goat and the outhouse while also trying to open the store on time for customers, causing quite an eruption.[48]

Instead of a goat, some jokers would grab a pig from the pig-pen and let it loose in the house, or a hen would be pushed through an open window to cause havoc in the kitchen. One time a rooster was pushed down a stove pipe from the roof in the hope that it would frighten the occupants of the home when it

A Night of Retaliation

MR. WILLIAMS AND his wife lived just north of Oakes store in Alliance, Alberta. They were likeable people as they kept dairy cows, which supplied the townspeople with milk. However, they also "kept chickens, turkeys and Guinea fowl, the latter being very noisy birds. These birds would get out into the street and when somebody came along with a team, they would set up a terrible commotion. This didn't do much for the nerves of the horses or their owners! One Halloween night a bunch of the boys gathered up all of Williams' chickens, turkeys and Guineas, crated them up and took them down to the station where they put the crates in a boxcar and billed them to Edmonton!" The story did not provide any details of how Mr. and Mrs. Williams reacted to their missing birds, if they ever got them back or if they were compensated in some way.[49] ●

came out the bottom. In this case, sadly, the rooster ended up dying as it did not survive the fall. Other recipients of Halloween pranks found their sheds had been tipped over, or they had to walk three miles in order to find their buggy. One man offered a five-cent reward for information regarding his missing buggy whip. Wooden doorsteps were removed from people's homes or from stores in town.[50] In one town, a number of plows ended up on the street in front of the livery barn.

Sometimes the pranks backfired. Two boys decided that tipping over an outhouse in their town would be a good idea, but when the outhouse was pushed over, one boy fell into the excrement-filled hole. He had to go home and get changed and washed before they could continue with their Halloween activities.

Good Luck, Bad Luck and Other Superstitions

Whether they took seriously signs of good or bad luck, or had their fortunes told, homesteaders could readily recall their involvement with paranormal activities. While some homesteaders were skeptics and viewed fortune-telling solely as entertainment, others were what would have been called "superstitious." Today, this term has negative connotations and is considered a pejorative by some, as it can be dismissive of traditional folk beliefs or customs. In this context, the term has been retained, as it refers to beliefs that even the homesteaders themselves viewed with a combination of suspicion and reverence.

Graveyards at night were often associated with the spirit world, ghosts and malevolent beings, so many people were reluctant to be in a cemetery when it was dark. Homesteader Sidney May recounted the time a young man was challenged by his friends to go to the cemetery and find an open grave that had been prepared for a funeral the next day.[1] To test his mettle, he had to walk around the grave three times, then stick an iron peg into the ground beside the grave just as the big clock struck midnight. He said he wasn't afraid and that he would do it. He wore a long black overcoat, and when he drove in the peg, it went through the tail of his coat, pinning him down. Because it was so dark, he did not realize what he had done. When he tried to walk away, he was pulled back. Thinking that the spirits had come for him, he "yelled blue murder." He calmed down when he realized his friends were laughing at his predicament.

Another homesteader had an experience in a graveyard that left him shaken, especially since he fell into an open grave.

> Walter Ralph of Elnora, Alberta, was visiting and staying with his friend Harold Burningham. He was courting a girl from a neighbouring homestead. One evening, he stayed until dark and then started back to Harold's. Walter hurried as fast as possible. (It should be mentioned that just a short time before this, Harold Burningham had sold a little plot of the southwest corner of his farm to be used as a cemetery. The plot had been fenced and contained very few graves.) Walter hurried onward, cautiously as there was much brush and rough ground to contend with and scarcely a good trail to follow. Finally, he located the cemetery and decided to cut across it and take a shortcut home. He was still hurrying when all of a sudden he felt himself falling, coming to a sudden stop in a cold, damp and utterly dark place. He was really in shock when he suddenly realized where he was. He was out of that grave which he had fallen into, in dead of night, in one bound, and raced home as fast as his legs could carry him. He awoke Harold and it was some little time before he could really talk coherently to tell of his experience. He [was so rattled that he] had no recollection of climbing over the fence when leaving the cemetery although the place was well fenced all around.[2]

Percy Thomson's uncle was taken aback one time when he thought he saw an apparition on the prairie.[3]

> He was travelling across the Qu'Appelle Valley one dark night when he saw something white moving slowly across the valley. After watching it for some time, it suddenly became filled with a glowing light. My uncle hollered hello, the light went out and the answer came hello. Rather than a floating spirit or ghost, he found out that it was actually a man with a white sheet over him to keep away the mosquitoes. He had lit a match to light his pipe.

Sadie McCallum recalled the common belief that she and her fellow homesteaders lived near a haunted lake.[4] She said that on summer nights, balls of light would float haphazardly on the upper banks of the lake. People who were travelling home late at night would be shocked and alarmed by the lights that seemed to dance on the opposite shore. One time, she said, a homesteader had a "ball of light whirling about the wheel of his cart for some distance." Many believed that the lake was occupied by some kind of supernatural being or force. It was not until a number of years later that homesteaders began to wonder if the lights came from gas or phosphorus seeping from the earth.

Homesteader Mary Jordan from the Busby district also had an experience with mysterious lights that frightened her.[5] Her daughter, Lily, said that her mother was very superstitious. Late one evening, Mary looked out the window of their farmhouse and saw lights flashing in the nearby slough. She thought that it was fairies dancing. She made the younger children crawl under the bed so they were hidden, and she nailed quilts over the windows and door. Then she and the older children sat up all night so they would be prepared to fend off the fairies. Mary was concerned because she believed that fairies were not always friendly or compassionate; rather, they had the potential to be malicious and vindictive. If they were of the evil type, they could negatively influence people's lives through the use of their magic.

Many homesteaders hoped to learn what the fates had in store for them and tried a variety of methods to ascertain what

Four people playing with a Ouija board, ca. 1940. Their fingertips are placed on the planchette, which moves to answer questions asked by someone in the group. NA-4950-34. COURTESY OF LIBRARIES AND CULTURAL RESOURCES DIGITAL COLLECTIONS, UNIVERSITY OF CALGARY

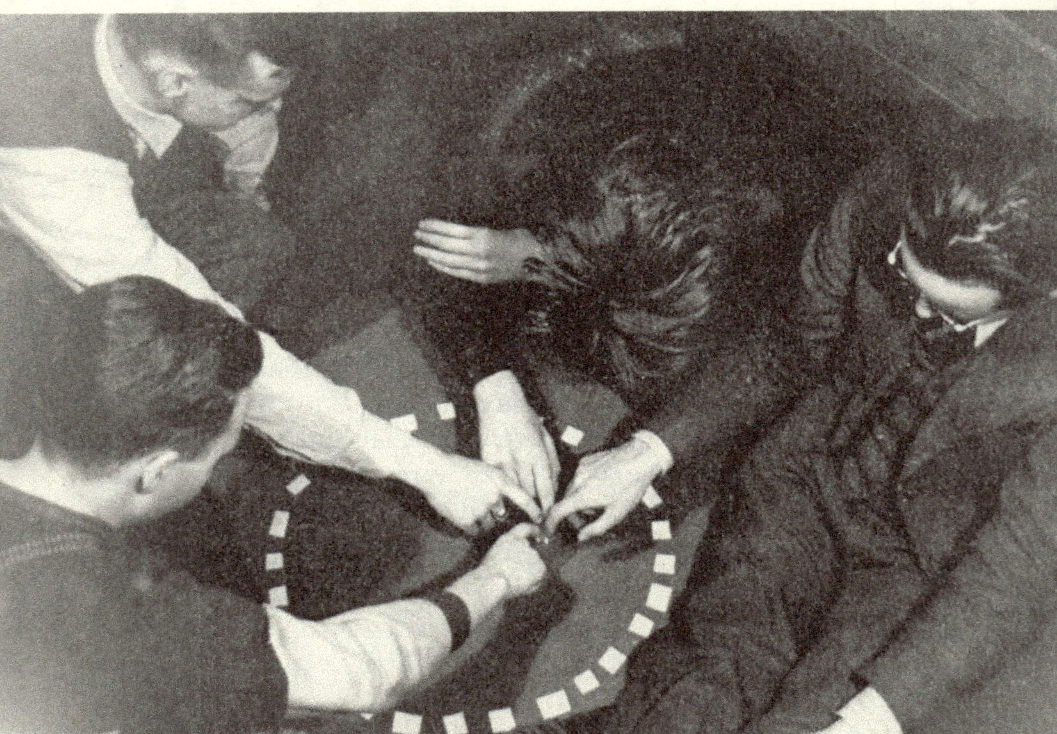

they should expect in the future. Lena May Purdy said that many people she knew "had a good deal of faith in an Ouija board."[6] A Ouija board was a flat board that contained each letter of the alphabet as well as the numbers 0 to 9, and the words "Yes," "No" and "Goodbye." The Ouija board was believed to be a magical device that provided a link between the paranormal world and the real world and could answer questions posed by the players. Questions could pertain to the past, present or future. At least two people would place their fingertips on the planchette (a teardrop-shaped piece of wood), ask their question and then watch as the planchette moved across the board, seemingly on its own. It would move from letter to letter to spell out words or would go to the Yes or No answers. If there was no response, it would move to Goodbye.

Cartomancy was another popular pastime for those who gathered for an evening's entertainment. Using a regular deck of cards, the fortune teller would ask the person who wished to know their fortune to shuffle the deck and then turn over the top card. Alternatively, a person could randomly choose a card from a deck that had been shuffled by the fortune teller. Once the card was identified, the fortune teller, who knew the meaning behind each card, would tell the person what it meant. For instance, if the upturned card was the ace of hearts, it meant that the person would be receiving a letter from a loved one, a visit from a friend or some other kind of pleasant news. If a seven of diamonds was revealed, the person faced a future of mockery or would be involved in a foolish scandal, while the ten of diamonds referred to a future journey or a change in residence.[7] Charles Pigeon remembered how popular cartomancy was in his area. "All of the neighbours would gather for a game of cards, but once the game was done, they would gather around to hear a man named Charlie tell them their fortunes with the cards." Charles did not feel that his neighbours were getting a real reading. As he said, Charlie "read the cards, telling girls what they wanted to hear or what they didn't want other people to hear."[8] In Admiral, Manitoba, Mrs. John Childs used to tell people's fortunes by cards; however, she would never tell fortunes on Sundays. Any other day of the week was fine with her, and she would start shuffling the deck as soon as someone expressed an interest.[9]

Mary Anderson stated that in her community, reading tea leaves or coffee grounds (also known as tasseography) was popular.[10] Neighbours would gather for afternoon tea or coffee. For tea leaf readings, each person would be given a teacup and saucer. When there was about a tablespoon of tea left in their cup, they would swirl the cup three times using their left hand. With the same hand, they would then invert their teacup over the saucer. The teacup would be left in this position for one minute, then it was rotated three times and turned upright with the handle facing south. The tea leaves that remained in the teacup after this process were read.[11] Shapes were identified in the tea leaves, and they were interpreted to give an indication of what the future held for the person who had drunk the tea. For instance, if the tea leaves were in the shape of a badger, the person would live a long life as a prosperous bachelor. If one could discern the shape of a bear, there would be a long period of travelling ahead. If a deer was depicted, the person would be involved with disputes and quarrels. A dog was a favourable sign that meant the person had faithful friends, while an elephant meant a future of good health.[12]

A similar process was used for reading coffee grounds. The coffee had to be quite strong, as it would be swirled in the same fashion as the tea when most of the coffee was drunk, and then inverted onto a saucer. After waiting a while, the sediment remaining in the cup would be read for any forms or patterns. The bottom of the cup represented the past, the midsection referred to the current time and the rim told the future. If the coffee grounds fell toward the handle, it foretold love and relationships; across from the handle referred to wealth; while the bottom of the cup referred to home and family.[13]

Palm reading, also known as palmistry, was another common form of entertainment. When telling the future, palm readers would first take into account the type of hand the person had and the natural elements their hand was associated with. For instance, a person with a square palm and short fingers had "earth hands," which meant they were practical and reliable. A person with long palms and short fingers had "fire hands" and were presumed to be passionate and empathetic, while those with square palms and long fingers, or "air hands," were curious or anxious. Those with long palms and long fingers had "water

Who Will We Marry?

MRS. ALBERT WEBSTER of Admiral, Manitoba, claimed to be able to read fortunes using tea leaves. Young school-girls, when they heard that she was going to tell fortunes on a particular day, would make sure to put extra tea leaves into their thermoses. When they had finished their lunch, they would run down to Mrs. Webster's place with their thermos. As one girl exclaimed, "[She] was always able to tell us the initial of who we were going to the next dance with, or who we would marry!"[14] •

hands." They were seen as creative and sensitive. After the hand type was identified, the hand reader would begin to read the palm's topography. The fleshy areas of the hand, referred to as mounts and plains, revealed the person's attributes, while the folds, creases and lines were used to predict the person's future.[15]

One homesteader, Elias Parmlee St. John, remembered the time he came across a hand reader when he went to town.[16] He mentioned that he was a very skeptical individual and didn't "entertain many superstitions." However, since he had some time to spare, he decided to get his palm read by a fortune teller who had set up shop.

> I came out of the Eaton's department store in Winnipeg in December 1915 and, looking across the street, saw the sign "Hands Read" in an upstairs window and I said to myself, that is a fake but I will go up and investigate it. Do you know that I got the surprise of my life? The hand-reader described my family, even the little girls we had adopted. She spoke of my wonderful wife and all the things she could turn her hand to. She even spoke about our mineral rights of over 3,000 acres we have on the ranch and advised me against leasing them which I forgot and leased to Imperial Oil later.

Pregnancy, Babies and Superstitions

THE SOCIAL NORMS of the time revolved around marriage and having large families. Such an expectation began in adolescence, when girls tried to predict how many children they would have in the future. Some counted the number of seeds inside an apple they had chosen to eat, with the number of seeds predicting the number of children they would bear. Others plucked heads off an oat or wheat stem and counted the number of grains, while others tried dropping an egg white into a glass of water to see how many times the egg white divided. The number of divisions would predict the number of children. Some girls would count the number of X's in the palm of their right hand, or they would pick a dandelion that had gone to seed and then blow the seeds into the wind. The seeds left on the stem predicted the number of children.

Once they were older, married and pregnant, predictions would be made regarding the baby's sex. It was believed that if the baby kicked a lot or if the mother gained more weight than usual, the baby would be a boy. If the mother happened to drop a knife during her pregnancy, she would have a boy. If she dropped a pair of scissors, she would have a girl. If the mother slept on her left side, she would have a boy. If she slept on her right, she would have a girl. If she started craving sweets, she would have a girl. If she craved salty foods, she would have a boy. Sometimes a woman would suspend her wedding ring over her stomach. If it started swinging in circles, the baby would be a girl, while a ring moving back and forth in a straight line predicted a boy. If a mother experienced morning sickness throughout her pregnancy, she would be having a girl. If morning sickness was not a problem, she would be having a boy.

The mother's body changes also led to predictions as to a baby's sex. If the mother carried the baby high or out front, it was going to be a boy. If she was carrying it low or wide, it would be a girl. When it was time to have the baby, superstitious beliefs continued. A sharp knife would be placed under the mother's bed while she was in labour. It was believed that doing this would cut her labour pains in half.[17]

Once the baby arrived, the day of the week they were born became an issue for discussion as people believed each day determined the future characteristics of the baby. The fortune-telling rhyme "Monday's Child," written in 1838 by English novelist Anna Eliza Bray, became a popular prophecy:

Monday's child is fair of face,
Tuesday's child is full of grace,
Wednesday's child is full of woe,
Thursday's child has far to go,
Friday's child is loving and giving,
Saturday's child works hard for a living,
But the child that is born on the Sabbath day,
is fair and wise and good and gay.[18]

Even the naming of the baby caused some superstitious concern. For instance, some believed that if a child was named after a deceased relative, the child would be doomed to an early death or would eventually be called away by the spirit of the dead. Others had a more positive approach to naming babies after relatives, as they felt that the deceased relative's spirit would protect the baby throughout their lifetime. Others believed it was unlucky to call a child by his or her name before they were christened, while others became anxious if the baby's name contained thirteen letters (as he or she would then have the devil's luck). ●

It all puzzled me as to how she knew all of this information. I could not understand it and wonder if there is a power that exists that we don't understand.

William Tarzwell of Sherman, Manitoba, had an experience with a fortune teller who was able to help him locate some missing horses.[19] The horses, William's best team, had been missing for a couple of days, ever since his hired man had left them out in a field to graze on their own. Each day, William and some friends rode out to try and find the horses, but they never had any luck. One day they stopped for dinner in a small town east of Admiral. A man who overheard their conversation about the horses suggested they get in touch with another man who lived in that town and who was very successful in helping people. William did not believe in fortune tellers but decided to give it a go. He came across the man, who was working on his roof. The man came down the ladder and proceeded to tell William that his horses were in a corral and that they were being treated well. He told him the exact location of the horses and how many miles it would take to get there. He also mentioned that the horses had William's brand on them. Along with the information about the horses, he told William that he and his wife would have a baby girl. To William's amazement, everything the fortune teller predicted turned out to be true. He was able to retrieve his horses, and in time he became the proud father of a baby girl.

Just as fortune-telling was an entertainment for some and a thought-provoking pastime for others, many homesteaders held their own superstitions regarding

Superstitions surrounded all aspects of childhood. In this photograph from 1909, two young brothers pose with their baby sister. AUTHOR'S COLLECTION

signs of good and bad luck. Whether they strongly believed these superstitions or not, many homesteaders were aware of practices that might produce good or bad events in the future. Here are some examples of beliefs about good luck:

> For good luck, always spit on your finger and cross the toe of your boot when you see a white horse.
>
> If you find a four-leaf clover in the field, you will have good luck.
>
> If you find a pin on the floor, pick it up and you will have good luck.
>
> Hang a horseshoe over the door with the open end up so that your luck can never run out.
>
> Carrying a rabbit's foot in your pocket will bring you good luck.
>
> The first person to see a robin in the spring will have good luck.
>
> Two people saying the same thing at the same time unknowingly is a sign of good luck.
>
> Expressing a hope for the future and crossing your fingers will result in good luck.
>
> If you see a new moon, turn over your money in your pocket for good luck.
>
> If you are the first to see a new moon over your right shoulder, you will have good luck.
>
> If the palm of your left hand itches, you will receive something good.

Martha Todd recounted the old adage that if you can find the end of the rainbow, you will discover a pot of gold.[20] She then told the story of how her neighbour decided to set out to find the end of the rainbow one day. When he came back, he said "he didn't quite believe it because every time he moved to get closer to the rainbow's end, the rainbow seemed farther away." Martha also mentioned that if you saw a double rainbow, you had to make sure you made a wish on it so that it would come true. Elias Parmlee St. John didn't believe in good luck signs.[21] Rather, he was quite practical about what good luck meant for him. As he said, "The best luck I know is if a friend gave me a check for $5,000!"

As for bad luck signs, homesteaders were able to point out many superstitious actions that could lead to misfortune and misery in the future. According to Ella Otterson, if a garment was put on inside out, it had to be worn that way until midday, otherwise bad luck would prevail.[22] In the same vein, Sam McWilliams recounted how an acquaintance was so superstitious that he refused to put his hunting vest on properly after he discovered that he had put it on backward one morning.[23] Sam said that he wore it that way all day as he was afraid of bad luck. Mrs. W.H.S. Gange stated that if a person put a garment on inside out by mistake, bad luck would be heading their way.[24]

Ellenor Merriken remembered a fellow homesteader named Mr. Bidleman who couldn't tolerate her litter of black kittens.[25] While most people believed that a black cat crossing their path led to bad luck, Mr. Bidleman was so superstitious that even the sight of the kittens ruined his day. Ellenor recounted:

> One fall when our cats had been real prolific, I had thirteen black kittens and every one followed me wherever I went around the farm. One day, as I was on my way down to see my friend Martha, I met a team and buggy with two men from town, bent on a hunting expedition. Meeting thirteen black cats was too much for Mr. Bidleman, who at best was a superstitious fellow. He stopped suddenly, wheeled the horses around and beat it back to town. I will never forget the expressions he used in relation to black cats spoiling his hunting trip.

There were a number of other well-known bad luck superstitions that made an impression on homesteaders:

> It was unlucky to start a new job on Friday, but not unlucky to keep on working if the job was already started a day or two

before. A person could even start late on Thursday evening in order to work on Friday without facing the consequences of bad luck.

Letting a fork drop on the floor at mealtime meant bad luck, as did putting two axes on the grindstone at the same time. Hanging up a calendar before January 1 was also a sign of bad luck in the future.

Bad luck would come to those who did unnecessary work on Sundays (i.e., the Sabbath day).

Breaking a mirror meant seven years of bad luck.

Walking under a ladder also meant bad luck.

Thirteen people seated at a table meant that one would die before the end of the year.

The thirteenth day of any month was always an unlucky day.

Used brooms should not be brought into a home that you are moving into as they will cause bad luck.

Slaughtering a pig for home use in the dark of the morning will result in bad luck.

Spilling salt meant a day of bad luck, as did a bird flying into a window or getting into a house.

Some people believed that mirages were bad omens, as was looking at the moon through a window or hearing a rooster crowing at night.

Swallowing a fruit pip was bad luck as a tree would grow inside you.

Being married on a wet day or on a Friday was a sign of bad luck, as was losing your wedding ring.

Getting out of bed on the wrong side meant bad luck, as did putting the left shoe on first and singing before breakfast.

If you broke a dish, you had to break two matches or you would have bad luck. (The idea was that breaking two matches would prevent further dishes being broken, as it was believed that breakages occurred in threes.)

Killing a spider was to be avoided. If you wish to live and thrive, let the spider run alive.

Dropping a comb meant bad luck, as did placing shoes on a table.[26]

If you set out on a trip but had to return to your house, you had to sit down before starting out again, otherwise you would have bad luck.

You would have bad luck if you cut your hair on Friday.

One homesteader recounted instances of both good and bad luck, as well as romance, set out in a simple rhyme about crows. As she said, "See one crow, good luck. Two crows, bad luck. Three a wish and four a kiss."

As for how to circumvent these bad luck signs, one homesteader suggested touching wood, crossing your fingers or throwing a pinch of salt over your right shoulder.

While it is not based on good or bad luck, water-witching, also known as dowsing, was an aspect of farm life that roused curiosity among the homesteading crowd. This was a method of finding water sources, which were critical for homesteaders. A person who had the "gift" (i.e., the ability to witch water) would take a Y-shaped branch from a willow tree. This branch was known as a divining rod. The water witcher held the two ends of the Y fairly loosely and started walking across a yard or field. When there was a strong downward force pulling the end of the branch toward the ground, it meant that water was nearby. By the time the water witcher was directly above the water source, the pull would become so strong that the witcher had to grip the two ends firmly; otherwise the stick would drop to the ground. While some firmly believed that water-witching worked and was a reliable method for finding water, others were more skeptical. They believed that the practice was based on superstition, and all agreed that though water-witching sometimes worked, sometimes it didn't.

Sidney May speculated that some people had the ability to water-witch because an electric current from running water met with a current in their body, which turned the rod. He said it "works more with people with plenty of electricity in their body. Some people don't have much," so it didn't work for them.[27]

Some homesteaders would try to dig wells on their property based on their own intuition or their hope that water was available where they planned to dig. Others relied on family members, friends and neighbours who had the water-witching skill. Tobias Lanegraff, for example, indicated that his father always used a forked willow to find water before he dug a well.[28] Marion Anderson of Newdale, Manitoba,[29] and Martha Todd of Indian Head, Saskatchewan,[30] were both well aware of the practice and knew which neighbours they could rely on if they needed any water-witching done. Paul Gehlert of Stony Plain, Alberta, told of the time he was ready to dig a well on his land in order to have a ready source of water for his family.[31] As he wrote in his memoirs, a neighbour happened to stop by on that particular day and ended up offering his advice based on his water-witching abilities.

> I went and made a bunch of five-inch rails and dragged them out for cribbing, and then started digging. Joe Trautman [a neighbour] came over and asked if I was sure I was getting water. I said, "I don't know. I am just digging and will find out." He walked a few steps away and found himself a willow. He walked around with the willow where I was digging and said, "Keep on digging where you are. You will get water." I dug down with the spade till I could not throw out any more dirt. I got my brother Elbert and we had to start using the bucket and pulling it up. We were down now thirteen feet and the wife called us in for dinner. I then took the shovel and struck it in the northeast corner of the hole. The shovel flew to the side and the water was coming in. I had to holler for the ladder. When we had eaten dinner and came out, the water had risen to six feet from the ground. There was water for as long as I was on that farm, that was thirty-five years.

John Olson, who lived near Young, Saskatchewan, recounted the time when he decided that he needed a well on his homestead.[32] He relied on the skill of the local water witcher to find a source of water, but things could easily have gone awry as his father, Lars, offered his input into the process.

> Someone in the district could witch for water. Mr. J. Gunnarson, a bachelor, homesteader and lay preacher, who lived a couple of miles east, was gifted with this know-how and he came over and witched for water while I did the fencing. When [I returned home], I started to dig, but got no water. [I asked my father,] did you move the stick that Gunnarson put up? Yes, I did, Lars answered. In what direction did you move the stick? Closer to the barn. What did you do that for? I thought it'd be handy to have the well as close to the barn as possible was the logical answer. I dug where the stick was first put up [by Gunnarson]. The side where I dug got wet. I dug down about thirty feet and water was coming in fast. I had several loads of stones ready for cribbing. As soon as the well was finished, I brought the cattle over. Father made the watering trough.

Many farmers in the Admiral district of Manitoba relied on the water-witching gift of such individuals as Eldon Kerbyson and Gunner Sahlen when they wanted to locate water on their land. However, other farmers were skeptical about water-witching. One fellow was very doubtful about the process until he discovered that he had the ability to do it himself, while Jack Moir completely disavowed this seemingly supernatural event. As he used to say to his fellow farmers, "You might just as well put your hat on your head and run like hell and where it falls off, dig your well!"[33]

There were also stories of farmers who were taken in by those who claimed to be water witchers. In one case, two men came to Admiral claiming that they had the ability to find water. They were hired by a farmer who lived north of Admiral for a negotiated price. They arrived at the farm and dug down quite a few feet with their shovels before they quit for the day. During the night, when the farmer and his family were asleep, they returned and

Three men dig a well in Airdrie, Alberta, in 1907. *L–R:* Frank Van Sickle, Fred Van Sickle and Lafe Van Sickle. NA-599-5. COURTESY OF LIBRARIES AND CULTURAL RESOURCES DIGITAL COLLECTIONS, UNIVERSITY OF CALGARY

poured a few barrels of water into the hole in the ground. In the morning, when they reappeared, they claimed that the well was a success, collected their money and left the area.[34]

"The Pig Is Generally the Best Weather Forecaster"

Some homesteaders relied on the changing behaviours of farm animals, birds, wild animals and insects to predict the weather. Such creatures quickly react to environmental signals like changes in the barometric pressure and fluctuations in the humidity, and they will flee, look for shelter or act in a strange manner. Their heightened senses mean that they can hear, feel and smell any environmental changes that are occurring, changes that people are completely unaware of. By watching for unusual behaviour around or in the farmyard, homesteaders could ready themselves for oncoming rainstorms, blizzards and warm or cold weather. From time to time, they could also make predictions about early springs or long hard winters.

Many animals and birds behave differently as different weather patterns approach—so much so that homesteaders began to watch for this "out of the ordinary" behaviour. Whether they were watching the wild birds, insects or their own farm animals and poultry, homesteaders came to rely on the creatures in and around the farmyard to predict the weather so they could prepare themselves before storms or other types of inclement weather approached. In other words, the behaviour of the farm animals helped homesteaders survive.[1] For instance, John Hamer remarked on the change in his horses' behaviour when a storm was drawing near.

> Horses seem to know if there is a very bad blizzard coming. On December 31, 1909, my horses came up into the yard. The Pinto was running around in a circle and the rest were following. She had her neck arched and was acting more

frisky than usual. About 3 o'clock, it began to snow with a strong wind from the northwest. I went to the barn, opened the door, and called them. They came in on the run. In about half an hour, there was a terrible blizzard. But it didn't last long as some. Quit about 2 o'clock in the morning. So, I figured the Pinto knew more about weather than I do.[2]

D.H. Maginnes had a similar experience when his animals had a better sense of the weather than he did.[3] He said, "I remember one time I wanted to hitch up the oxen in the yard and go somewhere but they resisted. I couldn't get their heads over the tongue of the yoke. They broke away from me and made straight for the barn. Inside of a quarter of an hour, we had a terrific hailstorm." Charles Bray could tell when a rainstorm was on the way by the behaviour of his cattle.[4] "If there was a wind, his cattle, which were out on the range, could smell when a storm was coming, and they would immediately start heading for home to seek shelter in the barn."

Homesteaders noticed other odd forms of animal behaviour that occurred around the farm. Some mentioned that their dogs would start eating grass or would roll around on the ground if a rainstorm was imminent. Others said that if you looked out the window in the morning and the dogs were not in the yard, it meant that it was too cold to go outside. Mrs. J.M. Telfodd noted that if a dog chased its tail, a wind would soon blow in,[5] and Mrs. C.A. Stewart said that her cats would jump about and fight if the weather changed.[6]

Cattle would seek shelter by a barn if a storm was imminent. Photo ca. 1919. NA-2637-2.
COURTESY OF LIBRARIES AND CULTURAL RESOURCES DIGITAL COLLECTIONS, UNIVERSITY OF CALGARY

Mrs. Ed Wilson also reported seeing unusual behaviour one morning, but it was not due to an impending storm or any kind of change in the weather patterns.[7] Rather, it was caused by the lunar cycle. She said, "A few years ago, I went out early as usual to get the cows. My hens were all fussing around, my horse was almost unmanageable and the cows just crazy. The light was very strange and all at once I remembered there was a partial eclipse of the sun that morning."

Others noticed that insects behaved differently if a storm was approaching. Mrs. Jay Laycock said that if there were more wasps around than usual, a rainstorm would soon follow.[8] Others believed that rain would occur if a number of horseflies suddenly appeared and started biting. Similarly, if mosquitoes were furiously biting at night, it meant that rain would arrive the next day. Frank Baines noticed that bees would fly into their hives before a storm,[9] while Charles Sargent believed that crickets chirping at night was a sure sign of rain.[10] Instead of watching flying insects, John Thiessen noted the behaviour of ants in his farmyard.[11] He said that if ants made banks of dirt around their holes after a rainstorm, more rain would be forthcoming. Not all insect behaviour foretold wet weather. If spiders spun their cobwebs on the bushes and they glistened with dew in the early morning in fall, a homesteader could bank on a good day for harvesting.

Some homesteaders focused on the behaviour of their farmyard birds. For example, one homesteader reported that if his chickens stayed out in the rain, it would rain all day, but if they ran for shelter, it would only be a shower. Mary Kajewski believed that if birds began flocking together, or if prairie chickens began congregating near the barn door, a storm would soon occur.[12] John Fetsch felt that the flying and running of his turkeys foretold a storm.[13] J.H. Sand believed that when birds were flying low and fast, a storm was coming.[14] Many other homesteaders studied the behaviour of the wild birds that flew in the vicinity of their farmhouse. Charles Sargent, for example, said that if ducks made their nests a long distance from the slough, it was a sign of the wet year that was to come.[15] Lila Pope indicated that when snowbirds came in flocks, they would be followed by a snowstorm,[16] while Mrs. J.M. Telfodd reported that honking geese were honking for the onset of winter.[17] Also, if the geese were migrating

Groundhog Day

GROUNDHOG DAY, WHICH occurs on February 2 each year, is a "cross-quarter day," which means that it falls midway between the winter solstice and the spring equinox. Many believe that this is the perfect date for predicting early or late springs. A number of homesteaders were familiar with the concept of Groundhog Day, as they referred to it in their memoirs when discussing how to predict the weather. For instance, Mary Kajewski,[18] Charles Sargent[19] and Mrs. D.A. Moorhouse[20] all indicated that if February 2 was bright and sunny and the groundhog saw his shadow, he would get scared and go back into his burrow for six weeks, which meant that there would be another six weeks of winter. If it was a dull day, the groundhog would stay out of his hole, he would not see his shadow and there would be early spring. •

south, it was likely that snow would soon follow them from the north. Martha Todd noted that if ducks and geese had a profuse amount of down, it would be a cold winter.[21]

Other birds foretold more pleasant weather conditions. If homesteaders saw crows early in the year, it meant that spring was just around the corner (but not right away). However, if one saw robins, spring was near. If meadowlarks began singing at sunrise, it meant that it would be a fine day. Another sign of good weather was ladybirds on the flowers in the garden.

Like his fellow homesteaders, Charles Davis from the Glaslyn area of Saskatchewan was familiar with animals and birds and how they could predict the weather.[22] However, he was also very knowledgeable about wild animals and their reactions to changing weather patterns as well as how vegetation reacted to moisture levels. In his memoir, he gave a thorough account of the signs that he looked for in order to prepare himself for future weather conditions. He also provided tips for those who were caught in lightning storms and other adverse conditions.

> Pigs are the only animals that can see the wind ... If you see them racing in circles, trying to catch their own tails, you can be sure of heavy winds and rain. If birds are nesting low in the brush or trees, high and strong winds will prevail for many weeks. Muskrats building high mounds in the fall means that lots of snow will fall during the winter. If leaves have fallen off the trees before the first week in November, expect a long cold winter. If bears are prowling in December, this indicates that an easy winter will follow. Migratory birds moving south in September and October means that an early winter is coming. If fish leave shallow water for deeper levels before October, there is going to be a hard winter ahead. If there are clouds in the sky, look out for a steady rain, and if they persist, there will be a long rain that will last from one to three days.
>
> If a hen calls for her chicks insistingly, to brood, rain is near. Birds of the air scurrying, as if they are being chased, means that a storm or tempest is forecast. When the bloom of the dandelion closes, rain will come down. When the leaves turn top to bottom, there will be a wind, followed by a rain that will soon spot them. Take no shelter under trees, for lightning often strikes. Those who wear rubber boots in the rain will be protected from the lightning. For those who are fearful of the tempestuous thunderstorm, the safest place to be is to rest in stockinged feet between woolen blankets in bed. If caught out in a very bad thunderstorm, in open country, avoid the higher land. Keep calm as a heated body becomes moist and is receptive and will make itself into a static conductor.
>
> The pig is generally the best weather forecaster when he or she jumps around like an animal gone loco. When this happens, it's ten to one that wind or rainstorms are approaching. If pigs are steadily carrying mouthfuls of bedding to their favorite corner of the sty, they are telling us, as plain as your face, to prepare for cooler and wetter weather. Frogs are also good predictors. If you hear an extra chorus

Weather Sayings

CERTAIN KINDS OF wildlife behaviour, repeated over many years, resulted in homesteaders believing in long-term forecasts, particularly about lengthy cold winters with vast amounts of snow, or predictions about when it was a good time to seed their crops in the spring. These beliefs developed into common sayings among the homesteaders, some of which are listed here.[23]

If muskrat houses are built large and high above the water, there is going to be a hard winter ahead.

If muskrats build big houses, it means that it will be cold in the winter, but little snow. If houses are built smaller, there will be lots of snow.

If animals grow a heavy coat of fur in the fall, it means a long cold winter ahead.

Spring has arrived when frogs were heard for the third time.

Coyotes howling presaged cold weather.

When wolves howl, there will be frost.

If frogs croaked very loudly in the evening, then there would be rain.

When frogs started to croak in spring, it was time to seed the wheat.

If jack rabbits turned white by the time the snow came, or before, there will be a severe winter. If they stay brown after the snow comes, the winter will be mild.

Anytime you see a lizard or garter snake sunning itself in the grass, or on the road, it will rain in twenty-four hours.

Coyotes howl before a change of weather. ●

Two young homesteaders, George and Grace Allen, feed their pigs in the Pine Lake district of Alberta, 1917. NA-2767-19. COURTESY OF LIBRARIES AND CULTURAL RESOURCES DIGITAL COLLECTIONS, UNIVERSITY OF CALGARY

of shrill croaking, especially in the early spring from a congregation of them, the spring skies will open with luscious drenching rains. Bullfrogs continually croaking in the fall is an omen that everything will be fine for all. If he hops to rocks ashore, a sunny fall is in store. If frogs in the froggery begin to roam, then you should stay at home. Crickets in the walls or the hearth give hints of the weather to come. When its fiddling legs give a shrill resonant sound and continue till after midnight, then it will be bonnie and bright the next day. If their fiddling is harsh and coarse, stormy weather will come in force. If gophers are chatting to each other outside of their gopher holes, soon spring weather will begin. Should the gopher start to roam, you should never go far from home. If he naps outside his home, rain and wind is sure to come.

Winds, Crescent Moons, Mirages and Northern Lights

Given that weather was so important to the lives of homesteaders, it was not a surprise to find that many relied on local adages—that is, they tried to forecast the weather based on past experiences, repeated over several years; social customs; and generational traditions and beliefs. Whether they were trying to ascertain the environmental effect of the prairie winds, the ominous-looking clouds, sundogs or mares' tails, many homesteaders were aware that such events could foretell high or low temperatures, or the advent of calm or stormy days. While they were not predictors of weather, northern lights were sometimes a cause of concern, and many homesteaders were less than impressed with mirages, given their deceitful qualities.

Trying to determine what the weather was going to be like for the day was an important facet of homesteading life. Homesteaders were keen to know which way the wind was blowing in order to ascertain whether the temperature would be getting chillier or warmer, or whether a storm could be brewing. Typically, winds from the north or northeast meant that cold weather was on the horizon, while winds from the west and south predicted warm weather. Other winds predicted rain storms. Koozma Tarasoff stated, "If the wind begins to blow from the S.E. and it follows the sun to the west, then rain is expected to fall ... In our district, near the junction of the North Saskatchewan River and Eagle Creek, if clouds came from the west towards Eagle Creek, and then turned off along that creek, a heavy rain and hail storm was expected to occur."[1]

The most common method for discovering which way the wind was blowing was described by homesteader Robert Widdess who lived on the vast plains of Rocanville, Saskatchewan.[2] He said, "There never was much trouble telling which way the wind was blowing. Even in the days before the trees began to grow, the blades of grass would usually indicate the wind direction. But at times when it was calm, the way to tell was by putting your finger in your mouth to moisten it, then hold your finger up in the air. The part of the surface that feels a little cool shows the direction from which the breeze is coming." Other homesteaders had a method for ascertaining the strength of the wind without leaving their homes. They would fasten a length of logging chain to a post in the yard. If the chain stood straight out in the wind, the wind was too strong for any kind of outdoor work to be done. Ella Otterson said that she never used the chain method for telling the velocity of the wind, but at different times when she had been out driving a team, the wind was so strong that she had to hold the reins with both hands to keep them from being jerked away from her. She had also seen winds so intense that chickens and turkeys, which had not sought cover in time, were blown across the yard.[3]

From time to time, serious wind-related events could occur. These strong winds not only caused damage but also threatened lives. Many homesteaders told tales of living through these types of disastrous events. John Ludlow's neighbour had an experience with high winds in which a two-by-four board was picked up from his barn and driven endwise through the side of his house. "Granaries, that were twelve foot by sixteen foot structures, were picked up by the wind and smashed."[4] Felix Belliveau recounted how "one couple took refuge behind a school in a windstorm and a barn blew by as they waited for the wind to subside. Their buggy had also been turned upside down behind the horse."[5] He related another story about a "fellow [who] was in a barn with his team of oxen and the barn blew off of them." Another homesteader stood against his shack door to try to keep the wind out and to keep the shack on its feet. If the wind had been able to get into the house, the strength of the wind would have blown the house away. Harriet Stueck recounted how her father's barn blew down two different times due to the strong winds,[6] while another homesteader remembered how often roofs were torn off and granaries were entirely moved from their foundations. Frank Baines said, "[A] wind at Waldron blew a house to pieces and killed a man and woman." This same wind "blew a piece of half-inch board right through a green standing poplar tree ... and left a foot out of each side."[7]

Edna Staples McIntosh told of the time her family experienced their first windstorm.

> It was dead still outside and we wondered if it was a tornado or something that was coming. The sky was so black and we just stood outside and watched it. The air was just still and then it hit us. We had to hold a pillow at the windows to keep them from breaking. It was just like a sheet of black; it was dirt [mixed up with the wind] ... Nothing grew, not even the weeds on the summerfallow ... It just finished everything. We had a good garden before this, but those storms just dried the land out so, you know, it was terrible.[8]

The Evans family also remembered their first windstorm.[9] Daughter Reta reported that the family was somewhat naive at first about the dangers associated with oncoming storms, but they soon learned how alarming such storms could be.

> We'd stop, look up, and sure enough, way to the south and east was an enormous wall of soft sand color. First thought was to get to the house ... Then back outside to watch and stay as long as we dared. The whole world was a funny yellow now and that wall of color was darker and nearer. It had become big rolling clouds piling higher and higher up the sky. And anticipating who knows what, we raced around for the sheer pleasure of the unexpected. First, little puffs and pieces of wind, then rough gusts, caught at our hair and clothes. Lids, or whole tin cans, in the yard were blown up in the air, way, way up, and dropped again. The birds glided and wheeled in circles. We laughed, watching the chickens scurrying for shelter while being pushed by the wind, noisily objecting with their feathers all fluffed out in anger and their tails blown almost backward. Tumbling weeds came from nowhere and sped across the yard and fields to pile up against the fences. Horses would come galloping home or race in the pasture and whinny. Even the cows made an attempt at running. This was

> a fun time and it lasted a very short while—a matter of minutes. We waited for the big boiling storm to catch right up to us ... Suddenly the wind hit, full of choking dust ... Mom, who was braced against the open door, [started calling for us], "Come inside. What's the matter with you? Do you want to be blown away?" It never did get that bad [as we always made sure to be inside when the storm hit], but she told that us that if ever we were caught away from the house, we should lie down on the ground.

Kenelm Luttman-Johnson, who lived south of Willow Bunch, Saskatchewan, recounted his story of the storm that he and his wife experienced in 1913—far more dangerous than the windstorm described by Reta Simons, as it was a cyclone that threatened their lives.[10] One day they decided to go into town for supplies, using a team of horses hitched to their democrat. Arriving at town, they detached the democrat in front of the mercantile and stabled the team. The stable was built into the side of a hill. As Kenelm said, "The heat was stifling. The storekeeper, a friend of ours, insisted we stay to supper at his shack. He made a small fire and lit the lamp. It was getting very dark, then the cyclone hit. The area was flat, surrounded by hills on the west, north, north-east and south. Open to the northwest and southeast. The storekeeper laughed when he [looked out the window] and saw my wagon spin. I told him this was no laughing matter." Kenelm, realizing how dire the situation was, felt that they would be lucky if they could survive the storm. He told the storekeeper to douse the fire and the lamp. He peered out the window and saw the clouds rolling off the hills at ground level. He grabbed his wife with one hand, and with the other he held the door, saying to her that when the shack collapsed, they would run outside where they would be safer. As the shack was hit, he opened the door, pulled his wife with him and made her lie down on the ground. He lay on top of her to protect her. They and the shopkeeper survived, but Kenelm and his wife were both "covered with little bruises from neck to heel." Their teenage son, who had stayed at their homestead, crawled under a table when the roof blew away. He was unhurt. The stable was undamaged and their team of horses was safe. The storekeeper's shack was destroyed, and the remains of the democrat, when it was found, were "nothing more than matchwood."

Robert Widdess, in his memoirs, gave an account of a cyclone he experienced when he was a young boy in the late 1890s in Rocanville, Saskatchewan.[11] He remembered that the second storeys of almost all the buildings in town were blown off. He was also impressed by the force of the cyclone when it hit the homestead where he was staying at the time. As he said, "The water in the well was actually drawn out, and the well was dry after the storm passed over. I was the boy who got the last pail of water from the well just before the storm burst and tried to pull another after because the pail had been knocked over by the cyclone. The well was dry." He described a peculiar incident that occurred just a few days later.

> My brother and I were driving out to Moosomin in a buggy. About halfway out, we were overtaken by a very heavy rainstorm. We turned off the road and pulled up with the horse's back to the fury of the wind and crawled under the buggy for shelter ourselves. The rain stopped just as suddenly as it had started, and we looked out and the ruts in the road were covered with shiny little fishes. It's hardly right to say covered, sprinkled would be a better term. But they were fish. There was no doubt about that ... tiny little fellows ... but fishes nevertheless.

With the strong winds, soil would drift and bank up against houses, barns and fences, as seen in this photograph from ca. 1920. NA-4357-2. COURTESY OF LIBRARIES AND CULTURAL RESOURCES DIGITAL COLLECTIONS, UNIVERSITY OF CALGARY

Prairie Wind Humour

GIVEN THEIR COMMON experiences, many homesteaders appreciated a good joke about the never-ending winds on the prairies.[12]

One fellow said it was so windy that when he was siding up his homestead shack, he just held the nails up and the wind blew them in.

There was the case of the men on the trail near Lake Johnson. They stopped at a halfway house. This halfway house was poorly constructed. It was a windy night. They had to get up during the night and remove the castors from the bed to keep it from blowing across the room.

In 1906, a visitor claimed that the wind in Saskatchewan was so bad that to keep his cap, he had to take it off and stand on it.

A rancher in Alberta went to town with a team and box sled in late winter. A chinook came up and he started for home.[13] It was thawing so fast, the team was trotting on the snow while the box sled was on the ground. He whipped up his teams, but he could not get the box sled on the snow as it was thawing so fast.

One man said that there were some terrible windstorms at times throughout the prairies. One storm blew his well clean out of the ground and stood it up alongside of the barn. He got an auger and bored a hole in the side of the well, put in a piece of pipe and a spigot, and he had all the water he wanted.

There are some heavy winds out on the open prairie. A man left his tractor sitting near the line fence. When he went out to get it, his neighbour was using it. The wind had picked it up and blew it over the fence onto the neighbour's land.

A homesteader tried to fence his quarter-section. He dug all the post holes, but along came a high wind and blew every one of those post holes out of the ground. He went out to retrieve them the next day, but they were so out of shape from bouncing all over the prairie that they were useless and he had to write them off as a total loss.

A hen undertook to lay an egg with her back to the wind. The wind was blowing so hard that she laid the same egg six times.

One homesteader stated that he and his family members never went outside when the winds were wild because if they did, their ragged worn-out clothes would flap them to death.

Instead of a joke, homesteader Eloise Anderson recounted a family story about the wind in Saskatchewan.[14]

> The funniest story I ever heard was about how my father wrote to my mother before she and I left Nebraska [to go homesteading in Saskatchewan]. He said she would not need to bring her clothespins up here, as there was no wind in Saskatchewan. It may have been living in the heavy timber that fooled him, or was there actually a year when it wasn't windy? He came first, located the homestead, put up buildings and then my mother and I came out. She immediately realized that she really needed her clothespins! ●

While Robert and his brother were shocked to see fish on dry land so far removed from any lake, there was a logical explanation for this strange event. A cyclone had likely moved over a lake and sucked up the fish into its vortex. The cyclone then travelled a number of miles before losing its strength and depositing the fish on the ground.[15]

Homesteaders could predict weather patterns by determining the direction of the wind. They also tried to forecast long-term conditions, particularly drought, by the colour of the sunset. As Ella Otterson noted, "Red or glinty sunsets, south-west winds and little dust devils or whirlwinds meant days of dry weather ahead. A very fiery red sunset meant hot winds the next day while continuous fiery red sunsets would foretell a long period of drought."[16]

Homesteaders dreaded drought conditions, as lack of moisture meant hardship for the family. It could even mean the end of their homesteading life, as crops cannot survive without rain. Given that homesteaders relied on payment for threshed grain, one year of drought could have serious economic consequences from which the family might not recover. Charles Sargent noted that experience taught many farmers that their biggest enemy was drought and not frost, as many anticipated when they first settled here.[17]

Mary Rogers Berkner remembered the serious drought conditions that her family lived through.[18]

> [We] hardly got into June when the weather turned extremely hot; it grew progressively worse until the thermometer registered 104 and 105 in the shade day after day, with not even a hint of a breeze or a drop of rain. Crops soon began to show the effects of the intense heat, the sloughs and ponds dried up one by one, until there wasn't a drop of water anywhere, with the exception of the Saskatchewan River and some of the larger creeks. Even the prairie grass looked dead.

Norman McDonald also remembered a year when he and his family experienced drought.[19] They were able to harvest only seventy-eight bushels of wheat off a hundred acres—in a normal year, with rain, they averaged about fifteen bushels per acre.

He mentioned that the only place the wheat would grow was in the low areas, and even then it was very sparse. Another year, along with the drought, they had a grasshopper infestation. With the little amount of wheat that was able to grow, even in the low areas, the crop was wiped out by these ravenous insects. As Norman wearily stated, "They did a lot of damage."

Frank Baines of Crescent City, Saskatchewan, remembered the summer of 1889 as the driest period of time he had ever lived through.[20] There was only one rain shower all summer. Sam McWilliams also remembered those long scorching summer days when, he said,

> it was so hot and dry, the prairie got so hard, we could not hold a walking plow in the ground. The prairie cracked open so badly, young turkeys and chicks and suckling pigs fell into these cracks and many were lost. The mother of these birds and animals would move along and the farmer could not find them and they perished. I also saw my father's wagon, all four wheels down in these cracks, right up to the axles. The wagon had to be pried up before the team could pull it out.[21]

Like Fred and Sam, Harve Carson reminisced about those hot dry days, especially one year when there was no rain. He described it succinctly: "It was so dry one summer that a cat couldn't spit at a dog!"[22]

Instead of considering the colour of the sunsets, some homesteaders tried to predict rain conditions by analyzing the shape of the crescent moon. Maggie Whyte described how one had to specifically note the horns of a "new" moon,[23] which occurs when the sun and moon are aligned so that most of the moon appears to be black.[24] If the horns, the two ends of the crescent, are inclined upward, this means that "water wouldn't be able to run out." Maggie referred to this type of moon as a "dry moon," with no rain predicted for the future.

If the moon looked like it was standing on end, the water would fall out and it would rain.

Rather than looking at the horns of the moon, D.H. Maginnes believed that if there was a ring around the moon, a rainstorm would occur within the next day or two: "The bigger the ring, the longer the storm."[25] He also stated that the number of stars located in the ring indicated the number of days that the storm would last. Other homesteaders believed that the number of stars referred to the number of days before a storm began.

Another way to predict rainy weather was to scrutinize the clouds. Mrs. J. Telfodd told how her family watched for "mares' tails" in the sky.[26] Mares' tails were feathery streaks of clouds that looked like the flowing tails of horses. If these cloud shapes were seen, there would be rain the next day. Charles Sargent offered a variety of predictors for rain in the forecast.[27] He said that if one saw a rainbow in the evening, this was regarded as a sure sign of rain the next day. (To see a double rainbow was a sign of good luck.) He also believed that if the weather was clear in the east in the evening, it would rain the next day. If there was a three-day wind from the east, there would be a three-day rain on the prairies. (A three-day rain was called a "million-dollar rain," as it usually meant a reprieve from extremely dry conditions.) If the sun went down behind a thick cloud after a long dry spell, there would be rain, but if a rim of light on the western horizon appeared below a rain cloud, it meant that the rain would clear up the next day.

Many homesteaders feared hailstorms due to their sudden, destructive nature and would keep a keen watch during the spring and summer months for thunderstorm clouds: multi-level ominous-looking vertical clouds.[28] This type of cloud could produce lightning, hard rain and hail—hard pellets of ice, sometimes as large as golf balls, that would rain down. Hail would destroy crops and cause great harm to those who were not able to find shelter in time.

John Gilbert Wren lived through a vicious hailstorm that occurred on August 2, 1916.[29] He said that the hailstones were huge, the size of hen's eggs, and were destructive. A beautiful standing crop of wheat that he had nurtured was pounded flat

Powder Horn and Hunting

ACCORDING TO ONE proverb, "If you are able to hang your powder horn on the hook of the new moon, it will be a dry month. If it is so dry that the twigs crackle under your foot, you may as well hang up your horn as it is useless to go hunting."[30] ●

on the ground within fifteen minutes. His chickens and ducklings lay dead or dying in their pen. The windows in his home were broken, and holes were punched into the roof that let in the rain that followed the hailstorm. While he suffered the damaging effects of the storm, he noted that his neighbours, who lived less than a quarter of a mile away, did not have hail. Rather, they just had rain with no negative repercussions.

Susan Tucker remembered that her family experienced hail a number of times while they were homesteading.[31] Sometimes the hail was the size of small stones, while at other times it was as large as tennis balls. After a hailstorm, she said that it often looked like it had snowed, as the fields were flattened and covered with white ice. Frank Baines said that he drove his cattle to his destroyed oat crop after a hailstorm in the hope that they would eat the oats and the crop wouldn't go to waste.[32] The cows ignored the crop and instead walked over to the next field to eat grass for a meal. Oresa Williams recalled a hailstorm that occurred on her family's homestead.[33] She reported that it came with such force that it broke all of their windows and scattered the evening meal across the room.

Dorthea Calverley was a small child when she was subjected to a terrifying hailstorm while she was visiting her grandparents.[34] She remembered the events clearly.

> Late one afternoon, Grandma summoned me inside when Collie, the dog, pulled me to the door. He dived under the table as the first rumbles of thunder became audible in the

Some hail was the size of golf balls. In this photograph, ca. 1926, surveyor D.A. Nichols is holding two hailstones and standing in front of his tent, which was damaged by the hailstorm. PA-1036-277. COURTESY OF LIBRARIES AND CULTURAL RESOURCES DIGITAL COLLECTIONS, UNIVERSITY OF CALGARY

west. Grandma took one look at the suddenly risen, threatening, yellowish cloud that marked the dust billow before a black boiling stratus burst in front of a towering cumulus that seemed to stretch up forever. She had only time to race upstairs to shut the windows and also the doors and windows downstairs, when Grandpa drew old Billy (the horse) up with his flank against the east end of the house [away from the storm]. Grandpa tumbled out and into the kitchen for he had seen the characteristic white streaks against the black murk that heralded a hailstorm. What a storm! Flash upon flash and roll upon roll. After a short pause, came a crack like a gigantic whip. Before one could catch their suspended breath again, hail the size of golf balls descended almost as one consignment of ice. Before one of the adults, carrying a heavy quilt, reached the West window, to hold it against the glass, the panes were already broken out and ice balls were hurtling in. I was under the table with Collie but I distinctly remember stones hitting the floor and bouncing up to twitch the chenille drapes in the doorway. It must have been heavily wind driven. At last, it was over. Fortunately, the peak of the roof faced the storm, and started the broadside, for only a few shingles were split, but the siding on the house was also split in one or two places. In the lee of the house, Old Billy had been somewhat protected. As the house door was opened, he had considered himself invited in, buggy and all until shafts in the front wheels jammed in the doorway. I don't know where the cows were, but dead chickens especially clucks and little ones littered the yard. The runoff from the cloudburst swept some down the draw where the garden had been, now a junior muddy Missouri [River] bloodied with the torn petals of the once flamboyant crimson poppies. We went out to inspect the fields. The incredibly tall, thick wheat, not quite binder cutting time ripe, lay like a mattress, compacted a foot or so high, where only a day or so earlier, I had become completely lost in it.

The northern lights, or aurora borealis, were a naturally occurring phenomenon that did not have any negative or dangerous elements associated with them. Rather, they were beautiful, vivid, multi-coloured streams of bluish-green or purple light that would twist and turn across a clear sky at night. Depending on how far north homesteaders were located, the northern lights tended to appear between September and April each year. Some homesteaders noticed a noise that seemed to accompany them. James Tulloch, for example, said that the northern lights made a noise like the rustling of an umbrella on a windy day,[35] while John Fetsch remembered it "as a murmuring noise like crushing soft paper."[36] For those who had never experienced northern lights before, the first encounter could be a disturbing and scary experience. Eloise Anderson said,

> When I was about ten years old, we saw such magnificent northern lights that they were awe-inspiring but to some folks they were terrifying. It was like a huge purple umbrella directly overhead and it would draw up and narrow then spread out lower and lower. My mother and I were alone and we clung to each other as we looked at it. A neighbour boy was bringing the cows home and thought it was a cyclone and left the cows, got on his horse and galloped home in terror.[37]

Sundogs and Cold Gray Suns

THE TERM "SUNDOG" refers to a bright spot in the sky surrounded by a halo during daylight hours. When homesteaders saw a sundog, many took it as a forecast for debilitatingly cold temperatures. Mrs. Charles Archer said that if a sundog appeared on the horizon, it meant that intensely cold weather would be arriving shortly and that a person "should not be caught too far from home because of the danger of freezing."[35] Similarly, Ella Otterson believed that a cold, gray sun predicted cold weather or a storm.[39] If there was a haze in the northwest along with a brisk wind, a blizzard would be imminent.

Homesteaders new to the western prairies were naive about weather conditions. Many had never seen a sundog before and didn't know what to expect. A.J. Riley was one of those new homesteaders, and he tells a humorous story on himself.[40]

> The first time I saw a sundog, my brother happened to be up first. He pulled the blind up and said "Come out! My, what a lovely sun dog." I jumped out of bed and grabbed my rifle. "Keep quiet," I said to my brother, "I will see if I can shoot it." I thought it was some animal that I had not seen so far. •

Rose Feist of Clyde, Alberta, recalled the night that she and her neighbours saw the northern lights.[41] While everyone around her appreciated the beauty of the night sky, the horses were less than enthused.

> One evening on the way to the Christmas concert at our school, the stars were so bright, no city lights to dim their brilliancy, the Milky Way showed every star in the Galaxy. The Northern Lights were so bright they practically seemed to be streaming to the ground. This night they made a great deal of noise, hissing loudly as they moved as waterfalls from

> the sky. "How beautiful!" we all said, but our horses thought differently, pulling our sleigh with all of us going to the concert. They reared up and started to get out of control. Dad had to get out of the sleigh and try to calm them down before we had a runaway across the fields. They did not like those bright, noisy, hissing Northern Lights.

In her memoirs, Mary Morrison recalled how the northern lights turned out to be a learning experience for a couple of young Manitoban girls.[42] Their mother had studied astronomy when she was young and had brought her textbooks with her when she travelled to the western prairies. She had her daughters study the positions of the stars and the yearly almanac relating to the weather. One night there was a clear sky, and they all went outside to watch the northern lights dance across the sky.

> The great drawback was, they could not stay out long in the cold without getting nipped by Jack Frost. Sometimes,

For some homesteaders, the northern lights were an awe-inspiring brilliant display of natural beauty. Set against the snow-covered ground, streams of blues and greens dipped in every direction across the night sky in a show of brightly moving colours that went on for hours. Others were not so appreciative of the northern lights. They panicked when they saw them as they feared that the end of the world was at hand. This northern lights display was near Selwyn, Yukon, ca. 1900. NA-1466-37, BY J. DOODY. COURTESY OF LIBRARIES AND CULTURAL RESOURCES DIGITAL COLLECTIONS, UNIVERSITY OF CALGARY

> while watching the stars, they were treated to such grandeur, words cannot express. Great shafts of varied colored lights suddenly shot up from horizon to zenith, then sank again then from west to east like a great scroll, unfolding slats of light, then again like a great army marching in step. But it was so cold, so cold. Dearly as they loved to watch it all, the intense cold drove them into the house and as the windows were always covered with frost, there was no chance to watch from there.

Along with northern lights, mirages were another common phenomenon that occurred on the western prairies. According to Frank Baines, a mirage indicated a difference of temperatures between the upper and lower layers of the atmosphere.[43] He believed that mirages often preceded a thaw in spring. Over the years, many homesteaders experienced mirages. Charles Sargent, for example, stated that he would often see trains travelling upside down when the real train underneath was not visible.[44] John Ludlow said, "I have seen mirages where it would seem you could see through a hill, things would seem to be lifted up, and brought closer to you."[45] He also said that he had heard lots of stories about all the towns that people had seen, even though the towns were hundreds of miles away. Frank Kusch remembered seeing mirages on the prairies, particularly in the mornings.[46]

The McLeod family, who originally hailed from the United States, settled in the Stavely area of Alberta on April 5, 1905.[47] A few months later, they saw a mirage when they arose one morning. They could clearly see the cutbank of the river that was located east of their homestead. The women in the family, who had not yet been to the river, decided to pack a picnic lunch and set out on foot. They believed they would be back at home shortly after the lunch hour. "At 4:30 that afternoon they staggered in, completely tired out. They had walked till noon before they gave up and stopped for lunch. There was no sign of the cutbank." Then they walked back home. They later found out that the cutbank was over twelve miles away.

Mabel Hawthorne was also deceived by a mirage one morning.[48] She wanted to purchase a hen from a neighbour who lived seven miles away. One morning, she said,

> there was a lovely "mirage" which seemed to bring our places very close together. So she arranged that Lawrence (her son) would go over and carry the hen home in a bag. So he started away nice and early and arrived at the neighbour's about noon, had dinner there and rested a while, then started back. He didn't make the return trip as fast as he did going. Mabel and her husband were getting very uneasy about his long absence when he "blew in," very hungry and so tired and foot weary.

Mabel then realized the error she had made, as the distance was much farther than what had appeared in the mirage. As she said, "That is what a 'mirage' can do in the west. It is so deceiving you think you are close, when you are actually far away."

Ernest Bishop also remembered the mirages that he used to see when he was a child on his family's Saskatchewan homestead.[49] As he said, "Buildings miles away would look quite near and small shacks would look like tall elevators." One morning, a couple of land hunters who were on their way to Carnduff stopped in at their place. There was a mirage that appeared to indicate the town was only a short ways away. Ernest's father told them that the town was actually ten miles from their homestead. The land hunters didn't believe him and said that he was just "spoofing them." They decided to keep on walking and have breakfast in town. Ernest's story doesn't tell what happened to them, but the land hunters likely didn't make it to town for at least another three hours, too late for breakfast.

Mary Morrison offered a different perspective on the mirages that she could see from her homestead.[50] Instead of focusing on the deceptiveness of the mirages, she was entranced by the different scenic views they offered her in whatever direction she looked. She most often saw mirages during the winter season. As she recalled,

> The sun would set on a perfectly white plain, no dark object visible, everything covered with the white mantle of snow. After sunrise in the morning, the plains seem to be dotted with houses and trees. In one direction would appear a range of hills, in another a vast lake, and you would imagine you saw ships upon it, then the scene would change. When you looked again, you would see the same old familiar prairie.

Weather Proverbs and Phrases

MANY HOMESTEADERS, WHEN describing weather conditions, resorted to using proverbs. Others recounted local phrases, used analogies and oxymorons, or made jokes. What follows is some of the weather lore from that time.[51]

Rain before seven, clear before eleven.

Red sky at night, shepherd's delight. Red sky at morning, sailor's warning.

As dry as chips.

As cold as hell.

As dry as dust or tinder.

As hot as Lucifer.

As wet as a drowned rat.

As the weather is on Monday morning, so it will be all week except for Friday.

The north wind doth blow and we shall have snow.

Cold enough to freeze the tail off a cast iron monkey.

As cold as molasses in January.

Foggy morning, sunny day.

Wind in the east, fit for neither man or beast.

Seeing a rainbow at night means a fine day tomorrow.

Evening red, morning grey, brings to us a better day.

As dry as a powderhouse.

As cold as a stepmother's kiss or a pussycat's nose.

The last three days of the month governs the weather for the next three weeks.

Eighty days after a heavy fog, there will be a heavy rain.

Three white frosts and then rain.

A blue snow is a sign of spring; it is the last snow of the season.

Heavy snow between Christmas and New Year will be followed by six weeks of very severe cold weather.

When it is raining, if you can see enough blue sky in a break in the clouds to make a man a pair of trousers, it is going to clear up.

Three days of an east wind brings three days of rain.

If it rains while the sun is shining, it will rain again tomorrow.

If your tobacco is so damp you have to smoke more matches than tobacco, then you are in for a wet spell. The same applies if the salt is so wet it will not sprinkle out of the cruet.

And lastly, a joke: How do I know that it's raining cats and dogs? I stepped in a poodle. •

The weather was variable on the prairies. Knowing what type of weather you could be facing in the future was important to daily survival. All members of the family learned to spot certain weather signs, and many tried to predict the days to come. Perhaps John Thiessen found the best way to sum up the various weather conditions on the prairies. He said, "The weather is so changeable that when you go into a field to work, you have to take with you a straw hat, fur cap, raincoat and sheepskin coat. And if you leave any of these items at the end of a field, you may need them by the time you reach the other end of the field."[52]

Conclusion

In this book I delved into the lives of those homesteaders who settled across the Canadian western prairies. Many people of different nationalities came together for a common purpose: to work the land, to eke out a living and to strive for a better future. But did they create a common folklife? Did they become unified through their daily efforts?

Folklife exists where a community spirit has been created by those who share their knowledge and skills. It includes people's personal stories and backgrounds, their experiences, their beliefs and their social norms, as well as their interests and hobbies. Folklife refers to the recreational activities that families enjoyed, such as concerts, dances and picnics, visiting the neighbours, playing jokes on one another, attending the country fairs, taking part in community organizations, and catching up on the latest news. Homesteaders eagerly anticipated getting together so they could regale each other with stories of horse thieves and bank robbers, or share predictions relating to inclement or pleasant weather conditions. Superstitions were also shared among members of the community, with many watching out for signs of good and bad luck. Some would place their hands on Ouija boards or have others read their tea leaves, the palms of their hands or playing cards, as many people were keen to know their futures. And the proverbs, witticisms or adages that were used in casual conversation helped to bind the homesteading community together, as did the telling and retelling of tall tales.

Landmarks and place names were important for community development. Recognizing distinctive geographical sites and being able to discuss them with others, or use them as guides for directions, unified neighbours. Community members worked together to create new names for towns and villages, schoolhouses, lakes and even their favourite bird-hunting or berry-gathering sites. The shared knowledge of how and when their communities developed, building by building, indicates the high level of community involvement at the time, as does the recognition of notable people in their areas. Many of those notable people were admired for their generosity, positive spirit and helpfulness in the community. Others became renowned for the particular skills they possessed or their physical prowess.

Chores also united those who lived on the western prairies. Working in the fields, tending the crops, feeding and taking care of farm animals, or labouring in the farmhouse, doing such domestic tasks as cleaning, washing, cooking, baking and raising children, were all common activities that everyone who lived on the prairies could relate to. Hunting game, snaring small animals or fishing were also chores that many homesteaders had to undertake in order to have meat or fish on the table, while others had to make trips to town to pick up supplies. Travelling across streams and lakes could be hazardous, and occasionally homesteaders and their wagons became mired in mud. Advice on the best places to cross and how to avoid problematic roads were common topics of conversation among the homesteaders.

Children had their own folklife that took the form of the stories they told each other, the types of homemade toys they played with, the kinds of pets they took care of and the games and social activities they took part in. Walking to and from school with other children, developing a warm camaraderie with those who were the same age, was a highlight, as was the annual Christmas concert, where schoolchildren and teachers worked hand in hand to get the schoolhouse ready for the festivities.

The examples collected in this book make it clear that a shared folklife emerged during the homesteading era on the prairies. One homesteader, Ellenor Merriken, was well aware of the changes in her community—how different types of people had immigrated and migrated into the area, and how they all came together to create a new society. In her memoir, she wrote:

> As the land was gradually being settled, we found that we had a community of many different nationalities. People came from all parts of the world, many of whom could not

> speak the language, but each one had something to contribute. We were all encouraged to hold on to the old traditions and culture from our homeland. We were strangers in a strange country, determined to get ahead on our own and get along with each other; that is what makes a country strong. Canada has a wealth of traditions, brought in by pioneers from older lands. This has culminated in a gracious and new atmosphere, different from any place I have ever known; free and easy and friendly towards all, yet dignified.[1]

Even though people faced daily challenges, they became fond of the prairie region that they eventually called home. Having neighbours who were facing the same struggles and hardships helped to unite those who worked on their homesteads. Whether they were sharing farm equipment, helping with building bees or lamenting over crops destroyed by hail, the homesteaders came to rely on each other for support and friendship. Homesteaders enjoyed each other's company when they met in town, when they attended community picnics or dances, or when they met each other at sports events. Debating and literary clubs, as well as

A happy homesteading family in 1912. AUTHOR'S COLLECTION

other organized charity-based clubs, helped to heighten community involvement. Whether the homesteaders were working on their quarter-sections or taking part in social events, their common interests and pursuits united them.

One other aspect that bonded people was the love of the land. One homesteader's love was so strong that he hoped to be buried on the prairie so he would never have to leave. This homesteader was likely not alone in having these thoughts. Many came to feel the same way. Once homesteaders held the title to their land in their hands, they not only had pride in their accomplishments but also felt a sense of belonging to the land as much as the land now belonged to them. As generations of their families evolved, as their friendships deepened and as their community involvement matured, their love for the prairies became stronger and stronger year after year. No matter where they came from, the hardships and work that they endured, the camaraderie and pride that they developed, led to a sense of belonging. They may have yearned to return to their mother country or birthplace from time to time, but their 160-acre homestead on the Canadian western prairies became their home, a place they never wished to leave.

Now when I die, as die I must,
will you bury me here where I placed my trust?
The prairie I loved so faithfully,
will ring its lullaby for me.
My spirit will be free evermore to roam
on this beautiful land that I now call home.[2]

Notes

1 Dora Mitchell. (n.d.). Memoir. "Far Horizons." Accession No. A 278, PAS.

INTRODUCTION

1 Prior to the region being divided into the three provinces of Alberta (1905), Saskatchewan (1905) and Manitoba (1870), it had been known as the North-West Territories (1870–1905) and Rupert's Land (1670–1870).

2 For a detailed discussion of the settlement process in Canada and commentaries on the distinctions in timing and progress of development, see A.S. Morton, "History of Prairie Settlement," Part 1 of *Canadian Frontiers of Settlement*, vol. 2 (Macmillan Canada, 1938), pp. 1–194.

3 Revisions to the act did occur over time with regard to ages; number of acres broken, cropped and harvested; residency requirements; and specifications with regard to a habitable home.

4 Being the head of a household meant being legally responsible for dependents (e.g., children).

HUNTERS, COWBOYS, TRAPPERS, EGG COLLECTORS AND BANJO PLAYERS

1 James Tulloch. (1897). Pioneer Folklore Questionnaire, PAS.

2 Graham Chandler, "Selling the Prairie Good Life," *Canada's History* (2016), https://www.canadashistory.ca/explore/settlement-immigration/selling-the-prairie-good-life.

3 The United Free Church of Scotland (based on Protestantism) existed between 1843 and 1900. During that time, members of the church became concerned with educational reform, particularly with educating the poor, and set up schools in order to provide free public education to children. Religious instruction was also included. For more information, see K. Stewart, "Education and the Free Church," *The Monthly Record* (2003), on the Christian Study Library website, https://www.christianstudylibrary.org/article/education-and-free-church.

4 Sidney S. May. (1901). Pioneer Folklore Questionnaire, PAS.

5 Fred Baines. (1883). Pioneer Folklore Questionnaire, PAS.

6 Charles Davis. (1882). Pioneer Folklore Questionnaire, PAS.

7 Tobias Lanegraff. (1906). Pioneer Folklore Questionnaire, PAS.

8 Marie Jordens. (1884). Pioneer Folklore Questionnaire, PAS.

9 The United States also had a homesteading program in place where potential settlers could obtain 160 acres of free land for a small registration fee. Refer to the *Homestead Act of 1862* (https://www.archives.gov/education/lessons/homestead-act). It was not unheard of for individuals to register for homestead land in the United States, sell their property (after they had gained title), then

take their profits, move north to western Canada and register for another 160 acres of free homestead land under the Canadian system.

10 Lena May Purdy. (1883). Pioneer Folklore Questionnaire, PAS.

11 John Thiessen. (1905). Pioneer Folklore Questionnaire, PAS.

12 Marion Anderson. (1883). Pioneer Folklore Questionnaire, PAS.

13 The term "mush" refers to oatmeal porridge.

14 Eric Neal. (1906). Pioneer Folklore Questionnaire, PAS.

15 John Evans. (1892). Pioneer Folklore Questionnaire, PAS.

16 Isabel Muirhead. (1883). Pioneer Folklore Questionnaire, PAS.

17 Memoir and photograph. "A Glimpse of the Aron Johnson Pioneering Days." Received from Brad Johnson of Regina, Saskatchewan, in June 2023.

18 A switch refers to a hair extension. In the late 1800s, women who wanted longer hair would have a switch made that could be attached to their own hair (near the roots). This longer hair could then be twisted, braided or made into a bun. For personal use, real hair would be saved after brushing. It was untangled and laid out flat, and the ends were then sewn onto a thin cord. A thicker cord was sewn onto the thin cord, with a loop left in the centre. When the woman applied the switch to her head, the loop would be attached to her hair. People who earned money by making switches would either purchase hair from others or would use hair given to them by their clients.

19 Albert Christianson. (1910). Pioneer Folklore Questionnaire, PAS.

GREENHORNS, SNIPE HUNTERS AND ROAD APPLES

1 Eric Neal. (1906). Pioneer Folklore Questionnaire, PAS.

2 Archie Althouse. (1906). Memoir. "Life on a Saskatchewan Homestead." Accession No. RE 2930, PAS.

3 Charles Cantlon Bray. (1883). Pioneer Farming Experiences Questionnaire, PAS.

4 Gordon Stewart, "The W.C. Stewart Family," *Golden Echoes: A History of Galahad* (Galahad Historical Society, 1980), p. 217.

5 Musk is a spray with a very potent odour that is difficult to get rid of. The musk is discharged from two glands near the base of a skunk's tail. It is discharged in such a powerful stream that a skunk can hit a target that is up to twelve feet away.

6 Percy Thomson. (1910). Pioneer Folklore Questionnaire, PAS.

7 "Memoirs of Mr. Charles A. Johnston," Pioneer Legacy: Bowden and Districts (Bowden Chamber of Commerce, 1979), p. 404.

8 Eric Neal. (1906). Pioneer Folklore Questionnaire, PAS.

9 Robert H. Wooff. (n.d.). Interview. Accession No. C 130, PAS.

10 Lucy Johnson. (1903). Memoir. "Against the Wind." Accession No. RE-2878, PAS.

11 Mary Rogers Berkner. (n.d.). Memoir. "Berkner Family." Accession No. A 454 339, PAS.

12 For more information on the Barr Colonists, see Lynne Bowen, *Muddling Through: The Remarkable Story of the Barr Colonists* (Douglas & McIntyre, 1992).

13 Grant MacEwan, Between the Red and the Rockies (University of Toronto Press, 1952), p. 93.

14 John Milton Singleton. (1911). Pioneer Experiences Questionnaire, PAS.

15 Ken Doolittle. (1905). Memoir. "My Pioneer Days in Saskatchewan." Accession No. RE 321 #36, PAS.

16 John Potts. (1894). Pioneer Experiences Questionnaire, PAS.

TRAVELLING THE TRAILS

1 Grant MacEwan, *Power for Prairie Plows* (Western Producer Book Service, 1974), p. 7.
2 C. Howard Shillington, *Historic Land Trails of Saskatchewan* (Evvard Publications, 1985).
3 C. Howard Shillington, *Historic Land Trails of Saskatchewan* (Evvard Publications, 1985), p. 17.
4 Mary Edith Alicia Kajewski. (1899). Pioneer Folklore Questionnaire, PAS.
5 George Shepherd. (1900). Pioneer Folklore Questionnaire, PAS.
6 Ella Otterson. (1903). Pioneer Folklore Questionnaire, PAS.
7 William Affleck. (1906). Pioneer Folklore Questionnaire, PAS.
8 William Gange. (1894). Pioneer Folklore Questionnaire, PAS.
9 Eloise Anderson. (1910). Pioneer Folklore Questionnaire, PAS.
10 Harriet May Stueck. (1886). Pioneer Folklore Questionnaire, PAS.
11 Sidney S. May. (1901). Pioneer Folklore Questionnaire, PAS.
12 Percy Thomson. (1910). Pioneer Folklore Questionnaire, PAS.
13 John Laidlaw. (1882). Pioneer Folklore Questionnaire, PAS.
14 Mrs. J. Meredith. (1907). Pioneer Folklore Questionnaire, PAS.
15 John Hamer. (1910). Pioneer Folklore Questionnaire, PAS.
16 Norman McDonald. (1883). Pioneer Folklore Questionnaire, PAS.
17 Roads or bridges built with logs were known as "corduroy" roads or "corduroy" bridges.
18 Albert Christianson. (1910). Pioneer Folklore Questionnaire, PAS.
19 Flora Kennedy. (n.d.). Memoir. "From East to West." Accession No. A310, PAS.
20 Tobias Lanegraff. (1906). Pioneer Folklore Questionnaire, PAS.
21 Fred Baines. (1883). Pioneer Folklore Questionnaire, PAS.
22 Captain A.L. Brick, "Rev. J. Gough Brick and his Shaftesbury Mission Farm," *Brick's Hill, Berwyn and Beyond* (Berwyn Centennial Committee, 1968), pp. 8–9.
23 This particular York boat was owned by the Hudson's Bay Company and had a crew of nine men including one steersman. It often made the trip from Edmonton to Athabasca and Slave Lake, completing their route in Grouard in northern Alberta.
24 "The Calgary-Edmonton Trail," *Beyond Our Prairie Trails* (Carstairs History Book Committee), pp. 35–36.
25 Ruth B. Upton, "Our Journey to the Peace," *Brick's Hill, Berwyn and Beyond* (Berwyn Centennial Committee, 1968), pp. 152–153.
26 Egges Halfway House was located forty-five miles north of Edmonton. It was built in 1898 and had a post office as well as a telegraph office.

WATER, WATER, EVERYWHERE! CROSSING STREAMS AND FORDING CREEKS

1 John Fetsch. (1910). Pioneer Folklore Questionnaire, PAS.
2 Frank Baines. (1883). Pioneer Folklore Questionnaire, PAS.
3 Mrs. Richard (Lillian) Miles. (1884). Pioneer Folklore Questionnaire, PAS.
4 Eric Neal. (1906). Pioneer Folklore Questionnaire, PAS.
5 "Memoirs of Mr. Charles A. Johnston," *Pioneer Legacy: Bowden and Districts* (Bowden Chamber of Commerce, 1979), p. 415.
6 A ford refers to a shallow place in a river, stream or lake where there would be good footing when crossing.
7 J.H. Sand (1910). Pioneer Folklore Questionnaire, PAS.

8 Charles Davis. (1882). Pioneer Folklore Questionnaire, PAS.
9 Mrs. L.J. Adler. (1910). Pioneer Folklore Questionnaire, PAS.
10 Mrs. Ella Mott. (1887). Pioneer Folklore Questionnaire, PAS.

"IT'S TA GOOMBO. IT WA' STICK TA' Y' TEETH IF'T HAD THE CHANCE."

1 The "Halfway Place" would have been a stopping place for travellers.
2 Eloise Anderson. (1910). Pioneer Folklore Questionnaire, PAS.
3 John Ludlow. (1905). Pioneer Folklore Questionnaire, PAS.
4 "H.G. Neufeld Family," *Bridging the Years: Nipawin, Saskatchewan* (Nipawin Historical Society, 1988), p. 731.
5 Isabel Muirhead. (1883). Pioneer Folklore Questionnaire, PAS.
6 The whipple tree refers to a swinging leader bar—a wooden or metal bar behind the horses, between the horses and the wagon. The tugs of a harness are attached to this bar. It was a required piece of equipment, otherwise the horses would not be able to pull the wagon.
7 Kathleen Lennox Smith. (n.d.). Memoir. "Memories of Kathleen Lennox Smith," Accession No. R-E3289, PAS.
8 The land across the prairies had been surveyed by federal government surveyors and marked with posts in mounds. Homesteaders could read the numbers on the surveyed posts and know where they were or how far they were from their own registered homestead.
9 Charles Davis. (1882). Pioneer Folklore Questionnaire, PAS.
10 Ella Otterson. (1903). Pioneer Folklore Questionnaire, PAS.
11 Mary E. Birkett. (1905). Pioneer Folklore Questionnaire, PAS.
12 Charles Sargent. (1911). Pioneer Folklore Questionnaire, PAS.
13 James Tulloch. (1897). Pioneer Folklore Questionnaire, PAS.
14 Felix Belliveau. (1902). Pioneer Folklore Questionnaire, PAS.
15 Clara Hoffer. (1905). Pioneer Folklore Questionnaire, PAS.
16 Elizabeth E. (Robinson) King, "Reflections," *Forests, Furrows and Faith* (Boyle and District Historical Society, 1982), p. 358.
17 Mrs. D.A. Moorhouse. (1911). Pioneer Folklore Questionnaire, PAS.
18 Mrs. J.M. Telfodd. (1910). Pioneer Folklore Questionnaire, PAS.
19 Percy Thomson. (1910). Pioneer Folklore Questionnaire, PAS.
20 John Thiessen. (1905). Pioneer Folklore Questionnaire, PAS.
21 Harve Carson. (1883). Pioneer Folklore Questionnaire, PAS.

CYPRESS TREES, BEAVER DAMS AND RED DEER ANTLERS

1 Mrs. E. Howard Olmstead. (1885). Pioneer Folklore Questionnaire, PAS.
2 Charles Davis. (1882). Pioneer Folklore Questionnaire, PAS.
3 Harriet May Stueck. (1886). Pioneer Folklore Questionnaire, PAS
4 Tobias Lanegraff. (1906). Pioneer Folklore Questionnaire, PAS.
5 Percy Thomson. (1910). Pioneer Folklore Questionnaire, PAS.
6 Mary Ann McMurdo. (1904). Pioneer Experiences Questionnaire, PAS.
7 Ella Otterson. (1903). Pioneer Folklore Questionnaire, PAS.
8 Mrs. W.H.S. Gange. (1894). Pioneer Folklore Questionnaire, PAS.
9 Robert Shaw. (1905). Pioneer Folklore Questionnaire, PAS.
10 John Hamer. (1909). Pioneer Folklore Questionnaire, PAS.
11 Mrs. J. Meredith. (1907). Pioneer Folklore Questionnaire, PAS.
12 "An Historical Study of the Smoky Lake Region," *Waskatenau: 1867–1967* (County of Smoky Lake, 1967), p. 1.
13 Janet Downie. (1901). Pioneer Folklore Questionnaire, PAS.

14 John Thiessen. (1905). Pioneer Folklore Questionnaire, PAS.

15 Dorothy Gush. (1968). Memoir. "Prairie Years 1905–1909." Accession No. A 266, PAS.

16 "Reminiscing," *Bucking Poles and Butter Churns* (North Lone Pine Women's Institute, 1972), pp. 83–84.

17 "Place Names of this Anthology," *Between River and Lake* (Warspite—Victoria Trail Historical Society, 1988), p. 4.

18 Mrs. Ed Wilson. (1905). Pioneer Folklore Questionnaire, PAS.

19 William Glock, "Points of Interest," *A New Beginning: Irvine and District* (20 Mile Post Historical Society, 1989), p. 5.

20 Mrs. Ella Mott. (1887). Pioneer Folklore Questionnaire, PAS.

21 James Tulloch. (1897). Pioneer Folklore Questionnaire, PAS.

22 In Gerald Flood, *Shy Boy from Lost Horse Hills*, cited on the LostHorseHills website, https://losthorsehills.wordpress.com/.

23 Frank Kusch. (1883). Pioneer Experiences Questionnaire, PAS.

24 Charles Sargent. (1911). Pioneer Folklore Questionnaire, PAS.

25 Shirley Manary, "Cowhide Coulee," *Bridging the Years: A History of Eastbank, Windfield, Hattonford and East Mahaska* (Hattonford History Book Committee, 1982), pp. 223–224.

26 Lucy Johnson. (1903). Memoir. "Against the Wind." Accession No. RE-2878, PAS.

I CAN LOOK AS FAR AS MY EYES WILL CARRY AND THERE IS NOTHING TO SEE

1 Census statistics of 1901 indicate that 54 percent of the population in Saskatchewan was male. This percentage increased to 59 percent by 1906 and did not decrease to the 56 percent level until 1916. The unequal numbers of men and women becomes more obvious when marital status is taken into account. Single males in 1901 outnumbered single females by a ratio of 1.32 to 1; this increased dramatically to 1.74 to 1 by 1906, 3.5 to 1 by 1911 and dropped back to 2.81 to 1 in 1916. (1916 *Census of the Prairie Provinces*, Population and Agriculture).

2 Statistics indicate that the number of married men and women increased substantially, although it appears that thousands of married men did not bring their wives with them, at least until the husband had improved the homestead to some degree. For instance, in Saskatchewan, the 1911 figures show that approximately 91,000 men classified themselves as being married, while only 82,000 women claimed this marital status. However, as development increased, the number of families also increased in the province of Saskatchewan. In 1901 there were 19,235 families reported, but this increased to 66,009 in 1906, 120,751 in 1911 and 150,292 in 1916. (1916 *Census* and *Census of the Northwest Territories*, 1906.)

3 Mrs. Richard (Lillian) Miles. (1886). Pioneer Folklore Questionnaire, PAS.

4 Mrs. H. Teece. (1885). Pioneer Folklore Questionnaire, PAS.

5 Lottie Meek. (1884). Pioneer Folklore Questionnaire, PAS.

6 John Fetsch. (1910). Pioneer Folklore Questionnaire, PAS.

7 William Colby Reesor. (n.d.). Memoir. Accession No. 77.57 SE, PAS.

8 George Shepherd. (1908). Pioneer Folklore Questionnaire, PAS.

9 Quoted in Marjorie Wilkins Campbell, *The Saskatchewan* (Rinehart and Company, 1950), pp. 280–281.

10 Marion Anderson. (1883). Pioneer Folklore Questionnaire, PAS.

11 Mary Morrison. (n.d.). Memoir. Accession No. MG9 A81, PAM.
12 Betty Iredale, *Stories of the Sod Shack and Other Reminiscences* (Hemlock Printers, 1991), pp. 14–16.
13 John Fetsch. (1910). Pioneer Folklore Questionnaire, PAS.
14 Mrs. Ella Mott. (1887). Pioneer Folklore Questionnaire, PAS.
15 John Ludlow. (1905). Pioneer Folklore Questionnaire, PAS.
16 Warren Smith, "The Peter McEachern and D.C. Smith Family History," *80 Years of Progress* (Westlock History Book Committee, 1984), pp. 619–20.
17 Mary Morrison. (n.d.). Memoir. Accession No. #MG9 A81, PAM.
18 Harriet May Stueck. (1886). Pioneer Folklore Questionnaire, PAS.
19 Mrs. Ed Wilson. (1905). Pioneer Folklore Questionnaire, PAS.
20 Eric Neal. (1906). Pioneer Folklore Questionnaire, PAS.
21 Harry Martyn. (1913). Pioneer Folklore Questionnaire, PAS.
22 John Hamer. (1910). Pioneer Folklore Questionnaire, PAS.
23 Albert Christianson. (1910). Pioneer Folklore Questionnaire, PAS.
24 Charles Davis. (1882). Pioneer Folklore Questionnaire, PAS. Snow blindness refers to the eye pain and discomfort or temporary loss of vision caused by too much exposure to UV light.
25 John Henry Foerster, "A Mornington Boy's Experience in Alberta," Along the Fifth: A History of Stony Plain and District (Stony Plain Historical Society, 1982), p. 154.
26 William Affleck. (1906). Pioneer Folklore Questionnaire, PAS.

EVERYTHING FROM "HOME ON THE RANGE" TO SHAKESPEARE

1 Marion Anderson. (1833). Pioneer Recreation and Social Life Questionnaire, PAS.
2 Melodeons were button accordions. They were also known as squeezeboxes.
3 It was interesting to read the history of how this song became a Christmas favourite. It was originally based on a horror story in which a pair of newlyweds decided to play hide-and-seek. The wife hid in a box. When the lid snapped shut, she could not escape. The husband could never find her. Thirty years later, her body was discovered. For more information, refer to https://en.wikipedia.org/wiki/Legend_of_the_Mistletoe_Bough.
4 John Evans. (1892). Pioneer Folklore Questionnaire, PAS.
5 For more information, refer to https://en.wikipedia.org/wiki/Comb_and_paper.
6 Mrs. Charles Archer. (1902). Pioneer Experiences Questionnaire, PAS.
7 Anna Born, *Changes: Anecdotal Tales of Changes in the Life of Anna Born* (Bindery Publishing House, 1995), p. 42.
8 Harriet Gerry. (n.d.). Memoir. "The Year I Grew Up." Accession No. A 603, PAS.
9 Betty Iredale, *Stories of the Sod Shack and Other Reminiscences* (Hemlock Printers, 1991), p. 33.
10 Tobias Lanegraff. (1906). Pioneer Folklore Questionnaire, PAS.
11 Eloise Anderson. (1902). Pioneer Folklore Questionnaire, PAS.
12 Robert Shaw. (1905). Pioneer Folklore Questionnaire, PAS.
13 Mary Kajewski. (1899). Pioneer Folklore Questionnaire, PAS.
14 Harry Martyn. (1913). Pioneer Folklore Questionnaire, PAS.
15 To read the original lyrics, refer to https://en.wikisource.org/wiki/Reuben_and_Rachel. For the playground parody, see https://en.wikipedia.org/wiki/Reuben_and_Rachel.

16 Norman McDonald. (1883). Pioneer Recreation and Social Life Questionnaire, PAS.
17 George Williscroft. (1898). Pioneer Folklore Questionnaire, PAS.
18 Grace Carr. (1910). Memoir. "What I Remember of Pioneer Days in the Wood River District." Accession No. RE 2849, PAS.
19 Dora Mitchell. (n.d.). Memoir. "Far Horizons." Accession No. A 278, PAS.
20 Sue Harrigan. (1980). Memoir. "The Courageous Pioneers." Accession No. RE-626, PAS.
21 "Johann and Anna Paulson," *They Came From Many Lands* (Foam Lake Review, 1985), p. 716.
22 James M. Minifie, *Homesteader: A Prairie Boyhood Recalled* (Macmillan of Canada, 1972), p. 105.

FOLKLIFE THROUGH POETRY

1 G.G.D., "Manitoba," *The Nor'-West Farmer* (April 1886), p. 451.
2 Kay Gregoire, "Rosa Story: From Poland to Prosperity," *Forests, Furrows and Faith* (Boyle and District Historical Society, 1982), pp. 535–36.
3 *A Tribute to the Many Indomitable Men who Homesteaded in Manitoba.* Poem. Accession No. 176 Homesteading Poem, RG 17D1, PAM.
4 J.W. Riley, "The Hoss," *The Nor'-West Farmer* (April 1886), p. 451.
5 Memoir and photograph. "A Glimpse of the Aron Johnson Pioneering Days." Received from Brad Johnson of Regina, Saskatchewan in June, 2023.
6 Robert Chase. (1902). Pioneer Folklore Questionnaire, PAS.
7 *I'd Like to be a Boy Again.* Poem. Accession No. 70.454/5 SE, PAA.
8 Archie Althouse. (1906). Memoir. "Life on a Saskatchewan Homestead." Accession No. RE 2930, PAS.
9 Andrew Twedt, "The Pearly Gate," *Bridging the Years: Carmangay and District* (Carmangay and District History Book Committee, 1968), p. 218.
10 This poem was published in *The Nor'-West Farmer*, April 1886, p. 451.
11 Julia Anna Asher. (1950). Memoir. "Grandma's Childhood: Pioneer Life in Southern Alberta." Accession No. MG8 B10, PAM.
12 Margaret M. Stewart, "Our Western Prairie," *Back Over the Trail* (The Acadia Women's Institute, 1967), p. 80.

FRIENDSHIPS AND GOOD TIMES

1 Florence Kenyon. (1895). Pioneer Experiences Questionnaire, PAS.
2 Lillian Butler. (1911). Pioneer Experiences Questionnaire, PAS.
3 Josie A. Jones, "Jones' Family Memories," *In the Bend of the Battle: A History of Alliance and District* (Alliance Lions Club, 1976), pp. 417–18.
4 Albert Elderton. (1909). Pioneer Experiences Questionnaire, PAS.
5 Kathleen Lennox Smith. (n.d.). Memoir. "Memories of Kathleen Lennox Smith," Accession No. R-E3289, PAS.
6 Kathleen Keyser. (1894). Pioneer Experiences Questionnaire, PAS.
7 Mrs. John C. Knaus. (1906). Pioneer Experiences Questionnaire, PAS.
8 Wayne Nelson, "Harry Nelson," *Golden Echoes: A History of Galahad* (Galahad Historical Society, 1980), p. 183.
9 Etta Robinson. (1914). Memoir. Author's Family History.
10 Ellenor Ranghild Merriken, *Looking for Country: A Norwegian Immigrant's Alberta Memoir* (University of Calgary Press, 1999), p. 94.
11 Elsie Campbell. (1905). Pioneer Experiences Questionnaire, PAS.
12 Charles Edward Kieper. (1954). Memoir. "The Life of a Pioneer." Accession No. A75, PAS.

13 Emily Wright Millar. (1976). Memoir. "Beyond the Sunset." Accession No. A 210, PAS.

14 Bridget Slater Carson, "Patrick and Emelia Carson," *Between River and Lake* (Warspite—Victoria Trail Historical Society, 1988), p. 175.

15 Blackout was another popular card game at the time. It was based on bidding and following the trump card. Each player would place bids on their hand as to how many plays they could win. Once the cards are dealt (beginning with one each and continuing up to ten cards each, depending on the number of players), the first card left in the pile is turned over. It identifies whether spades, hearts, clubs or diamonds are trump. The players play each round, and by the end it is determined whose bet was correct and whose was not. Those who did not get the number of bids that they expected would have their bid blacked out on the scorecard.

16 The term "birds" was slang for women's get-togethers.

17 George Shepherd. (1908). Pioneer Housing Questionnaire, PAS.

18 Grace Carr. (1910). Memoir. "What I Remember of Pioneer Days in the Wood River District." Accession No. RE 2849, PAS.

19 Archie Althouse. (1906). Memoir. "Life on a Saskatchewan Homestead." Accession No. RE 2930, PAS.

20 Marion Anderson. (1883). Pioneer Experiences Questionnaire, PAS.

21 Mrs. Amanda Aikenhead. (1900). Pioneer Experiences Questionnaire, PAS.

22 "Water Glen," *Ponoka 1904–1954: 50th Anniversary* (Ponoka Herald, 1954), p. 45.

23 Alfred Mann. (1882). Pioneer Experiences Questionnaire, PAS.

24 Susan Tucker. (1905). Pioneer Experiences Questionnaire, PAS.

25 Olive Phelps. (1933). Memoir. "Memoirs of Crescent Lake." Accession No. YF 560, PAS.

26 Ellenor Ranghild Merriken, *Looking for Country: A Norwegian Immigrant's Alberta Memoir* (University of Calgary Press, 1999), pp. 93–94.

27 Emma Brydon. (1965). Memoir. "Short Sketch of Edge Hill District." Accession No. MG9 A59-62, PAM.

COMMON PHRASES AND CASUAL CONVERSATION

1 All phrases in this list were taken from the Pioneer Folklore Questionnaires, PAS.

2 Memoir and photograph. "A Glimpse of the Aron Johnson Pioneering Days." Received from Brad Johnson of Regina, Saskatchewan in June, 2023.

NEIGHBOURS HELPING NEIGHBOURS

1 Herman Ehrlich. (1906). Pioneer Experiences Questionnaire, PAS.

2 *By the Old Mill Stream* (Holmfield History Book Committee, 1982), p. 95.

3 Ernest Ludlow. (1905). Pioneer Experiences Questionnaire, PAS.

4 Mrs. Sorine Franks. (1911). Pioneer Experiences Questionnaire, PAS.

5 John Singleton. (1911). Pioneer Experiences Questionnaire, PAS.

6 Christopher Atkings. (1906). Pioneer Experiences Questionnaire, PAS.

7. The mail that they are referring to here was likely from the Dominion Lands Office in Ottawa, Ontario. This was the department that handled all of the homestead requirements.

8 The Stanley Mills Company was located in Toronto, Ontario. It offered hardware items as well as stoves and ovens for sale.

9 In this case, freight referred to the heavier wooden boxes or crates of materials that had been ordered.
10 Herman Collingwood. (1977). Memoir. "My Life History from 1904 to 1970 in Saskatchewan." Accession No. RE 36, PAS.
11 Dorothy Gush. (1968). Memoir. "Prairie Years 1905–1909." Accession No. A 266, PAS.
12 Harriet Gerry. (n.d.). Memoir. "The Year I Grew Up." Accession No. A 603, PAS.
13 Frank Baines. (1883). Pioneer Farming Experiences Questionnaire, PAS.
14 Brian Harris and Eva Harris Northey, "C.K. Harris," *Brick's Hill, Berwyn and Beyond* (Berwyn Centennial Committee, 1968), p. 43.
15 Edith Brong Frederickson, "Charles Brong Family," *Brick's Hill, Berwyn and Beyond* (Berwyn Centennial Committee, 1968), p. 61.
16 Harriet Gerry. (n.d.). Memoir. "The Year I Grew Up." Accession No. A 603.
17 Edith Stilborn. (1883). Pioneer Farming Experiences Questionnaire, PAS.
18 Arthur Tilford. (1902). Pioneer Farming Experiences Questionnaire, PAS.
19 Emily Wright Millar. (1976). Memoir. "Beyond the Sunset." Accession No. A 210. PAS.
20 Robert Widdess. (1883). Pioneer Farming Experiences Questionnaire, PAS.
21 Charles Cantlon Bray. (1883). Pioneer Farming Experiences Questionnaire, PAS.
22 Edith Stilborn. (1910.) Pioneer Farming Experiences Questionnaire, PAS.
23 Emily Wright Millar. (1976). Memoir. "Beyond the Sunset." Accession No. A 210, PAS.
24 Mrs. Sorine Franks. (1911). Pioneer Experiences Questionnaire, PAS.

MAIL-ORDER CATALOGUES

1 The first edition of the catalogue was created in 1884. For more information on the history of the mail order catalogue business in Canada, refer to "Canadian Mail Order Catalogues—History" on the Library and Archives Canada website, https://www.bac-lac.gc.ca/eng/discover/postal-heritage-philately/canadian-mail-order-catalogues/Pages/catalogues-history.aspx.
2 Andrew Salamon. (1906). Pioneer Experiences Questionnaire, PAS.
3 Kathleen Keyser. (1894). Pioneer Experiences Questionnaire, PAS.
4 Florence Kenyon. (1895). Pioneer Experiences Questionnaire, PAS.
5 Lena May Purdy. (1883). Pioneer Experiences Questionnaire, PAS.
6 Lena Bacon. (1904). Pioneer Experiences Questionnaire, PAS.
7 For more information, refer to "The Ancestor of Amazon: The T. Eaton Company Mail Order and Catalogue Building," on the Heritage Winnipeg website, https://heritagewinnipeg.com/blogs/the-ancestor-of-amazon-the-t-eaton-company-mail-order-catalogue-building/.
8 Pearl Stone, "Health," *Beyond Our Prairie Trails* (Carstairs History Book Committee), p. 144.
9 Annie Norris, "Just Reminiscing," *Calahoo Trails: A History of Calahoo, Granger, Speldhurst, East Bilby and Green Willow* (Calahoo Women's Institute, 1975), p. 62.
10 Nannie Walker, "Clintberg Story," *Forests, Furrows and Faith* (Boyle and District Historical Society, 1982), p. 360.
11 Theresa McDonough. (1985). Memoir. "Some Memories of the Alexander Taylor Family, Pioneers of Bresaylor, Saskatchewan and of Mary Isabella Taylor Mack and her Family and their Growing Years on the Prairies." Accession No. A550, PAS.

12 A.J. Riley. (1904). Pioneer Folklore Questionnaire, PAS.
13 "Ladies' Summer Dresses," *Eaton's Spring/Summer 1901 Catalogue*, p. 4.
14 "Spring and Summer Styles for 1901," *Eaton's Spring/Summer 1901 Catalogue*, p. 90.
15 "Milestones and Memories," *Buried Treasures: The History of Elnora, Pine Lake and Huxley* (Elnora/Pine Lake History Book Association, 2009), p. 124.
16 Alexander Cameron. (1902). Pioneer Experiences Questionnaire, PAS.
17 Stephen Hall. (1903). Pioneer Experiences Questionnaire, PAS.
18 Joseph Hammerschmidt. (1904). Pioneer Experiences Questionnaire, PAS.
19 Alfred Riley. (1904). Pioneer Experiences Questionnaire, PAS.
20 Elnora History Committee, "Early Settlers of Elnora District," *Buried Treasures: The History of Elnora, Pine Lake and Huxley* (Elnora/Pine Lake History Book Association, 2009), p. 4.
21 Gladys Holmes. (1901). Memoir. "Autobiography of Gladys Carscallen Holmes." Accession No. RE 2148, PAS.
22 William Colby Reesor. (n.d.). Memoir. Accession No. 77.57 SE, PAS.
23 Claude Hellekson, "A Sure-Fire Vote Getter," *Bridging the Years: A History of Eastbank, Windfield, Hattonford and East Mahaska* (Hattonford History Book Committee, 1982), p. 223.

CHILDHOOD FRIENDS, GAMES AND TOYS

1 Grace Carr. (1910). Memoir. "What I Remember of Pioneer Days in the Wood River District." Accession No. RE 2849, PAS.
2 Dora Mitchell. (n.d.). Memoir. "Far Horizons." Accession No. A 278, PAS.
3 Peter Kozdrowski, "Peter and Pauline Kozdrowski," *Between River and Lake* (Warspite—Victoria Trail Historical Society, 1988), p. 288.
4 "August Roenspies, Sr.," *A Cross in the Clearing: A History, 1903–1980* (Phillips Publishers, 1980), p. 86.
5 Pearl Stone, "Children's Innovations," *Beyond Our Prairie Trails* (Carstairs History Book Committee, 1995), p. 143.
6 Dora Mitchell. (n.d.). Memoir. "Far Horizons." Accession No. A 278, PAS.
7 The first Eaton's Beauty doll was created in 1900. They ranged in price from $1.00 for the smaller dolls to $10.00 for the larger ones. Initially, the "the bisque heads were shoulderheads (the head and shoulder plate were all one piece) with sleep eyes and curly mohair wigs...The bodies were made of kid leather and were jointed at the knees, hips, elbows, and shoulders." For a history of the Beauty Doll, refer to Evelyn Robson Strahlendorf, "The Eaton Beauty Doll: 'The Doll We Will Never Forget,'" on the Canadian Museum of History website, https://www.historymuseum.ca/cmc/exhibitions/cpm/catalog/cat2101e.html.
8 Ella Dickie, "Games Children Played," *Along the Fifth: A History of Stony Plain and District* (Stony Plain Historical Society, 1982), p. 165.
9 Elizabeth E. (Robinson) King. "Reflections," *Forests, Furrows and Faith* (Boyle and District Historical Society, 1982), p. 359.
10 "Milestones and Memories," *Buried Treasures: The History of Elnora, Pine-Lake and Huxley* (Elnora/Pine Lake History Book Association, 2009), p. 125.
11 Florence Allen, "Lonnie and Florence Allen," *Along the Fifth: A History of Stony Plain and District* (Stony Plain Historical Society, 1982), p. 197.
12 Anna Born, *Changes: Anecdotal Tales of Changes in the Life of Anna Born* (Bindery Publishing House, 1995), pp. 38–39.
13 Lena May Purdy. (1883). Pioneer Folklore Questionnaire, PAS.
14 Geroge H. Gunn. (1956). Memoir. "Children's Games in the Red River Settlement." Accession No. MG9 A78-2, PAM.

15 Allen Weigl, "Allen Weigl," *Forests, Furrows and Faith* (Boyle and District Historical Society, 1982), pp. 657–59.

16 Gloria Kay Kolmatycki, "Gloria Kay Kolmatycki," *Forests, Furrows and Faith* (Boyle and District Historical Society, 1982), p. 364.

17 Nannie Walker, "Clintberg Story," *Forests, Furrows and Faith* (Boyle and District Historical Society, 1982), p. 363.

18 Reta Evens Simons, *It Rained at Harvest Time: Memoirs of the Forever Prairie* (Reask, 2017), pp. 11–12.

19 Manfred Prokop, "Canadianization of Immigrant Children: Role of the Rural Elementary School in Alberta, 1900–1930," *Alberta History*, 37, no. 2 (April 1989): pp. 1–10.

20 For more information on skipping rhymes, refer to the Skip-Hop website, https://www.skip-hop.co.uk/interactive-skipping-rhymes/.

21 Cecelia Hellum, "Otto and Wasylena Hellum," *Between River and Lake* (Warspite—Victoria Trail Historical Society, 1988), p. 249.

22 Katherine Schurko, "Miss Ellen Lee," *A Place of Our Own* (Fisher Branch Historical Society, 1982), pp. 33–34.

23 Frances M. Crawford, "The Christmas Concert," *Beyond Our Prairie Trails* (Carstairs History Book Committee), pp. 402–403.

A PARADISE OF PETS

1 Fred Baines. (1883). Pioneer Folklore Questionnaire, PAS.

2 Clarissa L. Bean. (1905). Pioneer Experiences Questionnaire, PAS.

3 Harriet May Stueck. (1886). Pioneer Folklore Questionnaire, PAS.

4 Mary Rogers Berkner. (n.d.). Memoir. "Berkner Family." Accession No. A 454 339, PAS.

5 Marion Anderson. (1883). Pioneer Folklore Questionnaire, PAS.

6 Grant MacEwan, *Power for Prairie Plows* (Western Producer Book Service, 1974), p. 21.

7 Elias Parmlee St. John. (1908). Pioneer Folklore Questionnaire, PAS.

8 Robert Eckel, "Noah August Eckel," *Bucking Poles and Butter Churns* (North Lone Pine Women's Institute, 1972), p. 157.

9 Sue Harrigan. (1980). Memoir. "The Courageous Pioneers." Accession No. RE-626, PAS.

10 Mae Turner, "The Walter Rector Family," *80 Years of Progress* (Westlock History Book Committee, 1984), p. 723.

11 "The Matthew Sanders Family," *Bucking Poles and Butter Churns* (North Lone Pine Women's Institute, 1972), p. 244.

12 Lulu Wilken, "Homesteading in Saskatchewan," *Canada West Magazine*, vol. 7 (1977), p. 33.

13 Josie A. Jones, "Jones' Family Memories," *In the Bend of the Battle: A History of Alliance and District* (Alliance Lions Club, 1976), pp. 417–18.

14 "Milestones and Memories," *Buried Treasures: The History of Elnora, Pine-Lake and Huxley* (Elnora/Pine Lake History Book Association, 2009), p. 126.

15 Elnora History Committee, "Elnora 1916," *Buried Treasures: The History of Elnora, Pine-Lake and Huxley* (Elnora/Pine Lake History Book Association, 2009), p. 6.

16 Loyd and George (Alex) McMillan, "The George and Maggie McMillan Family," *80 Years of Progress* (Westlock History Book Committee, 1984), p. 640.

17 Ellenor Ranghild Merriken, *Looking for Country: A Norwegian Immigrant's Alberta Memoir* (University of Calgary Press, 1999), pp. 70–71.

18 Annie Condon. (n.d.). Memoir. "Northern Lights: A Story of Pioneer Days in Saskatchewan." Accession No. A 535, PAS.

19 Ellenor Ranghild Merriken, *Looking for Country: A Norwegian Immigrant's Alberta Memoir* (University of Calgary Press, 1999), pp. 70–71.

20 Jessie, Hugh and Faye Nisbet, "Nisbets of the West," *Pioneer Legacy: Bowden and Districts* (Bowden Chamber of Commerce, 1979), p. 502.

21 Ethel McClymont, "The Denning Family History," *Forests, Furrows and Faith* (Boyle and District Historical Society, 1982), p. 231.

22 Olive Phelps. (1933). Memoir. "Memoirs of Crescent Lake." Accession No. YF 560, PAS.

23 Glen Carmichael, "Barnyard Stories," *Along the Fifth: A History of Stony Plain and District* (Stony Plain Historical Society, 1982), p. 159.

24 Nick Sherwin, "The Sherwin Story," *80 Years of Progress* (Westlock History Book Committee, 1984), p. 758.

25 Mrs. W.T. Billing. (n.d.). Memoir. "An English School Marm in Saskatchewan." Accession No. A 160, PAS.

26 "Gust Wallin," *Brick's Hill, Berwyn and Beyond* (Berwyn Centennial Committee, 1968), p. 58.

27 Ellenor Ranghild Merriken, *Looking for Country: A Norwegian Immigrant's Alberta Memoir* (University of Calgary Press, 1999), p. 106.

28 Eloise Anderson. (1902). Pioneer Folklore Questionnaire, PAS.

29 D.H. Maginnes. (1906). Pioneer Folklore Questionnaire, PAS.

30 Alfred Mann. (1882). Pioneer Experiences Questionnaire, PAS.

31 Olive Phelps. (1933). Memoir. "Memoirs of Crescent Lake." Accession No. YF 560, PAS.

32 James M. Minifie, *Homesteader: A Prairie Boyhood Recalled* (Macmillan of Canada, 1972), p. 127.

33 James M. Minifie, *Homesteader: A Prairie Boyhood Recalled* (Macmillan of Canada, 1972), p. 103.

34 Betty Iredale, *Stories of the Sod Shack and Other Reminiscences* (Hemlock Printers, 1991), p. 32.

35 Evelyn Olson. (1991). Memoir. "Memories Are Such Fragile Things." Accession No. X 173, p. 15, PAS.

36 "William Donner," *Back Over The Trail* (The Acadia Women's Institute, 1967), p. 114.

37 Lucy Johnson. (1903). Memoir. "Against the Wind." Accession No. RE-2878, PAS.

38 Arthur James Wheeler. (1906). Pioneer Farming Experiences Questionnaire, PAS.

39 Martha Ann Todd. (1894). Pioneer Folklore Questionnaire, PAS.

40 Rena Michael (n.d.). Memoir. "North Battleford," Accession No. R-E3198, PAS.

41 Oda Becker, "Conrad Becker and Descendants," *Along the Fifth: A History of Stony Plain and District* (Stony Plain Historical Society, 1982), p. 232.

42 Mary Morrison (n.d.). Memoir. Accession No. MG9 A81, PAM.

43 Alfred Bagehot Estlin. (n.d.). Memoir. "The Old Commission Trail." Accession No. P5039 F6, PAM.

44 Gordon Wolseley Stewart. (n.d.). Memoir. "Memoirs of Gordon Wolseley Stewart." Accession No. R-E1222, PAS.

45 John Evans. (1892). Pioneer Folklore Questionnaire, PAS.

46 Elsie Campbell. (1905). Pioneer Experiences Questionnaire, PAS.

47 Annie Gamroth Strachan, "Peter Gamroth Family," *Golden Echoes: A History of Galahad* (Galahad Historical Society, 1980), p. 131.

48 Ellenor Ranghild Merriken, *Looking for Country: A Norwegian Immigrant's Alberta Memoir* (University of Calgary Press, 1999), pp. 106–107.

49 "Price and McTavish," *Bridging the Years: Nipawin, Saskatchewan* (Nipawin Historical Society, 1988), p. 63.

50 Dorothy White Gladwin, "The White Family," *Bridging the Years: A History of Eastbank, Windfield, Hattonford and East Mahaska* (Hattonford History Book Committee, 1982), p. 186.

51 Dave Koelln, "Coming to the Peace," *Brick's Hill, Berwyn and Beyond* (Berwyn Centennial Committee, 1968), pp. 267–69.

52 Julia Anna Asher. (1950). Memoir. "Grandma's Childhood: Pioneer Life in Southern Alberta." Accession No. MG8 B10, PAM.

53 W. Roland Murray. (1981). Memoir. "The Murray-Hurlbert Homesteads," Accession No. M6089, Glenbow Archives.

54 Evelyn Slater McLeod. (1977). Memoir. "Restless Pioneers." Accession No. 77.39, PAS.

55 Annie Norris, "Mr and Mrs Steve Dozorec," *Calahoo Trails: A History of Calahoo, Granger, Speldhurst, East Bilby and Green Willow* (Calahoo Women's Institute, 1975), p. 84.

56 Reta Evens Simons, *It Rained at Harvest Time: Memoirs of the Forever Prairie* (Reask, 2017), pp. 25–26.

"A WONDERFUL SOCIAL SPIRIT IN THE COMMUNITY"

1 George A. Harris. (1955). Memoir. "Some History and Pioneer Experiences of Heward, Sask. from its Settlement in 1900 to 1914." Accession No. 623, PAS.

2 Lee-Enfield rifles were British-made while Ross rifles were Canadian-made. Large numbers of the Ross rifle were produced in 1910, with many more produced in 1911 for the Canadian military. They were excellent rifles for hunting and target shooting, but they jammed when used in the trenches during the war years. Jamming occurred so often that many soldiers went against orders to use them, threw them away and sought Lee-Enfield rifles. For more discussion on the Lee-Enfield/Ross controversy, see the "Ross Rifle" article in the *Canadian Encyclopdia*, https://www.thecanadianencyclopedia.ca/en/article/ross-rifle.

3 World War I ran from July 28, 1914 to November 11, 1918. As Canada was part of the British Empire, the country was directly involved as soon as Great Britain declared war on Germany in August 1914. Tens of thousands of Canadian men answered the call to serve within the first months of the war.

4 This refers to the members of the Rifle Association being called to war.

5 The Argyle Rifle Association, based in Argyle, Alberta, faced a similar situation. The association was formed in 1912 for the purpose of rifle practice. However, with the advent of the war, the club came to a standstill as many of the members headed off to serve in the army.

6 Ernest Bishop. (n.d.). Memoir. "Pioneer Days of the District." Accession No. A 31, PAS.

7 This rifle was designed by Edward Maynard, a dentist, in 1851. It became known for its accuracy during the American civil war (1861–65). For more information, see Bill Marr, "Maynard Model 1 Breechloading Carbine," June 7, 2015, on the Rifleshooter.com website, https://rifleshooter.com/2015/06/maynard-model-1-breechloading-carbine/.

8 Nell Williams, "Some Memories of Griffin Creek," *Brick's Hill, Berwyn and Beyond* (Berwyn Centennial Committee, 1968), pp. 35–36.

9 Clara Johnson and Phyllis Alcorn, "Argyle District," *In the Bend of the Battle: A History of Alliance and District* (Alliance Lions Club, 1976), p. 24.

10 *History of Rimbey, Alberta: 50 Years of Progress* (Rimbey Historical Committee, 1952), p. 43.

11 The term "horsehide" refers to the ball that was to be played. In this case, the ball would have been covered in horsehide.

12 "Hamiota: The Baseball Capital of Manitoba," *Hamiota: Grains of the Century* (Hamiota Centennial History Committee, 1984), p. 256.

13 The game of football in the late 1800s and early 1900s would be referred to as "soccer" today, given that it was often described as a "kicking game" and different from American football.

14 "Sports and Recreation," *Hamiota: Grains of the Century* (Hamiota Centennial History Committee, 1984), pp. 240–41.

15 "Carstairs Football," *Beyond Our Prairie Trails* (Carstairs History Book Committee), pp. 508–509.

16 "Sheho Football Team," *They Came From Many Lands* (Foam Lake Review, 1985), pp. 55–56.

17 Freda Purmal. "Ernest Redpath 'Jake' Fullerton, 1882–1975, Circle Five Ranch," Our Foothills (Priddis and Bragg Creek Historical Society, 1975), pp. 439–441, https://braggcreekhistoricalsociety.ca/wp-content/uploads/2020/08/our_foothills_bragg_creek.pdf.

18 George H. Hambley, "Game of Lacrosse," *Trails of the Pioneers* (D.W. Friesen & Sons Ltd., 1956), pp, 95–96.

19 Leslie Tetley, "Pine Lake Sports," *Buried Treasures: The History of Elnora, Pine-Lake and Huxley* (Elnora/Pine Lake History Book Association, 2009), pp. 307–309.

20 A militia formed in a community refers to a fighting organization of non-professional soldiers. The members, who could be as young as sixteen years old, learned how to follow rules and understand military jargon. They practised drills and did target shooting. They also tended to take part in official military service when called upon to do so.

21 Bob Mason, "Ice Sports," *Basswood, 1878–1978* (Centennial Book and Home Day Committee, 1978), p. 57.

22 Freemasonry began in the thirteenth century in England and Scotland. It involved local guilds of stonemasons, the regulations surrounding their trade, and determined how they interacted with clients and authorities. For more information relating to the history of freemasonry and how the organization transformed over the centuries, refer to the article on Freemasonry at the Britannica website, https://www.britannica.com/topic/Freemasonry.

23 For instance, in 1910, there were twelve men from the Foam Lake district of Saskatchewan who wished to become Masons. They constructed their lodge in Sheho, Saskatchewan. "Foam Lake Masonic Lodge, No. 79," *They Came From Many Lands* (Foam Lake Review, 1985), p. 117. For more information on the history of Masonry in the Canadian West, see http://ivanhoe142.org/wordpress/about-us/early-masonic-history-in-the-canadian-west/.

24 The member of the Masonic Lodge had to be a Master Mason. A Master Mason is an individual who has achieved all three masonic degrees of Entered Apprentice, Fellow Craft and Master Mason.

25 Eventually, youth groups were organized so that young men and women could become involved in the masonic family. The youth group for men, Demolay, was founded in 1919, and the youth group for women, Job's Daughters, was founded in 1920. Given that these groups were founded outside of 1867–1914 (the focus years of this book), no details have been provided.

26 *By the Old Mill Stream* (Holmfield History Book Committee, 1982), p. 69.

27 "Social and Fraternal Organizations," *Hamiota: Grains of the Century* (Hamiota Centennial History Committee, 1984), pp. 207–208.

28 "Foam Lake Lodge No. 68," *They Came From Many Lands* (Foam Lake Review, 1985), p. 119.

29 Those in need included individuals who were ill, widowed, orphaned or otherwise in distress.

30 Audrey Kulak, "The Stony Plain Women's Institute," *Along the Fifth: The History of Stony Plain and District* (Stony Plain Historical Society, 1982), p. 122.

31 Evelyn Olson. (1991). Memoir. "Memories Are Such Fragile Things." Accession No. X 173, PAS.

32 Lena May Purdy. (1883). Pioneer Experiences Questionnaire, PAS.

33 Lena Morin, "The History of Pickardville," *80 Years of Progress* (Westlock History Book Committee, 1984), p. 64.

34 "Health Care," *Hamiota: Grains of the Century* (Hamiota Centennial History Committee, 1984), p. 203.

35 Other community groups got involved with fundraising efforts for the hospital. They included the Oddfellows, Orangemen, Foresters, the Orrwold Ladies' Aid and the Ladies of Pope, as well as a number of private donors.

36 Aaron Biehn. (1898). Memoir. Accession No. RE 514, PAS.

37 This song was composed by Alfred, Lord Tennyson, in 1849. For a copy of the lyrics, refer to https://www.poetryfoundation.org/poems/45383/the-princess-sweet-and-low.

38 This song was composed by Tell Taylor and was very popular in 1910. For a copy of the lyrics, refer to https://digitalcommons.conncoll.edu/sheetmusic/280/.

39 "Early Entertainment," *Beyond Our Prairie Trails* (Carstairs History Book Committee), pp. 271–72.

40 Lena May Purdy. (1883). Pioneer Experiences Questionnaire, PAS.

41 "Social Life of Pioneers in the Waskatenau Area," *Waskatenau, 1867–1967* (County of Smoky Lake, 1967), p. 13.

42 "Entertainment," *Beyond Our Prairie Trails* (Carstairs History Book Committee), p. 270.

43 Mrs. W.T. Billing. (n.d.). Memoir. "An English School Marm in Saskatchewan." Accession No. A 160, PAS.

44 William F. Mills, "The Box Social," *Along the Fifth: A History of Stony Plain* (Stony Plain Historical Society, 1982), p. 173.

45 Nellie Anderson, "The Scales District," *Trails of Tail Creek Country* (Edith Lawrence Clark, 1972), p. 181.

46 "Early Entertainment," *Beyond Our Prairie Trails* (Carstairs History Book Committee), pp. 270–71.

47 "Gambling," *Beyond Our Prairie Trails* (Carstairs History Book Committee), p. 386.

WINNING PRIZES AT THE COUNTRY FAIRS

1 Edith Stilborn. (1883). Pioneer Farming Experiences Questionnaire, PAS.
2 Joseph C. Wilson. (1904). Pioneer Farming Experiences Questionnaire, PAS.
3 Pasterns are the area of the leg between the fetlock and the hoof.
4 Charles Cantlon Bray. (1883). Pioneer Farming Experiences Questionnaire, PAS.
5 Toulouse geese are large domestic birds from southwestern France.
6 Judges of the "dressed poultry" category evaluated how well the poultry were defeathered and washed, how the heads and feet were removed, how well the evisceration was done, as well as the presentation aspects of the birds.
7 The Carmangay and District Home and School Association, "Carmangay Agricultural Society Fair," *Bridging the Years: Carmangay and District* (Carmangay and District History Book Committee, 1968), pp. 100–108.
8 The term "bacon hogs" refers to Irish Tamworth hogs, which provide excellent quality hams and bacon.
9 "George Spady," *Along the Fifth: History of Stony Plain and District* (Stony Plain Historical Society, 1982), p. 514.
10 Chickens with four feet suffer from a genetic birth defect called "polymelia." The cause of this anomaly is unknown. For more information, refer to http://www.poultrydvm.com/condition/polymelia.
11 "Griffin Creek: From the Files of the Peace River Record," *Brick's Hill, Berwyn and Beyond* (Berwyn Centennial Committee, 1968), pp. 29–30.
12 The Hudson's Bay Baby Contest was a nationwide contest based on cuteness. For more information, see Mark Collin Reid, "Oh, Baby," *Canada's History*, November 2019, https://www.canadashistory.ca/explore/museums-galleries-archives/oh-baby!
13 A scuffler is a piece of farm machinery that is used for turning up the dirt between rows of crops such as potatoes, beets, onions and turnips. It also helps with controlling weeds, as the plant roots become exposed to the air and die.
14 "Irvine Agricultural Society," *A New Beginning: Irvine and District* (20 Mile Post Historical Society, 1989), p. 131.
15 "George Spady," *Along the Fifth: History of Stony Plain and District* (Stony Plain Historical Society, 1982), p. 515.
16 "Special Days in Bowden's History," *Pioneer Legacy: Bowden and Districts* (Bowden Chamber of Commerce, 1979), p. 203.
17 Dominion Day commemorated the formation of Canada on July 1, 1867, as a dominion with an allegiance to the British crown. It became a national holiday in 1879.
18 Olive Phelps. (1933). Memoir. "Memoirs of Crescent Lake." Accession No. YF 560, PAS.
19 "Agriculture," *Hamiota: Grains of the Century* (Hamiota Centennial History Committee, 1984), pp. 46–47.
20 Ethel Collier, "Social Life in Bowville," Bridging the Years: Carmangay and District (Carmangay and District History Book Committee, 1968), pp. 155–60.
21 "Early Entertainment," *Beyond Our Prairie Trails* (Carstairs History Book Committee), p. 270.
22 Letter from Dan Kennedy to Harry Scrivner. Posted January 24, 1954, Accession No. R-IS4, PAS.
23 A collection, in this case, refers to an agreed-upon amount of money if the rider could successfully stay on the horse.
24 The Carmangay and District Home and School Association, "The Carmangay Stampede," *Bridging the Years: Carmangay and District* (Carmangay and District History Book Committee, 1968), pp. 106–108.

25 Flossie Boice (Trace), "The Boice Family," *Buried Treasures: The History of Elnora, Pine-Lake and Huxley* (Elnora/Pine Lake History Book Association, 2009), p. 33.

26 Laura Matz. (1978). Memoir. "My Pioneer Days in Saskatchewan." Accession No. R-E321 #15, PAS.

27 Laura Matz. (1978). Memoir. "My Pioneer Days in Saskatchewan." Accession No. R-E321 #15, PAS.

28 *History of Rimbey, Alberta: 50 Years of Progress* (Rimbey Historical Committee, 1952), pp. 36–37.

29 Grant MacEwan, *Power for Prairie Plows* (Western Producer Book Service, 1974), p. 10. A "guy rope" is a rope that has been fixed to the ground in order to secure a pole, tent or other structure.

30 MacEwan, *Power for Prairie Plows* (Western Producer Book Service, 1974), p. 10.

31 MacEwan, *Power for Prairie Plows* (Western Producer Book Service, 1974), p. 11.

32 The average lifespan of an ox is fifteen years.

33 MacEwan, *Power for Prairie Plows* (Western Producer Book Service, 1974), p. 11.

DANCING THE NIGHT AWAY

1 Bertha Shaw Myer. (n.d.). Memoir. "My Pioneer Days in Saskatchewan." Accession No. R-E321 #19, PAS.

2 Patrick J. O'Toole, *Rhymes of a Homesteader* (Hamley Press, 1947), p. 58.

3 Nell Williams, "Some Memories of Griffin Creek," *Brick's Hill, Berwyn and Beyond* (Berwyn Centennial Committee, 1968), pp. 35–36.

4 Harry Bell. (1955). "A Short History of the Gladmar Community," *History of Gladmar*, Accession No. IF 86, PAS.

5 "Social Life of Pioneers in the Waskatenau Area," *Waskatenau: 1867–1967* (County of Smoky Lake, 1967), p. 13.

6 Robert Jackson Barnes, "Hard Time Fun," *Along the Fifth: A History of Stony Plain and District* (Stony Plain Historical Society, 1982), p. 173.

7 Mrs. W.T. Billing. (n.d.). Memoir. "An English School Marm in Saskatchewan." Accession No. A 160, PAS.

8 Julia Anna Asher. (1950). Memoir. "Grandma's Childhood: Pioneer Life in Southern Alberta." Accession No. MG8-B10, PAM.

9 Sue Harrigan. (1980). Memoir. "The Courageous Pioneers." Accession No. RE-626, PAS.

10 Bill Gwin, "Rimbey Entertains over the Years," *Over the Years, 1892–1982* (Rimbey History Book Committee, 1983), pp. 69–70.

11 Herman Collingwood. (1977). Memoir. "My Life History from 1904 to 1970 in Saskatchewan." Accession No. RE 36, PAS.

12 John Fetsch. (1910). Pioneer Folklore Questionnaire, PAS.

13 Patrick J. O'Toole, *Rhymes of a Homesteader* (Hamley Press, 1947), p. 40.

14 Ethel Collier, "Social Life in Bowville," *Bridging the Years: Carmangay and District* (Carmangay and District History Book Committee, 1968), pp. 155–58.

15 Annie Norris, "Old Time Dances in Calahoo," *Calahoo Trails: A History of Calahoo, Granger, Speldhurst, East Bilby and Green Willow* (Calahoo Women's Institute, 1975), p. 144.

TAKING THE FAMILY TO THE PICNIC

1 Mabel Wilson Hawthorne. (1905). Memoir. "My Reminiscence of Fifty Years on the Saskatchewan Prairies." Accession No. RE 2991, PAS.

2 Archie Althouse. (1906). Memoir. "Life on a Saskatchewan Homestead." Accession No. RE 2930, PAS.

3 Aaron Biehn. (1898). Memoir. Accession No. RE 513, PAS.

4 Annie Norris, "Old Time Calahoo Picnics," *Calahoo Trails: A History of Calahoo, Granger, Speldhurst, East Bilby and Green Willow* (Calahoo Women's Institute, 1975), p. 144.

5 Rose Feist, "The Heywoods: The Story of my Parents who Pioneered in the Clyde District at the Turn of the Century," *80 Years of Progress* (Westlock History Book Committee, 1984), p. 502.

6 "Memoirs of Duncan Campbell," *Pioneer Legacy: Bowden and Districts* (Bowden Chamber of Commerce, 1979), p. 437.

7 Samuel Jackson. (1878). Pioneer Experiences Questionnaire, PAS.

8 Claude Hellekson, "The Picnic," *Bridging the Years: A History of Eastbank, Windfield, Hattonford and East Mahaska* (Hattonford History Book Committee, 1982), p. 222.

9 "The Aubrey 'Jack' Davies Story," *Back Over The Trail* (The Acadia Women's Institute, 1967), pp. 107–108.

SHOPOWNERS, STRONG MEN, JUSTICE-KEEPERS AND CRIMINALS

1 The Carmangay and District Home and School Association, "Carmangay," *Bridging the Years: Carmangay and District* (Carmangay and District History Book Committee, 1968), pp. 6–8.

2 Ernest Bishop. (n.d.). Memoir. "Pioneer Days of the District." Accession No. A 31, PAS.

3 William Munro, "Busby's Early Years," *Busby's Busy Years: 75th Anniversary Edition* (Busby History Book Committee, 1989), pp. 5–6.

4 Foam Lake Composite School Students, "History of Sheho and District," *They Came from Many Lands* (Foam Lake Review, 1985), pp. 61–62.

5 Lena May Purdy. (1883). Pioneer Experiences Questionnaire, PAS.

6 "Agriculture and Progress," *Ponoka 1904–1954: 50th Anniversary* (Ponoka Herald, 1954), pp. 29–31.

7 The Foam Lake Historical Society, "Early Settlements," *They Came from Many Lands* (Foam Lake Review, 1985), pp. 4–5.

8 Albert Elderton. (1909). Pioneer Experiences Questionnaire, PAS.

9 Joseph Bonas. (1903). Pioneer Experiences Questionnaire, PAS.

10 Lena Bacon. (1904). Pioneer Experiences Questionnaire, PAS.

11 "Chinese Residents of Alliance," *In the Bend of the Battle: A History of Alliance and District* (Alliance Lions Club, 1976), p. 128.

12 "The Savoury History of Chop Suey on the Prairies: Reflections of Ponoka," *Ponoka News*, September 14, 2011, https://www.ponokanews.com/community/the-savoury-history-of-chop-suey-on-the-prairies-reflections-of-ponoka/.

13 Lila Pope. (1904). Pioneer Folklore Questionnaire, PAS.

14 Mary Kajewski. (1899). Pioneer Folklore Questionnaire, PAS.

15 Percy Thomson. (1910). Pioneer Folklore Questionnaire, PAS.

16 Harry Martyn. (1913). Pioneer Folklore Questionnaire, PAS.

17 Lena May Purdy. (1883). Pioneer Folklore Questionnaire, PAS.

18 Letter from Dan Kennedy to Harry Scrivner. Posted January 24, 1954, Accession No. R-IS4, PAS.

19 "Jumping Johnny," *Pioneer Legacy: Bowden and Districts* (Bowden Chamber of Commerce, 1979), p. 391.

20 Lila Pope. (1904). Folklore Pioneer Questionnaire, PAS.

21 Lena May Purdy. (1883). Pioneer Experiences Questionnaire, PAS.

22 Murdock Matheson, *Looking Backward over my Fifty Years in Saskatchewan* (self-published, 1960), pp. 32–33.

23 "Sharphead," *Ponoka 1904–1954: 50th Anniversary* (Ponoka Herald, 1954), p. 40.

24 Nell Williams, "Griffin Creek: Neighbours and Others," *Brick's Hill, Berwyn and Beyond* (Berwyn Centennial Committee, 1968), pp. 36–37.

25 Charles Sargent. (1911). Pioneer Folklore Questionnaire, PAS.

26 "Price and McTavish," *Bridging the Years: Nipawin, Saskatchewan* (Nipawin Historical Society, 1988), p. 63.

27 Sam Vickar. (1906). Pioneer Experiences Questionnaire, PAS.

28 Ernest Bishop. (n.d.). Memoir. "Pioneer Days of the District." Accession No. A 31, PAS.

29 "The Attempted Robbery of a Lang Bank," *Lang Syne: A History of Lang, Saskatchewan* (Lang Syne History Book Committee, 1980), p. 85.

30 A freebooter is a lawless opportunist or adventurer.

31 A posse is a group of armed men organized by a sheriff.

32 George H. Hambley, *Trails of the Pioneers* (D.W. Friesen & Sons Ltd., 1956), pp. 15–16.

33 The Forshee elevator siding was located between Rimbey and Bentley, Alberta.

34 *History of Rimbey, Alberta: 50 Years of Progress* (Rimbey Historical Committee, 1952), pp. 37–38.

JOKES, ANECDOTES AND HALLOWEEN TRICKS

1 John Alexander. "Boyle Memories," *Forests, Furrows and Faith* (Boyle and District Historical Society, 1982), p. 174.

2 Nell Williams, "Griffin Creek: Neighbours and Others," *Brick's Hill, Berwyn and Beyond* (Berwyn Centennial Committee, 1968), p. 37.

3 A cow who has "freshened" has recently had a calf and her milk production has begun. A "caked bag" refers to udder edema, where there is an excess of fluid in the udder.

4 Betty Iredale. *Stories of the Sod Shack and Other Reminiscences* (Hemlock Printers, 1991), p. 39.

5 Olive Phelps. (1933). Memoir. "Memoirs of Crescent Lake." Accession No. YF 560, PAS.

6 Susanna Liesemer, "Mr. John Bender," *Bucking Poles and Butter Churns* (North Lone Pine Women's Institute, 1972), p. 287.

7 M. Stevens, "Chuckles over the Years," *Over the Years: 1892–1982* (Rimbey History Book Committee, 1983), p. 638.

8 Harve Carson. (1883). Pioneer Folklore Questionnaire, PAS.

9 Charles Davis. (1882). Pioneer Folklore Questionnaire, PAS.

10 Anna Born, *Changes: Anecdotal Tales of Changes in the Life of Anna Born* (Bindery Publishing House, 1995), pp. 11–12.

11 "The Flim-Flamming of a Porter," *Pioneer Legacy: Bowden and Districts* (Bowden Chamber of Commerce, 1979), pp. 339–340.

12 Charles Edward Kieper. (1954). Memoir. "The Life of a Pioneer." Accession No. A 75, PAS.

13 Erdman Rosnau. "Chivarees," *From Bush to Bushels: A History of Bruderheim and District* (Bruderheim Historical Society, 1983), p. 209.

14 Charles Sargent. (1911). Pioneer Folklore Questionnaire, PAS.

15 John McChesney. (1904). Pioneer Recreation and Social Life Questionnaire, PAS.

16 "John A. MacDougall Family," *From Bush to Bushels, A History of Bruderheim and District* (Bruderheim Historical Society, 1983), p. 359.

17 Mrs. Charles Archer. (1902). Pioneer Folklore Questionnaire, PAS.
18 William Boyle. (1910). Pioneer Folklore Questionnaire, PAS.
19 "Reminiscences of Fred Williams," *Bridging the Years: Carmangay and District* (Carmangay and District History Book Committee, 1968), pp. 424–26.
20 "Milestones and Memories," *Buried Treasures: The History of Elnora, Pine-Lake and Huxley* (Elnora/Pine Lake History Book Association, 2009), p. 125.
21 Marion Anderson. (1883). Pioneer Folklore Questionnaire, PAS.
22 Betty Iredale, *Stories of the Sod Shack and Other Reminiscences* (Hemlock Printers, 1991), pp. 35–37.
23 Anna Born, *Changes: Anecdotal Tales of Changes in the Life of Anna Born* (Bindery Publishing House, 1995), pp. 36–37.
24 Rusty Roberts, "Memoirs," *Calahoo Trails: A History of Calahoo, Granger, Speldhurst, East Bilby and Green Willow* (Calahoo Women's Institute, 1975), p. 181.
25 Marion Anderson. (1883). Pioneer Folklore Questionnaire, PAS.
26 John Alexander, "Boyle Memories," *Forests, Furrows and Faith* (Boyle and District Historical Society, 1982), p. 174.
27 Elias Parmlee St. John. (1908). Pioneer Folklore Questionnaire, PAS.
28 Marion Anderson. (1883). Pioneer Folklore Questionnaire, PAS.
29 Ethel Krisher, "Amusing Anecdotes," *Busby's Busy Years: 75th Anniversary Edition* (Busby History Book Committee, 1989), p. 178.
30 "The Thundermug," *Pioneer Legacy: Bowden and Districts* (Bowden Chamber of Commerce, 1979), p. 255.
31 Letter from Dan Kennedy to Harry Scrivner. Posted January 24, 1954, Accession No. R-IS4, PAS.
32 Viola Cameron. (1975). Interview. Accession No. 81.279, File No. 17, PAA.
33 Allen Weigl, "Allen Weigl," *Forests, Furrows and Faith* (Boyle and District Historical Society, 1982), p. 658.
34 Lena May Purdy. (1883). Pioneer Experiences Questionnaire, PAS.
35 A teacherage refers to a teacher's place of accommodation, like a house or a building with multiple living quarters.
36 David Stammen, "History of the Math Stammen Family," *A Cross in the Clearing* (Phillips Publishers, 1980), p. 24.
37 Henning Bergstrom, "Mr and Mrs John Bergstrom," *They Came from Many Lands* (Foam Lake Review, 1985), p. 319.
38 Frank Roenspies, "Frank Roenspies," *A Cross in the Clearing* (Phillips Publishers, 1980), p. 87.
39 A.J. Riley. (1904). Pioneer Folklore Questionnaire, PAS.
40 "Vernon Seibert Story," *Busby's Busy Years: 75th Anniversary Edition* (Busby History Book Committee, 1989), p. 556.
41 *History of Rimbey, Alberta: 50 Years of Progress* (Rimbey Historical Committee, 1952), p. 7.
42 *History of Rimbey, Alberta: 50 Years of Progress* (Rimbey Historical Committee, 1952), p. 8.
43 John Fetsch. (1910). Pioneer Folklore Questionnaire, PAS.
44 Isabel Muirhead. (1883). Pioneer Folklore Questionnaire, PAS.
45 Dorothy White Gladwin, "The White Family," *Bridging the Years: A History of Eastbank, Windfield, Hattonford and East Mahaska* (Hattonford History Book Committee, 1982), p. 186.
46 Ernie Sanders, "Sanders Family," *In the Bend of the Battle: A History of Alliance and District* (Alliance Lions Club, 1976), pp. 525–27.
47 "Halloween Pranks," *Beyond Our Prairie Trails* (Carstairs History Book Committee), p. 388.

48 "The Roy Misner Family," *Golden Echoes: A History of Galahad* (Galahad Historical Society, 1980), p. 181.

49 Ernie Sanders, "Sanders Family," In the Bend of the Battle: A History of Alliance and District (Alliance Lions Club, 1976), pp. 525–27

50 "Halloween Pranks," *Beyond Our Prairie Trails* (Carstairs History Book Committee, 1995), p. 388.

GOOD LUCK, BAD LUCK AND OTHER SUPERSTITIONS

1 Sidney May. (1913). Pioneer Folklore Questionnaire, PAS.

2 Elnora History Committee, "Elnora 1916," *Buried Treasures: The History of Elnora, Pine-Lake and Huxley* (Elnora/Pine Lake History Book Association, 2009), p. 6.

3 Percy Thomson. (1910). Pioneer Folklore Questionnaire, PAS.

4 Sadie McCallum. (1900). Pioneer Folklore Questionnaire, PAS.

5 Lily Taylor, "John and Mary Jordan," *Busby's Busy Years: 75th Anniversary Edition* (Busby History Book Committee, 1989), p. 99.

6 Lena May Purdy. (1883). Pioneer Folklore Questionnaire, PAS.

7 For more information on cartomancy, see Mimi Matthews, "Nineteenth Century Fortune-Telling" on the Victorian Web website, https://victorianweb.org/history/matthews.html.

8 Gwen Coppock, "Charles A. Pigeon," *In the Bend of the Battle: A History of Alliance and District* (Alliance Lions Club, 1976), p. 490.

9 "Special Events," *Admiral: Prairie to Wheatfields* (Admiral History Book Club, 1978), p. 87.

10 Mary Anderson. (1902). Pioneer Folklore Questionnaire, PAS.

11 For more information on the process of reading tea leaves, see Aliza Kelly, "Your Essential Guide to Tasseography," *Allure*, May 17, 2018, https://www.allure.com/story/how-to-read-tea-leaves-tasseography.

12 For more tea leaf symbols and their connotations, refer to A Highland Seer, *Tea-Cup Reading and Fortune-Telling by Tea Leaves*, dated 1881. It is available at https://www.gutenberg.org/files/18241/18241-h/18241-h.htm#3.

13 For more information on coffee ground readings, refer to artsybot, "Turkish Coffee Fortune Telling," https://www.instructables.com/Turkish-Coffee-Fortune-Telling/.

14 "Special Events," *Admiral: Prairie to Wheatfields* (Admiral History Book Club, 1978), p. 87.

15 For more information on palm reading, see Aliza Kelly, "A Beginner's Guide to Reading Palms," *Allure*, December 2, 2021, https://www.allure.com/story/palm-reading-guide-hand-lines.

16 Elias Parmlee St. John. (1908). Pioneer Folklore Questionnaire, PAS.

17 Many of these superstitions were found in Rosalind Franklin, *Baby Lore: Superstitions and Old Wive's Tales from the World Over Related to Pregnancy, Birth and Childcare* (Diggory Press, 2005).

18 See "Monday's Child Poem: Your Child's Personality by Day of the Week," on the famlii website, https://www.famlii.com/mondays-child-day-of-the-week-nursery-rhyme-predicting-childs-personality/.

19 "William and Evelyn Tarzwell," *Admiral: Prairie to Wheatfields* (Admiral History Book Club, 1978), p. 318.

20 Martha Ann Todd. (1894). Pioneer Folklore Questionnaire, PAS.

21 Elias Parmlee St. John. (1908). Pioneer Folklore Questionnaire, PAS.

22 Ella Otterson. (1903). Pioneer Folklore Questionnaire, PAS.

23 Sam H. McWilliams. (1884). Pioneer Folklore Questionnaire, PAS.

24 Mrs. W.H.S. Gange. (1894). Pioneer Folklore Questionnaire, PAS.
25 Ellenor Ranghild Merriken, *Looking for Country: A Norwegian Immigrant's Alberta Memoir* (University of Calgary Press, 1999), p. 106.
26 Dropping a comb could also mean good luck, particularly if you made a wish before picking it up (Jacqueline Pearson, Correspondence, March 29, 2023).
27 Sidney S. May. (1901). Pioneer Folklore Questionnaire, PAS.
28 Tobias Lanegraff. (1906). Pioneer Folklore Questionnaire, PAS.
29 Marion Anderson. (1883). Pioneer Folklore Questionnaire, PAS.
30 Martha Ann Todd (1894). Pioneer Folklore Questionnaire, PAS.
31 Paul Gehlert, "Digging a Well," *Along the Fifth: A History of Stony Plain and District* (Stony Plain Historical Society, 1982), p. 158.
32 Olson Family. (n.d.). Memoir. "The Pioneers on South Half Section of 17-33-27-W2nd." Accession No. A 319, PAS.
33 "Early Water Supply," *Admiral: Prairie to Wheatfields* (Admiral History Book Club, 1978), p. 26.
34 "Early Water Supply," *Admiral: Prairie to Wheatfields* (Admiral History Book Club, 1978), p. 26.

"THE PIG IS GENERALLY THE BEST WEATHER FORECASTER"

1 In some cases, the farm animals also helped to reassure homesteaders when there was a storm. As one homesteader stated, "I watch my horses in a storm. If they're not afraid, I'm not."
2 John Hamer. (1909). Pioneer Folklore Questionnaire, PAS.
3 D.H. Maginnes. (1906). Pioneer Folklore Questionnaire, PAS.
4 Charles Cantlon Bray. (1883). Pioneer Folklore Questionnaire, PAS.
5 Mrs. J.M. Telfodd. (1910). Pioneer Folklore Questionnaire, PAS.
6 Mrs. C.A. Stewart. (1912). Pioneer Folklore Questionnaire, PAS.
7 Mrs. Ed Wilson. (1905). Pioneer Folklore Questionnaire, PAS.
8 Mrs. Jay Laycock. (1902). Pioneer Folklore Questionnaire, PAS.
9 Frank Baines. (1883). Pioneer Folklore Questionnaire, PAS.
10 Charles Sargent. (1911). Pioneer Folklore Questionnaire, PAS.
11 John Thiessen. (1905). Pioneer Folklore Questionnaire, PAS.
12 Mary Kajewski. (1899). Pioneer Folklore Questionnaire, PAS.
13 John Fetsch. (1910). Pioneer Folklore Questionnaire, PAS.
14 J.H. Sand (1910). Pioneer Folklore Questionnaire, PAS.
15 Charles Sargent. (1911). Pioneer Folklore Questionnaire, PAS.
16 Lila Pope. (1904). Pioneer Folklore Questionnaire, PAS.
17 Mrs. J.M. Telfodd. (1910). Pioneer Folklore Questionnaire, PAS.
18 Mary Kajewski. (1899). Pioneer Folklore Questionnaire, PAS.
19 Charles Sargent. (1911). Pioneer Folklore Questionnaire, PAS.
20 Mrs. D.A. Moorhouse. (1911). Pioneer Folklore Questionnaire, PAS.
21 Martha Ann Todd. (1894). Pioneer Folklore Questionnaire, PAS.
22 Charles Davis. (1882). Pioneer Folklore Questionnaire, PAS.
23 This list was compiled from responses to the Pioneer Folklore Questionnaire, PAS.

WINDS, CRESCENT MOONS, MIRAGES AND NORTHERN LIGHTS

1 Koozma Tarasoff. (1898). Pioneer Folklore Questionnaire, PAS.
2 Robert Widdess. (1883). Pioneer Folklore Questionnaire, PAS.
3 Ella Otterson. (1903). Pioneer Folklore Questionnaire, PAS.
4 John Ludlow. (1905). Pioneer Folklore Questionnaire, PAS.

5 Felix Belliveau. (1902). Pioneer Folklore Questionnaire, PAS.

6 Harriet May Stueck. (1886). Pioneer Folklore Questionnaire, PAS.

7 Frank Baines. (1883). Pioneer Folklore Questionnaire, PAS.

8 Edna Staples McIntosh. (1974). Interview. Accession No. C 117, PAS.

9 Reta Evans Simons, *It Rained at Harvest Time: Memoirs of the Forever Prairie* (Reask, 2017), p. 27.

10 Kenelm Luttman-Johnson. (1905). Pioneer Experiences Questionnaire, PAS.

11 Robert Widdess. (1883). Pioneer Folklore Questionnaire, PAS.

12 These examples of humour have been taken from the Pioneer Folklore Questionnaire, PAS.

13 A chinook refers to warm, westerly winds. At times, these winds could be incredibly strong.

14 Eloise Anderson. (1902). Pioneer Folklore Questionnaire, PAS.

15 For more information on raining fish, refer to "Can It Rain Fish?" at the West Texas A&M University website, https://www.wtamu.edu/~cbaird/sq/2013/04/30/can-it-rain-fish/#:~:text=Waterspouts%20suck%20up%20lake%20or,away%20from%20where%20they%20started.

16 Ella Otterson. (1903). Pioneer Folklore Questionnaire, PAS.

17 Charles Sargent. (1911). Pioneer Folklore Questionnaire, PAS.

18 Mary Rogers Berkner. (n.d.). Memoir. "Berkner Family." Accession No. A 454 339, PAS.

19 Norman McDonald. (1883). Pioneer Folklore Questionnaire, PAS.

20 Frank Baines. (1883). Pioneer Folklore Questionnaire, PAS.

21 Sam H. McWilliams. (1884). Pioneer Folklore Questionnaire, PAS.

22 Harve R. Carson. (1883). Pioneer Folklore Questionnaire, PAS.

23 A "new moon" refers to the beginning of a lunar cycle. There is a new moon every month. For more information, refer to Bob Berman, "What Is a New Moon? When Is the Next New Moon?" *Almanac*, March 7, 2024, https://www.almanac.com/what-new-moon.

24 Maggie Whyte. (1883). Pioneer Folklore Questionnaire, PAS.

25 D.H. Maginnes. (1906). Pioneer Folklore Questionnaire, PAS.

26 Mrs. J.M. Telfodd. (1910). Pioneer Folklore Questionnaire, PAS.

27 Charles Sargent. (1911). Pioneer Folklore Questionnaire, PAS.

28 These types of clouds are also known as cumulonimbus clouds. For more information, refer to the Met Office website, https://www.metoffice.gov.uk/weather/learn-about/weather/types-of-weather/clouds/low-level-clouds/cumulonimbus.

29 John Gilbert Wren. (1907). Pioneer Experiences Questionnaire, PAS.

30 Charles Sargent. (1911). Pioneer Folklore Questionnaire, PAS.

31 Susan Tucker. (1905). Pioneer Experiences Questionnaire, PAS.

32 Frank Baines. (1883). Pioneer Experiences Questionnaire, PAS.

33 Oresa Williams. (1890). Pioneer Folklore Questionnaire, PAS.

34 Dorthea Calverley. (1985). Memoir. "Memories of a Pioneer Child." Accession No. R85-269, PAS.

35 James Tulloch. (1897). Pioneer Folklore Questionnaire, PAS.

36 John Fetsch. (1910). Pioneer Folklore Questionnaire, PAS.

37 Eloise Anderson. (1902). Pioneer Folklore Questionnaire, PAS.

38 Mrs. Charles Archer. (1902). Pioneer Folklore Questionnaire, PAS.

39 Ella Otterson. (1903). Pioneer Folklore Questionnaire, PAS.

40 A.J. Riley. (1904). Pioneer Folklore Questionnaire, PAS.

41 Rose Feist, "The Heywoods," *80 Years of Progress* (Westlock History Book Committee, 1984), p. 503.

42 Mary Morrison. (n.d.). Memoir. Accession No. MG9 A81, PAM.
43 Frank Baines. (1883). Pioneer Folklore Questionnaire, PAS.
44 Charles Sargent. (1911). Pioneer Folklore Questionnaire, PAS.
45 John Ludlow. (1905). Pioneer Folklore Questionnaire, PAS.
46 Frank Kusch. (1883). Pioneer Folklore Questionnaire, PAS.
47 "The McLeod Families," *Bridging the Years: Carmangay and District* (Carmangay and District History Book Committee, 1968), pp. 436.
48 Mabel Wilson Hawthorne. (1905). Memoir. "My Reminiscence of Fifty Years on the Saskatchewan Prairies." Accession No. RE 2991, PAS.
49 Ernest Bishop. (n.d.). Memoir. "Pioneer Days of the District." Accession No. A 31, PAS.
50 Mary Morrison. (n.d.). Memoir. Accession No. MG9 A81, PAM.
51 All information for this section has been taken from the Pioneer Folklore Questionnaires, PAS.
52 John Thiessen. (1905). Pioneer Folklore Questionnaire, PAS.

CONCLUSION

1 Ellenor Ranghild Merriken, *Looking for Country: A Norwegian Immigrant's Alberta Memoir* (University of Calgary Press, 1999), pp. 93–94.
2 Reg Breen, excerpt from "Home Sweet Home," *Buried Treasures: The History of Elnora, Pine Lake and Huxley* (Elnora/Pine Lake History Book Association, 2009), p. 38.

Bibliography

ABBREVIATIONS

PAA—Provincial Archives of Alberta
PAM—Provincial Archives of Manitoba
PAS—Provincial Archives of Saskatchewan

ARCHIVAL SOURCES

"A Glimpse of the Aron Johnson Pioneering Days." Memoir and photograph. Received from Brad Johnson of Regina, Saskatchewan, in June 2023.

Adler, Mrs. L.J. (1910). Pioneer Folklore Questionnaire, PAS.

Affleck, William. (1906). Pioneer Folklore Questionnaire, PAS.

Aikenhead, Mrs. Amanda. (1900). Pioneer Experiences Questionnaire, PAS.

Althouse, Archie. (1906). Memoir. "Life on a Saskatchewan Homestead." Accession No. RE 2930, PAS.

Anderson, Eloise. (1902). Pioneer Folklore Questionnaire, PAS.

Anderson, Marion. (1833). Pioneer Recreation and Social Life Questionnaire, PAS.

———. (1883). Pioneer Experiences Questionnaire, PAS.

———. (1883). Pioneer Folklore Questionnaire, PAS.

Anderson, Mary. (1902). Pioneer Folklore Questionnaire, PAS.

Archer, Mrs. Charles. (1902). Pioneer Experiences Questionnaire, PAS.

Asher, Julia Anna. (1950). Memoir. "Grandma's Childhood: Pioneer Life in Southern Alberta." Accession No. MG8 B10, PAM.

Atkings, Christopher. (1906). Pioneer Experiences Questionnaire, PAS.

Bacon, Lena. (1904). Pioneer Experiences Questionnaire, PAS.

Baines, Frank. (1883). Pioneer Experiences Questionnaire, PAS.

Baines, Fred. (1883). Pioneer Folklore Questionnaire, PAS.

Bean, Clarissa L. (1905). Pioneer Experiences Questionnaire, PAS.

Bell, Harry. (1955). "A Short History of the Gladmar Community," *History of Gladmar*, Accession No. IF 86, PAS.

Belliveau, Felix. (1902). Pioneer Folklore Questionnaire, PAS.

Berkner, Mary Rogers. (n.d.). Memoir. "Berkner Family." Accession No. A 454 339, PAS.

Biehn, Aaron. (1898). Memoir. Accession No. RE 513, PAS.

Billing, Mrs. W.T. (n.d.). Memoir. "An English School Marm in Saskatchewan." Accession No. A 160, PAS.

Birkett, Mary E. (1905). Pioneer Folklore Questionnaire, PAS.

Bishop, Ernest. (n.d.). Memoir. "Pioneer Days of the District." Accession No. A 31, PAS.

Bonas, Joseph. (1903). Pioneer Experiences Questionnaire, PAS.
Boyle, William. (1910). Pioneer Folklore Questionnaire, PAS.
Bray, Charles Cantlon. (1883). Pioneer Farming Experiences Questionnaire, PAS.
———. (1883). Pioneer Folklore Questionnaire, PAS.
Brydon, Emma. (1965). Memoir. "Short Sketch of Edge Hill District." Accession No. MG9 A59-62, PAM.
Butler, Lillian. (1911). Pioneer Experiences Questionnaire, PAS.
Calverley, Dorthea. (1985). Memoir. "Memories of a Pioneer Child." Accession No. R85-269, PAS.
Cameron, Alexander. (1902). Pioneer Experiences Questionnaire, PAS.
Cameron, Viola. (1975). Interview. Accession No. 81.279, File No. 17, PAA.
Campbell, Elsie. (1905). Pioneer Experiences Questionnaire, PAS.
Carr, Grace. (1910). Memoir. "What I Remember of Pioneer Days in the Wood River District." Accession No. RE 2849, PAS.
Carson, Harve. (1883). Pioneer Folklore Questionnaire, PAS.
Chase, Robert. (1902). Pioneer Folklore Questionnaire, PAS.
Christianson, Albert. (1910). Pioneer Folklore Questionnaire, PAS.
Collingwood, Herman. (1977). Memoir. "My Life History from 1904 to 1970 in Saskatchewan." Accession No. RE 36, PAS.
Condon, Annie. (n.d.). Memoir. "Northern Lights: A Story of Pioneer Days in Saskatchewan." Accession No. A 535, PAS.
Davis, Charles. (1882). Pioneer Folklore Questionnaire, PAS.
Doolittle, Ken. (1905). Memoir. "My Pioneer Days in Saskatchewan." Accession No. RE 321 #36, PAS.
Downie, Janet. (1901). Pioneer Folklore Questionnaire, PAS.
Ehrlich, Herman. (1906). Pioneer Experiences Questionnaire, PAS.
Elderton, Albert. (1909). Pioneer Experiences Questionnaire, PAS.
Estlin, Alfred Bagehot. (n.d.). Memoir. "The Old Commission Trail." Accession No. P5039 F6, PAM.
Evans, John. (1892). Pioneer Folklore Questionnaire, PAS.
Fetsch, John. (1910). Pioneer Folklore Questionnaire, PAS.
Franks, Mrs. Sorine. (1911). Pioneer Experiences Questionnaire, PAS.
Gange, Mrs. W.H.S. (1894). Pioneer Folklore Questionnaire, PAS.
Gange, William. (1894). Pioneer Folklore Questionnaire, PAS.
Gerry, Harriet. (n.d.). Memoir. "The Year I Grew Up." Accession No. A 603, PAS.
Gunn, George H. (1956). Memoir. "Children's Games in the Red River Settlement." Accession No. MG9 A78-2, PAM.
Gush, Dorothy. (1968). Memoir. "Prairie Years 1905–1909." Accession No. A 266, PAS.
Hall, Stephen. (1903). Pioneer Experiences Questionnaire, PAS.
Hamer, John. (1909). Pioneer Folklore Questionnaire, PAS.
Hammerschmidt, Joseph. (1904). Pioneer Experiences Questionnaire, PAS.
Harrigan, Sue. (1980). Memoir. "The Courageous Pioneers." Accession No. RE-626, PAS.
Harris, George A. (1955). Memoir. "Some History and Pioneer Experiences of Heward, Sask. from its Settlement in 1900 to 1914." Accession No. 623, PAS.
Hawthorne, Mabel Wilson. (1905). Memoir. "My Reminiscence of Fifty Years on the Saskatchewan Prairies." Accession No. RE 2991, PAS.
Hoffer, Clara. (1905). Pioneer Folklore Questionnaire, PAS.

Holmes, Gladys. (1901). Memoir. "Autobiography of Gladys Carscallen Holmes." Accession No. RE 2148, PAS.

I'd Like to be a Boy Again. Poem. Accession No. 70.454/5 SE, PAA.

Jackson, Samuel. (1878). Pioneer Experiences Questionnaire, PAS.

Johnson, Lucy. (1903). Memoir. "Against the Wind." Accession No. RE-2878, PAS.

Jordens, Marie. (1884). Pioneer Folklore Questionnaire, PAS.

Kajewski, Mary Edith Alicia. (1899). Pioneer Folklore Questionnaire, PAS.

Kennedy, Dan, letter to Harry Scrivner. Posted January 24, 1954, Accession No. R-IS4, PAS.

Kennedy, Flora. (n.d.). Memoir. "From East to West." Accession No. A310, PAS.

Kenyon, Florence. (1895). Pioneer Experiences Questionnaire, PAS.

Keyser, Kathleen. (1894). Pioneer Experiences Questionnaire, PAS.

Kieper, Charles Edward. (1954). Memoir. "The Life of a Pioneer." Accession No. A75, PAS.

Knaus, Mrs. John C. (1906). Pioneer Experiences Questionnaire, PAS.

Kusch, Frank. (1883). Pioneer Experiences Questionnaire, PAS.

Laidlaw, John. (1882). Pioneer Folklore Questionnaire, PAS.

Lanegraff, Tobias. (1906). Pioneer Folklore Questionnaire, PAS.

Laycock, Mrs. Jay. (1902). Pioneer Folklore Questionnaire, PAS.

Ludlow, Ernest. (1905). Pioneer Experiences Questionnaire, PAS.

Ludlow, John. (1905). Pioneer Folklore Questionnaire, PAS.

Luttman-Johnson, Kenelm. (1905). Pioneer Experiences Questionnaire, PAS.

McDonald, Norman. (1883). Pioneer Folklore Questionnaire, PAS.

Maginnes, D.H. (1906). Pioneer Folklore Questionnaire, PAS.

Mann, Alfred. (1882). Pioneer Experiences Questionnaire, PAS.

Martyn, Harry. (1913). Pioneer Folklore Questionnaire, PAS.

Matz, Laura. (1978). Memoir. "My Pioneer Days in Saskatchewan." Accession No. R-E321 #15, PAS.

May, Sidney S. (1901). Pioneer Folklore Questionnaire, PAS.

May, Sidney. (1913). Pioneer Folklore Questionnaire, PAS.

McCallum, Sadie. (1900). Pioneer Folklore Questionnaire, PAS.

McChesney, John. (1904). Pioneer Recreation and Social Life Questionnaire, PAS.

McDonald, Norman. (1883). Pioneer Recreation and Social Life Questionnaire, PAS.

McDonough, Theresa. (1985). Memoir. "Some Memories of the Alexander Taylor Family, Pioneers of Bresaylor, Saskatchewan and of Mary Isabella Taylor Mack and her Family and their Growing Years on the Prairies." Accession No. A550, PAS.

McIntosh, Edna Staples. (1974). Interview. Accession No. C 117, PAS.

McLeod, Evelyn Slater. (1977). Memoir. "Restless Pioneers." Accession No. 77.39, PAS.

McMurdo, Mary Ann. (1904). Pioneer Experiences Questionnaire, PAS.

McWilliams, Sam H. (1884). Pioneer Folklore Questionnaire, PAS.

Meek, Lottie. (1884). Pioneer Folklore Questionnaire, PAS.

Meredith, Mrs. J. (1907). Pioneer Folklore Questionnaire, PAS.

Michael, Rena. (n.d.). Memoir. "North Battleford," Accession No. R-E3198, PAS.

Miles, Mrs. Richard (Lillian). (1884). Pioneer Folklore Questionnaire, PAS.

Millar, Emily Wright. (1976). Memoir. "Beyond the Sunset." Accession No. A 210, PAS.

Mitchell, Dora. (n.d.). Memoir. "Far Horizons." Accession No. A 278, PAS.

Moorhouse, Mrs. D.A. (1911). Pioneer Folklore Questionnaire, PAS.
Morrison, Mary. (n.d.). Memoir. Accession No. MG9 A81, PAM.
Mott, Mrs. Ella. (1887). Pioneer Folklore Questionnaire, PAS.
Muirhead, Isabel. (1883). Pioneer Folklore Questionnaire, PAS.
Murray, W. Roland. (1981). Memoir. "The Murray-Hurlbert Homesteads," Accession No. M6089, Glenbow Archives.
Myer, Bertha Shaw. (n.d.). Memoir. "My Pioneer Days in Saskatchewan." Accession No. R-E321 #19, PAS.
Neal, Eric. (1906). Pioneer Folklore Questionnaire, PAS.
Olmstead, Mrs. E. Howard. (1885). Pioneer Folklore Questionnaire, PAS.
Olson Family. (n.d.). Memoir. "The Pioneers on South Half Section of 17-33-27-W2nd." Accession No. A 319, PAS.
Olson, Evelyn. (1991). Memoir. "Memories Are Such Fragile Things." Accession No. X 173, p. 15, PAS.
Otterson, Ella. (1903). Pioneer Folklore Questionnaire, PAS.
Phelps, Olive. (1933). Memoir. "Memoirs of Crescent Lake." Accession No. YF 560, PAS.
Pope, Lila. (1904). Folklore Pioneer Questionnaire, PAS.
Potts, John. (1894). Pioneer Experiences Questionnaire, PAS.
Purdy, Lena May. (1883). Pioneer Experiences Questionnaire, PAS.
Reesor, William Colby. (n.d.). Memoir. Accession No. 77.57 SE, PAS.
Riley, A.J. (1904). Pioneer Folklore Questionnaire, PAS.
Riley, Alfred. (1904). Pioneer Experiences Questionnaire, PAS.
Robinson, Etta. (1914). Memoir. Author's Family History.
Salamon, Andrew. (1906). Pioneer Experiences Questionnaire, PAS.
Sand, J.H. (1910). Pioneer Folklore Questionnaire, PAS.
Sargent, Charles. (1911). Pioneer Folklore Questionnaire, PAS.
Shaw, Robert. (1905). Pioneer Folklore Questionnaire, PAS.
Shepherd, George. (1900). Pioneer Folklore Questionnaire, PAS.
———. (1908). Pioneer Housing Questionnaire, PAS.
Singleton, John Milton. (1911). Pioneer Experiences Questionnaire, PAS.
Smith, Kathleen Lennox. (n.d.). Memoir. "Memories of Kathleen Lennox Smith," Accession No. R-E3289, PAS.
St. John, Elias Parmlee. (1908). Pioneer Folklore Questionnaire, PAS.
Stewart, Gordon Wolseley. (n.d.). Memoir. "Memoirs of Gordon Wolseley Stewart." Accession No. R-E1222, PAS.
Stewart, Mrs. C.A. (1912). Pioneer Folklore Questionnaire, PAS.
Stilborn, Edith. (1883). Pioneer Farming Experiences Questionnaire, PAS.
Stueck, Harriet May. (1886). Pioneer Folklore Questionnaire, PAS
Tarasoff, Koozma. (1898). Pioneer Folklore Questionnaire, PAS.
Teece, Mrs. H. (1885). Pioneer Folklore Questionnaire, PAS.
Telfodd, Mrs. J.M. (1910). Pioneer Folklore Questionnaire, PAS.
Thiessen, John. (1905). Pioneer Folklore Questionnaire, PAS.
Thomson, Percy. (1910). Pioneer Folklore Questionnaire, PAS.
Tilford, Arthur. (1902). Pioneer Farming Experiences Questionnaire, PAS.
Todd, Martha Ann. (1894). Pioneer Folklore Questionnaire, PAS.
Tribute to the Many Indomitable Men who Homesteaded in Manitoba. Poem. Accession No. 176 Homesteading Poem, RG 17D1, PAM.
Tucker, Susan. (1905). Pioneer Experiences Questionnaire, PAS.
Tulloch, James. (1897). Pioneer Folklore Questionnaire, PAS.
Vickar, Sam. (1906). Pioneer Experiences Questionnaire, PAS.
Wheeler, Arthur James. (1906). Pioneer Farming Experiences Questionnaire, PAS.
Whyte, Maggie. (1883). Pioneer Folklore Questionnaire, PAS.

Widdess, Robert. (1883). Pioneer Farming Experiences Questionnaire, PAS.
———. (1883). Pioneer Folklore Questionnaire, PAS.
Williams, Oresa. (1890). Pioneer Folklore Questionnaire, PAS.
Williscroft, George. (1898). Pioneer Folklore Questionnaire, PAS.
Wilson, Joseph C. (1904). Pioneer Farming Experiences Questionnaire, PAS.
Wilson, Mrs. Ed. (1905). Pioneer Folklore Questionnaire, PAS.
Wooff, Robert H. (n.d.). Interview. Accession No. C 130, PAS.
Wren, John Gilbert. (1907). Pioneer Experiences Questionnaire, PAS.

BOOKS

Admiral: Prairie to Wheatfields. Admiral History Book Club, 1978.
Along the Fifth: History of Stony Plain and District. Stony Plain Historical Society, 1982.
Back Over the Trail. The Acadia Women's Institute, 1967.
Basswood, 1878–1978. Centennial Book and Home Day Committee, 1978.
Between River and Lake. Warspite—Victoria Trail Historical Society, 1988.
Beyond Our Prairie Trails. Carstairs History Book Committee.
Born, Anna. *Changes: Anecdotal Tales of Changes in the Life of Anna Born*. Bindery Publishing House, 1995.
Bowen, Lynne. *Muddling Through: The Remarkable Story of the Barr Colonists*. Douglas & McIntyre, 1992.
Brick's Hill, Berwyn and Beyond. Berwyn Centennial Committee, 1968.
Bridging the Years: A History of Eastbank, Windfield, Hattonford and East Mahaska. Hattonford History Book Committee, 1982.
Bridging the Years: Carmangay and District. Carmangay and District History Book Committee, 1968.
Bridging the Years: Nipawin, Saskatchewan. Nipawin Historical Society, 1988.
Bucking Poles and Butter Churns. North Lone Pine Women's Institute, 1972.
Buried Treasures: The History of Elnora, Pine Lake and Huxley. Elnora/Pine Lake History Book Association, 2009.
Busby's Busy Years: 75th Anniversary Edition. Busby History Book Committee, 1989.
By the Old Mill Stream. Holmfield History Book Committee, 1982.
Calahoo Trails: A History of Calahoo, Granger, Speldhurst, East Bilby and Green Willow. Calahoo Women's Institute, 1975.
Campbell, Marjorie Wilkins. *The Saskatchewan*. Rinehart and Company, 1950.
Chandler, Graham. "Selling the Prairie Good Life." *Canada's History* (2016), https://www.canadashistory.ca/explore/settlement-immigration/selling-the-prairie-good-life.
A Cross in the Clearing: A History, 1903–1980. Phillips Publishers, 1980.
80 Years of Progress. Westlock History Book Committee, 1984.
Forests, Furrows and Faith. Boyle and District Historical Society, 1982.
Franklin, Rosalind. *Baby Lore: Superstitions and Old Wive's Tales from the World Over Related to Pregnancy, Birth and Childcare*. Diggory Press, 2005.
From Bush to Bushels, A History of Bruderheim and District. Bruderheim Historical Society, 1983.
Golden Echoes: A History of Galahad. Galahad Historical Society, 1980.
Hambley, George H. *Trails of the Pioneers*. D.W. Friesen & Sons Ltd., 1956.
Hamiota: Grains of the Century. Hamiota Centennial History Committee, 1984.
History of Rimbey, Alberta: 50 Years of Progress. Rimbey Historical Committee, 1952.

In the Bend of the Battle: A History of Alliance and District. Alliance Lions Club, 1976.

Iredale, Betty. *Stories of the Sod Shack and Other Reminiscences*. Hemlock Printers, 1991.

Lang Syne: A History of Lang, Saskatchewan. Lang Syne History Book Committee, 1980.

MacEwan, Grant. *Between the Red and the Rockies*. University of Toronto Press, 1952.

———. *Power for Prairie Plows*. Western Producer Book Service, 1974.

Matheson, Murdock. *Looking Backward over my Fifty Years in Saskatchewan*. Self-published, 1960.

Merriken, Ellenor Ranghild. *Looking for Country: A Norwegian Immigrant's Alberta Memoir*. University of Calgary Press, 1999.

Minifie, James M. *Homesteader: A Prairie Boyhood Recalled*. Macmillan of Canada, 1972.

Morton, A.S. "History of Prairie Settlement." Part 1 of *Canadian Frontiers of Settlement*, vol. 2. Macmillan Canada, 1938.

A New Beginning: Irvine and District. 20 Mile Post Historical Society, 1989.

O'Toole, Patrick J. *Rhymes of a Homesteader*. Hamley Press, 1947.

Our Foothills. Priddis and Bragg Creek Historical Society, 1975, https://braggcreekhistoricalsociety.ca/wp-content/uploads/2020/08/our_foothills_bragg_creek.pdf.

Over the Years, 1892–1982. Rimbey History Book Committee, 1983.

Pioneer Legacy: Bowden and Districts. Bowden Chamber of Commerce, 1979.

A Place of Our Own. Fisher Branch Historical Society, 1982.

Ponoka 1904–1954: 50th Anniversary. Ponoka Herald, 1954.

Prokop, Manfred. "Canadianization of Immigrant Children: Role of the Rural Elementary School in Alberta, 1900–1930." *Alberta History*, 37, no. 2 (April 1989): pp. 1–10.

Reid, Mark Collin. "Oh, Baby. *Canada's History*, November 2019, https://www.canadashistory.ca/explore/museums-galleries-archives/oh-baby!

"The Savoury History of Chop Suey on the Prairies: Reflections of Ponoka." *Ponoka News*, September 14, 2011, https://www.ponokanews.com/community/the-savoury-history-of-chop-suey-on-the-prairies-reflections-of-ponoka/.

Shillington, C. Howard. *Historic Land Trails of Saskatchewan*. Evvard Publications, 1985.

Simons, Reta Evans. *It Rained at Harvest Time: Memoirs of the Forever Prairie*. Reask, 2017.

Stewart, K. "Education and the Free Church." The Monthly Record (2003). On the Christian Study Library website, https://www.christianstudylibrary.org/article/education-and-free-church.

They Came From Many Lands. Foam Lake Review, 1985.

Trails of Tail Creek Country. Edith Lawrence Clark, 1972.

Waskatenau, 1867–1967. County of Smoky Lake, 1967.

Wilken, Lulu. "Homesteading in Saskatchewan." *Canada West Magazine*, 7 (1977), p. 33.

Index

Page numbers by province are listed at the end of the index. Page numbers *in italics* indicate a photograph.

SANDRA ROLLINGS-MAGNUSSON is an Associate Professor of Sociology at MacEwan University. She has studied western Canadian homesteaders for over thirty years. Since receiving a Master's Degree from the University of Regina and a PhD from the University of Alberta, she has written numerous academic journal articles on homesteading life and lectured on a number of homesteading topics. She has also written four books, *Tales from the Homestead: A History of Prairie Pioneers, 1867–1914* (Heritage House), *Heavy Burdens on Small Shoulders: The Labour of Pioneer Children on the Canadian Prairies* (University of Alberta Press), *Women Homesteaders on the Canadian Prairies* (KDP Publishing) and *The Homesteaders* (University of Regina Press).